Trek Into Nuba

Trek Into Nuba

Ian Mackie

The Pentland Press
Edinburgh – Cambridge – Durham – USA

To Marion and to the other kind people who encouraged me

© Ian Mackie, 1994

First published in 1994 by
The Pentland Press Ltd
1 Hutton Close
South Church
Bishop Auckland
Durham

British Library
Cataloguing-in-Publication Data
A catalogue record for this book
is available from the British Library.

ISBN 1-85821-200-6

Typeset by Carnegie Publishing, 18 Maynard St., Preston
Printed and bound in Great Britain by Bookcraft (Bath) Ltd.

To
all the peoples of the Nuba Mountains
and
to
my Father who said, 'Keep a record of it all.'
Then he said, 'Now write a book about it.'

Contents

	Foreword	ix
Part I	ABDEL MAGID	
	Beginnings	1
	Northwards to the Sudan	18
	Nile Passage	21
	Arrival	27
	Settling In	44
	Into Kordofan	69
Part II	NUBA	
	The Mountains	76
	Maroor (Trek)	88
	The House on the Hill	101
	Deep South	104
	Talodi	107
	Day Off	112
	Land Without Water	117
	The Body in the Grass	125
	The Scorpion	129
	At Home	131
	Abu Anga	136
	Back on the Trail	140
	Revelations	144
	Sibr	150
	Settlement of Soldiers	154
	Back to the City	157
	The Lecture	160
	Zikr	163
	Athena (an idyll)	169
	Virtuoso	175
	Of Horses, Armour and a Sword	178
	Happy Return	188
	Tegali	195

Entertaining Ladies   202
Worms in the Bath   204
Habibala's Party   207
The Nuba Gathering   210
Excavations   214
Horse Trek   223
Seseiban   229
Problems of Water   239
Tribal Troubles   253
El Azraq   257
The Python   262
Deep Nuba   266
Troubled Times at Talodi   273
The Flood   286

Part III   ABU HABL
A Tale of the Mountains   306
Back into Harness   314
The Well   332
The Nurse   337
Domestic Duties   343
Taming the Abu Habl   347
Finale   386
Footnote   389

Appendices   390

Maps   411

Foreword

by the Rt Hon David Steel KBE, MP

At the age of eleven, I sailed with my parents aboard a British India steamship company liner to Mombasa, beginning memorable years in Kenya. We took the Suez Canal route, and at Port Sudan encountered the 'fuzzy wuzzies', young men who swarmed aboard as porters and cargo loaders, others of whom dived into the sea in pursuit of coins thrown by the passengers – part of a regular, lucrative entertainment.

In my travels in East Africa as a boy, and, later, throughout much of Africa as an MP I have, oddly enough, never set foot in Sudan itself. In these recent years, the news from there has been of grim civil strife, but I looked forward to learning more of the country when I heard of the forthcoming publication of *Trek Into Nuba*.

The memoirs of a retired Scottish colonial civil servant specialising in agriculture do not at first sight seem a promising vehicle for information, still less entertainment. Yet one could not be more wrong, for Ian Mackie has written a vividly enthralling account of his life in Sudan during the last war.

It makes exciting reading. He almost drowns; he is almost killed by a rock-face fall; an 18-foot python ends up being slain, rather than slaying; he is stung by a scorpion; and, most surprisingly of all, an eagle drops a snake into his moving car, which is immediately evacuated by everybody including the driver of the still-moving vehicle. All of this is told with verve and self-deprecating humour.

There is also the wit of tedium; his Arab examinations; falling asleep in the saddle of his horse; the bouts of malaria; the enforced, isolated companionship of ghastly people. The life of the different native peoples is colourfully described: the activities of the witch doctors, the accidental and natural deaths of people he knew, tribal conflicts and customs all appear as lively, written photographs.

I laughed out loud at his account of the five-person 'dinner dance', at his summons by the governor to play the organ in church for a visiting Welsh bishop, at the life of the Russian couple, which ended when the wife hit her engineer husband on the head so hard with a saucepan that he was knocked unconscious, at his vain attempt to introduce selective castration of cattle.

This is an account of a life which has gone – of pioneering in Africa. It bubbles along with fresh fascination on every page. Mr Mackie can be both funny and moving. He certainly preaches the gospel of soil conservation and irrigation in a manner unknown to the textbooks. This is a joy to read.

Part I – Abdel Magid

Beginnings

Early on a grey autumn morning in 1942 I lay alone, very alone in a drab war-time hotel bedroom in Liverpool knowing that in a few hours' time my whole lifetime's experience was about to change to something unknown and unpredictable – new people entering my life, travel by sea, danger and, no doubt, excitement, with, beyond all this, the great unknown. Africa! The prospect of living in a new land, the need to speak Arabic and to work with tropical soils: at this time of the morning, in this cold and alien setting, I knew only too well how inadequate I was.

Everything had happened so quickly. I had been given one week's notice to make all the necessary preparations – obtain tropical kit, inoculations – say farewells – there had been no time to think of what it really meant. But now, uncertainties struck with full force. When one is young the effects of separation and change are impossible to predict. In war-time, enforced change for millions of people was extreme as they hurried from the security of home, often for the first time, into circumstances far beyond their experience or desire, perhaps to be away for years.

In going to Africa, I was fulfilling an ambition and had no cause to complain: but somehow, that did not make it easier.

At the start of the war I was a student of Agriculture in Edinburgh and had decided to specialise in 'Colonial Agriculture'. This was regarded as a 'reserved' occupation and given priority over military service (as far as I was concerned) because, even with the urgency of war, the Empire still had to be staffed with trained recruits.

Many of my friends had been called up – some to be killed in the early days of fighting – but tribunals which examined my position insisted that my future role overseas would better serve the country's needs. So, life at university continued through grim early war years, amid restraints which stifled the imagination and made student life a drab experience. These few years passed, and it was with a sense of escape that I clutched my degree, eager for what lay ahead.

Everything then had happened in rapid succession. I applied for a post in the Anglo-Egyptian Sudan, was invited to London for interview, then accepted, all in a matter of days. In these years jobs were to be had in many overseas territories and it was not uncommon for Agricultural students to seek work in the Empire, but from the days of childhood my hopes had focused on one country only – the Sudan. The Sudan? That vast area of land south of the Sahara Desert described often as a wilderness or, 'certainly not a white man's country'. What could have awakened an interest in a place so remote from anything I had yet experienced in life?

It is seldom easy to pinpoint the influences which shape major directions in one's life, but in choosing the Sudan I was probably responding to attitude of the times. The days of my childhood were still 'glorious' days of Empire in which Britain had a special destiny, or so its people thought. Children were reared on tales of the country's victorious heroes. These were not the flimsy heroes of modern times, but were giants of their day encapsulated in myth. They were presented as examples to follow and usually seemed more than human.

Two such heroes were a regular diet of childhood – General Gordon of Khartoum, and David Livingstone the missionary explorer. The stories of their African experiences had worked away in my mind so that Africa had become to some degree a romantic obsession. These thoughts were encouraged by the family, particularly Father, who had a restless urge to travel, an urge he fulfilled in large measure. From earliest childhood I was taken to the harbours of Scotland to look at ships while Father dreamed his dreams of foreign parts.

Perhaps I would become a missionary, explorer, adventurer. Would I ever have my own porters and trek the African bush? At that time these were not impossible dreams; there was still unknown territory in darkest Africa and, in their ignorance, people spoke occasionally of 'savages'.

But how could I ever make a beginning? Would it be possible to break away from the security of family to penetrate such an exciting world?

Two things occurred to make it easier for this to happen: first, there was the war which uprooted people and made foreign travel commonplace. The second was my discovery that it was possible to study with the object of going overseas. My town background did not deter me. I saw an opportunity and prepared to study Colonial Agriculture.

It had all grown from there and now, alone in Liverpool, there was time to marvel that I was on my way at last. I had travelled from Scotland by rail the previous day, and what a journey it had been. It was as if I had travelled in a dream: as if the whole experience was unreal. My heart still beat faster, not just because of the coming journey or even because of going to Africa – another important event had happened only hours before leaving home.

I had known Marion six months: she was serving in Edinburgh in the forces and we had met on many occasions, times which I knew were happy for both of us. I had worked for a time on her father's farm and we walked the hills together while I spoke of my dreams of Africa. One day we cycled to the side of Loch Tay where we sat, entranced by a peace so much in contrast to a world at war. I knew that very soon I would be leaving for Africa, and perhaps we would never see each other again. I proposed to her with faltering words; she looked into my eyes and said, simply, 'No.' Slowly now she spoke of our uncertain future: we could be parted for years, and time might change our feelings.

Next day she saw me off at Ballinluig station. We said our farewells and I huddled dejectedly in the corner of a compartment, as I returned home to prepare for departure. To go then, with such a sense of loss, suddenly made the future seem bleak.

But a miracle happened! Hours before leaving she phoned unexpectedly to wish me a safe journey. I asked her to come to my home where we could really say our goodbyes. We met again at the station, moments which were for me thrilling beyond words. I asked her again, and this time she said she would wait for my return – we were engaged to be married! Then, once again we were on that same crowded platform, with family and friends; but my eyes were on one person only, absorbing pictures, images, which would have to last through the years ahead.

What a start to a journey! Even here in the hotel room with all the uncertainties, I felt surges of happiness. There was everything to work for, much to achieve, and the intervening years would pass.

I was unable to lie any longer so I rose and dressed and tried to concentrate on the immediate problem of the journey. My instructions read: 'Report to floating dock for transit.' There was no mention of ship, route, or destination, all of which was regarded as classified information. No doubt at the 'floating dock' everything would be made clear.

This was a time of secrecy when, of all things, information about the movement of ships had to be hidden from the enemy. Rooms and passages in the hotel carried the reminder 'Walls have ears', so I was travelling in ignorance, not knowing ship, route or even the port of arrival. The time it would take to reach Khartoum in the Sudan, or for that matter whether I would get there at all – these were just thoughts at the back of the mind.

In 1942 few places in the world were so inaccessible as the Sudan, with the Mediterranean closed to shipping, the Suez Canal blocked, and Japanese submarines prowling the East African coast. Worse than all of these, packs of U-boats in the Atlantic were taking heavy toll of convoys. It could only be an eventful journey.

The one vague promise I had been given was that I would arrive some-where on the East African coast: thereafter it would be up to me to reach the Sudan. In the event, it took three months merely to get to my 'job'. The war situation for Britain was at its lowest ebb. In Africa, the British Army had retreated far into Egypt. The Battle of the Atlantic was poised on a knife-edge. To leave the country then raised inevitable questions: when, if ever, would I be able to return home? But there was a great spirit of optimism: everyone knew the tide would turn and it was only a question of time. Here, in Liverpool, with its bomb-damaged streets thronging with soldiers and sailors, I was something out of place, an object of curiosity, perhaps even suspicion: a civilian in plain clothes. Yet it was easy to sense a heart-warming togetherness with this great family of determined people. I had become one very small part of the great adventure.

A taxi dropped me at the dock entrance; a gate clanged behind, sealing off that familiar world and bringing me to the reality of the war.

I stood alone in an open shed with time passing, and no one showing any interest in me: then, three other men in civilian clothes turned up. We were all bound for Africa: hesitantly, we admitted, for the Sudan. Together we waited for something to happen or someone to advise us of our next move, because there was no ship here – just an empty floating quay. Hours passed. No one was disposed to tell us anything: if only someone would acknowledge our existence.

By mid-afternoon we were tired and hungry when a naval officer in-formed us that we would soon be collected. My three fellow-travellers were chatting freely to one another, while I stood apart in awkward silence, my mind full of the events of the day before. As early as this, with the journey still to begin, I was discovering, as I had always pictured myself, that I was uncomfortable in company – a loner with little to say.

But still we waited. The dockside clock registered 5 p.m. when, at last, we were told to pick up our baggage and move to a side door. It came as a relief that at last something was happening. A customs examination followed in which it was evident that it was quite uncommon for civilians to leave Liverpool in war-time. After a careful scrutiny we were bundled into a canvas-covered truck and the entrance was carefully tied, leaving us seated on our baggage in darkness. Another weary wait, then the truck set off, swaying from side to side as it rattled over rough dockside roads.

Uncertainty, tiredness and hunger made the journey seem like an uncomfortable dream, then, with a swerve which landed us in a heap on the floor, motion stopped, and we waited minutes for the next event in our lives. Outside, there was a confusion of new sounds. Marching feet, doors clanging shut, the roar of an engine, shouting voices, all spoke of a crowded dockside.

Now, hands fumbled with the canvas, and we blinked at the sudden inrush of daylight. Outside was a black wall – the side of a ship! I jumped to the ground and looked up towards the boat deck of what seemed a gigantic vessel. There were a number of gangways with streams of khaki-clad men pouring up, and overhead, derricks lifted nets full of kitbags and boxes.

Everything now happened in a rush. We were led up a steep gangway and entered the main foyer of this great ship. A white-coated steward took us to a little office where our identities were carefully re-checked, then we were led through a maze of passageways to our cabin.

The prospect of relaxing on a bed, followed by a wash, then a stroll to the dining room, was very appealing after the dreary day at the quay, but any such comfortable prospect was dashed when I looked at the cabin, our home for the next few weeks. How could four people exist in this confined space? I counted the bunks and got a further shock – there were six in tiers of three at either side, which left floor room for three standing men, provided they stood to attention. At the far end, a miniature hand-basin with a proportionally small mirror provided the only other furnishings to the cubicle. Cases went below the bottom bunk, and a little rack beside each bunk was the full extent of storage space. Above the mirror, a black-painted porthole looked down like a blind eye, and beside it was printed the text: 'Shut before dark. Wear life-jackets at all times.'

There was room only for two people to move in the cabin at the one time, so I dumped my case on a middle bunk and set out to explore the ship. Corridors thronged with air force officers wandering restlessly, like myself. They looked at me in some wonder, the only civilian in sight.

Now that I was aboard and accepted. I found myself free to move from deck to deck, until an occasional notice barred the way. I was travelling first-class with officers, while somewhere lower in the ship were the other ranks.

It was difficult with all the bustle and cheerful chatter to associate this scene with danger, and with war. One got caught up with the carefree spirit of the mass; there was an excitement and pleasure to be part of the crowd.

Up on the boat deck I pushed my way though heavy canvas screens into bright daylight. The deck was already being paraded by officers, both army and air force, from a variety of units. I looked down on the dockside so far below and noticed that loading was almost finished, with top hamper being secured and, along the hull, heavy steel doors clanging shut with a sound of finality. No doubt we four, the only civilians among thousands of military, had been left to the last.

A brass plate beneath the bridge gave my new habitation an identity – MV *Rangitiki*, New Zealand Shipping Co. Ltd. To me this was a splendid ship, originally part-cargo, part-passenger. She must have been a luxury vessel in pre-war days, as I quickly discovered spacious, well-decorated public rooms, albeit now just a bit shabby. The ship had recently come from the Argentine with meat and had been rapidly turned round to carry thousands of soldiers, who were crammed into high tiers of bunks, in every conceivable space. Even with the drabness of war the ship had a dignity and majesty, as if it could brush off U-boats with disdain. Nevertheless, it was comforting to see the rows of substantial-looking lifeboats that lined the boat deck.

A voice boomed through the Tannoy: 'All new arrivals return to cabins for emergency instruction.'

A tide of people filtered downwards. In the cabin with my three fellow civilians, the only available space was on a bunk where I lay down to await events. Two air force officers squeezed in beside us; our new cabin-mates. They looked startled for a moment: what had they been thrown among? To be landed with the only civilians in the ship! However, when we were shaving, or in our bunks, we all looked the same, and were gradually accepted as normal, possibly as 'boffins' with some mysterious contribution to make to the war effort.

A ship's officer came from cabin to cabin, clipping out instructions and handing over information dockets. His voice faltered a second at the sight of us, then: 'Lifeboat twelve, port side, report to station 8 p.m. Meal sitting three. Collect life-jackets from store immediately.'

He moved on, and I waited my turn to rise. Somebody had the useful information that 'sitting three' was about to start.

With life-jackets collected and laid on our bunks, we found our tables in the dining room, and were ushered to our seats by a white-coated steward, as if we really mattered. In this great room, already crowded with a sea of chattering officers, a silence fell as our plain garb was scrutinised then, slowly, they started to speak again, and we were both accepted and forgotten.

The appointments were magnificent: the menu promised foods seldom seen in war-time Britain. It occurred to me that a military machine capable of a show such as this after years of war must speedily put paid to Hitler. War or no war, everyone present was settling in for a cruise which, at least for a limited period, would offer some compensation for what lay in the future.

The meal over, an alarm bell rung and the company made leisurely progress to its appointed lifeboats. Sailors gathered us into ragged lines with the reminder that when the ship was going down we had better turn up sharper, or else. . . in fact, when real emergencies came, no one needed prompting!

By now it was obvious the ship was ready for sailing. All activity had stopped, and there was an ominous silence as if it was straining at the leash, poised to go. Other ships, nearby, looked in an equal state of readiness. The decks were crowded as people looked thoughtfully towards the land, the question in everyone's minds: 'When shall I return home again?' We stood patiently as the sun set through layers of thin cloud, and even when it was dark, decks remained crowded with people, reluctant to lose sight of 'home'.

It was late when I summoned up courage to go down to the cabin and to the ordeal of our crowded quarters. It would be a form of torture to have to live in such a cramped style, but it was doubly so to me, because of my solitary nature. The remoteness of Africa had provided much of the appeal which drew me towards it, and here I was squeezed into this crowded space with people to whom I had nothing to say. My three fellow civilians had hit it off well, but I had some nervous impediment which kept me apart.

I lay squeezed into my bunk, alert and uncomfortable. It was after 11 p.m. that the cabin began to vibrate and the rumble of the engines sounded deep in the ship. The vibration increased, then through it came the steady beat of pistons.

We must be moving down the Mersey towards the Irish Sea, towards the many lurking dangers – submarines, mines, bombs. In these first moments in this stuffy, confined space, imagination ran riot. How could this great vessel conceal itself from the many lurking predators? In an emergency, how could so many people scramble from bunks and along corridors to the distant lifeboats? A torpedo might even strike beneath our porthole.

Wide awake, my mind tossed around a confused mixture of uncertainties and homesickness. To think that my entire life experience was focused into this uncomfortable cell, little roomier than a coffin. The utter confinement, the hissing of the ventilation system, the clattering of feet along corridors, a shout from some distant part: all produced a confused bedlam of discomfort. When would I ever be able to return to Marion? It had happened so quickly, and then I was waving goodbye from the train . . . My father had said, 'Keep a record of everything that happens, and send it home when you can.' How much he would have liked an opportunity to go to Africa! To travel in Africa: what would it be like? Heat, vast tracts of country, much of it unpopulated – would I trek over this country? Would I see where General Gordon struggled so hard to overcome the slavers, or perhaps where he made his stand against the Mahdi and his dervishes . . .?

Creaks and grunts from the other bunks told a tale. There was little sleep that first night.

The ship by now was moving to the waves, and faster engine beats told that we were heading out to sea.

I wakened to an appalling silence.

The engines were still. There was scarcely a sound in the ship. What now? I became aware of a faint chorus of seagulls, a strangely comforting sound. There was nothing warlike in this motionless calm, so I settled for another sleep. A little clear speck on the porthole showed the first light of morning.

Six a.m. and the corridors were alive with pounding feet as curious passengers climbed to the boat deck to solve the mystery of our whereabouts. In the cabin the ritual of shaving and dressing got under way in rota. It took some considerable time, as each of us took turn at the little basin.

Finally I surfaced to swallow clear, crisp air and to look with surprise on mountains which could only belong to Scotland. It became clear that this was the Clyde estuary. On all sides was a vast armada – liners, tankers, cargo boats, supply vessels, possibly eighty in number scattered over the wide estuary. In spite of this accumulation of power, an air of soft peace seemed to cloak the scene. The hills, heather-topped and crowned with fleecy clouds, cancelled out the many symbols of war, so that I leaned on the ships's rail in a rapture that such beauty should replace the anticipated dangers of the night.

An interesting and pleasant day followed, because, between eating good meals and watching the bustle of shipping, there was no call on our time, and it was not even necessary to wear the clumsy life-jackets. The lumpy shapes of air-defence balloons trailed their cables on all sides, and at several points, cruisers, destroyers and an aircraft-carrier were being serviced by a fleet of small craft.

I tried to identify the larger ships but most were complete strangers including a mixed bag from Holland, Norway and Poland. Here was an Allied fleet which, by its very size, was obviously poised for some major strategy of the war. In fact, the convoy was on its way to reinforce the desert army, now under a new general – Montgomery. Somewhere were a few vessels destined for Burma, to relieve the hard-pressed armies there in their struggles with the Japanese. Here were tens of thousands of men heading for an uncertain destiny, some to live and some to die: and yet to judge by my own ship, setting out cheerfully as if only on a great adventure.

We lay anchored in the Clyde for five whole days. On the fourth, some fresh excitement came with the arrival of four more ships, one of them a big three-funneller attended by two destroyers. On the sixth day our ship up-anchored, then, without any fuss, moved out through the boom-barrage, towards the open sea.

Was it to be a solo dash across the ocean? The *Rangitiki* performed some manoeuvres close to the Isle of Arran, then returned to the same peaceful moorings. Word went round the ship that the ship's radar was being tested.

Mid-morning of the seventh day and semaphores were flashing from ship to ship. Two destroyers edged through the boom, then, with an amazing lack of fuss, anchors were raised and ships gathered into line astern, to form a procession miles long, until it appeared as if every vessel there was on the move.

Even to be merely a humble spectator of this scene, one felt a thrill of pride – so many great ships all heavily laden with men and equipment, gave the impression of an irresistible armada. It was wonderful to be part of it.

Every rail was crowded with excited spectators, all relieved to be on the move at last.

The three-funnelled liner took the lead, with the *Rangitiki* fifth in line. Each ship had its own armaments and these, together with the naval escort, must deter any enemy at sea. It remained for me to discover the vast spread of ocean this convoy would cover, and how slender the almost invisible escort was as it patrolled the horizon, too far away for comfort.

Out into the open sea, the line turned westwards across a bar of choppy water, causing queasings in a multitude of stomachs. Now, a miraculous change of order took place: the ships formed into seven or eight long columns with the larger vessels and several significant-looking cargo ships herded into the middle. On the outer rows were the smaller ships. It was a source of comfort to find our ship tucked into the centre, while steaming out proudly in front was the large three-funnelled ship which we dubbed 'the Commodore's ship'. All the flashing lights and flag signals controlling the entire organism came from this vessel, and when every ship had reached its station, a brave display of flags signalled full steam ahead, and the whole pack advanced into the unknown.

Each ship followed a drogue marker trailed from the ship in front so that stations were kept exactly. The first zig came as a surprise when, like a flock of sheep turned by the bark of a sheep-dog, each vessel swung simultaneously to starboard and so began a long zig-zag journey through the ocean, designed to put any enemy submarines off the scent.

It was so well-organised and reassuring that we went cheerfully to dinner that first evening and enjoyed a good meal, followed by a sing-song in the crowded, smoky lounge. Late into the night crowds thronged the darkened decks, pacing up and down, back and forwards, in twos and threes, all in earnest conversation. I pursued my solitary way, content to be alone, yet uncomfortable at not being one with the small group of civilians, even though they, too, were heading for the Sudan. I was one of the last to leave the deck to creep silently into my bunk, but this time, to sleep. The new sounds of creaks and squeaks as the ship lurched to the swell were scarcely noticed.

Next morning the sea was coated with a thick grey fog, hiding everything except the dim outline of the nearest ships. Sensing the mass of fog-shrouded shapes slipping over the black water gave the silence of the boat deck a spectral quality, as if these were ghost ships manned by spirits. Passengers, however, were preoccupied with their own problems. Each foot of rail supported a seasick soldier. The pale-faced sufferers abandoned themselves to discomforts more real than the possibility of a submarine attack.

Four p.m. and the fog was still thick. Sudden alarm-bells clanging and the Tannoy bawling 'Emergency Stations!' The sound of aeroplanes, invisible above the fog . . . Guns pound at the sky, then the engine sounds are silenced, with only gunfire remaining. What has happened?

Now there is total silence. People look at each other and wait; the sailors lean nonchalantly on the rails while a long half-hour passes. No explanations are given; then comes the 'All Clear'. Slowly the crowd melts away as the convoy beats on through the fog. An unpleasant rumour, never to be confirmed or denied, sweeps though the ship – 'Two British Sunderland Flying-boats shot down in error.' The possibility of this tragedy left us silent – could it be that our protectors had been destroyed? But so much was at stake that secrecy in all things was maintained.

That day I unearthed three books from a case. They were *The Forsyte Saga*, an Arabic dictionary and *A History of the Sudan*.

In the days that followed, the *Saga* was quickly read; the dictionary looked at then put away, as on my own, Arabic words had neither shape nor sound. I would just have to wait until I arrived in the Sudan to learn the language.

The history came as a surprise: I had grown up to believe that world history was essentially that of Britain, with a few bits added here and there. Never had I guessed that the Sudan itself was a cradle of early civilisations many hundreds of years before Victorian explorers 'opened up' central Africa. For the first time I read in depth about the Mahdi and the death of General Gordon, and I began to understand that in any conflict, heroism is not confined to one side in battle.

'. . . the Mahdi trekked with his small band to the comparative safety of the Tegali hills. He stopped with his weary and ragged little army at Jebel Gedir in the most remote and inaccessible region of the tangled Nuba Mountains . . .' This weary and ragged little army eventually captured the entire Sudan and killed General Gordon!

In the days that followed in this crowded ship I found an escape world in these remote and inaccessible regions, reading, then dreaming of days that would surely come in the not-far-distant future. It was difficult to find a quiet place to read as every corner and seat was cluttered with people, and the cabin was a place to keep out of whenever possible.

That night, after the alarm, I walked the decks alone once more, long after the ship was settled for the night. My mind ranged from subject to subject. With each passing day, thoughts of the future were taking over from memories of the past. Prospects for my life in Africa were as uncertain and unknown, as was the secrecy of this journey at sea.

A new morning, bright and clear, encouraged a large crowd on deck, so that walking was difficult in the congested ways. The boat deck was reasonably crowded, but down in the well of the ship, on the hatches and lower riggings, were half-clad soldiers, everywhere, in solid mass. No walking here! It was merely a pack of humanity stretched out wherever possible, but mainly standing, sitting or clinging to rigging in what, at times, were perilous positions.

There was no sign of sickness now. Some men were reading, some writing or talking, many stared blankly at the ships of the convoy. Indeed, the convoy on the blue water was a splendid spectacle. Ships, at first glance, appeared stationary relative to one another, and it came as a surprise to see the water surging towards the ship then slipping silently past, at what seemed a remarkable speed. If a neighbouring ship edged a little forward or slipped behind, it immediately caught the eye; indeed our neighbours became familiar friends, and were so close that movements aboard could be clearly seen.

At our port side, bow for bow, the black-funnelled, armed merchant cruiser *Maloja* ploughed on impassively, with guns ranging fore and aft. Slightly to our bow was a modern Polish liner; we discovered its name was *Sibjak*. It was a poor sailer, rising with the slightest waves and giving its passengers an uncomfortable time. A stately tall-funnelled liner sailed astern – the *Samaria*, crowded with soldiers like our own, and riding the seas steadily, with the air of a seasoned veteran. An old naval cruiser, gloomy in its dark camouflage, plodded on beyond the *Maloja* and behind the Commodore's ship. Other vessels had their special characteristics which became part of the unchanging scene, and the dogged pace of the convoy reminded one of mute and determined wolves stalking a prey.

All manner of entertainments were on the go, with playing-cards well to the fore. Housey-housey was in full swing, and a piano played nostalgic songs. It was all cheerful enough as men adapted themselves to weeks of shipboard life.

A little NAAFI shop opened aft, where tea, buns, cigarettes and chocolates were on sale. It became customary to start queuing at least two hours before opening time, presumably not because of any need for provisions, but it was as well sitting in a queue as anywhere else.

That evening the alarm went off again sending people rushing frantically in all directions, fetching life-jackets or heading for lifeboat stations. We all stood for over an hour in the cold air while booming sounds came from the horizon. Faintly, destroyers could be seen turning and twisting, while the convoy sailed on – the cruiser moved over to the fringe of the convoy, but now there was silence.

As darkness fell, the all-clear sounded and, with relief, we went for our delayed evening meal.

Next morning we wakened once more to the awful silence of stopped engines. This was a dreadful mystery. Why should the ship stop in mid-Atlantic unless there was a breakdown? The silence was, however, reassuring and it was decided to open the porthole for the first time, as it was now daylight. The entire convoy was stationary!

Feet, by now, were pounding the corridors. To a man, we threw on some clothes and hurried on deck where earlier risers already crowded the port rail. There, only a mile away, was the great liner *Queen Mary*, also stationary, and with bows pointing towards the British Isles. The sight of the grey-painted monster made the heart thrill with pleasure. Here was a tweak at Hitler's nose! That our convoy could halt deliberately to hold business with the greatest troop-ship of all! The cheek of it made us laugh.

The halt lasted relatively few minutes with, presumably, some exchange of personnel or equipment taking place, then engines started once more, and the convoy regained speed. The *Queen Mary* steamed off towards Britain with wonderful grace, alone.

With the sun rising in flaming red, the convoy commenced a wide turn southwards and with this mid-ocean meeting over, I could look forward to the prospect of glorious heat and, beyond, Africa and work. The sight of the sun straight over the ship's bow encouraged me to bring out the books on Africa, to begin some serious study. I found my own secluded corner beneath a lifeboat and spent long, solitary hours trying to prepare my mind for what lay ahead.

The sea that day was glassy calm, but by evening a remarkable change took place. The sun disappeared behind a wall of black cloud and a high sea built up, making the ship, big as it was, rise high to the waves. With darkness I had the deck to myself, pacing backwards and forwards across the width of the ship, anticipating her movements. Red sparks rose from the funnels but, otherwise, everything was black and it was hard to believe that on all sides was this great invisible armada.

Back in the cabin a game of cards was in progress. I slipped into bed and soon fell asleep.

Was it midnight? All hell let loose. Clamour of bells and shouting voices. The ship heaved as never before and, in a second, we were all tangled in bedding, while struggling to put on some clothes. Six men in such confined space with the ship bucking through a storm, was a nightmare confusing the senses. Out into the gangways at last: joining the mad stampede to the boats.

I joined ranks of huddled shapes standing in bitter cold. Wind howled through the ship's rigging and a mist of salt spray drenched everyone. Sailors had already loosened ropes supporting the lifeboats in what seemed a futile exercise with such a storm.

Dejectedly, everyone became resigned to the bitter inevitable, crouched, shivering in utter misery. Minutes passed and still the ship battled into the waves; there was no sound apart from the crashing of the storm. Was it an hour that passed in this way? If it was only an hour, this short period of time fills a large space in memory, and puts other periods of hardship into perspective.

The all-clear sounded again. Wet and stiffened we staggered back to our bunks, to hide for warmth beneath now dampened sheets.

By morning the storm had subsided, although there was still a bit of movement. It seemed a miracle that all of the ships were steaming on as normal, instead of being scattered far and wide. How many tens of thousands of men had suffered that bitter night of storm on deck throughout the convoy? But what did that matter when compared with the ever-present possibility of loss due to enemy action?

A cold, grey day followed, with surly waves and storm clouds but, by the next morning, the sun was perceptibly higher and a new warmth animated the company. The last day or two had been strained and gloomy but now spirits rose, and that earlier impression of a holiday cruise came seeping back.

There was a church service this day. The room was packed as a red-robed padre spoke words full of meaning to me, then we sang the hymns of home – a home, by now, slipping far into the past.

A morning dawned when we found the convoy sailing due east at reduced speed towards a coastline covered by low cloud. I was gripped by a wave of excitement – my first sight of Africa!

The ships drew into a single line while the destroyer escort worked inwards. A periscope rose from the water close by, and up from the water came a submarine bearing the colours of Holland. Slowly we moved into a wide river-mouth – this was Sierra Leone; the first stage of the long journey to the Sudan was safely over.

I looked on with rapture as I saw my first Africans in a hollowed-out canoe getting loud cheers as each ship sailed by. Now we were rounding a bend in this inlet and I was looking at a town with picture-book buildings, palm trees, mist-capped hills – Freetown.

Three long, weary days were spent there amid stifling heat. The entire convoy had crowded in to be serviced by a fleet of small craft. Below decks it was like an oven and, as no one was permitted ashore, people sought in vain for cool places to while the hours away. The thousands of military aboard the *Rangitiki* patiently lived these days out, the most dreary days of all: days of nothingness.

A morning dawned when unexpectedly and without warning, the entire convoy got under way again. Just clear of land, the ships formed up in the same familiar ranks, then veered southwards on the long trip to the south Atlantic.

There followed blissful days sailing over blue waters with a cool breeze sweeping the ship. There was a dreamy quality about this time, as if wars could never be: I lay, reading, in the shade of the lifeboat by day and, at night, watching the black finger of the ship's mast circling the stars; occasionally I stayed there the entire night, sleeping on the hard deck with my lifejacket as a pillow.

One morning the ship tilted perceptibly to port. In our neighbouring ship, the *Maloja*, a group of nurses dressed in white lined up to perform morning exercises, and it seemed our entire complement of passengers crowded the rails to cheer them on. This became a regular entertainment on the *Rangitiki*, with viewpoints booked well before the exercises were due to begin.

The second night from Freetown, a tramp vessel clearly marked *España* blundered between the ranks of the darkened convoy, too close to some ships for comfort.

By now, the southern stars were climbing the sky – the Southern Cross, the Scorpion and other new constellations held my interest. The usual playful schools of porpoises danced at the ship's bows and a graceful, solitary bird, the albatross, glided high overhead.

Father Neptune came aboard as the convoy crossed the Equator but there were so many first-time voyagers that only a few representatives received treatment at his hands. This was a day for special celebration which finished with a concert, held on a rear hatch, with solid tiers of people on every side. Some appeared to dangle from the ship's rails by fingertips to have a view, but no one fell overboard.

Next day, the mood was different. Two soldiers had died, 'through over-exposure to the sun' it was said. In mid-afternoon, another crowd gathered as the canvas-wrapped bodies were consigned to the deep. The service was read to the accompaniment of total silence: from the many thousands of people in this large convoy, here was the first waste of human life.

A story went round the ship that a German raider was loose in the South Atlantic – some said, a 'pocket battleship'. This was enough to maintain a level of excitement, so we were not taken by surprise when there came another alarm and, once again, stood expectantly at our appointed stations. This time conditions were both calm and warm, and we took it in our stride, looking around with interest to identify anything unusual.

Nothing happened, except that our constant follower and companion, the *Samaria*, suddenly released volumes of white steam and began to slip back, out of the convoy. The rest of the ships steamed on, apparently unheeding, while we watched anxiously as it disappeared out of sight below the horizon. Thoughts of this defenceless ship wallowing alone with a German raider near at hand led us to fear the worst, but next morning a cheer went up when the *Samaria* was seen creeping back to its usual station in the convoy.

The weather was becoming cooler again as the southwards progress continued: a low bar of cloud stretched down the eastern horizon which was conjectured to be close to the African coast. Then, things began to happen. A mass of flags festooned the Commodore's ship and it suddenly peeled off eastwards followed in turn by ships at random, from all parts of the convoy. This procession headed towards the cloudmass, to Cape Town in the Union of South Africa where Table Mountain was just visible with its cloud cap.

The major part of the convoy continued in a more easterly direction, then the *Maloja* took in hand another line of ships, veering in towards Port

Elizabeth, leaving a much-reduced force following at the heels of the cruiser. It was obvious, by now, that we were bound for Durban, with, this time, the promise of some days ashore.

Next morning we awakened to different rhythms as the ship slowed on its approach to land. Tall, white buildings grew up and the long arm of a pier reached out towards us.

A clear voice bridged the last mile: a voice singing 'Land of Hope and Glory, Mother of the Free,' and there at the end of the pier stood a solitary figure – the Lady in White, welcoming us as she did most other arrivals at this period of history.

The effect was magnificent: it held us in its thrall – we were among friends in this new country.

Northwards to the Sudan

Merely to go ashore was a sufficiently exciting prospect but that the shore should be African at last, had the quality of a dream. Soon after docking we four civilians were instructed to transfer to another ship, a Dutch liner, the *Volendam*, berthed not far away. This time, our tiny cabin had only four berths.

The harbour, like any other one in war-time, was filled with grey, dingy ships, ranging from sleek ocean liners to antiquated tramps with massive smoke-stacks. Beyond the harbour I looked with pleasure on exotic trees and shrubs, and listened to the cheerful chatter of negro voices. Ships seemed filled with a choice of food I had not seen in years, making war seem too far off to matter. After bomb-drenched Liverpool, Durban was an oasis of plenty, yet, should Hitler's forces win the battle for North Africa, the entire continent would be at his mercy.

Five days we spent in this paradise, then in the middle of the night the throb of engines told us we were heading once more for the open sea.

The convoy, this time, numbered about thirty ships and, again, ours was placed in the middle. The majority of soldiers on the *Volendam* were white South Africans, heading for the Middle-East fighting. Days passed by in the same languid way, with concerts and sing-songs and a number of 'international' boxing competitions to while the hours away. Eight days out of Durban the convoy split into two sections – the starboard column with escorts bearing east towards Asia, leaving ten ships and one cruiser continuing up the African coast.

Next day, high mountain-tops visible above a belt of cloud turned out to be Madagascar, and this time, six more ships left. The cruiser now led the *Volendam* and another three vessels westwards, toward the coast of Africa. For the first time we were told our destination – Mombasa, the end of our journey at sea. One morning the ship crept painfully slowly towards a rain-drenched mainland, past little palm-decked islands, and into the security of Mombasa harbour.

There was a feeling of elation that the long days at sea were over, and thoughts of torpedoes and enemy action could be put aside for good. Yet that had been the easy part. What happened now? How did one travel from Mombasa in Kenya to Khartoum in the Sudan?

When we finally struggled from the ship with our baggage, several things became clear – there would be no more ships to take us up the coast to Port Sudan and no one had the slightest interest in our future progress. Military personnel were being transported from the ship with the usual precision, but as for four civilians, it seemed that no one wanted to know us.

There was no consul to advise us, hotels had no accommodation to spare, police disputed our right to be there. Arguments waxed hot then, when it seemed we might as likely be sent back by ship to England, we were unceremoniously put aboard a van and driven to Malindi, a military staging post north of the town.

The camp commandant met us warily, and tactfully advised us to get the first possible train to Nairobi, where we might find others of our ilk. No one here was impressed by the important anonymity of our garb.

It took four more days before railway officials conceded to let us travel, but these days were memorable ones. We inhabited a bamboo hut on the fringe of a coral beach, and I had freedom to make my solitary explorations of this new tropical world. I walked mile after mile and discovered crops and plants that I had previously only seen in the pages of textbooks – sisal-hemp, pineapple, plantains. I watched men climbing coconut palms with splendid ease. There were bright-coloured butterflies, great spiders – in fact, these were days full of excitement, days which reinforced my high expectations of Africa.

By the time our seaside stay was over, I knew that there was one way only to get into the Sudan, namely to follow the line of the Equator across Kenya and Uganda, then to sail the long Nile passage to Khartoum. On a map the journey looked feasible, but the means of travelling were uncertain, and unknown for much of the way.

An overloaded train puffed away from Mombasa on the long stretch to Nairobi. I was separated from my three companions, fortunate to find a seat. I watched in rapture as heavy locomotives pulled the long string of coaches up the steep escarpment, until the sea became a faint line in the distance.

On the escarpment now, I sat back and marvelled at every new spectacle. The compartment was hot, with people packed so that there was no room for movement. By darkness, I struggled unsuccessfully for sleep: the ship's cabin seemed luxurious in comparison with this. I saw the dawn, with its glowing colours opening out wide vistas, and discomfort was forgotten.

By mid-morning the spectacle of a crowded game reserve had me in rapt attention. Animals were teeming there in thousands. Now time passed easily until, in the early afternoon, the train reached Nairobi.

I found my three fellow travellers. They had resolved to go into the city for a meal and to organise the next stage of their journey to Khartoum. I told them I would continue into Uganda at once, so they went their way, and I went mine.

I was gripped with a sense of relief to be alone after so many crowded weeks; alone and able to make my own decisions. In fact, I ultimately reached Khartoum in advance of the others.

A train was due to leave for Uganda, so I quickly climbed aboard, then remembered I had not eaten at all that day. There was no service of food on this train, so I had to wait until the following day to eat, but somehow that did not matter. Fewer people were travelling now, and I was able to stretch out and relish the scene as the railway line led over the great central rift valley, taking me deeper into the heart of Africa.

I saw flamingo-covered lakes, then, as darkness fell, the line climbed into highlands with the temperature getting lower and lower, so that I shivered as the train crossed the Equator. By morning we were in the soft afforested landscape of Uganda.

Kampala had the look of a pleasant little colonial town, peaceful and beautiful. Exotic plants covered buildings; the people, dressed in bright-coloured garments, looked cheerful and prosperous.

I went by taxi to the Imperial Hotel where, at last, I was made to feel welcome, and was allocated a spacious room with my own private bathroom; comfort at last! There followed ten wonderful days in which the local Agricultural Department took me in hand to show me tropical agriculture at its best. I discovered that Uganda was indeed a rich country. I saw tea being picked and dried, rich juices extracted from sugar cane: the red, iron-rich soil seemed capable of growing anything. Meanwhile, I had used up all my money, and it took an urgent telegram to Khartoum to make me solvent again.

When the ten days had gone there came the first opportunity to travel westwards to the Nile. I was offered a lift by a district commissioner who was heading for a spell of duty in the west, to Butiaba on Lake Albert, the very starting point of the Nile Passage. This was unbelievable luck, as I was beginning to despair of ever getting out of the country. I left Uganda knowing that it was a land which had everything in its favour, and I felt grateful for the knowledge I had gained there about tropical agriculture.

Nile Passage

The road drops steeply to the Lake Albert depression. We stopped to admire a red sun setting over the towering Mountains of the Moon in the Belgian Congo. Here were the fountains of the Nile: I had arrived at the very heart of Africa.

My kind host left me on a little jetty at Butiaba, on the shore of Lake Albert. By now it was night. A little steamer with some barges tied to its sides was fitfully lit by a few light-bulbs, but there was no one in sight as it was late. I wandered through the huddle of sheds which constituted the port, then climbed a gang-plank to the ship's deck. Doors leading into the ship were locked: there was only silence.

I put my cases on the deck and lay down beside them, to sleep. Despite this discomfort I was asleep in minutes. I wakened in daylight with somebody shaking me. A bearded figure wearing a naval-type cap said, 'Where the hell did you come from?'

I struggled up and explained my destination, and how I had got this far. 'You have not a hope of getting on this ship: it has been booked solid for months.' Apparently parties regularly travelled to and from the Sudan, but no one ever just turned up as I had done.

'I don't need a cabin,' I pleaded, 'just let me travel with you, I can look after myself.'

'Sorry,' he said, 'I would like to help, but. . .' He thought for a minute, then, 'Well, there is no reason why you can't travel in one of the barges with the cargo.'

I was overcome with relief; it did not matter how I went as long as I was moving in the right direction. I tested my luck further.

'Can I buy some food on the ship?'

The Captain, for such he was, smiled. 'Yes, why not? You can come in and eat after the other passengers are finished.' So, it was all amicably arranged. I found a comfortable corner among some gunny sacks on a barge, and settled in to await the arrival of the passengers.

A long, hot day followed. I befriended a black crew member who was fishing from the ship's rail. The waters of the lake teemed with fish and they were so easily caught that there was soon a heap of them on the deck.

*Twenty-second birthday, 27 October
1942, Uganda/Sudan frontier.*

Barge on source of Nile.

White Nile river steamer.

Late in the afternoon a bus emptied out the ship's passengers, a mixed group of military personnel and civilians – no aeroplanes were available at this time to fly from Khartoum to Central Africa so the Nile route had become an important artery. They moved into their comfortable berths and, perhaps, wondered at the poor 'white' who was settled in among the cargo. Indeed, I did have companions; a mixed assortment of livestock, including goats, which apparently had the freedom of the barge.

The Captain called out to me, 'Keep an eye open for scorpions!' then the ropes were untied and the ship set out into the vast lake.

I had dinner in the little dining room, then, back on the barge again, I had a wash from a bucket of lake water, and finally settled down to enjoy the journey. It was a never-to-be-forgotten night. The little family of boats was beating its way towards the Nile and I settled into the deep bed of sacks to look at a starlit sky, over which sheet-lightning occasionally flashed. Fireflies flickered beads of light before my eyes. The animals, my close neighbours, were settled down for the voyage.

In the middle of the night a sudden tropical shower had me burrowing for cover, but I slept and wakened at first light to find we were approaching a shelving beach bearing the sign: 'Rhino Camp'. The barge ran onto the sand; some passengers left the boat, others joined and, as there was to be a six-hour halt, I set out into the jungle to explore. I found that most of the trees and wild flowers fitted into my basic understanding of botany, and the hours passed more quickly than I realised.

In a village close by, a market was in progress. A bustle of naked tribespeople gathered round the various products, some of which were quite unrecognisable – what could have been slabs of hippo-fat, snake-meat, insects of some kind, and a range of vegetable products: yams, cassava and others, were finding a ready market.

The ship's whistle pulled me hurriedly from the scene, and I was settling back into the barge when the Captain called, 'Come aboard, there's a cabin for you. Make yourself comfortable.'

I was home and dry, accepted on the passenger list – in another fourteen or so days of travel, I would reach my destination. At last I had identity, a sense of 'belonging'. I was no longer the outsider, and I was with my own kind.

The boat made its way into the river with the navigable channel shifting from side to side. At one point when gliding close to the west bank, a statuesque

Floating islands of papyrus. Through the Sudd.

Nile Passage, Sudd.

elephant stood just a few yards away – I could see the light in its eyes. Then came reserves with countless hordes of wild animals gathered to drink at the river-bank – the home of white rhino and buffalo. In places, long lines of crocodiles basked in the sun, and the water was speckled with the eyes and ears of hippos, so many that it appeared as if we would run aground on them.

A soldier lay on the upper deck shooting ruthlessly at the river animals as if it was his considered view that they had no right to be there.

Next morning the ship tied up at Nimule, where the river tumbles over rocks and necessitates a transfer to motor transport for the next 100 miles. The sign 'Anglo-Egyptian Sudan' caught my eye. I had arrived

Nilotic tribesmen.

at the country of my choice, although a long river journey still remained.

This was an occasion for contemplation. I walked beside the river, then sat for some time on a rock beside the tumbling waters. The date was 27 October, 1942 – my twenty-second birthday.

A small fleet of estate cars stood waiting for the passengers and I thrilled at the sight of the words 'Sudan Government' on the epaulette of a driver. It was a tight squeeze once passengers and luggage were packed in, and I just managed a seat in the last vehicle.

The cars set off along a dust road close to the river, and from the first moment it became obvious that our vehicle had a serious steering defect. We swayed from side to side of the road, but the driver seemed determined to keep up with the other cars.

Several miles passed in this way, until we were shouting to the driver to stop. He began to slow down, but too late. The car slid into a ditch, rolled on its side then gently turned over. I was showered with broken glass and seemed part of a tangled heap of people, but, somehow, we all climbed out, with little more than a few bruises.

The other cars were far out of sight and now began a long, long wait. With no other traffic on this road, it was only when the cars reached the next town, Juba, that it was discovered the tail-ender was missing. We were eventually collected and, disconsolately now, sat nursing our wounds.

I, for one, pondered over this welcome. Submarines and bombs had all failed to interrupt the journey: it had taken a car in the middle of the African jungle. By now, I was sated with spectacle and was anxious only to get to Khartoum. It would be a relief to settle down to work!

Safely aboard another river steamer for the next 1000 miles, there followed day after day through the Sudd swamps, turning and twisting between the all-encroaching masses of elephant grass and papyrus reaching as high as the top deck of the ship. With its cluster of six barges it beat its way over the top of small floating islands of papyrus. This was a long, monotonous stretch, then the Sudd lessened, and there were firm river banks once more.

The boat stopped at mission stations and trading-posts which served the various nilotic races. Nuer, Dinka, and Shiluk, each people distinctive with their special fascination. These were peoples almost untouched by modern civilisation, except to witness the arrival of river steamers such as ours.

The current was faster now as it left the Sudd carrying the boat along with it at greater speed. The forest was slowly changing to savannah grass. The change seemed complete when we saw Arabs riding on donkeys, followed, a little further on, by long strings of camels.

By the time the river journey ended at Kosti I had had my fill of boats of all kinds, and was looking with some excitement at a semi-arid landscape, one with which I was likely to become familiar in years to come.

The boat stopped at a jetty beside a railway bridge – the first bridge in that long reach of river: twelve days' journey from Uganda. Now it remained only to cross this bridge by train, followed by one more day of travel to reach journey's end.

Arrival

I could tell by the numbers of mud-brick houses that Khartoum was drawing near. My eyes picked out lines of earthworks, probably part of the city's defences against the Mahdi. The scene looked as it must have done in General Gordon's day.

With the long journey at an end, I was tense with excitement as the train squealed to a halt. What would happen now? Would anyone come to meet me? My only advice was to report to the Agricultural Department. There were no station platforms, just red sand which, in seconds, was crowded with white-clad Arabs.

I made out a group of white people, conspicuous with their pith helmets, pushing through the throng. They were apparently searching for some new arrival to the city. I was throwing my bags to the ground when there came a shout:

'There he is!' They pushed their way towards me. 'Keep your hands off him, he's mine!' 'He's arrived at last: well done!'

My hands were shaken enthusiastically, they patted my back, and there were smiles on every side. They apparently did things in style here. It turned out that included in the group were government department heads, some military officers, and one distinguished-looking man, introduced as the Civil Secretary. Two reporters, notebooks at the ready, shouted questions. After my solitary journey I felt confused with this sudden prominence.

One slightly built man took my arm, introducing himself as the Director of Agriculture; the very man who controlled my destiny.

'You are coming home with me: you must need a rest.' These words were just what I most wanted to hear.

At this period, at the end of the Sudan's own war in Eritrea against the Italians and with Rommel's campaign in Egypt going on, the Sudan was isolated. British staff had had no leave home for several years and my arrival from the south was an event which spelled out hope to them. Here was an occasion to celebrate. In some respects it was a sign that the war was being won.

Next day the *Sudan Star* carried the news of my arrival, and journey. More alarming were statements I was supposed to have made about impending

Agricultural Headquarters, 1942.

victory over Hitler. Whether or not I had actually said these things was irrelevant; it was what people wanted to hear.

My Director drove me along palm-fringed roads to his home on the banks of the Blue Nile. He allocated a servant for the period of my stay with him, and in a matter of minutes I luxuriated in a marble bath, feeling at peace with the world, and sated with a warm sense of security.

I spent a week in Khartoum becoming acclimatised to this new hot country and learning what the work of an Inspector of Agriculture amounted to. In just a few days it became commonplace to move among the Sudanese people, to shop at the market-place and to listen to the guttural, incomprehensible Arabic language. I did not know a word of Arabic.

People were assigned to show me round. On my second day there came a disappointment – my vision of trekking through the African bush was thwarted with the news that it was necessary for me to spend an initial year at an irrigation scheme learning about the country before I would be ready for anything more ambitious. A whole year! It seemed like a life sentence, yet it was reasonable enough: there was obviously a great deal to learn.

The Director sat me in his office, and after looking at maps of the country he explained how complex was its agriculture, varying as it does from the arid north to the tropical south. He outlined its sheer size, its many different races – and yet with very few white inspectors in charge of agriculture: some worked close to the desert using irrigation water from the rivers, others amid tropical jungle. He spoke of his main interest and concern, namely the question of soil erosion. 'The desert is spreading, and people don't take time to observe.'

The following advice was passed on to me with some sense of passion: 'Remember, the future of the Sudan rests in its soil and its people: get to know and understand them both. They shall remain long after we British are gone.' My first briefing and he was referring to the possibility of the British leaving the country some time in the future!

He added, 'You will be working on equal terms with the Sudanese one day, and may even have a Sudanese superior.' Today, these words may not seem significant, but they were prophetic. Few people working there fifty years ago could visualise anything other than the status quo: after all, the Union Jack still flew bravely over a great and intact Empire. After a lifetime of service in Africa, the Director's words were worth heeding: they influenced me greatly throughout my years in the country.

I was given a long typewritten list of over 100 items to purchase or acquire during that busy week. It included trek table; chairs and bed; mosquito net; pots and pans; bush-shirts and shorts (all made to measure at the suq); a 'housewife' with needles, thread and thimble; and a full-dress uniform with a striking pith helmet bearing the department's badge. My last purchase was a cumbersome black steel box (guaranteed white ant-proof) and described as a trek-box, though much too clumsy for trekking as I discovered later. Barclays Bank, Khartoum Branch, accommodated me with an account, but once everything was purchased, the account was very nearly empty.

At headquarters I received the briefing for my first post to Abdel Magid, an irrigation scheme in the Gezira, a flat wilderness of clay soil between the two Niles. The scheme was named 'The Alternative Livelihood Scheme', described as a 'great social experiment' designed to settle poor tribespeople in villages and agricultural holdings, with the hope of raising their living standards. It was much in the public eye at that time although war had intervened. It was also a reminder that the Sudan was not a colony. British rule was apparently serving other functions than merely that of exploitation. The scheme and its objectives were explained to me in detail but no amount of explanation could have prepared me for the sheer scale of the operation. So many thousands of acres, with only two inspectors in charge.

I was to share the running of the scheme with a senior inspector, Alex Graves, who had many years of service in the country. During the week in the city his name kept cropping up in conversation – 'A hard worker, a hard nut, difficult to get on with' – 'You will probably get on all right with him, but . . .' Obviously headquarters regarded him with unease, though with grudging respect. I had yet to learn about the great divide between city office-wallahs and the workers in the field.

The prospects for this year in the Gezira were, however, far from comforting. In all the excitement of this new life one important thing had been lacking: namely, news from home. Four months had passed since leaving Scotland, and there were times when my engagement to Marion on that last evening was like a dream. Had it actually happened? Would she write to me? I knew that in war-time, letters often took several months to reach the Sudan: but it was a cause for worry. On the last day before leaving the city, mail reached Khartoum. There were two letters from Marion. Holding these tightly and trembling in my eagerness, I tore them open. She loved me: she was missing me! It seemed almost unbelievable that it could be so. Aren't moments like these among life's happiest?

A hurdle had been cleared. I thought: now for the Sudan, Abdel Magid, Alex Graves, and work! I was ready for them all.

That day I crossed the White Nile to Omdurman to see the Mahdi's Tomb. I enjoyed being part of the congested life of people and animals. Then I stood on the spit of land where the Blue and the White Nile unite: here, General Gordon had looked in vain for the arrival of Kitchener with his relieving army.

The evening was spent experiencing city night-life – an open-air cinema followed by a visit to a 'cabaret' where the only significant entertainment was that of three matronly chorus-girls, presumably all that were available in war-time, singing: 'There were three little sisters in their teens; one loved a soldier, one loved a sailor and one loved a man from the Marines.'

Next morning at dawn I said goodbye to the Director, then, with a laden car, was driven by a sleepy driver to the station.

The station was quiet and deserted in the thin morning light. It looked as if I was to be the only traveller. There was a reserved compartment and soon my bits and pieces were heaped on the floor; that is, apart from the steel trek-box containing all my clothes which was placed in the hands of a guard at the rear of the train. Left alone, I watched the sun edging over the horizon.

This was such a contrast to the noisy welcome of a week before. What would the coming year hold for me? This man Alex Graves, my sole 'white' companion at Abdel Magid, was he as formidable as they said? Tropical crops grown under irrigation – I hoped that allowances would be made for my ignorance of the country.

With a jolt the train pulled away (on the short sixty-five-mile journey). Warm crimson light flooded the compartment. Leaving the city, retracing last week's journey, the suburbs looked as untidy as before; only now, they were bathed in the softest glow, giving them an unreal beauty. Now, I felt I could view the scene from the eye of experience. My hat boasted the department's badge – I was an Inspector of Agriculture: but what did that really mean?

A fine film of dust filtered through the window joints. Heat was building up. I opened the window but quickly closed it as streamers of dust poured in. The landscape looked flat and uninviting. Even though not far from the capital, it had the bareness of a desert. Surely very little rain fell here. In the distance a line of trees marked the proximity of the Blue Nile.

Water made all the difference between fertility and a desert. That was the first obvious lesson to be learned in this barren land. Water – soil – and people: it had been said these were the ingredients of my job. Heat-mirages like sheets of water sent shimmering images into the sky. Here was the famous Gezira – a wide-spread plain, fertile, though absolutely parched.

Time was passing; a ceiling fan purred busily, but it had little effect in this heat. Unexpectedly the train juddered to a halt. There was no sign of a station – then I saw a post bearing a name: Abu Usher. My stop! Time to get out: my heart gave a jump. Opening the door I quickly threw my kit out and was stepping to the ground, when a grey open box-car swept up in a cloud of dust. A stalky, khaki-clad figure stepped out, eyeing me up and down for a few moments before extending a hand and saying, 'Welcome lad, Alex Graves is the name,' in a gravelly sort of voice. My first impression was of khaki shorts reaching below kneecaps; then, higher up, a lantern jaw topped by steely blue eyes. His grip was hard. Here was no soothing father-figure: at first glance, not the kind of person to tolerate deficiencies in others.

Preoccupied as I was I scarcely noticed the train's departure, taking my box with it and almost all my clothes. Guards obviously did not read baggage-labels in the Sudan! The box shuttled up and down the line for three weeks before the 'careful' guard decided to drop it at Abu Usher.

A bad start. But Alex made no comment, except to say I could wear his spare clothes until mine arrived. I looked at his shorts and wondered.

We loaded the car, and Alex said, 'Let's head for home.' What could home be like in such a wilderness?

He drove flat out over the plain; there was nothing so sophisticated as a road. The high earth bank of a canal came into view. I was given a first lesson on irrigation at Abdel Magid.

'The scheme is thirty miles further on: it takes twenty-four hours for water to reach us from the Sennar Dam. If the water-need is not carefully calculated a canal bursts its banks or crops shrivel up.' He looked at me silently, but with the corner of a grin on his face. Here was something I had to learn, and fast.

The lesson continued. I listened as carefully as I could; subsequent explanation might be less forthcoming.

'We have 40,000 acres here: you and I are responsible for it. Some Sudanese supervise the tenants who grow the crops.' Information poured from his lips. I could scarcely comprehend it due to the novelty of the journey, which commanded most of my attention.

'The White Nile Alternative Livelihood Scheme, as it is called, is an important social experiment to give security and income to poor tribesmen who own no land. Each cultivator grows ten acres of crop consisting of five acres cotton, three acres millet and two of oilseed simsim with dubia, a type of bean. The Government keeps part of the income to pay for irrigation and other overheads.

'The scheme is divided into separate canal units; each is supervised by an agricultural sheikh. We have to make sure the whole thing works.'

A lot more was said on the journey to my new home. What I did not understand then, quickly became apparent in the days that lay ahead.

We left the canal to continue over another plain: mile after mile without a vestige of vegetation to give scale to the scene. A trail of dust fanned out behind. Alex's eyes were mere slits against the fierce light. Searing hot air made me withdraw my arm from the sides of the car. There was never a more inhospitable environment – only flat cracked clay and burning sunlight.

Then came a scattering of animal skeletons, with one recently dead camel

The 'Boys' on arrival, Abu Guta, 1942. Ibrahim is second from the right.

hidden beneath a curtain of jostling vultures. Suddenly, a strip of green stretching to the far horizon: a young cotton-crop! The land was now worked into a patchwork of geometrical shapes, each little section with its own dry water-channel – most of it unplanted, as if waiting my arrival. Mile after mile of this: the scale of it was staggering. Alex said that, together, we would be 'growing' fifty square miles of crops, an area so vast as to have little meaning for me at that time.,

The entire world of Abdel Magid was one of straight lines and squares, with only occasional mud-hut villages spaced at regular intervals to relieve the eye. This scheme could well be a worthwhile effort to improve the lot of poor nomadic people, but what a place for them to spend their lives! I thought it was time for me to say something.

'Do you find the scene monotonous?' – the best I could raise.

'Haven't got time to think about it,' was all I got in reply.

At last a grove of thorn trees came into sight, almost the only trees I had seen. There was a little suq at its edge. This must be home. Shimmering images settled to the ground as we approached this little forest, and Alex

33

Introducing 'new' technologies. Cultivation, Abdel Magid.

drove into an avenue leading to a clearing at its centre. Here stood two
squat houses, about 100 yards apart, surrounded by irrigated gardens. A
rather attractive oasis, I thought, and all, like the crops, depending on water
coming from the Blue Nile, so many miles away.

As at a signal a line of smartly clad natives came out to welcome us. Alex
described them as 'the boys', though it appeared that boys came in all ages,
including some with grey hair. I was introduced to them in turn – Sherif,
Ahmed, Ali, Ibrahim Sullieman; and others who could well have been garden-
ers. They were an impressive group, tall and very black-skinned; that is, apart
from Ibrahim who was on the small side. He caught my eye because of the
width of his smile, and the fact that he seemed to find me of some special
interest as he shouldered my gear into a room in Alex's house.

I was ushered in. It was remarkably cool inside, after the fierce heat of
the journey. The house was furnished with some style, indicating a female
influence. The lady of the house was in Khartoum doing war-work. The floors
were of polished tiles, with wide and airy corridors. What more could one ask?
I quickly discovered the house had its snags. The only energy sources were
paraffin and dung pats, or the occasional bag of charcoal; all water including
that for drinking came from muddy canals which were used for washing camels
and various unmentionable purposes; sanitation was by means of a bucket in
an out-shed – a bucket which was liable to disappear from beneath one at
unfortunate moments. We sat down to lunch on the verandah.

Home, Abdel Magid.

At work, Gezira, Abdul Magid.

Alex said, 'You can stay here for a few days before moving next door.'

I thought of my meagre furnishings and asked him, 'Are both houses the same?'

'Exactly the same. Of course, you will need boys of your own.'

I wondered for a moment what would I need 'boys' for. Then Alex gave a loud yell, making me jump. 'Ibrahim!'

The little black 'boy' padded in on bare feet.

'Take him,' Alex said, 'he's yours. Do what you like with him as long as he gets paid £2 monthly. You can get a cook later.'

I had no choice in the matter; not that I had any opinions to offer. Ibrahim was smiling benignly, as if fully understanding his fate and not intending to complain.

I said, 'How do you do, Ibrahim.'

'*Salaam Aleckum*,' came the response.

A plateful or two was quickly eaten. Alex wiped his mouth and stood up. 'Time for work. Just come with me. Watch and listen.' Hardly an hour at Abdel Magid and I was starting work!

He drove me to the office at the side of the suq, where, again, a line of figures, khaki-clad clerks and native agriculturalists this time, were introduced to me. In his own private office I sat as inconspicuously as I could while Alex got down to work. In a few minutes his feet were on the desk and his chair tilted back as, one by one, natives were ushered in. I had seen a long queue waiting outside: it seemed that this afternoon's work consisted of discussion and argument on a wide range of issues. There were policemen, poorly clad cultivators, more smartly dressed Arabs described as 'agricultural sheikhs', and what I took to be a merchant.

The constant flow of Arabic, sometimes heated, as men gesticulated wildly to accompany their arguments, bewildered me. Occasionally Alex explained what was going on. I was pleased to see that a twinkle seldom left his eye. Each man left in turn, apparently satisfied with the outcome. From this very first hour it was apparent that Alex was in his element: he was absolutely in command of each situation and exercised some power – a mixture of awe and regard – over all who came to him. He had a way of making the sourest face open up into smiles. Whatever Khartoum might say about him, he could certainly get on with the local people. We finished the day by touring a corner of the scheme, discussing the factors involved in growing crops under irrigation.

It had been a long, long day. We drove home at sunset and, after a wash,

Waterspill onto road – CLAY!

A village sage.

Gezira dweller with wives and child

sat down to dinner, followed by drinks on the verandah. At midnight, and not a minute before, I was able to escape to bed and solitude beneath the mosquito net. Sleep did not come easily; the new noises of frogs and crickets saw to that.

5.30 a.m. – Ibrahim opened the net, a cup of tea in his hand. He gave me the morning greeting in Arabic, then the word for 'tea', and from that moment became an effective language instructor. He laughed at my mistakes and repeated words carefully, until they became 'fixed'. This role alone was worth his £2 salary.

That first morning I was sent alone to Abu Idiena canal to instruct a group of sheikhs in wheat growing, a crop they had never seen before. Alex told me I was to be given the responsibility for growing 6,500 acres of wheat on the scheme, so I should get down to it at once and introduce the crop to the people. My inability to speak the language apparently did not give him any concern. This was his method – a few words of explanation, then I was sent out alone. He was impatient if I hesitated and even liable to walk away if I asked more questions. If the job was inadequately done, even in these first few days, he did not spare me. I just had to learn or life became unbearable.

It was a hard school, but it was also an effective one. In fact, very quickly I could drive round the scheme with a feeling of confidence. Alex never offered praise or expressed satisfaction at my efforts, but there was the concealed reward of being treated as an equal.

Surprisingly enough, despite what had been said in Khartoum, we were getting on quite well together. In fact, I also quickly became submerged in Abdel Magid, beneath its work, its language and its people. There was nothing else to act as a diversion – no radio, no newspaper and no books. It was a world apart.

One week after my arrival Ibrahim and I flitted to the empty house next door, where Mahomed Omer from the tribe of Dongola in the north joined my 'staff'. Mahomed the cook was indeed an acquisition. He was middle-aged, wise and gentle. Not only could he transform the rough products of the suq into something palatable, he shared future hardships without complaint, and became a friend.

My next acquisition was a horse, for which a groom was needed. This gave me an establishment of four: a houseboy, cook, driver and groom. They occupied a little community of huts at the back of the house where Mahomed also had his kitchen.

In the late evenings it became a custom to have the 'boys' into the house where I could practise my Arabic on them. The early stumbling words gradually extended to become sentences, so that I was able to learn from them not only their language, but also about their country and the people's customs. Ibrahim was a particularly devout Moslem and was ever willing to discuss his faith. Some of our earliest discussions were on the subject of religion. He would say, 'We Moslems are continually bowing in prayer to Allah, why are Christians never seen to pray?' To answer these questions often stretched more than an understanding of Arabic!

The office chief clerk, Suleiman Effendi, took it in hand to teach me the written language, a more intractable problem which I never fully resolved. I also discovered a new form of recreation for the evening hours, namely writing up a diary of the day's events, a hobby which provided hundreds of busy hours in the years ahead.

Khartoum had said that I must learn to handle a horse. I kept putting this off even though Bakhit, a cross Arab thoroughbred and a beautiful horse at that, waited for me to show an interest in him. Abdulahi, the groom, brought him round regularly for my inspection, then rode him along the canals to exercise him.

39

Finally, one Friday, the local rest day, I took life in my hands and called for the horse to be saddled. The boys were fully aware of my doubts where riding was concerned, so they gathered round to watch the entertainment.

'Don't put your weight on the stirrups!' 'Grip the saddle with your knees!' 'Hold him on a tight rein!' 'Don't fall off!'

Advice came in large supply, but I was preoccupied with the horse and how far I would have to fall, when the inevitable happened. The groom stood back, the boys retreated, then Bakhit for some reason went into reverse. He tossed his head as if having decided to show who was boss, then trotted towards the nearest canal – the most uncomfortable motion I had ever experienced. At the canal, fortunately, he decided to stop. The boys were watching with interest. I dug in my heels to encourage further movement and it worked. Bakhit set off along the canal bank in a wild gallop. My first moments on a horse and I was going like the wind!

The following five minutes provided material for subsequent nightmares. How did I stay in the saddle? I shall never know, but finally I returned a winded, slightly jaded Bakhit to the groom.

'Well done!' 'Good riding!' came the comments. Little did they know!

Somehow I mustered sufficient courage to try again later, so that gradually Bakhit began to tolerate me and riding became more bearable. Horse-riding at Abdel Magid, however, remained a minority interest mainly because there was seldom time to indulge it.

By now the scheme had been divided into two sections of equal area. Alex looked after his area and left me to run mine, consisting of land at the very tail-end of the scheme. In a few short weeks land was blanketed with green crops – wheat, cotton, millet, and lubia, a pulse grown to improve the diet of the local people. It was a time of frantic endeavour in which I averaged eighty to a hundred miles daily, encouraging often reluctant cultivators to tend their crops. On many occasions they had gone on a journey when the water arrived, despite a 'foolproof' system of communication, namely messengers on donkey-back. Areas of flooding or drought indicated the lazy, and made tempers short. All too often, bad practice was blamed on Allah with a shrug of the shoulders and: 'It was Allah's will' the invariable excuse.

One afternoon a swarm of locusts descended on a corner of my land, destroying several hundred acres of cotton, then flew off eastwards leaving one more problem to be solved.

Seven weeks from the day of arrival I still had not enjoyed a single rest day; then, one morning, Alex surprised me by suggesting, 'Let's take a day off!'

A day off could only mean leaving the scheme and, true enough, after breakfast we drove westwards leaving the growing crops and heading straight into that flat Gezira plain of nothingness. Soon we were in a wide circle of clay soil in which the horizon was a continuous level line with nothing to relieve it. Occasional little mounds of earth had been raised as markers. There were twenty-five miles of this, then a gradual transition to sand, the precursor of great rolling dunes close to the White Nile.

We arrived at a village which was almost buried in sand. The car churned its way to the largest of the houses, surrounded by a high mud-brick wall topped with broken glass. I was introduced to the owner, the local Omdah who was obviously pleased to welcome Alex to his home, his arms outstretched.

'Allah bless you. Welcome! Come into my humble home.'

Alex's eyes were alight with pleasure at meeting an old friend. A sparkling, laughing exchange of conversation followed as we crossed a courtyard to his mud-brick house.

We were ushered to a low divan. The Omdah elegantly arranged his robes then sat on a cushion at our feet. I looked round the large room, bright with painted walls, each one draped with a splendid Persian carpet. Otherwise, furnishings were sparse, consisting of animal skins stretched out on the floor, a large inlaid (and valuable-looking) cabinet, and a few little tables.

This was more like the Africa I had hoped to find. I had a feeling of release at being away from the never-ending grind at Abdel Magid, even though only for a single day. It was bad luck that my introduction to the country had been to an intensive agricultural scheme. Yet I was learning about the people and the language, as the Director had said.

I was able to understand the gist of the conversation – about the Omdah's camels. I watched Alex as he talked. There was nothing patronising in his attitude: this was not a colonial 'type' talking down to a native – very far from it. The Omdah was laughing heartily at Alex's expense! Would I ever be able to relate so easily to the Sudanese people?

Servants carried in a large circular platter laden with food which was placed before us. It contained a large joint of lamb with a variety of salads and spices. We tore off bits of meat with our fingers then dipped these into the sauces. It was excellent. Several servants crowded around offering fruit drinks, then they brought black Turkish coffee in little cups and much-needed finger bowls.

The meal was finished and we were rising when there came a cry from the courtyard, setting the company into a frenzy of action. The Omdah grabbed a rifle from the wall and rushed outside. Alex explained to me, 'Mad dog,' nodding his head knowingly, but making no attempt to join in the rush. Minutes passed, then came a shot – my first experience of rabies in Africa, one of the ever-present dangers.

When the excitement had passed we walked through the little village to look at the encroaching sand dunes. It was explained that as recently as twenty years before, the village had stood in a forest of acacia and palm trees. All of those had gone, leaving the houses at the mercy of blown sand. What could have happened in this short period to change the nature of the countryside: was it climatic change? Had the practices of the people changed in recent years? How was it possible after centuries of stability to turn a forest into a desert? I thought about the Director's advice to me concerning erosion and the progressive damage being done by it to the land. Surely the people would need to evacuate this village before very long?

But this was our holiday! Two camels were brought to carry us to the White Nile where, it turned out, we were to be taken for a sail in the Omdah's dhow. My first ride on a camel! Not a very great adventure, however, with the Omdah walking beside us over the mile or so to the river's bank. It was an important 'taster' however, and set me thinking with longing of days to come when trekking could well be an everyday experience.

Several boats were tied against a flimsy wooden jetty. We climbed aboard the biggest of these and were soon sailing gently beneath a billowing sail to the centre of the river, probably a mile wide. The ancient, weathered timbers of the boat radiated waves of heat and I could feel my skin crisping.

Alex suggested to me, 'Why not go in for a swim?'

The Omdah tied a rope round my waist and I slipped over the stern into the cool water. The boat sailed smoothly on beneath its great sail, and twenty-five yards behind I was pulled through the water, luxuriating in the coolness and reflecting on my good fortune that, in part at least, I had attained my heart's desire.

By the time our river trip was over, a crescent moon shone in the star-filled sky. Hundreds of camels and cattle were standing in the comfort of the cool water as we steered our way through this massive herd. Many of them were quite far from the shoreline, motionless and probably ruminating on their destinies. There came a sudden commotion in the water scarcely a hundred yards away. A camel disappeared beneath the surface and rose again; then we saw the flailing of a crocodile's tail. The Omdah jumped into the water; other men tried to reach the scene but long before they could get there it was pulled beneath the surface, leaving only gentle eddies to mark the spot. I thought of my recent swim not far away and felt grateful that crocodiles had a preference for camels.

That evening, with the day's holiday almost over, we crossed the Gezira plain once more. Alex headed eastwards, leaving the dunes behind and racing homewards over the featureless land. There was no compass in the car but he explained how an understanding of the stars gave a means of navigating, particularly by making use of the North Star. Since coming to the country, skies had been completely cloudless, leaving the stars like a chart above our heads. As expected we reached our main canal not far from the forest and got home in time for dinner.

Settling In

Weeks flew past. Each day brought its involvements with people. By now some were coming to consult me in the office, always stretching my abilities to speak Arabic to its limits. Only seldom did I call on Alex to resolve a special issue: he preferred me to solve my own problems without his help. I found that people would accept judgements provided I was absolutely certain of my case. When my vocabulary was limited they laughingly led me to the right word, thus helping me to encourage them to my way of thinking. I became accustomed to contending with noisy argument accompanied by wildly gesticulating arms – they loved to argue over the least point but when defeated, accepted it with good grace. I also found that most people did not have my sense of urgency for things to get done. They were apt to defer action until it was Allah's will that action should take place: this usually meant after long siesta or a prolonged family discussion.

It was easy to detect the source of most difficulties, mainly that people accustomed to the slow rhythms of nomadic or peasant life did not easily adapt to the urgent requirements of an irrigation scheme.

Pursuing my solitary way among the cultivators, drawn from many Sudan tribes, there was never any cause for nervousness or fear of the unexpected, except on one occasion.

It was a golden evening, the end of a long, hot day. In the west, broad diffused bands of colour spread out like a gigantic rainbow in tints of red, orange and green. I had a feeling of contentment; things were going well, most of the crops looked good, and Ibrahim would have a bath ready for me at home.

Flocks of sheep and goats were moving towards the villages in the gathering gloom. The scene was biblical. At the last bridge close to the Abu Guta forest where the house was situated, I drew up to let a flock squeeze its way over, before me. Suddenly my peace was shattered. A raucous yell came from behind, just a few yards away. With a start I turned – a white-bearded ancient was moving towards me with a curved sword raised, as if to smite. Me? What had I done? But his intentions were clear. His words did not need translation: they could only be: 'Heathen dog! Infidel! Son of a dog!'

There was fire in his eye. Had I paused to investigate I might have smelled alcohol on his breath, but there was little inducement for me to delay. I flicked in gears and shot forward, scattering both sheep and shepherds – only just in time! The sword descended where my arm had been a second before. There was one uncomfortable bump, then I was speeding towards the house. Turning into the drive I gulped. The sword-bearer was hot on my trail!

I rushed into the house. 'Ibrahim! Mahomed!' I called, banging the flimsy door behind me. The boys came in wondering; then, after words of explanation from me, Ibrahim set off at some speed into the trees. 'Coward,' I thought. My only defence was a bamboo donkey-stick. Mahomed and I stood behind the door, stick poised, expecting the worst.

Minutes went by: still there was no sound in the dark driveway. I opened the door, peered outside – then a white-clad figure stumped towards us, easily seen to be Ibrahim. He was in full grin.

'Come here,' he said, 'Follow me.'

We trailed behind him to the canal. A pathetic-looking, bedraggled old man sat on the bank, looking around him with bleary eyes. A sword lay in the dust nearby.

Ibrahim said, 'I picked up the *schiab* (old man) and threw him into the canal.' He was standing with arms folded, in heroic posture. It seemed more likely that a gentle shove had up-ended him into the water, but this was Ibrahim's day!

It was the only personal attack I had in the Sudan. It might have been a dream but for the neat slash on the side of the car just beneath the arm-rest. The old man was locked up for a spell, his sword was confiscated, and life resumed its usual tenor.

For a considerable time after this event, Ibrahim ruled the roost. Occasionally he shook his head slowly as he looked at me. Obviously his new charge required careful tending: it was as well he was in command! His brave efforts earned him a bonus of one additional month's wages, namely £2. At that time my monthly salary was £50: rather a good pay then. Hero he might be, but he was also developing a vain streak, slipping into the role of 'gentleman's gentleman' and exercising some authority over our sparse household. When I opposed his judgements he waved his head from side to side in exaggerated manner, and tut-tutted for everyone to hear. It wasn't easy to be angry with him and he usually got his way. Mahomed, the cook, bore with Ibrahim patiently. I found Mahomed to be completely honest

45

and, in the course of time, learned that he was the one to be depended on in an emergency.

After four months at Abdel Magid there had been no white visitors to the scheme. I was beginning to realise that I was circulating in an entirely male society. No doubt there are people who flourish when living apart from the opposite sex — presumably monks and hermits do — but I was a young man and on many occasions my attention was drawn to the veiled and furtive forms which occasionally came into view.

Sulieman Effendi invited me to his home for coffee. During the time in his little house we talked about his language, and he showed me a beautiful copy of the Koran. I was examining this when I noticed that he walked over to a little cupboard, spoke to it and fed it a biscuit. Belatedly it dawned on me that his wife had been shut in the cupboard for the duration of my visit. Where I was concerned, an embargo on female company had been decreed.

Magarin was just one canal in the scheme. It irrigated several thousand crop acres: the same long strips of cotton and millet stretching as far as the eye could see. It was neither the best worked land nor was it the worst — just average, so I had given it no unusual attention. I met the Agricultural Sheikh, as in other areas, then drove him around to inspect his cultivators' holdings.

There came a day when Magarin became more important to me. I had just left the Sheikh at his holding and was driving along minor canal six on the fringe of the scheme, when I saw an old cultivator waving to catch my attention, and hurrying as best he could over the sticky clay towards me before I passed by. I stopped.

The old man gasped out, 'Help me! You must help me. My daughter is dying. In Allah's name follow me!'

I followed him over the new-watered soil and was quickly almost knee-deep in the ooze. A figure lay in the young cotton crop, clay-spattered and still. Her blue robe had slipped from her shoulders showing, in spite of the mess of clay, an attractive female body. Then I saw a deep wound in her leg which had poured out blood and in which the thickness of sliced muscles could be clearly seen.

I bent down to look at the wound. How could such an injury have been conjured out of two frail people and a mattock? It didn't seem possible. She had been lying for some time: blood and clay beside the wound was caked and dry.

She opened her eyes and spoke to me, which came as a surprise. 'You

46

have come, praise be to Allah! *Ya moffetish!* (Inspector).' She lifted her hand for me to shake but made no attempt to conceal her body. I examined her damaged leg. The little dispensary at Abu Guta was probably ten miles away; I must carry her to the car – the sooner the wound was cleaned and sewn, the better.

As carefully as possible I eased her from the ground supporting the leg as best I could. She put her arm round my neck, then slowly we stumbled through the clinging clay. A shoe was sucked from my foot and it took the old man's strength to prise it from the mud.

I would have been forced to drop any other burden: the effort was almost too much. My heart pumped furiously and I tugged for breath in the blistering heat, yet I was only too aware of the very beautiful form in my arms. She was in her early twenties, I thought. Her body was slender as if she had not borne children: rather unusual where girls are married in the early teens. She had broad, pure-white teeth. Her cheeks wore tribal cuts, as I had often seen on men's faces.

Somehow the car was reached. I eased her into the passenger seat. Her father squeezed in to support her.

She was unconscious when I drove up to the dispensary. The little Arab doctor – Alex had called him Dr Hitler because of his little moustache – took her in hand.

I drove the father back to his village, then got on with the day's work. At this time, each day produced its own special excitement – the unexpected commonly happened – and in some respects the events of this day were not remarkable. Yet, somehow, there was a difference. To say the least, it was rare to be so close to a Moslem woman: by rights I should not even have gazed upon her.

That evening I sat at my lonely evening meal, thinking over the day's events. By now the muddied clothes had been pounded clean, and I was dressed in my usual evening wear of white shirt, flannels and cummerbund.

Was the girl recovering? It was too soon to tell. Perhaps I should ask. My mind struggled with the thought of this young person alone in an alien environment. Should I show an interest in her recovery; had I any responsibility towards her? Yes, she was a Moslem and the daughter of a cultivator, but did that really matter? Finally, I left the table and walked the mile to the dispensary. I would only ask how she was getting on.

The suq was empty, the dispensary door locked. Only silence. Dissatisfied with myself, and uncertain, I slowly retraced my steps. It was so difficult to behave naturally in this country where race and religion imposed such absolute barriers: was it wrong to visit an Arab woman in hospital?

Next afternoon I stopped work slightly earlier than usual and called in at the dispensary. A donkey stood with drooping head outside the hut. Inside, the girl's father was sitting cross-legged beside her. He rose as I entered and stepped back from the little string bed, bowing in silence. She lay, breathing heavily, as if in a fever. I asked the old man about her and at the sound of my voice her eyes flickered open, but only for a second.

Rather reluctantly, I thought, the father answered my questions. Her name was Miriam; they had left their village to find a holding here. Her mother was dead and they had no friends in the scheme. His daughter was unmarried; she was as good a worker as any man. He would say no more about her.

I left the hospital questioning in my mind my right to ask these things about a Moslem woman. Had it been a son there would have been no difficulty, but there was something intangible where the other sex was concerned.

I visited again the next day carrying with me a few flowers from the garden. She smiled and looked wide-eyed at the flowers as if not knowing what to make of them. Then she thanked me for my help. There was an appealing mixture of shyness yet willingness to speak. Her old father sat silently, just watching.

During the week that followed she slowly recovered. I visited the hospital perhaps more often than was proper. Dr Hitler obviously wondered at my interest. Her father usually stood at the door in silence. There was an irresistible attraction for me that at long last I could speak to my first Arab woman; and she was attractive, and now chattered on with a continuing sense of fun: she was so markedly in contrast with these veiled shadows which avoided me in the world outside. My interest was totally innocent, I told myself, yet for some guilty reason, I never told Alex about my hospital visits.

One day, I found that her father had taken her home on donkey-back. From that day on, Magarin No. 6 was inspected just a little more thoroughly than the state of the crops merited. Usually when I drove the length of the canal I could see her run over the cultivations to meet me. It was then difficult to drive on, although there were seldom more than a few minutes of conversation between us, about the simplest of things. 'Yes,' I told myself, 'we are friends. After all, we have shared an uncommon experience

together.' But there was, somehow, an intangible barrier which was total –
she, the simple cultivator, and me – well, what was I?

Then, one day, I drove the canal and she wasn't there. Another time,
and still she did not run to meet me. Something had changed which I did
not understand. I never saw her again.

The Agricultural Sheikh said they had gone from the scheme leaving
their crops untended. Was it because of me? I was troubled that this had
happened. Could it be because of race or religion: had my intrusion been
more than the father could endure? Or perhaps it was none of these things,
just the draw, homewards, to their village in the north.

Why does this little happening occupy my mind so many years afterwards? Is it because I can still picture her smile? And how easy it is, still,
to sense that slight body in my arms.

A short time afterwards, I took another woman to the dispensary. I was driving
the high bank of the main canal when I came upon a little knot of people
blocking the narrow road. There was a woman, her husband, some children
and a few interested bystanders. Some saddled donkeys stood nearby, quite
forgotten.

They all ignored me. It was obvious to me that the woman was in the
throes of childbirth. I waited in the background, and within a few minutes
could see a squalling infant being dangled by the ankles.

The husband came towards me smiling with pleasure. He shook my hand
then spoke with pride about the new arrival.

I thought that the appropriate thing was for me to offer them a lift to
Abu Guta, where I could place the wife in the hands of Dr Hitler. Rather
hesitantly she accepted, and with her baby and an old woman, probably her
mother, they climbed into the rear of the box-car.

We set off towards Abu Guta, leaving the husband to bring in the
donkeys. At the dispensary, I was about to leave in search of the doctor
when the family came to thank me. They were carefully concealed beneath
their robes, leaving only slits to peer through. She clutched the baby in her
wraps. Then they walked from the scene towards the village as if nothing
out of the ordinary had happened.

I told Dr Hitler about the event. He looked at me with a smile.

'But why bring her to the hospital, was she ill?'

I should have known better!

The District Commissioner was responsible for matters political. He dealt with tribal interfaces and matters of law and order. A native administration worked under the supervision of the DC who lived at Dueim on the White Nile, and who turned up as the occasion demanded. When a serious infringement of the law took place, a court was set up, and the culprit consigned to the local prison, not far from the suq.

The Agricultural Inspector, on the other hand, dealt with crops, livestock and the land, not to mention the occasional visit of locusts and similar troubles. The DC and Alex had worked together for years so that demarcations were blurred. It was not unknown for the DC to get his hands dirty occasionally, and as for Alex, he knew the tribes better than anyone.

It was something of an occasion when the DC appeared. Soldiers lined up for inspection, bugles blew and the Union Jack flew proudly over the suq. People looked on in silent admiration; at least they were silent, and there was never any trouble to upset the smooth tenor of life.

The DC was a popular figure who strode abut flicking a fly-switch. In general terms he supported the good works going on at Abdel Magid. Occasionally a young ADC came with him, learning his trade as I was doing. We put them up. The ADC stayed with me, so that two camp beds stood in the verandah and two lots of servants attended to our needs. I enjoyed these visits. We spent the late evening hours walking canal banks and talking in profound terms about our adopted country. We also both anticipated a future life of trekking with all the freedoms such a life would entail.

Superintending the local prison which housed maldoers from throughout the province, and the local primary school, were areas of interest shared by both departments. I was encouraged to have an involvement with both of them.

The school got frequent visits. The little boys (only boys) would, on every occasion, stand and chirp their school song as soon as I entered. The words of the song made glowing comment about Sacchlarides cotton, the variety grown at that time, and it finished with favourable reference to King George VI. With their performance over, it was expected that I should 'say something', which I always did with a few well-chosen words.

But it was the prison that most drew me.

A high, wired compound stood on the fringes of Abu Guta which housed many miscreants from throughout Blue Nile province. It was the Sudanese equivalent of Alcatraz, except that it was surrounded by an 'ocean' of barren clay where even a mouse could scarcely find a place to hide. In another way the comparison falls flat, because even to lean on the compound fence could have caused a general collapse. For some reason the prisoners found no urgency to leave Abu Guta. The few askaris on guard had a fairly easy life of it.

I enjoyed my evening visits to the prison, inhabited though it apparently was by murderers and other 'desperate' criminals. In truth, I didn't go with any reforming zeal; rather, I went for an evening's company and entertainment. The prisoners were more full of life and fun than the average run of people at Abdel Magid. As far as I could learn from these evenings, the prisoners' concept of law was much removed from that exemplified by British justice. For example, a sharp blow to the head or stab to the chest was fully justified if tribal or family honour was at stake.

There was always a restful atmosphere about the prison as if prisoners accepted the soothing monotony of prison life with equanimity. It sometimes struck me that the wire fence had the purpose of keeping people out rather than keeping them in.

Within the limitations of my understanding of Arabic we discussed matters politic and otherwise, but any serious conversation usually ended in laughter. The askaris meanwhile laid down their rifles to join in the fun.

On one occasion I learned from some forgotten source that an eclipse of the moon was due to take place during the evening. It occurred to me that I might study the effect of this eclipse on the 'simple' detainees. At the appropriate time I walked round to the compound. The askari on guard gave me a smart salute and let me in through the gates.

It may seem that to be locked in with a small tribe of murderers might bear comparison with Daniel entering the lions' den. Scarcely so, because I was soon seated with the usual group of miscreants around me, all in high good humour, as ever. There was something about prison life which appeared to bring out the best in them – an object lesson for prison authorities anywhere.

Time was passing. I kept looking upwards for the first sign of the eclipse – there it was at last! I halted the conversation then, dramatically:

'See, there, the moon shall disappear for a time!'

Silence descended. Fingers pointed to the moon. The shadows grew and the moonlit compound darkened.

They looked at me in wonder for some moments, as if to question my reason for obliterating the moon. For some time the spectacle commanded their full attention, then I heard the whispered words:

'*El hakooma ajib!*' (Isn't the Government wonderful!)

There seemed to be general acquiescence with this remark and slowly the conversation was resumed as if they were content to accept that here was yet another inexplicable act on the part of the Government.

The eclipse moved on and light returned. I thought it only right to disclaim the Government's power, and went into detailed explanation of the relative positions of sun, earth and moon, all of which they listened to with unbelieving silence.

I confessed in full, but it made no impact. As far as they were concerned the Government was wonderful – or, who knows, perhaps it was my leg that was being pulled . . .

Thoughtfully I returned home to find a stir in the house. The boys, too, had been out studying the phenomenon.

'What's wrong, Ibrahim?' I asked.

'There has been a great darkness. The moon lost its light, did you not see?'

'Yes, and what do you think caused it?'

'By the name of Allah I can't say, but Allah has good reason for everything. He must be angry!'

Again, I explained the eclipse.

'No! Never!' Ibrahim scorned my explanation. 'Raboona (the Creator) moves the heavens: he makes the rain to fall, so he can easily put out the light of the moon!'

There was a considerable element of truth in this explanation, so we left it at that and Ibrahim returned to his more-than-usually devout evening prayer.

A few days before Christmas a letter came from the Director to me. His retirement from the service, delayed by the war, was about to happen. It said: '. . .I have arranged for you to take up a job in Western Sudan that will involve you in a lot of travel, but first of all, complete your year in irrigation. . . .don't forget our discussion abut the erosion problem . . . keep this under your hat until you have official word from Khartoum.'

I had never given Christmas a thought, but here was a wonderful present, enough to keep me awake long into the night going over my old dream of trek, a dream that was going to become reality. Did Alex know, I wondered. I decided that it was up to him to raise the subject, so I tucked it into the back of my mind and started to count the days.

Eventually Alex said, 'What are you doing for Christmas, lad?' – as if I had a number of alternatives to choose from! There would be few people, if any, at Abdel Magid celebrating Christmas.

He went on, 'We are both invited to Wad Medani for a few days – everybody goes there for Christmas.'

This sounded a pleasant proposition, but a more attractive offer turned up which I could not refuse. A message from the ADC was laid on my desk; it read: 'Can you join me on a Christmas camel trek to the White Nile – Alistair.' Alistair, almost as young in the service as I was, shared my interest in trek; we had burned the midnight oil discussing the topic.

Alex agreed. I phoned Alistair, and arrangements for the great occasion were put in hand. As novices, we were going to trek the easy way, with an accompanying lorry preparing camps for our arrival.

On the 23 December, Alex shut up shop and left to join the festivities in the city. Alistair and I stowed our kit into a chunky administration lorry, and with Ibrahim and Mahomed as well as Alistair's servants aboard, we set off for the village of Geteina close to the White Nile.

The trek route was of Alistair's choosing. We were to stay overnight at the Geteina rest-house then set off before dawn on camels provided by the Omdah there. A long day of trek would bring us to the Nile, on the sunset of Christmas Eve. An entire day in the saddle! We were like children going on our first picnic.

A giant of a man, fully six feet eight inches tall, and every bit as black as Ibrahim, stepped from the Omdah's house on our arrival at Geteina. Once more came the warm spontaneous welcome which was so commonplace in the Sudan. He told us that his camels would be ready for us before dawn, and that it would give him pleasure to accompany us on the first few miles of our journey.

That night we lay in our camp beds within the high walls of the rest-house compound. Overhead, stars made shimmering patterns in the sky. The sound of rapid drum-beats drifted over from the village. Occasionally the bark of a dog or the rasp of a donkey lent noise to the throbbing air. I was wide awake: this was no time for sleep, there was too much to experience.

I thought of Alex among crowds of people in the town, with noise and Christmas celebrations. Would he really enjoy that? It seemed so unlike him. Here, all around, was the wonder of Africa and yet he chose crowds of people; was it just that he had seen it all before? Would I, one day, tire of it all? It didn't seem likely, then.

53

Suddenly came the voice of Ibrahim from a dream.

'*Salaam aleckum ya haderetak*!' (Greetings, excellency!).

Pitch darkness apart from a little lamp set on the trek table – he opened the net and passed in a cup of tea.

Servants were bustling about the compound. I could hear the grunting of camels outside. A tail-end moon hovered in the sky, large bats swooped silently overhead. So early, there was a different feel in the air. It was as if to move out into such a silent world was alien and forbidding.

Alistair and I quickly dressed and left the boys to pack up the gear and travel on to the point of our evening rendezvous.

The Omdah greeted us. Three beautifully dressed camels knelt, awaiting our pleasure. Up – up – the animals jolted; in the darkness, so high, the ground seemed far below. I sat cross-legged holding a single line from the camel's mouth, then, in single file, we swayed through the silent village and over on to the sand dunes which were scarcely visible in the darkness. The Omdah had explained his intention of leading us on our way until sunrise when he would leave us to our own devices.

We moved onwards in silence. I saw the North Star clear before us – then I gradually felt the immensity of silence and of space in a way quite new.

My dream! This was it! The encapsulated wonder of an African journey. As I watched the dawn unfolding I was struck with a feeling approaching reverence. Tears of emotion flooded my eyes at the perfection of the scene. If I had ever questioned that a desert could be beautiful, the evidence was before my eyes: I had never before imagined such beauty.

Even as we rode on into the strengthening light I felt impelled to record my mood:

A Desert Dawn

> Pale insipid dawn blending night with day
> A waning moon pales before the flush of the eastern sky
> The land is cold and grey.
> This is a sad and lifeless world
> Not yet awake,
> Mysteriously subdued.
> Three tall camels pace the rolling sands
> And in the hollows
> Wend the scattered rock and stunted scrub.

Travellers silenced by the pressing quiet
Of brooding nature, are borne towards some distant goal,
Far out of sight.
The air is still as nature holds its breath,
Death cannot be more quiet
And the camels' feet move noiselessly on sand.
Horizons are broad and flat,
Harsh and black against the whitening sky.
The scarce-visible track
Winds aimlessly,
Onwards through the arid waste.
Earth and sky: just nothing else
Except three intruders,
Moving particles, in an infinity of space.

But other creatures are abroad
That are more fitted to this scene,
Lizards dart out from the camel's foot
And stop motionless on rock,
Condemning the intruders with a baleful stare.
But the camels disdain them all
And step on unheeding.

There by the path lie some white-bleached bones,
One horn pointing starkly to the sky,
Victim of this thirsty land, a fitting tribute
To the dismal scene.
Deep purple paints the darker western sky
Pushing back the shadows of the night
And the east is golden.
At last the spell of darkness is undone:
The first bird rises fluttering from the ground,
The earth and life are moulded into one,
As day is ushered with this cheerful sound.
The presence of a solitary bird
Dispels the gloom that weighs upon the mind,
The knell of night is tolled and hope returns
These are the very moments
When the traveller knows his God.

The world is alive
Speech is not a sacrilege,
But voices are thin naked things
Slipping through the edge of space
Making silence the more desirable.

The traveller thinks of city-dwelling man
Locked within his artificial bonds
of concrete and of iron,
Blotting out the land.
How sad for him to live so separate
From life, so sunk in problems
Of his own escape.
He grows apart from nature, obsessed with that
Which hastens an inevitable fate.
Could he but have the soul
To break the bonds
To reach and grasp the very hand of God.
A traveller in lonely places knows these things.

A naked flame licks upward in the east:
The livid sun poised for its final leap,
An oval orb now flashing bands of light
Across the earth in gold and red.
The camels' shadows stretch out far behind
The icy moon is melting with the day.
Now comes that precious time of bliss
When for a fleeting spell,
Desert is another word for paradise.
New life suffuses into weary limbs
The camels' pace is quickened as they seek
To take most value
From this comfortable time.

To reach their goal, before the heat
Transforms the arid scene once more
To stark reality.

Too soon the softness of dawn changed into a fierce desert heat. The
Omdah said his goodbyes and shortly after, we stopped to breakfast – from

a water-skin and some sandwiches provided by Mahomed. Alone with our camels, the animals looked in wonderment at us, as we struggled to make the appropriate dismount noises – not very successfully as they danced round in circles before deciding to fold up!

Food over, we mounted again and experimented by trotting the animals, then going into a gallop. The land flew beneath us – how much easier it seemed than horse riding, and how comfortable, too.

There followed long hot hours as the sun slowly moved over the sky. Excitement had tired me. I was longing for journey's end. A number of aches called attention to my inexperience. Then it was sunset.

In the distance, a halo of light told of a welcoming camp-fire. The boys were all trekking novices like ourselves, but the campsite was well chosen. Our beds were already erected beneath date palms on the bank of the Nile. Mahomed sat cross-legged beside his pots, cooking our meal over an improvised hob. He looked in his element, waving a spoon as we dismounted. Ibrahim welcomed us as if we were returning from a major expedition. Alistair's servants, too, were bustling around, attending to our needs.

The river looked appealing and innocent. We discarded our clothes and plunged into the refreshing water. The current was swift and, quickly, we realised the danger of being swept out of our depths. Now, feeling just a bit foolish, we managed to struggle to the bank and to safety. Next morning a long line of crocodiles basked on that same beach. There was obviously still a lot to learn about the Sudan, before either of us was fit to take up the trekking life!

But it was Christmas Eve in an idyllic setting.

Dinner was appropriate to the occasion – monkey nut soup followed by guinea fowl with trimmings, sweet potato and something green (and un-known); this was followed by a salad of fruit, freshly picked from the Geteina gardens. Late into the evening we sat reminiscing over past Christ-mases and sharing nostalgic tales about our loved ones; it was an occasion for an attack of homesickness which we indulged to the full. Stars sparkled on the water: we would scarcely have been surprised to see the three wise men riding by.

Alistair took my breath away when, unexpectedly, he said: 'Let's kneel down and pray!'

– Kneel down and – ? We did so, and I found that here beside the gigantic Nile, praying came easily. I could see Ibrahim watching us.

We trekked in luxurious ease for two more days with our support team always in close attendance. I knew well enough that real trek would have little resemblance to this holiday, but it was a beginning.

Alex returned to the scheme in high good humour. He had had a good Christmas.

'You missed yourself, and people were asking why you didn't come to join in the fun,' he said.

He brought a few presents from people I had never met, but who expected a visit in the future. Here was another side to Alex: he was not just the 'loner' he appeared to be.

When we reached the office his humour quickly changed. A telegram from the province Governor read:

'Coming with the Governor General to visit scheme 7 – 8 January. Can you provide hospitality for six.'

Why was the GG, the King's representative in the Sudan, making this, his first visit to Abdel Magid? There was worse to follow: another message read:

'Be prepared to go to Tehran late March to advise Shah on project – will possibly mean three months absence: Mackie to run Abdel Magid until you return . . .'

The prospect of three months in Tehran was a pleasant one for Alex but not for me: only a few months in the country, then to be faced with the cotton and wheat harvest and all that that would involve. I expressed my doubts to Alex but he brushed these aside with – 'You'll manage.'

'What will I do with thousands of tons of wheat and cotton?' I asked.

'Oh, you will easily get rid of the stuff,' was all I could get from him. There was virtually no storage for crops on the scheme – but why worry, I thought, it will be made plain in the fullness of time.

Time passed in a frenzy of work. I seldom saw Alex: he did most of the desk work, I did most of the rushing around. Every single day the words of the song beat into my brain: 'Mad dogs and Englishmen go out in the midday sun.'

I had to constantly waken sleepy cultivators from siesta in their homes, as canals brimmed over with untapped water. It was the sheikhs' job to muster his cultivators, but they showed an equal tardiness to face the heat of the day. Somehow there was no major canal burst, and I was able to say with an enthusiasm equal to that of the cultivators:

'*Allah Karim!*' (Allah is generous).

The fertile Gezira clay carried oceans of cotton and wheat. It was a perfect picture: mile after mile of the stuff!

We felt satisfied with the work, as the day for the visit of His Excellency drew close. By now we had learned the reasons for his coming: he had a particular interest in the wheat crop which was to be used to feed General Montgomery's troops in Egypt. Indeed, an army officer was to be with the GG and arrangements for disposal of the grain were to be considered.

Ibrahim took a special interest in the impending visit. My dress uniform was extracted from the steel box, creases were ironed out and buttons polished, then I was persuaded that a dress rehearsal was essential. He placed the large topee on my head, did up the polished buttons and stood back to admire the effect.

'In Allah's name, you are really splendid!' he said with patronising pride. He called Mahomed to enjoy the show: apparently they found some pleasure in my new-found dignity.

But I did not feel able to share in their fun. I was feeling listless and unwell. Even Mahomed's cooking could not persuade me to eat. The day before the visit I was unable to rise from bed; trembling shivers moved over me in waves. It was Mahomed who recognised the symptoms.

'Malaria, *ya haderetak*! You must return to bed.'

How could it be malaria? I thought miserably about the many precautions that were taken as a matter of course – long canvas boots and long shirt-sleeves in the evening; indeed every effort was made to protect the flesh from mosquitoes. Then I remembered that ridiculous swim in the Nile: how doubly foolish it had been!

For several days I lay in misery, alternately sweating and shivering as the disease dictated. Time lost all meaning for me. Visitors arrived at the scheme: some of them were lodged in the house – I scarcely noticed and had no interest in them.

At one point a group of people sat round my bed. One of them touched my sweat-soaked forehead: I guessed that it was the GG. There was a scrub of beard on my chin. My uniform lay folded on the steel box; I sank into a fevered sleep even as the visitors left the room.

Alex visited me once or twice in the following days, but it was the boys who saw to my recovery.

The GG might as well not have come as far as I was concerned, yet there was a significant difference; arrangements for the wheat crop had been concluded. One-third of the crop was to be stored on the scheme to provide seed stock to meet the country's needs, the remaining two-thirds was to go by camel to the railway and thence to Egypt.

The crop was not yet ripe. Alex was due to leave for Tehran when harvesting started and it would remain for me to carry out the plan. But, I was as yet, too weak to care.

One week after the onset of the illness I was staggering about the scheme again. There was no time for a full convalescence: it was only work that mattered. I felt that I had let Alex down and drove myself all the harder.

The first cotton bolls ripened; the fields were gay with white and pink flowers. Families plucked at the lint then carried their produce to purchasing points throughout the scheme. Almost overnight, wheat adopted a golden tinge and its bearded heads nodded towards ripening.

Even now, many cultivators showed a reluctance to work and to harvest the crops. This was partly because the people had little interest in receiving money in the shape of paper notes but, more seriously, the weather had been unusually cold, causing an epidemic of pneumonia. Malaria was always endemic, and now thin, weakened bodies succumbed to the cold. It was a tragic time: long queues of mourners carried bodies of the dead for burial. Scarcely a family escaped. Faces were lined with suffering. It seemed cruel and unjust. Even in such sad circumstances, pressure had to be exerted to save the harvest. But there were holdings where cotton just fell to the ground and was lost.

This was another face to the Sudan, the face of suffering; one for which I had not been prepared. Most families did not even have wealth enough to provide blankets as protection from cold: in fact, I knew only too well that most families possessed virtually nothing at all. Abdel Magid was one of Africa's most advanced agricultural settlement schemes, and yet the simple peasant who worked it could scarcely have been poorer. Were the people being exploited? Or was it too soon in this young scheme for wealth to be fairly distributed? These questions were far beyond my ability to judge in these early days of my career.

The day arrived for his departure. I drove Alex to Abu Usher and saw him off on his long journey north. I had completed six months of my apprenticeship and was returning to the scheme in full charge, albeit temporarily. By now, the spoken Arabic language presented no difficulties, but there was sufficient to keep me on tenterhooks as each day unfolded.

Alex had left his desk tidy and ready for me to occupy, and arrangements for buying and transporting cotton were well in hand. Hundreds of camels travelled daily to the railway weighed down with heavy cotton packs. Irrigation had virtually stopped as crops were being left to ripen. In fact, normally blue skies carried patterns of fluffy clouds indicating that the rainy season was approaching. 'Rainy season' is scarcely the right term, because rains amounted to a very few heavy downpours spread over a two-month period, and not enough to sustain crop-growing.

One arrangement, however, had not been concluded and it concerned an area of decision from which, probably, Alex was glad to escape. It was made clear to me that I had to secure the many hundreds of tons of grain-seed wherever there was cover. 'Stow it into huts, empty inspectors' houses; anywhere – before the rains come and spoil it!'

No one had visualised the sheer space that so much wheat in 2-cwt. bags occupies. There was virtually no place for it to go! The weeks that followed had nightmarish qualities.

The people were ill and tired and had never harvested wheat before in their lives – it was like a 'strike'. They would not get down to harvesting – a laborious process involving cutting the crop with sickles. As in all areas of life, there were a few enthusiastic families who made a start, but it was all too slow, with the rains so close.

I gathered the sheikhs together to seek out an answer. Days passed by and I had a vision of failure, then the weather changed once again. Nights of bitter cold were replaced by normal warmth, and slowly people surfaced. One morning I realised that throughout the scheme families were busy; men cutting and threshing, women and children winnowing. Heaps of threshed grain lay everywhere. It was like a miracle.

Purchasing centres were set up at strategic points and grain was brought in, until hills of wheat, guarded by police, reared above the skyline. I then had to judge the best quality of wheat for keeping as seed; the remainder was bagged by gangs of labourers and finally dispatched to the armies in the north.

In the midst of harvest, a telegram reached my desk:

'Two threshing mills on their way from Khartoum by road. Use them to clean wheat seed.'

This was unexpected. What did I want with two threshing mills? Surely there was enough going on without the worry of threshing mills! With further thought I realised that hand-winnowed grain, still contaminated with dust and weed seeds, could scarcely be termed a good sample. Perhaps it was a sound idea, after all.

One machine eventually turned up at the office pulled by a primitive diesel tractor; it was a Swiss job, about the average size for a threshing mill. The mechanic in charge, Said by name, told a tale of woe.

'The other machine is embedded in the sand outside Khartoum; the mechanic there is waiting for you to send help to get him out.'

'How did you manage to get here; why did you not use your tractor to assist him?'

It seemed that this had not occurred to Said. 'It's a very big machine, it will never get here in any case.' This was not very helpful!

There was only one course of action – drop everything and head for the city to recover the stranded machine.

Said was sent back with his tractor the sixty or so miles. I went to our stores, hunted out rope and block and tackle, as well as several able-bodied men, then biting my nails in vexation, hit the trail north. It was merely an earth track; in fact, most of the way there wasn't even a track.

The machine, 'Clayton and Shuttleworth, England' on its bow, was indeed big. Bedded down to its axles in soft fluid dust, it looked gigantic, immovable. A clumsy old tractor had also expired into the dusty depths. Two forlorn mechanics sat there, disconsolately waiting for Allah to place them on firm ground again.

The struggle to unearth the monster, then to trundle it over the desert miles to Abdel Magid, was entirely epic. Arrive we did, twenty-four hours later. A telegram from the new Director lay on my desk:

'Report on performance of the threshing machines.'

Grr! I had no idea yet whether the things worked.

That evening the machines were lined up, belts crossed and clutches disengaged; the tractors groaned under the strain. I waited with bated breath: what would happen now? An almighty crash came from within the Swiss machine, boards scattered to the winds, then silence. Examination showed that white ants had been busy. It was towed behind the store-shed and forgotten.

From a safe distance I watched the 'monster' settle down to a roaring hum which spoke business. Clouds of dust dispersed in all directions, then the first grain was timidly poured in. It worked! Weeds fell beneath the machine, chaff and dust blew out in a cloud: a beautiful grain sample appeared at the rear. Now, with a large squad of labourers working in shifts, the machine worked on night and day, eating into the mountains of grain.

Then a new disaster struck. A great wind blew up from the west, indicating that the rains could not be far off. The sky had been getting heavily overcast: suddenly, in came swirling clouds of dust, packing nostrils, eyes and hair, so that work had to stop as people sought shelter. The *Haboob*, the notorious dust storm of the Sudan, carried vast amounts of eroded soil particles mile upon mile, leaving the land more impoverished than before. With visibility down to a few yards, and chewing and spitting mud, I went home.

The boys had sealed both doors and windows, but despite all their efforts the inside of the house was covered with a dust film: it had even penetrated drawers and cupboards. There seemed little hope for the

Said with machine.

crop now. I paced the floor in despair. But the storm passed away. Slowly sunlight filtered through and hope returned. Bags of wheat seed in hundreds were stacked under every possible roof in the scheme, into huts and empty houses. It was an uncomfortable, untidy job and it was almost impossible to keep an exact account of what was going on. Then Mahomed Omer stood before me looking sad and forlorn.

'My father is dying far off in Dongola, can you generously give me leave, together with a £10 advance in pay?'

I could hardly say no. In any case, Mahomed was proving a faithful servant: he could be trusted to come back. I gave him the advance, then as if it had ben previously worked out, Ibrahim came into the presence.

'*Ya haderetak*,' (Your Excellency: the name used when a special favour was about to be asked). 'I have a friend, Delil by name, who is a cook. He is waiting outside. Are you prepared to interview him? He can cook for you until Mahomed returns.'

'Bring him in and let me meet this friend.' A replacement cook at five minutes' notice: it sounded too good to be true! A rather old, wizened, though well-clad gentlemen was brought in. He was dressed in servant's garb, namely white robes and *emmah*, with green cummerbund. Another coincidence.

'*Haderetak*, I am privileged to enter your presence. I have ample evidence that I am an excellent cook!'

A wallet-full of glowing references was placed in my hand. A quick perusal showed what was apparently a distinguished career, feeding several prominent families. I should have taken time to ponder why he was seeking employment from such a lowly beginner. I might also have weighed up his weasel face and ferret eyes: he did not look lovable by any standards.

He did not stay long! It happened like this. . .

I quickly discovered that under the ministrations of Delil the kitchen accounts were increasing. It appeared as if severe inflation had struck the suq. Judging by arguments from the servants' quarters, earlier friendships were apparently dwindling. I had the impression that some of my hard-earned income was going on *marissa* (native beer).

Then Khartoum kindly sent two visitors for an overnight stay. My opinions of city agriculturalists reached a new 'low'. 'Idling in their Khartoum offices, playing squash in the evening, now sending people to pester me.' This subject was one of Alex's favourite topics of conversation with which I heartily concurred.

The visitors arrived, to study irrigation – at least, one of them did: a young Hungarian engineer. His partner proved to be his wife, an attractive young girl from Armenia with slanting dark eyes. They were war refugees. The engineer had been contracted to work in the Sudan and, evidently, I had to initiate him to the mysteries of irrigation.

They spoke neither Arabic nor English. I was singularly deficient in Hungarian and Armenian, yet we communicated after a fashion. She had a ready smile which was generously disported in my direction.

Things could had been worse!

Delil was sent to the suq with additional funds to hunt out the best piece of goat steak, and other delicacies.

That evening, we three sat on the verandah, passing the time exchanging smiles and nods, awaiting the arrival of dinner. My one bottle of whisky was on the table, much enjoyed by the visitors; I never touched the stuff.

Ibrahim sidled in to whisper that dinner would be a little later than expected. Well, for a special effort, that was acceptable. Half an hour passed. I called Ibrahim, only to be told the meal was still not forthcoming.

This was embarrassing. I apologised to the guests. They settled for another drink.

Finally, I could wait no longer. I went to the kitchen where I quickly discovered a singular lack of activity: there was no sign of a fire in the grate, the place was dead.

The cook! Where was he?

Ibrahim was hiding nervously behind a corner of the house.

'The meal, where is the cook?' My yell could have wakened the dead. With enthusiasm, I grabbed a firm hold of Ibrahim in case he too would melt from sight.

'Your Excellency,' Ibrahim said, his eyes wide, 'look over there!'

At the side of the compound wall, a figure lay, still as death. I bent over the prostrate form, fearing murder had been committed. The smell of beer wafted to my nostrils. He was blind drunk; dead to the world. The body muttered some unrecognisable words.

Red lights flashed before my eyes. Drunk! No dinner! My guests waiting – and drinking all my whisky! I could have torn him apart with my bare hands.

Deliberately, I walked to the water-house and filled a bucket to the brim. Ibrahim watched apprehensively as I returned to the recumbent figure, and, with relish, poured the contents over its face. The figure sat up, spluttering, made to rise; then, finding some hidden resource of strength, I picked him up and threw him over the garden wall.

Somewhat mollified, I returned to the puzzled guests to make a full confession and to my relief they laughed – the whisky must have exercised beneficial effects on both of them. The wife rolled up her sleeves with deliberation, then we all went to the kitchen to hunt out the means of making a stew.

The meal, and the making of it, was a success. Madam was a born cook. I could have given her a job there and then.

After lunch the following day, cooked by the same willing hands, both of the visitors were driven back to the city. That evening, Delil the cook was ushered in, sobered up and ready for duty. In his estimation, apparently, nothing unusual had happened the day before. I sacked him on the spot and all but threw him over the wall again. Great was his indignation! Never did he guess that I was so lacking in consideration, but, failing everything else, could he please get a reference?

He was ejected, minus the reference.

It was Ibrahim's turn for a reprimand. Fortunately, by this stage in my Arabic studies, I had learned words to fit the occasion.

He hung his head, then ventured, 'There was nothing I could do, it was the will of Allah!'

Out in the field, the threshing mill roared on night and day, but there were frequent hiccups, such as when, unaccountably, so much grain was poured into the machine that it became constipated and ground to a protesting halt. Such happenings were hard on the nerves.

Heat, rush and frustration: all were there, ingredients for premature old age. Then the labourers withdrew their labour: it was hardly a strike, they merely melted away. Perhaps there was justification for their disappearance. Lumping two-hundredweight sacks, one every twenty seconds – in and then out of the machine, amid a dust cloud and in burning African heat, was no sinecure. There were no other volunteers for the job. Persuasion and press-ganging proved futile. There the machine stood, taunting me with its silence, as did the remaining grain, filled as it was with dust and weed seeds.

Then came a flash of inspiration: a moment of genius, the kind that wins battles or discovers penicillin. What about the prisoners? Of course, the murderers and their friends in the Abu Guta prison compound! Some of them were giant Nuba from Kordofan Province; they would toss two-

Machine prisoners and me – grain harvest.

hundredweight bags like skittles. I rushed to the phone, negotiated with the DC and in a matter of hours everything was arranged.

Fifty prisoners with their attendant askaris took over the job and saw it through to its conclusion. They enjoyed every minute of what can only be described as slavery. The askaris had an easy time, as the prisoners showed no inclination to depart. There is a moral somewhere in this happening; it must say something about prisons, rehabilitation and the human mind. Had they been engaged as hired labour, without a doubt they, too, would have melted away.

At times, their exuberance went beyond acceptable limits.

At night, the machine presented an alarming spectacle. In the dry atmosphere, sparks of static electricity leapt from every corner, often with the sound of fire-crackers. I had visions of it all exploding into flame, so a criss-cross of wires was joined, in an endeavour to neutralise the charges. But with its spectral aura it was a thing of beauty: crowds gathered round to watch. Where the main driving-belts crossed a gigantic charge built up. A passer-by within four feet of this point received a shattering crack on the head as a miniature lighting flash struck. The prisoners quickly found entertainment value in this phenomenon. A simple bystander leaning thoughtfully on his staff was beckoned towards the crossed belt. Doubtful as to the reason for the summons, the selected victim moved foot by foot to the spot. Them came the thump; the poor unfortunate toppled head over heels, then ran off in terror, convinced evil spirits were in hot pursuit. The prisoners howled in merriment. I had to keep remembering the danger as they were not beyond having a laugh at my expense.

An adequate quantity of seed was dressed in this way, though some was bagged dirty, due to the imminence of the rains. Somehow, also, it was all stowed away into shelter, and the wheat saga come to an end, and I could breathe freely again.

An unfamiliar quiet settled over the scheme. The ground stood bare and empty. Most of the canals were dry.

It was a time for maintenance. In the villages ploughing co-operatives had been set up, and hundreds of bull-teams scratched the land's surface in preparation for next season's crop. Life became easier: I could now take an occasional day off.

Dr Hitler got married and I was invited to the wedding. This was no novel experience for the good doctor, as he already had two wives extant. He explained that a young girl had been proposed to him; he had not seen her, but it was a good arrangement. The wedding lasted four days; I attended one evening's celebration. This consisted of his male friends, including me, sitting in the yard of his house and feasting. The only females present were a troop of dancing girls, the Habasha from Abyssinia, who performed on these occasions and delighted the males present.

Ibrahim told me the performers were of low repute, actually dancing before men, of all things! The bride was not present at the wedding: it seemed that she came on the scene when the long festivities were over.

I also visited the nearest town, Wad Medani, in response to earlier invitations, and called at the nearest Syndicate irrigation scheme to learn how things worked on a purely commercial enterprise. Time passed pleasantly enough.

Alex returned in the fullness of time. I had been apprehensive as to how he would view the results of my efforts, but he was scarcely interested.

'Lad,' he said, 'I am transferred to a job in Kordofan Province – to be Senior Inspector of Agriculture, and what's more, I am taking you with me.'

It took time for this to sink in. 'I am going to Kordofan too?' I said, thinking he was perhaps joking.

'Yes, you will be trekking the Nuba Mountains, a very different job from what you have been doing here. I believe it is the kind of job you always wanted to do.'

'Yes, it is,' I said faintly, still hardly able to believe him.

'The Nuba are a great people – you will like them.' He went on to explain that they were a very primitive race, virtually 'stone-age', with the Nuba Mountains an isolated backwater which had few outside visitors. Yes, this was the kind of life that I had hoped for in Africa. It was what the Director had promised.

I told the boys. They were overjoyed. Even staid old Mahomed, long since back from his father's funeral, was pleased, even though to trek would be a very arduous life.

I was sent for one week's leave into the Red Sea Hills. When I returned Alex had already packed up and gone. I was due to follow him to Kordofan one month later.

Into Kordofan

The long year in the Gezira wilderness had come to an end. My apprenticeship was over.

I had a reasonable grasp of the language: I felt that I had some understanding of the Sudanese people, sufficient at least to feel for their state of poverty and to question its causes. My other remit, namely to understand the soil, was an ongoing source of interest, with the fertility of Gezira clay a revelation.

In several other respects I was now prepared for what could be a dramatically different life – trekking in the bush.

My personal establishment was, by now, adequate for immediate purposes. Ibrahim, Mahomed and the groom Abdulahi made a reasonable team. They were as enthusiastic for what lay ahead as I was. I could now ride Bakhit with confidence: he galloped only when asked! There were a few sticks of furniture in the house, constructed mainly from boards and nails, but pride of place went to a string-bed, with heavy carved legs made in the suq. The steel trek-box, which had indeed resisted attacks from white ants, was the only cupboard or wardrobe.

A move from the featureless Gezira to the mountains of Kordofan offered a prospect rich in uncertainty. Mountains were more than welcome, but what of the Nuba? A very different race and culture. Would it mean starting at the beginning again? I discussed the Nuba with the boys frequently. They spoke disparagingly of the naked Nuba and his primitiveness. I could detect an attitude of superiority because, in history, the Nuba had been cruelly driven by Arab traders from Kordofan to markets in the north.

Yet the boys were keen to go. It seemed that Ibrahim had friends in the Kingdom of Tegali, on the northern fringes of the mountains.

'These are good people; very black people,' he said. 'They are not Nuba but Arabs,' he was careful to point out.

I learned that the tribes of the Nuba Mountains were of both Nuba and Arab stock, and that at times this created problems, as their territories overlapped each other. All this was for the future!

The boys organised packing, and the day of departure dawned. Suddenly

I realised that I was leaving behind many friends at Abdel Magid. Apart from saying goodbye to the office staff who provided a farewell tea party, I thought I would just slip quietly away from the scheme. It didn't work out that way donkeys rode up to the door carrying some sheikhs, Dr Hitler, and several others who, I thought, would never have missed me.

The Arab is courteous at the best of times, but on the occasion of a departure he excels himself in kind words and gestures of friendship. Perhaps this has origins in his insecure nomadic inheritance, with its frequent separations. Words were not spared on this occasion. Glowing tributes heaped upon me amid a profusion of blessings. I had been a guiding light, a messenger from heaven. Tears would be shed, but, by the will of Allah, I would come back again!

This fond treatment could stir the faintest ego, but I had heard such expressions before: indeed, I was saying virtually the same in return! The Arab, I had found, is extravagant with praise and friendship, as he is also with his anger when aroused.

Then it was time to go! With the house locked up (a new inspector was already occupying Alex's home) we set off for the railway at Abu Usher.

I found that the farewell committee were unanimous in wanting to say a second lot of farewells at the station. They climbed aboard the lorry beside the sparse furnishings and Bakhit the horse, and off we went for the last time as far as I was concerned, away from the scheme and over the arid plain.

The railway station – that solitary hut and signal – witnessed another long hour of reminiscences and farewells, but, as the afternoon 'flier', as it was known, failed to turn up, my friends returned to Abdel Magid leaving us to continue as best we could without them. Mahomed, the car driver (there were many Mahomeds in my life), remained with us in case the train didn't arrive, a not-uncommon occurrence! Considerable patience with regard to railway travel was always exercised in the Sudan: an hour or two of lateness was neither here nor there.

Darkness fell. We were having a snack beside the rails when a distant light heralded the train's approach.

There was still time to stretch my legs, so I strolled over the flat plain at right angles to the line conjecturing upon coming experiences, when another train, pulled by a large Garrett double-ended locomotive, drew into a passing-loop beside the station. This was too much for Bakhit who had never previously seen such a monster, he reared on hind legs, broke his halter and careered off into the black desert out of sight.

The 'flier' drew in also. The previously silent desert was now a turmoil of belching steam. I ran to inform the engine-driver about the mishap, then set off in the car to search for Bakhit. We turned and twisted, fanning headlights in wide circles until the horse came into view, trotting now, but tossing his head in fear. At our approach Bakhit swerved and ran away. We had to chase him ruthlessly until, blown and sweat-lathered, he was roped to the car and led back to the station.

Fortunately the engine-driver was not in the least impatient: what did another half-hour matter, after all? He admired Bakhit, examined mouth and legs, then with a knowledgeable air declared him to be worth £30.

We all climbed aboard except for Mahomed the car driver, who set off back to the scheme, glad that it was all over. All the struggle had gone from Bakhit. He went quietly to a special horse-box with the groom, and settled down for the night. With a loud triumphant whistle directed at the empty desert, the train slowly picked up speed. Fortunately the boys had seen the gear safely into a wagon, so I could now relax in my compartment for some hours before entering into another new world.

That night the electric fan whirred gently overhead, and finally I slept deeply. I wakened to the early red light of dawn, and with a surge of excitement, remembered the significance of this journey.

At 6.30 a.m. Ibrahim entered with morning tea and my clothes for the day. He was bubbling with high spirits, as if to travel from Abdel Magid was the fulfilment of a lifetime's ambition. I was beginning to realise that he must be descended from the black people of Tegali (perhaps his mother was a slave), so in a sense he was probably going home to his people.

I looked out of the window to a still-parched landscape, although there was now a slight ground cover of thorn trees and yellow-dry grass.

The day hotted up. The track headed westwards over a plain of sparse savannah grass with a few isolated rock peaks reaching incongruously to the sky. Then came a belt of trees, and with what was a dramatic change of scene, the train thundered over the White Nile bridge at Kosti.

Kosti station bustled with people, mainly Arabs but also many blacks, possibly Nuba shouldering their way along the length of the train.

Women were shrouded in the usual blue robes held close to the face; many Arab men wore the elegant flowing robe so suited to the climate; most of the blacks were dressed in all manner of scraps of clothing with tattered shirts and out-at-knee trousers.

A *feki* (holy man) walked past, preceded by a cavorting dancer with some musicians beating drums and playing simple flutes. People reached out to touch him: he lifted his hands in blessing.

I climbed down to stretch my legs and have a look at Bakhit. He was travelling well in spite of the previous night's excitement.

There were no other Europeans in sight. A beggar asked for baksheesh, officials saluted me, and some children trailed at my heels. The heat and bustle, the shouted Arabic words, were now commonplace, and I scarcely noticed them. I saw the boys also walking through the crowd. Ibrahim was dressed, in the heat, in an old discarded raincoat I had brought from home.

There came a peremptory whistle from the engine, we climbed aboard, and headed into Kordofan Province. Hours passed, and Ibrahim served lunch in the compartment.

With each successive halt it was obvious that the proportion of black people increased: a complete mixture of Arab and Negroid types. Women were more careless of their dress, perhaps demonstrating a lessening of Moslem influence.

The scenery was also changing. Ground, covered with yellow withered grass and occasional patches of stronger thorn trees, indicated a higher seasonal rainfall. A group of hobbled, dappled ponies caught my eye, then in turn a string of gaily-clad camels each with a rider carrying a flat-headed spear, reflecting sunlight like a mirror.

Suddenly the landscape was like a sea of red sand, sometimes with rolling grass-covered hillocks. The train shuddered to a halt – 'Um Ruaba Station' a notice said. I climbed from the train, once again grateful for some exercise.

A smartly-dressed Arab stepped up and saluted.

'Are you the new Chief Inspector (*bash mofetish*) of the Nuba Mountains?' He had recognised my badge. He continued: 'I am the Omdah of Rashad, you will live in my town in the mountains.'

Apparently it was chance that we met here. Business had brought him to Um Ruaba. He told me that Rashad, which was indeed to be my headquarters, was still about 130 miles away.

Next, up came the station master who also congratulated me on my arrival. He said, 'Much of the traffic of the mountains comes through my station; I know we shall meet many times in the future.'

I learned what I could from him, then he asked me, 'But sir, I must know your name, please tell me.'

I told him it was a Scottish name – Mackie (I knew by now that most Sudanese recognised that 'Scottish' and 'English' were separate tribes).

He burst out laughing. 'Mr Mekie . . . Mr Mekie!' he tried again. 'Here is an omen. That is one of the names for the Prophet Mahomed. Your reign will indeed be good and benevolent!'

This was a pleasant start, indeed: a warm welcome to the province!

The train journey continued. At 2.45 p.m., at last, a glimpse of the Nuba Mountains, a hazy, dull mass rearing over the horizon. A prayer moved over my lips, arising out of uncertainties about the future. Alex had said that my new district was bigger than Scotland in area; could I cope with this on my own?

Ibrahim entered the compartment to pack my valise. I noticed him folding some red-coloured items among the bedding.

'Ibrahim, what are these red things?' I queried.

'Sir, they are women's frocks.' He was quite unabashed.

'Why on earth are you putting women's dresses in there?' I demanded.

'*Ya haderetak*,' he realised that a special politeness was now needed, 'they are for a lady friend in the mountains. This is the safest place for them.'

'Whose lady friend?'

'Mine,' he answered. 'I promise you that you shall meet her.'

With this tempting proposition the subject closed, because the train had stopped at Rahad station, our rail destination.

It was now sunset. Looking from the window I saw a little station surrounded by dunes. Men and animals cast long shadows over the vividly red sand.

A native agriculturalist, waiting exactly at the compartment door, stood smartly erect and saluted as I jumped to the ground. With words of welcome he handed me a letter from Alex who was at El Obeid, the province capital, fifty miles further along the track.

'Maki Effendi is my name!' he said.

Another Maki I thought; he laughed as I told him we shared our name with the Prophet.

The boys unloaded the gear. Bakhit climbed uneventfully down a ramp. At the rear of the train a squad was unearthing the furnishings from beneath a mountain of sacks, and crates of fruit. Saddles, boxes and planks emerged – the planks had boarded the train as one of my few items of furnishings: a bookshelf unit. A leg of my new bed was broken. Most items were decorated with fruit juice. Yet a good scrubbing and some well-directed nails would quickly put things to rights again. With the last piece reclaimed, the engine made a plaintive whistle, and the train slid out of the station, leaving me well and truly in a new world.

Maki Effendi had a department lorry at hand. It was loaded up and we drove over the soft sand to the nearby rest-house. I noticed the mysterious presence of a crate of tomatoes among the kit.

'Mahomed, where did the tomatoes come from?' I queried.

'Sir,' he said, eyes turning piously skywards, 'they are there thanks to the providence of Allah.'

A crescent moon bathed the village of Rahad in soft light. The village consisted of a small suq with several clusters of little mud and thatch houses, each with its own group of shade-providing trees. There was sufficient light to see the shape of a sharp mountain peak standing in splendid isolation to the south of the village.

The evening was beautifully cool. I sensed an atmosphere quite new to me, rich with a sense of mystery, in which it felt as if the unexpected could happen at any moment.

The lorry ground to a halt beside a larger house, standing alone, and almost buried beneath encroaching sand. A little compound round the rest-house looked like a gloomy cavern hidden beneath leafy trees; it was a far-from-cheerful place to spend my first night in Kordofan. I walked through the ghostly rooms with a paraffin lamp. Walls threw back echoes as from a tomb. The boys were welcome to inhabit the cook hut; I would sleep outside on the garden *mustabe* (platform)!

Maki Effendi left, with the promise that he would call in the morning to drive us all to Rashad in the mountains – that is, apart from Bakhit who was to be ridden there by the groom.

I now took time to open Alex's letter. There were words of welcome: actually, Alex was not a 'paper' man, so the note was quite brief.

' . . . Your predecessor left the mountains because of illness. The DC is at Rashad to meet you. Take time to look round. I will join you in a few days.'

That was about all! I had to go to my own headquarters and 'look round' until he turned up to tell me my job. As he wished!

Mahomed produced the evening meal. Tomato soup was on the menu. I sat in solitary state listening to the throb of drums from the village, then walked out into the soft warm sand to sense this new environment, before turning in for the night. Some desert rats, jerboa, came bounding up like miniature kangaroos. They studied me with curiosity then disappeared with great jumps, as with triggered elastic.

Then, lying beneath the mosquito net, I listened to the absolute silence. The boys were asleep; the drums still. I must have drifted to sleep because the moon was down the sky when I became alerted by sounds from the house. There was a soft light in one of the rooms; fleeting shadows passed before the meshed windows. I could think of no explanation: it was like a visitation of spirits from another world.

I climbed out of bed to peer through the window: the forms of a male and female were climbing into camp beds. I introduced myself, and discovered that like me they were birds of passage, using the rest-house before boarding the early-morning train for Khartoum in five hours' time. They were missionaries from the deep Nuba Mountains, off on furlough.

I returned to bed and they were away and out of my life by the time Ibrahim wakened me in the morning.

Part II – Nuba

The Mountains

We were all on the move by 6 a.m. Even Mahomed Omer was excited, his pots tied together in bundles – he was ready to go! Some chickens had found their way into the purloined tomato crate.

Ibrahim chattered on about joys to come when finally we reached our new home in Rashad. Abdulahi was preparing Bakhit and was about ready to set out on the long journey, a goatskin water-container hanging at the rear of the saddle.

Orange morning light set the dunes aflame. The high mountain peak seen on the previous night reared up from the plain in grand symmetry.

With the lorry quickly loaded and Maki Effendi driving, we churned our way over the sand across the railway line, and out of the village. Leaving the dunes behind, the track twisted through an acacia forest.

My first trek! I looked around ecstatically, immediately sensing a freedom, in contrast with the previous year's labour at Abdel Magid. But it had all been worthwhile: at least I had a better chance of survival than would have been the case a year before.

The track descended to a clay plain, then down sharply into a wide, dry watercourse. The lorry stopped. Maki Effendi began a long explanation of this watercourse, which acted as a main drain from the mountains during the rains.

'Its name is Abu Habl. Beware the Abu Habl!' he said. 'Many people have lost their lives here, particularly when the floods come. There are evil spirits here which delight in tormenting the traveller.'

Maki Effendi was educated and, presumably, a good Moslem.

'Do you really believe there are evil spirits here?' I asked.

He started the engine and the lorry charged up the other side of the watercourse.

'Yes, there most cerainly are!' He seemed anxious now that we should escape from danger. Little did I know at that time how important the Abu Habl would be to me in days to come!

Some Data on the Nuba Mountains (1942–1946)

For administration purposes divided into two 'districts' –

Eastern Jebels (Mountains) – Area 18,735 sq. miles. Population 156,400.
  Administered from Rashad.

Western Jebels – Area 12,756 sq. miles. Population 319,100
  Administered from Dilling.

Peoples of the Jebels – Ancient Nuba. Mixed Arab peoples including Kawahla,
  Hawazma, Buggara etc.

Rainfall – From 14″ in north of district, to 24″ in south of district.
    The rainy season is confined to the June–October period, and may fall on
relatively few days of heavy rainstorm within that period – particularly in
the north.
    To the north the waters of the mountains drain mainly into the Abu Habl
Khor (Khor translates as 'watercourse'). A khor is characterised by flash
floods: it is a dry river bed for the greater part of the year.

Communications – Sudan Post and Telegraphs Department provides communication by radio (morse) signals at Rashad and Talodi. Mail is brought in by
lorry in the dry season, and by animal carrier during the rains, when roads
are cut by fast-flowing watercourses. All travel is by horse or bull in the rains,
otherwise the Nuba Mountains are cut off.

Some distances –

Khartoum–El Obeid	(rail)	– 428 miles
Khartoum–Rahad	(rail)	– 385 miles
Rahad–Rashad	(road)	– 78 miles
Rashad–Talodi	(road)	– 152 miles
Rashad–El Obeid	(road)	– 140 miles
Talodi–El Obeid	(road)	– 247 miles

Crops of the mountains – Grown only in proximity of the scattered tribal communities.

Dura – various Sorghum millets: a food staple, but also grown for export
from the mountains.
Cotton – Short staple; rain grown for export from mountains.
Simsim (sesame) – main source of vegetable oil.
Ful Sudani – monkey or earth nuts.

Success in cropping depends on extent of the annual rains. In many parts
Dura is virtually the only crop grown.

Ibrahim peered round from the back of the lorry, listening. He shouted knowingly, 'Yes, there are jinns in the Abu Habl: I know that!'

Here was an intriguing start to my first trek. Was I to contend with evil spirits, as well as all the other hazards of trekking? There were, however, so many things to experience that jinns were forgotten, at least for the present.

This was my own district: many thousands of square miles of territory, with freedom to make my own programme and set my own hours: at least, it depended on what Alex had to tell me when he reached Rashad, in a day or two.

We were, by now, approaching the spectacular mountain peak – 'Gebel Dair' – I was given its name. It stands apart from the Nuba Mountains proper. Tall, finger peaks reached upwards to the topmost pinnacle, all of bright red rock. Many-coloured trees clung to its sides; it seemed a riot of colour in the morning light.

The road wended around a tumble of broken rock at the base of the mountain and into a grove of the tallest trees I had yet seen in the Sudan. To my surprise, Ibrahim knew them all by name. He clung to the side of the car and shouted: 'That is Tabeldi – Haraz – Dom Palm.' He had names for each kind – words which were to become a regular part of my vocabulary.

In a flat, sandy-bottomed cleft at the base of a cliff on the mountain's edge stood my first Nuba village. Red rock towered vertically, 2,000 feet above. Neat mud huts with tall pointed thatch were clustered together. It could have been a goblin village, dwarfed as it was by the mountain.

The inhabitants were certainly not goblins: tall, very black Nuba, clad in white robes, came out to meet us.

We drew in at a rest-house and the boys jumped down to organise a fire, and make breakfast. The headman of the village came forward to invite me to his home; he spoke Arabic, and said that I should meet his family. His circular little house was spotless and had some pieces of furniture of a quality I had seldom seen in Arab villages. The family lined up to shake my hand, then we all sat to drink coffee – several cupfuls of the thick black coffee favoured in the Sudan. An hour passed cheerfully in this way. Mahomed stood, hands on hips, at the rest-house door, conjecturing on the condition of a panful of congealing omelette.

A busy draw-well close to the village was surrounded by people and animals, with the water being raised to the surface by a hard-worked donkey. The rainy season was past for the year and people were now dependent on wells to supply their needs. It was interesting to observe that Arabs and Nuba worked side by side, apparently in harmony.

We drove from Sidra over a plain with tall yellow dead grass and acacia shrubs. The ridge of the Nuba Mountains drew closer, presenting a jagged edge to the sky and seemingly offering no means for the road to penetrate them.

Maki Effendi stopped the lorry at another village close to the mountains. Before the dust settled, a man came forward to greet us. It was quite obviously a poor village, but he prevailed on us to visit his home: he would not countenance refusal.

Inside a little house, I met his three wives and a number of children, and again we were offered refreshments. Men and women of all ages gathered at the doorway to listen as we talked. I was already noticing ways in which the Nuba differed from Arabs. Men and women were taking part equally in the conversation and showing a sense of fun that was infectious. The dignified stature of the Nuba appeared to give more force to their words. I sensed a good nature which would make them slow to take offence.

If this hospitality was typical of the mountains, my trekking progress would be slow in days to come.

It was, by now, after midday, and I was suddenly impatient to get into the mountains. We made our farewells and set off in a straight line towards the mountain-side. The lorry crossed a series of deep-sided watercourses, the drains from the mountains, which must have been raging rivers a few months previously. The road was now a bed of broken rock and stones, making the lorry bounce and almost jostling the boys to the ground.

In low gear the vehicle rushed upwards from the plain, now rounding hairpin corners so steep that wheels spun on the bare rock surface. The engine protested; steam appeared from the radiator. Maki Effendi crouched low over the wheel as if trying to encourage the labouring machine.

Half an hour of climbing and we stopped close to a sheer drop. I took time to admire the far-spreading panorama beneath. Gebel Dair, now in the distance, reached up in splendid isolation. To the north a flat plain stretched to the horizon, and to the desert.

We continued upwards on what was little more than an eroded camel track. Trees scraped the lorry's side. The air was cooler and, looking around, I could delude myself that this scene was from the Scottish Highlands in winter garb. Silver-barked trees resembled the birch; dead grass could be bracken. Overhead were the mountain-tops.

Now, a small plateau of tumbled rock – we turned and twisted between gigantic rock slabs: one was taller than a three-storey office block. I could see sweat trickling from Maki's brow, down to his shirt.

Headquarters, Rashad.

The worst was yet to come.

The lorry stopped, first gear engaged, then up, up over the steepest bit of track ever. Wheels appeared to clamber, slip and clutch at the exposed rock which now resembled a staircase – we squeezed between two vertical cliffs with echoes of the engine roaring in our ears: a precipice now with feet to spare, only one of the hazards. A final hairpin bend then a gently sloping track between high peaks. We were into the Nuba Mountains at last!

The excitements of the climb combined with the majesty of the scene had me almost in a state of shock. A year in an entirely flat plain of clay, and now suddenly, this.

Every few yards presented a new wonder to the eyes. Some trees were in gaudy flower. A gigantic rock pillar made me stare in wonder.

The driver, now relaxed and smiling, pointed to the rock and said, 'That rock is called Abu Anga's penis!'

I asked who Abu Anga was.

'During the Mahidiya he rose from being a local tribesman to leadership under the Mahdi. There was a rising of people here against the Turks.' He pointed beyond the peak to a great ridge of exposed rock reminding me of the hull of a submarine. 'See all the Nuba houses on the mountain tops?

Home, Rashad.

The new box-car/

Through the mountains villages are perched high on the skyline as a means of defence, but also because it is healthier there than in the hollows.'

Indeed, each hill showed Nuba villages on the skyline. I would need to be fit if my work involved going to Nuba villages.

We now, miraculously, crossed a little running stream, the first flowing water I had seen in the Sudan apart from the great Nile. In the distance a small cascade of water poured over a cliff. Maki Effendi pointed to a hedge beyond the stream – I recognised it as mulberry – in fact, this was the Rashad garden and, as it proved, an easy horse-ride from the village.

I walked through the garden in company with a little Arab gardener who smiled with pleasure at my arrival. I remembered my sparse diet in the Gezira, but here was a cornucopia – paw paw, mango, guava, lime, orange, banana, grapefruit, to name just a few; also cabbage, sweet potato, onion, carrot and green salads. Mahomed already carried a basket laden with more fruit than we could ever eat, a broad smile showing approval at this unexpected wealth. Ibrahim stood in rapture and, as ever, gave praise to the Almighty: 'Allah be praised: he is indeed bountiful!'

There was a last little climb over the shoulder of a hill and finally, two natural rock pillars marked the entrance to the village. My village! My new home! But a most unusual village!

I saw a little elevated plateau surrounded by crags. Here and there great rocks lay where they had fallen, some of them embraced by twisted tree-trunks. On every flat place there stood little groups of brightly-coloured little houses. In the middle of the village, a small square of rather ramshackle 'shops' indicated the suq.

We drove beyond the village to find flat ground spreading out like the broad end of a wedge. The shoulders of hills receded so that beyond and to the south lay a wide horizon of scattered, blue-tinted hills and multi-shaded forests. My district, as far as the eye could see, and beyond.

Attention was now focused on a castellated 'fort' flying the Egyptian flag and Union Jack at either side of the entrance. Headquarters! A little distance beyond, a track led to three European houses – the first one occupied by the DC, then an empty house and last of all, on the very edge of the forest, my own home.

Inside, Ibrahim found a letter. It read:

'. . . Welcome to Rashad. You will find some food in the cookhouse. Sorry to miss you. Am off on a month's leave. Look forward to meeting you on my return. Enjoy Rashad. Neil, DC.'

Mustaba, in my Rashad garden with Ibrahim.

The garden, Rashad.

As far as white company was concerned, apparently, I had the mountains to myself. Still, Alex was coming here soon to tell me my job. I stood at the door of the house and surveyed the hilltops crowned with little Nuba villages. I knew that I could certainly live here!

Next day was spent settling in, and exploring the village. The boys had their own little huts behind the house. There was a little rest-house in the garden for the use of visitors. The Inspector's house was in keeping with the environment, sitting comfortably beneath a thick straw insulating thatch. In the shrub-filled garden, and most attractive feature of all, stood a raised *mustaba* (platform), partially shaded by trees, with an outlook to the surrounding hills. Things could not have looked better, though the probability was that I would be constantly on trek and seldom at home.

I wandered through the village. Several people came to meet me and shake my hand. I entered the little primary school; the teacher welcomed me and introduced me to his class of twenty-five pupils, all boys.

I stood in admiration looking at my new office: it did indeed resemble a mountain-top castle. A *ziraa* (agriculture) clerk came out to welcome me and show me round. The DC occupied one side of the 'fort'; my premises were at the other side. Behind the main offices at the entrance, a continuous square of buildings facing to a central compound housed the various support services. In one of these, the Department of Post and Telegraphs provided morse communication with province headquarters at El Obeid. I quickly learned the importance of this office, because on entering the square, a smiling official come to meet me with a bundle of mail, including some letters from Scotland.

Every trek into the mountains was preceded by an exchange of messages, in case of accidents and the necessity of a search: something not too uncommon.

On my desk stood a heap of untidy files. I searched through these to learn the business of the mountains, but in vain; there was no precise record of past events, at least, nothing to sketch out the reasons for my being there.

There came a sudden clatter of horses in the office compound, followed by footsteps on the stairs. Three white-robed Arabs were ushered into the office. It took several seconds for me to pick out the Rashad Omdah who I had met previously at the railway station. Then, he was dressed in European clothes: now he wore the much more suitable garb of the Arab.

He spoke to me as if I was his guest in Rashad: 'May Allah bless you and make your stay with us a happy one.'

I was introduced to his friends, then – 'You have a horse, I am told, Come, ride with us to our village in the hills and share our hospitality.'

He pointed to a nearby hilltop – the hill I discovered was called Gebel el Omdah (mountain of the Omdah). I did not feel like a hilltop ride – in any case it would be another day yet before Bakhit reached Rashad from the railway, so his invitation was premature.

'I am a stranger here with much to learn.' I said. 'Let me settle in, then I will visit your home.'

We talked on over a cup of coffee.

'I have a wonderful horse which you can buy from me,' the Omdah said. 'You will be needing more horses for travelling through the mountains.'

I gathered that this was his main reason for visiting me so soon after my arrival. As yet, I had no idea how many horses I would need, but there was no harm in seeing this special animal.

'Bring it here then, and I may buy it.'

In fact, he returned the next day with a strong black Arab horse. I bought it, and, in my inexperience, paid over the odds. Its name, the Omdah said, was Gamr (Moonbeam) because of a white flash on its forehead. I handed over the money, and my friend departed with a satisfied smile on his face.

A very tall, jet-black Nuba entered the office at a quiet moment, when I was questioning in my mind when Alex would arrive from El Obeid. The visitor stood smartly to attention, saluted in best military manner, speaking meanwhile in a flood of words which I thought must be the Nuba tongue, but which I soon realised was pure gibberish. He wore a Bombay-bowler bearing a badge which declared in English: 'I am the village idiot.'

He took off his hat and showed me the badge with an air of pride. It turned out he was the *marasla* (message boy). I never found out whether he was a victim of shell-shock, or merely a 'worthy' on a soft wicket. His eccentricities were tolerated and in course of time, scarcely noticed.

He handed over my first telegram. It said, bluntly: 'Coming tomorrow. Alex.'

Alex did arrive next day, dust-covered from his long journey. Two vehicles arrived at the same time. One of them was a Ford box-car with a driver named Jacoub; both he and the car for my use in future travel.

It was a cheerful meeting.

'Nice to see you, lad. Will the mountains suit you?'

'I could not ask for a better station!'

85

I enthused on about the village, house, the people; indeed, everything I had seen here.

'Everybody in the Sudan wants to visit Rashad and to travel on to see the Nuba, but very few ever do,' Alex said.

We walked homewards for lunch in my new, and still sparsely furnished home. I felt a certain excitement that, at long last, I would get some specific information about my work. Alex went on in a more conversational tone than I had previously known:

'This is a good station but it has its snags. Be careful about your health: take no chances where food or water is concerned – many British officers have left the mountains on their backs!'

It was rather late in the day to give me this warning. Since coming to the country, the topic of illness or disease had not been raised. Now I was told of the diseases endemic to the mountains: how the Nuba had resistance to them but not Europeans or even Arabs.

'Food must be carefully prepared with all water filtered and boiled.'

I was quite aware of this and could trust Mahomed to look after the kitchen. But the prospect of disease was my least concern. I was too keen to be moving. Impatiently, I asked, 'What do you expect of me, here?' It was ridiculous to ask this so late, but work had never been discussed.

Alex continued at his own pace. 'Your new car is loaded with trek gear from my store. There are six pack-saddles with metal water-tanks, store boxes and tents. In all, you will have to get eight horses, two for riding and six for pack.'

I told him brightly, 'I bought a second horse from the Omdah here!'

Alex wasn't impressed. 'And you will have paid too much for it. You should have waited until the Talodi gathering – that is the place to buy horses.'

Talodi was in the south end of my district in pure Nuba country. I had heard this place spoken about. Its name generated some interest in the Sudan because of its chequered history.

'Now, about your work.' Alex unfolded cloth maps on a table and drew his finger over routes to be taken. 'Just get out on trek. Call at the main villages and meet people there. You will discover there is plenty that needs doing. Oh, and look at the soil as you go; find places where good crops will grow. Erosion has destroyed many areas; people may need to move.'

'And water?' I queried, because this was just a repetition of my original briefing in Khartoum.

'Yes, good land cannot be developed without permanent water supplies.'

Other ongoing work in the mountains was discussed late into the evening, until I felt that I understood how I could contribute to the departments's work, and could pursue my travels alone.

Next day, Alex drove south into the mountains saying that we would probably meet again in the next few days. He left with a typical parting shot.

'Remember,' he said, 'this is your district, it is now up to you. In future I will not come here without giving you advance warning of my plans.'

So, it was now up to me.

He left in a rush, his boys clinging to the inside of the box-car, and I was left alone once more, to prepare for my own departure in two more days' time.

I was sitting on the *mustaba* late that evening, writing up a diary in the light of a paraffin lamp, when the shape of Ibrahim materialised at my elbow.

'*Jenabo*, I have brought ladies to see you as I said I would.'

Two red-clad figures climbed onto the *mustaba* and held out fingers for me to shake. They never said a word, but stood with hands held elegantly before their faces. Ibrahim said something, then pushed them out of sight again. It was all very mysterious so I called Ibrahim back later.

'Who were the women, Ibrahim?'

'Oh, the young one is a cousin, the other is an aunt!'

This was hardly a sufficient explanation.

'But why did you bring them here?'

He was as cheerful as ever, teeth flashing in the light.

'I shall marry my cousin soon. I wanted them both to see you.'

It was to be hoped that they were sufficiently impressed with what they had seen. The cousin was only thirteen years old, an appropriate age for a girl to get married in the Nuba mountains.

Before leaving Rashad, Ibrahim persuaded me to take on a second house-boy. 'Every *bash-mofetish* has two house-boys,' he declared.

Ali, a boy from the Tegali people, was taken on at a salary of £1.50 monthly to look after the house and livestock during our times of absence. Livestock included a number of hens and a cow, purchased to keep us all supplied with fresh dairy produce when in residence.

The rear of the house already resembled a small farmstead and yet it was only four days since arriving in Rashad. I had quickly found that the local market place supplied only basic commodities, most of which held little appeal, so I would require to supplement these through my own farming efforts.

Mahomed had already proposed buying a small sheep flock. Having witnessed butchery practices in the suq I agreed with him.

Maroor (Trek)

The long-awaited day came. Off on *maroor* at last. This is what it's all about, I thought. We were all impatient to go.

This first day, however, was to be an experimental jaunt to Abu Gubeiha, only thirty-five miles to the south. In the yard behind the house everything was laid out in rows for inspection – steel boxes containing the many articles needed during weeks of travel: portable furnishings – table, chairs, beds and a folding canvas bath; water containers; kitchen equipment; and a small folding desk containing my papers and maps. I had found an ancient portable gramophone with a few records at the office, and these too were boxed, to provide future entertainment.

The car needed its own supplies: spare springs clamped to the vehicle's side and a number of four-gallon petrol cans secured in the body of the vehicle. By the time we were loaded up there was just enough room for the four travellers – Mahomed and Ibrahim made their own shelter among the boxes behind.

We spent the whole morning organising ourselves, having decided to leave after lunch. Mahomed had his own special boxes containing sacks of food – the dreary dried grains of the suq, although there was also a large container of fruit from the Rashad garden. It was obvious we would have to eat off the land as we travelled.

Alex had said there were less than twenty motor vehicles in the entire mountains, belonging to missionaries, or perhaps a Talodi merchant. In the case of a vehicle breaking down there would be no 'garage in the next town': we would have to make the necessary repairs ourselves.

After lunch, or what purported to be lunch, I went out to the car. Everything was ready and the boys stood around the vehicle waiting. A small crowd had gathered as news of our departure had gone round. Immediately I learned my first error – namely, that one should depart in secret and with the minimum of publicity. Several people squeezed in front of me saying that they were travelling my way and they wanted a lift. A mild old man, leaning pathetically on a stick, asked me to bear his weary body to Delami, where he had to visit ailing relatives. Thankfully, I told him we were heading for Abu Gubeiha in the opposite direction. Not in the least crestfallen, he said that would suit him, as he had ailing relatives there as well!

There were always people on the move in the mountains, usually walking with packs on their backs, sometimes riding on bulls. There were relatively few camels, and horses were for the rich – these were very few!

I decided to take no additional passenger and we were turning out of the compound when an old bent man, evidently a retired servant, thrust a few brightly coloured dinner-plates onto my lap. These, he said, were gifts from a previous employer and it would be an honour to him if the young inspector would accept them.

I had little option: the car was in gear and I shouted my thanks.

The boys were clad in a variety of ex-army clothes, their faces and heads wrapped in what looked like bath towels, to shield them from dust. A motley crew indeed! Hardly the staff of an affluent civil servant. My purse could not yet stretch to trek clothes for all and sundry.

The track, scarcely a road, dropped gradually from Rashad to enter a narrow gorge. There was little enough room to spare at either side, when, at a particularly steep point, we were suddenly confronted by a string of twenty laden camels. An awkward situation. Who was going to reverse?

Jacoub jumped from his seat, with signs of affronted dignity. He waved his arms, shouting, 'How dare you block the Inspector's path! Where are your manners? Get out of the way!'

This was easier said than done. Words of protest froze on the camel man's lips: after all, wasn't this a public thoroughfare? Were they holy men to predict the coming of such a person? I preserved a weak and passive neutrality as the animals were untangled and made to retrace their steps.

Nothing, it seemed, was going to stand in our way: there apparently was an element of divine right in our progress.

Half an hour later we were bowling through a thick, leafless forest. Ibrahim continued instructing me from behind: he certainly knew trees!

The first tree to catch the eye was the Um Tarag Tarag (the Mother of Paper), so named because of straggling strips of white bark hanging from every branch. 'It only grows on bad land.' Ibrahim said. True enough, the soil was gravelly and poor. Then came the Jir Jir, the Figl and others, each with its story.

The car bounced over dry watercourses, then drove through a broken-down village of grass huts surrounded by a herd of diminutive black cattle. Unlike their owners, one of the tallest African races, the cattle were miniatures.

I discovered that the few cattle in the mountains existed only in certain favoured areas.

For some reason, at this point (my notes tell me) Ibrahim interjected a jarring thought

'*Jenabo* – toilet paper: we have forgotten it!'

Here was a contingency, although I knew Ibrahim was considering my future alone (Arabs never use this commodity). We proceeded bravely on our way, without faltering.

The short journey passed like lightning. We were driving through a little mud and thatch village, up to a rest-house, and stopping – our day's trek already over.

I climbed from the car wondering what happened next. The boys unloaded, and in a matter of minutes Mahomed kindled a fire and got his cooking oddments gathered tidily around him. Ibrahim set up table and chairs, then, at the side of the rest-house, erected my bed with mosquito net. It took very little time before the bare little house was transformed into a dwelling appropriate to our short stay in the village.

The little houses of the village, some round, some square, were scattered at random round a wide clearing – people approached the rest-house, curious as to the new arrival. They were not as black as some of the peoples I had already met, though darker in skin than most Arabs.

Abu Jubeiha was the head town of the Hawazma tribe, though it only had a population of five or six hundred then.

Alex had taken time to explain the political organisation of the district: he had lived in the mountains in the past and was knowledgable about the tribes and their leaders. He spoke in warm terms about the Kingdom of Tegali, an ancient federation of tribes in the northern area, and ruled by its 'king', his 'fine old friend', Mek Adam. Most of the Tegali people had very black skin, though not all of them, but they were all Moslem and spoke Arabic.

The central government administration worked through tribal structures accepted by the people: it was a stable, secure system, where the atmosphere was friendly and there were few 'hiccups'. In historical terms this was quite remarkable because Tegali had supported the Mahdi not so many years before. Much depended on the man on the spot, and even with an Inspector of Agriculture, diplomacy was an essential aspect of his work.

Memories of past fighting lingered in stories told by the village sages. Most villages boasted past connections with the Mahdi himself.

The people of the village gathered round, watching idly as we organised

Buying provisions.

Abu Gubeiha.

our camp. I was told that Nazir Zbeir, head of the Hawazma, was out among his cultivations. The villages of the mountains had no network of communications – generally, the most speedy way information travelled was on donkey-back so it was very often necessary to wait patiently until the chief turned up after I arrived in a village.

I took the chance to wander round, accompanied by a talkative retinue. A little cotton ginnery, part of the remit of the inspector in peace time, was on 'care and maintenance' and well supervised by a little clerk named Ijazzi, who also cared for a neighbouring demonstration fruit plantation. There were a number of such gardens in the district intended to encourage the people to improve the range of foods in their diet. The Abu Gubeiha garden was a poor one; I guessed this was due to deficiency in the soil.

In the centre of the village square a large heap of millet, superintended by a clerk, represented another of my responsibilities. At this period of time there was a scarcity of food in several African countries and large quantities of grain were transported out of the mountains by camel-train, to the railway.

Even in this little village there was work for me to do. There were clerks to meet and to encourage, lists of figures to check, and there were always people with problems requiring attention.

A native sheikh came out of the crowd of shuffling spectators, shook my hand and asked. 'When do I get the £10 I was promised to deepen my silted well?'

I said I would discuss this with the Nazir when he arrived.

The market sheikh brought a chair and little table, set them in the middle of the square, and asked me to sit down. I sat down. I indicated to the crowd to follow my example which they did in a circle at my feet. Good-natured questions came from all sides:

'What is your name?'

'Do you have a wife?'

'Where are you from?'

I gave my answers, all of which were received with smiles.

Men, probably merchants, offered me gifts – a gourd containing lime-juice, some fruit, and even a useful-looking flyswat. This generosity was embarrassing, but more was to follow.

A path opened up at the approach of five white-robed and venerable grey-beards – before them, a boy led a sheep. Nazir Zbeir, small and bent, came forward from the group and grasped my hand warmly. Effusively, blessings rained on me: I was introduced to his followers and then the sheep was brought before me.

In silence now, the company watched as the animal's throat was cut before my gaze. Blood welled out: the animal staggered and fell. With traditional words of hospitality he offered me the carcass. I knew of this custom, and, with words which I hoped were also appropriate, offered it back for the benefit of the poor in the village.

With mature thought, this process of exchange, though unfortunate for the sheep, is a wonderful way of breaking hospitality barriers. Needless to say, on such occasions Mahomed hovered in the background with his butcher's knives at the ready!

Two rickety old basket chairs were now firmly placed nearby. I was ushered into one – Nazir Zbeir occupied the other – and so, commenced my first 'parliament' in the mountains.

People spoke out in loud voices from all parts of the crowd, not in a confusion of noise, but well ordered, as if sessions such as this were a common means of communication. Questions were asked and answered. It felt to me as if my presence acted as a form of catalyst between the people and the Nazir. They spoke with a form of semi-oratory, waving their arms to emphasise points. Others listened avidly, nodding or shaking their heads at appropriate junctures.

Alex had been right in emphasising that work would quickly become apparent as I proceeded on trek. My mind was open to the needs of the people: I had some understanding of the role of government as represented by my department. There was no point in promising what could not effectively be carried out.

The Nazir spoke rapidly with an excitable flow of words which raced from idea to idea. With our session over, and daylight drawing to a close, we walked together back to the rest-house – I noticed his characteristic shuffling walk as if his sandals were too big. We parted that night as old friends: there was something very homely about the Nazir, future negotiations with him should present very little difficulty.

A log fire burned close to the rest-house door. The boys, looking smart now in their white *jelibiyahs*, were waiting for me. The canvas bath was filled and fresh clothes ready for the evening lay folded nearby. A pleasant aroma of cooking lamb came from the general direction of Mahomed.

Later, in a world of my own, bounded by the circle of light from a little lamp on the trek table, I sat writing up the day's records. Dinner was over and the boys sat near the car talking over their own affairs.

I reflected over the day's events and prospects of many more days of this new, shifting life. It offered an attractive prospect then, shallow as my roots were. In some way it was the fulfilment of the dream. Here was freedom! A perfect life of adventure for a young man fresh in a career, and building up his reputation

Patterns would gradually evolve – it was unbelievable that so far I had had only one day of real trek, and that a short one.

A harsh grating noise forced itself on my attention. It came from the far side of the village. I walked over to find a primitive oil factory. In the light of wood fires a number of camels – I counted ten – turned endlessly in circles, grinding out sim-sim (sesame) oil from simple presses. The activity took place within high sheltering straw walls.

I stood entranced. There was a demoniacal quality to the scene in the flickering light. The animals worked blindfold, each under the charge of a boy. How much longer would such a scene take place? I knew that all this was soon to disappear. One little engine could do the work of ten camels and as many people.

At midnight I wakened suddenly to find the tall dark shadow of a man standing close to the net. I asked him what he wanted. Slowly he moved away towards the village without answering. I lay awake for a long time, only too aware of this new environment. An animals's cries came from the bush with startling clarity – was it a hyena? Snuffling sounds might come from a warthog. There were no pigs in this Moslem village.

Then it was morning.

Mid-morning and the Nazir walked me round some nearby cultivations. Crops of millet close to the village were poor, as could be seen by the small, withered stalks left after harvesting. We discussed the problems of over-cropping the land, and the possible means of improving crops. It surprised me to discover that no one among the Hawazma practised crop rotation; there was no awareness of how the fertility of soil could be improved, and no apparent effort was made to husband fodder to feed animals in the long dry season just started. These were primary requirements of good husbandry in any country, and yet they were not being applied here! Was it because land was plentiful, and simple villages like Abu Jubeiha could be finally transplanted to new land? I felt certain that, at least in part, Nazir Zbeir understood these questions but they did not rank in his priorities. Yet I had to admit the people had survived for centuries with this simple system, so perhaps it was not as clear-cut as I thought!

Back at the rest-house the Nazir joined me for coffee. An excited lady came to harangue us about some broken matrimonial vow. It was beyond my level of comprehension and I was grateful that such questions were outwith my area of remit. The Nazir turned her away angrily: this was a village squabble he knew about, and he had no patience with the woman.

We talked the morning away and he left, after extracting a promise from me to visit his home on my next trek. Unfortunately, on that occasion disaster had struck his people and he was too preoccupied to remember the invitation.

After lunch, in the full heat of the day when the village was asleep, we left for the next village of consequence: Kologi, just fifty miles to the south. I spread the simple cloth map of the mountains over my knee as Jacoub drove us away. This stretch of fifty miles was apparently uninhabited, possibly because of the absence of permanent sources of water.

We ran out of mountain! After some rocky knolls and stretches of eroded soil the track headed straight over an almost flat clay plain. I stopped the car to examine the soil: it was good. Trees also indicated the quality of the land. Out came my notebook. The soil was parched and cracked, and there would be no rain for another four or five months.

Was there underground water? Could wells be dug? It was early days yet to start searching for answers.

The map indicated that this unpopulated plain stretched eastwards to the Nile, over one hundred miles away. Travelling on, the land was now poor and gravelly. Mile after mile monotonously the same. We all sweated in furnace-like heat with the boys dug deep into the kit, making a kind of tent with their coats so that the hot air flowed over them.

There was little sign of mountains here, and no travellers, just leafless trees and dead grass. Then Jacoub put on the brakes as a lynx eyed us from the side of the track, the first canine predator we had seen. After a few moments it loped off into the bush. It was surprising to find so few wild animals, and yet, they too required water to exist.

A range of low hills with some rocky mounds before them came into view. We wended through thicker forest where clearings showed remnants of recent cultivation, then on to a slight elevation where Kologi village stood, headquarters of the Kowahla tribe, and our destination for the day.

At the largest hut, obviously the rest-house, I was surprised to see three white men standing as if awaiting our arrival. Quickly I picked out Alex's short stature; the other were apparently British Army officers of the Sudan Defence Force.

I was taken aback by this invasion of what I had been told was my district. Alex introduced them as recruiting officers from Khartoum, seeking to enlist tribesmen for service in the Middle East. I had heard on many occasions how the Nuba made excellent soldiers and very often rose to non-commissioned rank in the army. It was difficult to reconcile this fact with the historical picture of the Nuba as a slave to the Arab.

I took a back seat for the remainder of that day, not having an active involvement with the events; indeed, I was glad to have nothing to do with them.

Some men were enlisted and showed every sign of pleasure at their future prospects. They were in no position to understand the squalor of war, or the corruptive influences of city life, which had, as yet, cast no blight on this unspoiled area. These men, if they did return, could scarcely be expected to re-accept the simple life to which they had been reared. However, at this time, I, too, did not see things in this light. After all, the war still had a long time to run, and that was a consideration beyond all others. I was glad when they all left next morning with their campaign finished. Before going, Alex and I had a session alone with the local Nazir, who was named Mahomed. We talked over a number of questions to do with the area. Again, these centred on land and drought: there was evidently a serious problem of soil erosion close to the village. Alex asked me, as if I was on a holiday tour:

'Are you finding much of interest in your travels so far?'

'Everything is of interest,' I said, and went on to outline my first impressions – vast resources of land but no water!

'Take your time; you have only started, and don't forget it will take more than we can ever do to make much impression here. But there are some things we can do, if I can get the Government to move!'

'Such as?' I asked.

'Think, lad!' he said. 'For three or four months the land is saturated with water, then it dries out for the rest of the year: of course there are answers!'

'You mean, store the water?' I asked, thinking this very far-fetched.

'As I said, wait till you have had a good look round. There is a lot to learn but, remember, don't drive yourself too hard. If your health goes we shall all be the losers.'

They drove off leaving me deep in thought. Was it remotely possible that there were answers to the endemic problems of hunger and of thirst here in this vast belt of semi-arid Africa? Could the abundance of water from the rains be conserved for use over the seven dry months?

Nazir Mahomed wore Arab dress — this was still not pure Nuba country. He too, seemed not a little relieved that the visitors had gone. He wore the slight scrub of a beard: indeed, an apology for a beard. There was something European in his looks and outlook which was never far from my mind during our time together.

Kologi stood isolated from the other peoples of the Jebels although one track did lead from the mountains proper, through the village and to the river, and there was a little movement of riverain people which brought some trade to the village.

The Nazir brought me a donkey, and we rode out into the cultivations. As we talked about the land, people came forward to greet us – it eventually occurred to me that the people were being invited to a special celebration in the village that same evening. In effect, he was announcing:

'This is His Excellency Mr Meki, there will be a dance tonight in his honour!' He might have asked me first! With experience, I learned that the Kowahla had many attractive characteristics, foremost of these being their ability to enjoy themselves. Each and every day they seemed to be searching a cause for celebration, for festival or dance. Usually my arrival in the village provided a sufficient cause. I returned to the rest-house to prepare for the fray. Nazir Mahomed said that I would be 'collected' when my evening meal was over, then he rode off with his donkeys. This left me with two hours to condition my mind for the celebration.

I told the boys, 'We are all attending a dance tonight.'

Ibrahim shook his head doubtfully. 'Dancing is not good. No, nothing good comes from dancing. I will not go!'

Mahomed seemed equally unenthusiastic, as if dancing offended his scruples. The only reason he would give was a shake of the head. Well that was not going to stop me! I bathed, dressed for the occasion with cummerbund carefully wound, and sat down to dinner.

I could see preparations taking place two hundred yards from the rest-house. A moon had risen and there was sufficient light to see a large pile of wood being prepared for a bonfire. A crowd was gathering. What could well be rehearsals were taking place on drums, and violent surges of pulsating rhythm welled out in bursts.

The crowd thickened then moved *en masse* towards me. Nazir Mahomed

Kologi dancers.

headed the procession with, on one side, his lamp-bearer and on the other, his arms-bearer. This latter warrior carried a curved sword vertically before his face, and he looked prepared to swipe off my head should I decide not to join in the festivities.

A procession formed up – the lamp-bearer to the fore, the Nazir by my side, and then the military escort. The crowd gathered in a circle and in this order we marched to the clearing where the fire was already lit.

One lonely chair stood a comfortable distance from the fire with a little table like a plant-pot stand before it. The chair was for me: the Nazir sat cross-legged at my side, and the warrior stood behind us with his blade, as if ready for any emergency. With the lamp set before us and the crowd of about three hundred disporting themselves in a wide circle, the stage was set.

The musicians sat close to our right flank and ready for action. Nazir Mahomed clapped his hands to start the proceedings and music struck up energetically. The crowd began to stamp and sway to the beat and, from the first moment, the entire audience participated in the movement.

Some local drinks were placed on the table – I thought about the warning I had been given about drinking unsterilised fluids, but could not refuse them.

Up to this point I had rarely seen the naked Nuba I had so often heard about, mainly because this side of the mountains was largely under Moslem influence and bodies were mostly concealed, as in the Gezira. I looked round the crowd in the now bright firelight, and saw numbers of almost naked Nuba, men and women mixed at random, among the Arabs.

This had just registered, when six women, stripped to the waist, stepped into the arena and began dancing. They were all young and attractive with hair in hundreds of long plaits trailing to their waist. The drums, with an accompanying 'xylophone' made of hollow wooden tubes, broke into rapid, exciting rhythm. The girls moved singly within the circle, beating their feet to the ground and strutting, back straight, with breasts jutting forward, while arms and fingers moved in graceful postures.

The crowd swayed to the beat so that the whole scene was a harmony of sound and movement, making the blood flow faster and nerves tingle. In this confined world of flickering light, rhythm and beat, the effect was almost hypnotic. I looked over my shoulder to make sure our guardian had a firm grip of his sword, but was pleased to see he had disposed of it and was equally entranced with the dance.

Could it be – ? Yes, on the outskirts of the crowd Ibrahim and Mahomed were watching like everyone else.

The unexpected happened – one dancer, her body oily and reflecting light as if sheathed in copper, moved in my direction, closer and closer till her face almost touched mine. With a flick of her head her long hair slid over my face. What would happen next? I waited, expecting the worst: she seemed to be looking for some response from me and paused in her dance. I noticed that the entire gathering seemed to be looking with expectation in my direction.

The Nazir jumped up.

'*Shuf* (look)!' he said. 'This is what she wants you to do.'

He beckoned the girl towards him. She responded, swishing his face in like manner, whereupon he placed his left arm round her waist, pressed his cheek to her forehead, clicked the fingers of his right hand above her head and finally stamped his right foot on the ground in an exaggerated movement.

So that was the game! the Nazir gave me a meaningful look and sat down. It soon happened!

Another dancer sidled up, her hair stroked my face as in the previous case and as I rose I put my arm round her – she was rather small for me,

I had to bend down to reach her face – a snap of the fingers, a thump on the ground, and I sat down.

A cheer went up; the entire audience laughed. The dancer too smiled broadly. In turn, the other dancers went through the motions with me: then the music stopped – we were all breathless!

That was only the first dance of many. The company had an insatiable appetite. Hours passed by in noise, movement, and good humour. At one point I must have reached a minor degree of ecstasy because I found myself doing a few mincing steps with another dance group. Judging by the guffaws of laughter, heard above the drums, my efforts were appreciated: a few spectators almost rolled over in the fullness of their joy.

With this encouragement the Nazir was the next performer, jumping towards the nearest girl and making sallies back and forward with the same drumming foot beats.

During a halt in the dance I was invited to handle the musical instruments. I could tell they must need as much skill as any other musical instrument requires anywhere.

A melody was now tapped out which encouraged a raucous form of community chanting. The words were difficult to follow so the Nazir interpreted them in Arabic. They went like this –

> Marhuba I love you for your dancing
> Your beauty is from heaven
> Sleep with me tonight.

The next went –

> The inspector paid me for my cotton:
> The inspector paid me for my cotton.
> Fatna I can sleep with you tonight,
> The inspector paid me for my cotton.

– words which indicated there was an incentive for commercial activity in the mountains.

The fire was now a heap of embers. With sudden decision I stood up to thank the Nazir. The music stopped, the guardian discovered his sword, then I was paraded home to bed.

Ibrahim was waiting for me, presumably to tuck me in. I asked him, 'Did you enjoy the dance Ibrahim?'

He just shook his head, as before, without even venturing a smile.

The House on the Hill

I decided to spend one more full day with the Kowahla before continuing
south. The Nazir said there was much he wanted me to see, but there was
another important reason for taking time to explore the Kologi area.

I remembered that it was to this part of Nuba the Mahdi had come in
the early days of the Jihad[1]. He had reached Jebel Gedir close to Kologi
and had remained there for some months recouping strength among his
faithful followers in the mountains. On my trek map I had seen the
intriguing words 'Mahdi's Cave', and knew that I had to visit the area.

After breakfast, the Nazir arrived at the rest-house with two saddled
donkeys. We rode off, feet almost trailing to the ground. Cultivators were
threshing and winnowing grain. They all paused in their work to greet us.

All round the village the forest had been cleared, and there was evidence
of erosion. In places the topsoil was completely missing, leaving only sand
and stones. Nazir Mahomed, however, had little time for such matters. He
rushed me on to a group of houses where several people, men and women,
gathered round as if a meeting had been prearranged. An argument started
up – a question of land tenure: they spoke so rapidly that I could not follow
its course; however, the Nazir apparently did not need any help from me.
He pushed his side of the argument with finality then nodded to me as if
to say, 'See, I have got government backing in this matter!'

That seemed to clinch it, although I scarcely understood a word that was
being said.

The day passed busily – even in the heat of the afternoon there were
things to be done, until my bottom protested at such long contact with the
saddle.

When the day's work was over I told Nazir Mahomed of my intention
to visit the Mahdi's cave at Jebel Gedir. His eyes lit up at once and he
offered to act as guide.

We drove the few miles to a low rocky hill which was scarcely a mountain
but had evidently sufficed the Mahdi as a base. Now, it was a desolate enough
place with nothing in its favour except its remoteness from habitation. We

---

1 Jihad – holy war

climbed to a little cave leading a short distance into a broken rock face. Here it was that the Mahdi, after the example of the Prophet Mahomed, had gone apart to engage in prayer, continuously day after day, until he had summoned the spiritual resource to further his campaign. From this place it might be said ideas were shaped which, in time, rocked European governments and in some measure changed world history.

The Nazir talked on with enthusiasm about these glorious days when the Aulad Himeid, the Kowahla, and Hawazma of the Eastern Mountains had rallied here in their thousands.

We were walking between two little rock hills when the Nazir gripped my arm. 'Look,' he said, 'there is the Mahdi's house.'

The crumbling remains of a stone-built house, something rare in the mountains, stood at a place which could only have been chosen for its isolation. We looked at it silently for a few moments then he continued:

'My father was with the Mahdi at Khartoum when Gordon Pasha was killed. He told me often about these great days and how the Mahdi was a great holy man and leader.' He thought for a little, then added, 'Gordon Pasha was a great man too!'

It went through my mind that these events had happened little more than sixty years before that day.

By now the sun was setting, so we drove back to Kologi. The Nazir talked on. 'My father said that some of his people rode back to Gedir with the heads of British soldiers hanging from their saddles.'

I could but wonder how this warrior people had become the friendly people of last night's dance. What is there in the nature of man which can permit such change, perhaps as inevitable as the pendulum's swing?

In the late evening I was sitting alone at the rest-house. The moon was high and I was on the point of turning in, but my thoughts kept returning to that house on the hill and its connection with the Sudan's turbulent history. There was complete silence apart from an occasional dog's bark and the rustle of branches, as warm gusts of wind swept round the corner of the rest-house.

I felt impelled to return to this mysterious ruin to breathe the scent of history. I drove slowly and thoughtfully to Jebel Gedir, then climbed the broken path towards the little house. Trees stood gaunt and silvered in the sharp moonlight throwing shadow lines across the path.

My thoughts traced the history of the Mahdi – that history which I had read so assiduously in the shelter of the lifeboat, seemingly so long ago.

Sixty years before that evening, the Sudan was ruled from Egypt. An Egyptian army, officered mainly by Europeans, controlled the country in a way which paid little heed to the needs of the people. Into this cruel and starving country, ripe for release, a new star appeared: Mohammed Ahmed Ibn el-Sayid Abdullah – later to be called Mahdi (leader of the faithful) proclaimed a *jihad* in the name of the Prophet. He came as from nowhere. His fanatical faith inspired the tribes to follow him blindly, until a large army rose against the country's oppressors. It was, at first, simply armed, but indolent Egyptian forces were easily picked off so that gradually, inflamed by success, they moved from the Nile into Kordofan to Jebel Gedir. The people of Tegali joined the *jihad* and with a now substantial army, they moved northwards to invest El Obeid, finally starving the people, and massacring thousands.

A new army left Khartoum under the command of an Englishman, Colonel Hicks, to deal with this dangerous situation, consisting of 7,500 infantry and 1,000 cavalry. After virtually losing its way in the parched desert, it was routed by the 'dervishes'. Only a few hundred survived their slashing blades. The next stage of this historical epic was at Khartoum where, finally, Gordon Pasha was killed and the entire Sudan ruled by the Mahdi. In the end, the British Government was roused to take action and an army equipped with the latest weapons of the day overcame Moslem zeal at Omdurman. The beaten remnants dispersed back into the hills of Kordofan.

Walking this path alone in the dim light, it was easy to picture the hillside crowded with warriors, flags fluttering in the wind and signifying the tent of each emir.

I reached the ruins and sat inside on a flat boulder, listening to the wind shaking the grass. By the doorway a shadow became the broad figure of the Mahdi, a fixed humourless smile on his face, giving out absolute commands, utterly ruthless to anyone who deviated from the faith, even his own emirs.

I shivered a little and wondered at the struggles of man. The fighting and the suffering pass away; only the land remains – the land and God?

Yes, I had chosen the right life!

Walking back to the car I knew that here I had an ideal, namely to work for the harmony of the soil and the people. Yes, it was my ideal to promote such a harmony!

Or perhaps I was merely tired.

Deep South

Off south once more, the Nazir waved us from his village. Day was warming, and I had a relaxed feeling of being on holiday: after all, as far as the outside world was concerned I scarcely existed. Only Alex had a vague idea of my movements. It could be months before I saw him again, and there were no white men for a hundred miles around, as far as I knew.

I opened the cloth map in the hope of spotting a place of interest worthy of a visit; there was nothing, only a dotted line crossing a blank space, that is, apart from a few lines of watercourses. However, towards the end of the dotted line I read 'Jebel Tosi Rock Pictures' a suitable distance away for a midday meal-stop.

The Kologi hills were left behind and we crossed a steep-walled dry watercourse. The map read 'Khor Tira water till January' (the Arabic word for watercourse is *khor*). Many small excavations in the sand-base of the khor showed where men and animals had scratched out the last drops of water. Near the watercourse lay a broad plain of fertile clay soil. It occurred to me that if permanent sources of water could be found, it would support a considerable population. I stopped the car and walked along a dry river-bed into the bush, trying to think of an answer to this question – perhaps an earth dam could be built; perhaps deep storage holes could be excavated to trap the short rain floods. But how to do this so far from anywhere? If answers were as simple as that it would have been done before.

A few miles on we drove near a little ridge of rock no more than one hundred feet high and about a mile from the track. This must be Jebel Tosi. Jacoub drove through the scrub and stopped close to the rock wall. A group of gazelle, sheltering beside the rock. bounded off at our approach.

The boys unpacked to prepare lunch in a shady spot, while I set off to explore the ridge which rose almost vertically. Only after a long search did I find a way to the top. I sat on the highest point and my eyes were immediately arrested by a long line of shimmering blue mountains to the west. At last, real mountains – the Nuba Mountains proper!

Round the ridge in all directions, a forest of flat-topped acacia stretched to the horizon. Occasional tall rock needles stretched skywards. Centuries of weathering had sculpted rocks into strange shapes, but the plain consisted mainly of fertile clay unspoiled by the intrusion of man. No doubt for thousands of years men had hunted here, but had never settled, due to absence of water in the dry season. I jotted down some notes in my book.

Far to the south a great pillar of smoke rose from a forest fire; then, just too far away to make identification possible, a long line of animals strung out in singe file walked slowly through the bush. I peered until my eyes were sore but the shimmer made outlines obscure. Little lizards with gaudy red heads darted up to investigate me, then disappeared just as quickly.

The rock was dehydrating my body: I felt parched and moved on round the rock to search for the pictures, but without success. Back at the car I found Mahomed staring up at the rock. He pointed, and there exactly where we had parked were faint outlines of animals and trees painted in shades of amber and green. They depicted dynamic-looking hunters chasing buffalo, while women with exaggerated breasts looked on. Even here, in such remoteness, was evidence of a past civilisation!

I sat down to lunch. The boys crouched over their meal a few yards away: they always kept this discreet distance between us. I was always provided with table and chair, but they elected to eat seated on the ground, as was their custom. They were laughing. I asked them whether they had enjoyed the dance. Ibrahim said with a broad smile on his face:

'It was awful! It is wrong to be unclothed. These people are just stupid!'

'Why? Is it stupid to wear no clothes?' I asked him.

'It is wrong,' was all he could offer.

It was a pleasant meal: we were all cheerful and at ease, there was no hurry and the boys were enjoying the trek every bit as much as I was. I knew only too well it could not always be as carefree as this.

Leisurely, the car was repacked and we set of for Talodi, the southernmost point in the present trek and in pure Nuba territory.

Mile after mile we drove along the dotted line: the same monotonous bush, except that the track had assumed a surface like a sea in a storm. Wave after wave, fifteen feet between each crest, and eighteen inches from crest to trough; the bonnet of the car rose and fell like a wooden horse on a carousel. Our heads nodded up and down with the motion. This phenomenon could only have resulted from the flooding, then drying, of heavy clay soil, expanding then shrinking. In places, trees had been torn out by the moving clay and were thrown over the track.

There was ten miles of this: we were all feeling queasy, then the surface changed to gravel and we were again able to enjoy the luxury of speed. The long mountain range was now closer, then, suddenly, another track from the north converged with ours and rounded a lengthy strip of cleared forest. Obviously an unused airstrip.

Suddenly we were in Nuba. We drove through a village with all its inhabitants naked. They stood tall, beautifully proportioned figures, staring motionless as we passed. Five warriors armed with spears moved aside to let us by. One of them lifted a hand in salute.

The mountains now showed sharp jagged peaks with many deep valleys gashed into their sides. We had almost reached our destination!

Rounding the shoulder to a steep-sided mountain, Jacoub slowed down. He had been here before. He turned into a path through trees and drew up beside a long white house with a red iron roof. This was the Talodi rest-house: standing alone with no other buildings in sight, an inhospitable-looking, even forbidding place.

Talodi

I climbed steps to the raised balcony surrounding the house to examine what was, in effect, my home in the south. By any standards it was unattractive, consisting of an end-to-end row of rooms, high, echoing, and empty; white walls and tiled floors, with nothing to relieve the bareness. My few trek furnishings would be swamped by this relatively vast space; to sit inside at night with a small paraffin light would be like sitting in a cavern.

There was an uncomfortable feel about the place. Jacoub had said it was haunted. I decided to live in the garden and use the house as little as possible. The boys heartily concurred!

I looked from the balcony to the garden, if it could be so called; a low wall surrounded an area of dead grass and shrubs. There was a row of white stones close to the wall. A small graveyard in the garden? Obviously this had added to the house's reputation for being haunted.

I had an urge to investigate the unseen town, and walked round the base of the hill – there were other 'white' houses, all standing empty – then looked down on Talodi, spread out below in a broad 'V' where two mountains met. An untidy sprawl of flat-roofed houses filled the space between the mountains; a haze of dust hung over the scene. It looked unattractive, if not forbidding and I stopped at that point, deciding to delay my visit until the following day.

To look at Talodi was to look at history, though there were no visible monuments to past events. Here in its remote backwater, Talodi had a reputation which belied its size. Its often grim history included the ravages of disease, slavery, the gathering of armies and tribal conflict (the good parts of a history are seldom recorded).

Yellow fever, now fortunately under control, had once decimated the people, but the town still had a bad health record. Hot air trapped in the mountains engulfed the town for months at a time. In earlier years, Europeans, military and civilian personnel alike, had regularly to leave in a hurry or be carried away. In the rains Talodi is cut off totally for months, which doesn't help! Regiments of soldiers once encamped here under the command of British officers, in an endeavour to establish rule of law, Many never saw their homes again. Talodi was an unpopular station.

That Talodi house!

Much of this had been told to me in advance, so I viewed the town with jaundiced eyes, prepared to expect the worst.

Back at the rest-house the *mustaba* was already furnished with bed, table and chair. Dinner over, I sat in the lamplight writing my record in the stuffy heat of the garden. The boys had settled into their quarters at the rear. An oppressive stillness was disturbed only by crickets.

At the edge of visibility I could make out the gravestones. A figure suddenly stood before me – it seemed to materialise from the ground.

'Tahr Effendi, sir, and pleased to meet you!' it said.

I was comforted to see the familiar agricultural badge on his pith hat. He saluted smartly then sat down beside me, at my request. The bush telegraph had operated in its usual way, announcing my arrival. My own agriculturalist at Talodi; there was a lot to discuss!

Two important activities went on at Talodi then, under the aegis of the Agricultural Department and supervised by the native agriculturalist. The first of these centred on a cotton ginnery where rain-grown cotton, purchased from the Nuba, was ginned and dispatched by camel to the railway, a distance of perhaps two hundred miles. The second and much more interesting activity from my point of view was an important 'settlement experiment' being prepared with the end of the war in view. Nuba soldiers returning from war must be encouraged to resettle in their home territory: this experiment had been designed to provide information to this end.

We talked into the night and I took an opportunity to learn the politics of Talodi as Tahr saw them. Surprisingly, there was a 'club' for officials, which I was expected to join on my arrival.

Tahr left, and, late as it was, the boys – Ibrahim and Mahomed – came to the *mustaba*, with Jacoub hovering in the shadows behind them.

'We can't sleep here because there are jinns (evil spirits) in this place!'

'Jinns? Nonsense!' I tried to sound convincing, but if there was such a thing as a jinn it struck me that this was a perfect place to find one. 'What makes you think that?' I asked.

Mahomed added his contribution to the discussion: 'Jacoub tells us that everyone tells stories about this house.'

'Jacoub!' I called. 'What are you telling the boys?'

'*Jenabo*, it is just what people say, and I know that inspectors have refused to stay here.'

'Rubbish, there are no such things as jinns!'

This was the wrong thing to say to them; it was tempting providence and the boys knew it. I thought that the best thing we could do was explore the house together. I picked up the lamp and led them towards the door; perhaps their protests were half-hearted, because they followed me into the echoing rooms which were, of course, innocent and empty.

Then they began to laugh and Jacoub remembered – 'Of course, it is only during the rains that jinns come here.'

The rains were a long way off, so we went to our several beds in peace. Later, lying in the open, I looked at the sharp, black outline of the mountains. Part of the sky was radiant with stars in contrast to the blackness of the mountains. The stars were by now quite familiar to me, as each night I looked at them before going to sleep. The Plough to the north, just as I remembered it from childhood; but there were the Scorpion and the Southern Cross deeper in the south.

It was understandable that people here believed in the supernatural. In the stillness of the mountains with only soughing winds and stars and solitude, shadows could take substance and the mind create images. Yet there was something about the timelessness and space of the mountains which encouraged thought of another dimension – something beyond the merely physical. Such an awareness was coming to me: I looked to the black mountains, and the vast expanse of the sky.

Yes, there was a 'something': but jinns? I smiled to myself – never!

Talodi was very different from other places in the Nuba Mountains I had yet seen. The population consisted of a number of different races – Nilots, Nuba, Arabs and Fallata of indeterminate origin. The community was grouped accordingly so that it lacked the integration of a tribal village and was thus less welcoming. No chiefs waited for me and, at first, it seemed less friendly and spontaneous.

Tahr Effendi showed me the ginning factory where the season was over as the last of the cotton had been carried down from the hills. A small mountains of bales was being gradually transported by camel (there were eight thousand camels involved, Tahr said) the two hundred miles to the railway. A British engineer visited the ginnery twice in the year to inspect machinery: he was due to arrive before long to close the mill for the season, so there was very little here to interest me.

We drove on to the 'Dam Gamad Agricultural Resettlement Scheme for Returning Soldiers', a social experiment which had some priority in government planning at this time. It was hoped that information would be gathered from this experiment to assist them in making decisions on how to rehabilitate soldiers after the war. There were many hundreds of soldiers to consider. The scheme was still in its infancy.

Six miles south of the town, at a spot on the map named Dam Gamad, the first steps were being taken to create a new settlement. Land had been cleared and pegged out, with holdings and a little Nuba-style village being erected from scratch. Tahr Effendi had set the work in motion but surveying, well-digging, budgeting, hire of labour, transport of materials and so on remained to be done. It had to be tackled systematically or the information gained was likely to be worthless. A social experiment is always difficult, and this was to prove no exception!

I had been thralled by the freedom and spaciousness of trek, yet now I found a perverse pleasure in rolling up my sleeves and settling to this new project. It took three days of strenuous work to get things moving: one of the difficulties of trekking was having to leave operations until the next visit, weeks or months ahead.

At the end of the first evening I was taken to the 'club'. Tahr walked with me from the rest-house – there were no refinements in this town in the shape of street lighting or pavements. We came to an open square, where raucous Arabic music blared from a well-lit building surrounded by trees.

At our approach, the incumbents lined up to welcome me. One well-clad dignitary in smart European suit took me in hand and introduced clerks, merchants; indeed, all who apparently had some standing in the community. I noticed there were no Nuba present!

It was a cheerful occasion in which a variety of games were played, including a noisy form of dominoes which generated high excitement as the pieces thumped down on the table.

There was one Greek in the club, introduced to me as Mr Kosti. He spoke about the life of a merchant so far from civilisation and invited me to his home on some future occasion.

When the lights were dimmed, I walked home with a feeling of contentment thinking Talodi was a friendly place after all.

Day Off

It was Friday, 'Yom el Jummah', the Moslem day of rest.

I felt that it was time to get moving again, but, first of all, I wanted to spend a day among the pure Nuba. There were many of them in Talodi, but a dusty town was the wrong place to discover such interesting people.

Tahr agreed to accompany me, so we set off into the hills, where, as before, little Nuba houses perched high on the tops. It was like entering into a new country! Some trees were still green, and the landscape had more life in it. A number of people threaded the tracks, some carrying heavy loads on their heads, others driving animals. Most of them were completely naked, their bodies daubed with clay.

At a village fifteen miles from Talodi Tahr asked me to stop beside a large hut where a tall Nuba, wearing an Arab-style *jelibiyah* and carrying what could well have been a staff of office, was watching our arrival.

Tahr knew him. We shook hands. He spoke Arabic, and, pointing to his village higher on the mountainside, invited us to visit his home. Every person I passed on the well-beaten track paused to shake my hand. They gripped the fingertips, moving the fingers rapidly – an unusual sensation, but apparently the Nuba way of exchanging greetings. A group of men, strikingly naked and carrying spears probably ten feet in length, lined up to greet me, with broad smiles and words quite incomprehensible.

The Nuba language has roots quite different from Arabic. It is a language which has never been anchored by the written word as is the case with English or Arabic; consequently, it varies almost from valley to valley. Perhaps this is a reason for lack of cohesion in the race, and accounts for the ease with which they were picked off into slavery. By now I knew that when people are well-disposed, sign language is a sufficient way to communicate – I gripped one of the spears to test its feel and the warriors laughed approval.

The houses were indeed curious! They were built in defensive clusters of five huts, each joined by a high wall, forming a tight, in-looking circle. Each cluster belonged to a single family. The long entrance was a low, keyhole-shaped hole – we crawled through this and along a short tunnel to reach the central courtyard. This makes as secure a structure as clay walls

Typical Nuba beauties, married and unmarried, of tall, sturdy race.

Nuba wrestling.

Young Nuba girls.

can produce, and obviously arose as a means of protection from enemies, and probably also wild animals.

The walls were all brightly coloured in red, yellow or blue from native clays, giving an impression of gaiety and good hygiene, particularly as the ground was swept clean and free from any litter. How different, I thought, from the many Arab villages I had seen. There was an air of permanence here – the community was built to endure on its precarious hilltop.

Many Arab villages were simply dismantled by the people as erosion destroyed over-cropped soil, but obviously this was not the Nuba tradition. I had seen the hills carefully terraced round the villages, as if to conserve every inch of soil. Nuba were hunters, but they were also capable cultivators to judge by the surrounding landscape.

From this first day's experience with the Nuba I learned an important lesson: that nakedness and painted bodies do not necessarily indicate extreme states of primitiveness – here was a separate culture, well-developed in its own backwater.

It continued to surprise me.

The little enclosed compound jostled with people all very keen to speak and shake my hand. Their bodies were like polished ebony. Each little house apparently served a special purpose: the best-furnished one was the husband's own domain. It contained several items of carved (though clumsy) furniture, and the floor was covered with leopard and cheetah skins. Another hut was for the wives, of which there were several, with an age span of at least twenty years. The children, at least ten in number, had their own dormitory hut – the other two huts were for cooking and storing water, beer and food.

I sat with the husband in his hut and people crowded round to examine me, obviously a prize exhibit. Questions were showered about my clothes and the contents of pockets – my pen, watch, keys; each of these articles of curiosity to them.

A discussion on family life carefully interpreted by the Nuba to his wives caused howls of laughter.

'How do you manage to keep peace in the home with so many wives to contend with?' I asked.

'They just have to behave or they are shut out for the night! But what happens in your country?'

'Tell your wives that I am allowed only one wife, and in my country it is as likely that the husband can be shut out for the night by the wife!'

Of course, this just had to be a joke – they laughed on and on.

I was offered a drink of home-brewed beer. Fortunately they took it in good part when I screwed up my nose and refused to drink.

Now I was taken to see his hill-top cultivations. Outside the little tunnel a great armed Nuba – probably six feet eight inches tall – greeted me with the same finger grip. Some spark inside encouraged me to challenge him to a race up the hillside: he understood and, together, we raced up followed by a crowd, including many children, who sprawled over the rocks like a swarm of ants.

At the top he looked at me, smiling easily as I panted for breath. He slapped the palm of his hand into mine. The chief arrived with a breathless Tahr Effendi, bent double from his exertion. Then we moved over the smooth rock face, past little houses apparently planted on the virgin rock, towards the cultivations.

Most of the hillside was terraced and showed signs of good crops, recently harvested. I learned that animal manure was worked into the soil, something not seen in Arab cultivations.

By now, a crowd which must have been in excess of three hundred mobbed the hilltop so that we could hardly move. Partly to escape this crowd we were taken into another home, through its keyhole entrance. The usual confusion of greetings took place from the residents, noticeably a number of Nuba beauties, apparently relatives of my escort.

The girls crowded round: no shyness here. One of them ruffled my relatively long hair and dodged away laughing. Another stroked my face, talking all the time in incomprehensible Nuba. They were all tall and of impressive physique, their well-proportioned bodies shining with oil, no doubt a fashionable beauty feature. Such people must have an understanding of nutrition to generate such good physique, and, of course, there is no slouching in Nuba where water and other commodities are carried on the head up and down the hill every day of life.

It struck me that people like this scarcely needed the interference of government. What could a government give them apart from protection from outside interference? They appeared to have all they needed to satisfy their expectations. They were apparently managing rather well without the benefits of 'civilisation'. But it was ridiculous to form opinions of a race at this early stage – my first day there.

What a day it had been! We drove homewards: even Tahr had enjoyed the experience though he didn't say very much.

At the rest-house Ibrahim asked me what I had seen.

'A really marvellous people, and so happy!' I went on to tell some of our experiences.

'But they are *abd* (slaves) and naked!' he said scornfully, as if such people had no entitlement to my respect.

'Ibrahim,' I said firmly, 'they have well-built homes, are clean and well fed, and what's more, they look after their land more than others we have seen here.'

He was offended. I was making invidious comparisons. The subject was dropped and he disappeared to his quarters to sulk.

Land Without Water

The foothills around Talodi stood barren and eroded. Trees for miles around had been chopped to provide firewood: the land was approaching a state of dereliction. I drove round the area with some community leaders on this last morning before leaving town, and listened to tales of impending disaster. In the rains, watercourses broke their banks and spewed water into areas of the town; land was becoming barren, deeper wells were needed – 'what was the government going to do about it?'

The answer, of course, was 'probably nothing,' though I didn't say as much. However, my notebook was out and I took copious, important-looking notes, which gave some satisfaction.

Even this ancient community of Talodi, perhaps established for thousands of years, had recently undergone changes detrimental to the environment and the people. The brief I had been given was to observe these things and think them over, but the scale of the problem was so vast as to make any possible solution seem like a pipe-dream.

Mahomed had lunch ready on the *Mustaba*, and once I had gulped it down, everything was packed aboard and we left on our way northwards along the foothills of the Jebels. We were all relieved to be away from that house, yet I had nagging worries about leaving Talodi. I had a premonition about the place as if it could in some way command my future.

I brooded over events of the past three days. Was it inevitable that land should be progressively destroyed in this way? Why did people from a peasant culture not practise the simple husbandries – over-grazing and over-cropping went on relentlessly as if soil had limitless fertility. Was it the system of land tenure, or the lack of a system, that made people go on from year to year blindly taking the heart out of the land? Too often they shrugged their shoulders and said, '*Allah karim!*' (it is in the hands of the Almighty!) and that, therefore, was sufficient. On this first trek it had become apparent that the Agricultural Department of the Sudan Government had a big job on its hands in this territory. The trouble was that I *was* the Department – what on earth could one person possibly do?

Yes, it was a relief to be 'on tour' again, perhaps I would find some answers in what lay ahead.

Hot dusty miles swept past. We were heading northwards now along the foothills of the main mountain ridge when a jagged rock hill caught my eye; the mere bare-bones of a mountain. Close to its base I saw a depression surrounded by a clay bank – obviously an attempt by men to create a reservoir. I stopped the car and climbed out to examine the site.

The remains of grass houses stood close by; it looked as if they had recently been occupied, and the hollow dug in an attempt to provide a long-term store of water: its base of clay had cracks fully six inches in width.

My attention was arrested by seven graves, each piled over with layers of stones and carrying some fluttering rags, on sticks. There were four houses; there were seven graves. Obviously some disaster had struck the inhabitants to cause so many deaths, apparently about the same time! Had it been disease? Hunger? Disease and hunger are peril enough, add to this a scarcity of water, then life hangs by a thread.

I walked the watercourse leading to this pathetic little reservoir. Here was one answer to the quandary – *hafirs* (reservoirs), to trap the rivers when in flood. Was it only a matter of scale, effort, and capital to establish secure communities in places like this? Small *hafirs* which quickly dried up were common in the mountains.

I spent so long at this site that there was no point in continuing our journey, as the sun was setting over the mountain range. The boys by now were resigned to my whims, though they showed a distinct lack of enthusiasm to spend a night at such a remote place. The trek gear was grudgingly erected at the side of the track, a fire lit, and the usual evening routine commenced under the stars.

I had a busy evening of writing. It was almost time for bed when I remembered the gramophone hidden under a tarpaulin in the car. There followed an hour of music – *Tannhäuser*, the Pathétique, and 'the Funickle Man Who Had an Old Sow'! A varied programme, rather scratchy, but music nevertheless. The boys were neither amused nor appreciative. They could please themselves; to me it was rare entertainment.

Breakfast in this wilderness was a breathtaking experience. The sun crested the horizon and I sat absorbing the thrill of it. Even Ibrahim stood smiling in the orange glow. I had a strong inclination to linger here, perhaps even to examine the unusual hill at our back, but I decided to move on and not waste time. In minutes, with the car loaded, we were on our way.

Time passed effortlessly. It was a morning of shimmering heat where everything living hung without movement as in death. A goatskin of water slung on the side of the car gave a supply of cool though flat-tasting water. No doubt it was as poor-tasting as water can be, but often – yes very often – it seemed the best thing the world had to offer. In the Jebels people often asked for a drink from our skin, then smacked their lips with satisfaction. Water, the elixir of life, valuable beyond price when it is scarce!

We crossed a plain of variable soil types and came to one of the biggest khors I had yet seen. The map read 'Khor Tira Mandi'. It was steep-walled with a dry sandy base, about forty yards wide. It had been a frothing torrent a few months before, but now groups of Nuba women were scooping gourds of water from holes in the sandy base. They waved to the car, so I decided to stop at the neighbouring village to ask questions about the water position in this relatively populous area. Men came from their houses, and I joined a group in one little house, but none of them spoke Arabic. Sign language did produce a few answers: in the dry months they had to travel many miles from their homes to draw water from wells. The water got in this way was brackish. They suffered this hardship for several months each year.

Was it beyond the wit of man to conserve the vast flood-waters in sufficient quantity to span this period? It could be done if the will and the resource was applied.

My reserves of sign language exhausted, I rose to leave, and innocently turned to notice a little baby being nursed by her mother in a string bed. The mother rose quickly with fear in her eyes, and rushed with her baby from the hut. This response on her part shocked me a little, but when I thought about it, the sudden appearance of a white stranger into her home was cause enough for such a response. I realised then how easy it was to presume on a position of authority, and to expect a smiling acceptance wherever I went – in other words, to be patronising. It was a useful lesson.

How close can one ever get to a culture far removed from one's own? How long does it take to understand the customs, conventions, superstitions and traditions of another race? Perhaps it takes a lifetime of living with people and accepting their values. There is an assumption among many western peoples that African cultures are inferior to their own, and that they must inevitably change to ape the western way. That is a sad assumption. It was clear to me that in spite of the friendliness of the Nuba toward me on my travels, my understanding of them would be a mere caricature.

At the end of the day's trek we entered a narrow valley with high hills reaching up on each side. The road, the dry bed of a twisting watercourse, demonstrated why motor transport became impossible during the rains.

We stopped for the night at a little clearing, presided over by a tall Haraz tree in full leaf, the only one in sight bearing leaves, no doubt because its deep root-system reached down to a subterranean water-table. In the course of the evening Ibrahim told me the tale of the Haraz tree.

'When Raboonah created the world, all species of plants and animals were told to make obeisance to him. They all did so, except the Haraz tree. "I am the Lord of the forest," it said, "why should I make supplication to another lord?" The great creator learned of this, and, in his anger, condemned the Haraz, alone of the forest trees, to suffer the hot season in full leaf, then to cast them in the rains.'

It was always easy to recognise a Haraz because of its long-suffering canopy. Next morning I walked deep into surrounding bush, and stopped, intrigued at the sight of a python, coiled and basking only twenty yards from me. In the neighbouring trees a colony of heart-nosed monkeys chattered excitedly as I disturbed them at feeding time.

There must have been a water-hole in the valley, as our night's sleep had been disturbed by the sound of heavy creatures walking by, quite close to our beds. It surprised me that the boys had not been worried at the closeness of the animals: unlike jinns, they were no cause for concern!

We were now entering 'missionary country'. A limited effort by Christian missionaries was permitted in the mountains, and I had looked forward for some time to meeting an active missionary. Would I find an up-to-date Dr Livingstone, with his band of faithful followers? There must be some similarities, because missionaries remained isolated and immured for years at a time, even remaining through the rains, when other white people left the mountains for the good of their health. By now I felt some slight feeling of excitement at meeting again with white people, and being able to speak English once more.

The Heiban Mission stands at the base of a quite spectacular mountain range, which presents a jagged outline to the sky, where gigantic balancing rocks are poised as if ready to roll to the valley floor at any moment. A palm-fringed road leads to a cluster of white buildings, standing out boldly from the surrounding red soil. There are church, hospital, and school, representing the three main works of the missionaries, and it was pleasing to discover that they were there not only to convert the 'heathen', but also to raise the quality of the physical well-being of the Nuba. Their work went even beyond that indicated by the three main buildings, extending into agriculture and horticulture. Heiban provided interesting evidence of what can be done to improve land, and people's diet, by the careful application of primary husbandries.

The station at this time was a very attractive place at which to live. It was a veritable garden of flowers and shrubs, often patiently irrigated by hand, and, in the surrounding countryside, a wider range of vegetables and fruits were grown than anywhere else in the mountains.

Mr Nobbs, the missionary in charge, welcomed me like a long-lost friend and from the first moment spoke about seeds, plant diseases and treatments, and the state of the soil. In him I found a sounding-board for my thoughts, and at the same time, gained much from his long years of experience in the mountains.

It shocked me to find that in the past, missionaries had been virtually ignored, even resented, by government people touring the mountains. In spite of their considerable experience with the Nuba, their advice was seldom if ever sought, and very often inspectors passed through Heiban without calling on them.

Within minutes of my arrival the kettle was on, and I was sitting down to a cup of tea with a group of people eager for conversation with someone from outside their little world. I enjoyed my visits there. I enjoyed the sing-song round an old treadle organ in the evening, only it tended to make me feel very far from home.

I was taken to an area of forest some miles from Heiban which, because of native belief that it was haunted, was never visited by the local people. I saw virgin forest, thick and tropical, unlike all the surrounding countryside, where there was widespread evidence of soil deterioration due to destruction of the top growth by animals and men. It provided an illustration of what the area had once been like and also a warning of future dangers if soil deterioration continued.

To walk through that gloomy forest provided an eerie sensation. There was evidence of man's activities in the distant past in the shape of deep pits to trap animals and mounds of stones built to serve some unknown purpose.

Back at the little hospital I got my first real insight of the hold witch-doctors exercise over the peoples of the mountains. A Nuba family crowding round a very ill boy in a hospital hut sat silently and patiently as we looked at him wrapped up in bandages, and evidently on the point of death. He had had a fall which resulted in his injuries being treated by a witch-doctor; only when this treatment had proved ineffectual had they thought to bring

Heiban mission house.

him to the hospital – too late to save his life. This sort of happening was an everyday event: the witch-doctor was consulted first, only then did they come to the hospital.

The Sudan missionaries also were skilled as doctors, carpenters or agriculturalists like myself. They had obviously not come to the Nuba Mountains for personal gain like so many Europeans in Africa; in fact several in the Mountains had left good careers in order to serve in the country.

The homeliness of Heiban, the warm sense of love for the local people which was always apparent, made me reluctant to continue trek, but I never stayed more than one day at a time, and even that short period was spent at work of some kind, usually considering cropping problems or soil deficiencies around the station.

On our way northwards from Heiban the car squeezed past long lines of camels on their way to the railway station with Talodi cotton and grain: indeed, we had been passing such caravans from the moment of leaving Talodi. There were thousands of camels employed in this way, all of them brought down from the northern plains by Arab contractors. By the time of the rains every single camel would be out of the mountains and away to the northern plains again.

In the rains people rode only on the backs of bulls, which were sure-footed in wet clay.

North of Heiban, where the track crested a low hill, a vast plateau became visible, stretching to the horizon. It appeared to be completely unpopulated, possibly due to the scarcity of life-giving water. There was a tang of smoke in the air. Several miles to the north a bush fire, with a front over ten miles wide, advanced in a line towards us. It was still far away, yet, even at this distance it was possible to see trees exploding into flame.

I stopped the car and looked, fascinated, as the land, golden with its covering of dry grass, was transformed into a wilderness of black ash. By the look of it this fire was set to consume hundreds of square miles of bush, depriving man and animals alike of any means of sustenance.

This was a primary cause of soil erosion! Land having its heart burned out before my eyes, leaving only a wasteland of blowing dust.

We drove quickly through the fire line into a black, charred wilderness stretching as far as the eye could see. Larger trees had turned into smouldering pillars. Remnants of long-dead trees spoke of a history of previous fires, making a desert out of what had once been lush forest. Sheet erosion had already removed most of the topsoil, as there was no longer a protective canopy of vegetation to protect the soil from wind and violent rainstorms.

This first experience of bush fire held me in its thrall; the scale of destruction was so vast – could the cycle ever be reversed? Who started the fires? Was the spread of the desert into this lovely area inevitable? Could people ever be resettled in areas like this, with water sources drying up?

In sombre mood our journey continued northwards, past a high range of rocky hills with Nuba villages here and there, then down to a little plain with another mission station in its centre. What must once have been a beautiful landscape bore all the evidence of degradation to the extent that blown sand piled against the mission buildings.

An elderly couple came out of the Abri mission house: a striking pair, and, to me, the very epitome of missionaries. The husband was indeed a Livingstone figure, tall and bent with the years, his leathern skin could not conceal the sparkle of deep-set blue eyes which had the haunting look of the visionary. His wife, small and fairly stout, in a plain cotton frock, looked as if she could well be the prop and stay of the man, and of the mission. I soon found she could turn her hand to anything, being equally at home as nurse, woodchopper, teacher or cook. They were a couple radiating warmth and kindness, much loved by the Nuba who lived near the station: they were the kind of people one never forgets.

In some sense, they tried to adopt me, always urging me to return quickly, and treating me as if I was their special charge. Mr and Mrs Mills were almost at the end of a lifetime of service in the mountains. They looked forward bleakly to the prospect of retirement, trying to conjure an enthusiasm for a new life back home in Australia. Their stay had been extended, as his long-term ambition had been to translate the Bible into the Nuba tongue, a work by now almost done.

Mr Mills gave me a fascinating account of their twenty-five years at Abri – tribal uprising, opposition to their work – they had survived it all. He spoke of earlier years, when Abri was surrounded by virgin forest teeming with animal life: elephants, lions, most of the year round. He pointed to the scarred landscape, saying, 'Look at it now, and all in my lifetime!'

The Body in the Grass

On this first visit to Abri I stayed only a few hours. There were other places still to visit before returning to Rashad, and by now I had an urge to contact Alex, to unburden myself of thoughts and impressions accumulated so far.

With Abri behind us we drove once more through an ocean of golden grass into the mellow light of evening. Cool air tempted me into the back of the car, so I changed places with Ibrahim and stood above the kit, holding on to the driver's cab. The changing scene was exhilarating, as the blue-shaded mountains gathered the pallor of night: at such a time the whole of nature was a hymn of thanksgiving. With eyes half closed I tried to absorb its mood.

Mahomed stood at my side, equally entranced. At a point about ten miles from Abri he pulled my arm, pointing into the dead grass.

'Look, *Jenabo*, there – stop!'

I turned and saw a black shape lying motionless, and I nodded, thinking it was an animal of some kind, and didn't give it much thought.

A short distance further on Mahomed attracted my attention again.

'*Jenabo*, we should have stopped; that was a human body.'

A body! I told Jacoub to turn back along the trail. We scanned the grass in the growing darkness until . . . there it was, only a few yards from the track; the body of a woman, old and wizened, and naked. A spade was fixed to the side of the car, and it seemed right that we should bury her. I looked around, but there were no other people anywhere in sight.

How could an old lady like this have been left to die in such a remote place? The boys could offer no explanation.

Ibrahim called out with surprise, 'She is not dead! See her eyes!'

She was looking at us, eerily, through half-closed eyes. The water-skin was brought, but her lips remained tightly closed. She could not be persuaded to drink.

There was obviously very little life left in her pathetic little body: her grizzled white hair seemed to shine in the gloom. With difficulty I eased her up a little, but she groaned and flopped back, as if wanting to be left to die in peace.

I could not leave her there!

We carried her back to the car and cleared a place for her among the boxes. She never moved: her eyes were tightly closed and I thought she had died.

We drove back to Abri in very different humour from when we had left. Mr and Mrs Mills both came to the little mission dispensary as the car drew up outside, wondering who the unexpected arrivals were. When they looked at the woman and heard my story, Mr Mills shook his head.

'She is not dead yet, but I think you have wasted your time. We will put her on a bed, but there is nothing we can do for her.'

She was carried into a little hut, but within minutes she wriggled out of the bed and fell to the ground, as if, with the last spark of life, she wanted to escape back to the bush.

It was too late now for our journey north, so the boys unpacked at a little rest-house, while I went to spend an evening with the missionary and his wife. Twice again the old woman fell from the bed, and finally was rolled like a mummy in sheets in an attempt to restrain her movements. It was in vain. Next morning she was found lying in the grass, dead, outside the hut.

I had learned yet another fact about the Nuba, that it was not uncommon for old people, when approaching death, to go voluntarily to their death in the bush: something accepted by the family.

Perhaps the next time I found an old, worn, black body in the bush, I would be as well to drive on.

The next day's trek was through a remarkable countryside: if any nearer to civilisation it would become a magnet to the modern tourist. Aeons of wind erosion have sculpted hills and rocks into mile after mile of spectacular shapes. As we drove through natural arenas, and round fantastic rock pillars, I felt encouraged to write descriptions of the ongoing scene:

> . . . The lovely tulla tree can be seen on every side. It has vivid red bark and its trunk stands out conspicuously at a distance. Now, the silver-barked Sahab, like a stunted beech tree. Different bands of forest trees indicate how varied the soil is – sometimes rich clay, then in a few yards, eroded gravel with dwarfed scrub. Soil is more varied here than anywhere else I have so far seen.
>
> There are two Arabs walking, each carrying antiquated-looking rifles, something not uncommon here. Suddenly, a gigantic cone of virgin rock with a separate balancing stone on top, under which daylight can be seen.

Now a ridge of this same rock, about 150 feet high, with heaps of gigantic boulders piled along its base. The road wends into a grove of large-trunked trees resembling oaks, but with spines and tiny leaves (Ibrahim doesn't know this one!).

A little Nuba village, and we are waved to a stop by three Nuba soldiers in khaki shirts and shorts. With them is a group of naked villagers: they ask if I can give a young woman a lift to Delami, fifteen miles north from here. I agree, and she climbs aboard beside the boys, at the rear. Ibrahim looks embarrassed as he thinks nakedness improper. She is carrying a cloth-wrapped parcel.

This is now a strange landscape. Huge stones lie singly, scattered at random over the flat soil. They are all rounded, and some are as big as a house. We wend between them and are dwarfed. Slabs of rock lean against each other and now the *pièce de résistance*, an amazing pile of balancing rocks one on top of the other in descending size, and each quite separate from the one beneath. The structure is probably 120 feet in height. It would make a perfect text-book illustration on the subject of erosion.

We have stopped to look at this wonder: words cannot adequately describe it! On we go through tumbledown rock ranges with tall fingers reaching to the sky – trees cling to crevices.

There are twelve Nuba women waving and shouting as we pass. Their teeth flash white in contrast to the black of their bodies. They carry heavy water vessels on their heads. They are all very upright, though only the youngest have shapely figures because they have not yet borne any children.

We enter a grove of Doleib palms, a sure sign that water is close to the surface. Now sand dunes, and wheels spin as we crawl over a hill. Down again into a new scene – could be a moonscape! – black-jagged country with grim rock piles like tumbledown tombs. There are fat Baobab trees which fit well into the picture.

Round a corner: we stop just in time! A caravan of forty-five camels carrying my grain to the railway, still almost a hundred miles away, each with its four-cwt. load. Some of them feint to the side as we go by, even though they are haltered nose to tail.

Now a group of Nuba men armed with long spears. We are entering an area of cultivations with the dead straw of ripe millet making a brittle avenue – many animal skeletons at the base of a stumpy hill – Delami . . .

Delami, as far as I was concerned, was just an interesting suq where Mahomed might find a slightly better range of food than was the general case in the mountains. It was a trading centre where Arab met Nuba, and products were moved by camel to Er Rahad on the railway. People all wore the *jelibiyah* showing that we had moved into Arab country.

Merchants apparently welcomed my visits, as I was regularly encouraged into their little shops where I would be invited to sit and drink coffee in the hope of a sale.

Heaps of animal skins – leopard, cheetah, python and other – were for sale throughout the market. At that time a skin was priced at twenty piastres (one hundred piastres to the Egyptian pound): proud animals killed for the sake of a few pence!

The Scorpion

There was one more stopping point on that first trek before returning to Rashad and home, namely Um Berembeita, where there was a cotton ginning mill. It was also the most intensive grain-producing area in the Jebels, and likely to involve me in the future.

To reach the Um Berembeita rest-house the track crossed many miles of fertile clay soil, much of it uncultivated and with a high potential for cropping. Close to the rest-house Jacoub drove into a large dry watercourse clearly shown on my cloth map – the Abu Habl, at its upper reaches, the same one I had crossed when leaving the station at Er Rahad. This watercourse drained the northern mountains, pouring its water over a great flood plain, never reaching river or sea. It was also, as I had been told, haunted by jinns.

The rest-house stood on the banks of the Abu Habl.

The boys quickly took over the rest-house, which was, unusually, brick-built and once the home of an inspector. An uninviting house, it had something of the forbidding qualities of the Talodi house, but with one redeeming feature: a well-stocked demonstration garden.

That evening, after having met the people of the village, I sat alone at the trek table writing notes on the day's work, when Ibrahim came into the light of the lamp.

'*Jenabo*, have we got to stay here so close to the Abu Habl?'

By this stage I was becoming tired of stories about jinns. 'Don't tell me you are afraid again? There must be somewhere in the mountains safe from them!'

'But I told you about the Abu Habl: we shouldn't tempt providence by staying on its banks!' he protested.

I decided to be firm and stop this ridiculous talk.

'Ibrahim, I don't want to hear any more of these stories. There is nothing here. Go to bed!'

Ibrahim went off, crestfallen.

I thought for some time about the boys and their fears and how they apparently accepted spirits as indisputable fact, and not to be treated lightly. Well, I would walk along the bed of the Abu Habl in the darkness then tell them how foolish were their fears. I told the boys where I was going, then climbed down into the watercourse, and walked along its stony base.

It was very dark, and I could just see where to place my feet among the stones. The high earth walls seemed to tower over me and I found that occasionally I was looking over my shoulder. A slight shiver went up my spine: all this talk about evil spirits, it put silly ideas into a person's mind! I stopped to savour the silence, and to pit myself against a gathering fear, which, of course, was ridiculous.

A sudden excruciating pain pierced into the shin of my right foot. It came like a dagger. I hopped in agony, but strangely did not associate the pain with the supernatural – it was only too real! Slowly I hobbled back to the rest-house and into the light of the lamp, to flop in a chair. Then, as I looked at a red weal, already swelling, I knew that I had been stung by a scorpion – it had climbed over my sandals and stung into my bare ankle. In this dry place it was reasonable to expect there were no malaria-bearing mosquitoes, so I had not worn the usual protective clothing. The last thing I had thought about was a scorpion.

I called Ibrahim and ignored his, 'I told you so,' and other comments, and got him to bring a medical kit from the car. Somewhere I had learned that an appropriate treatment was to make the wound bleed, then rub in crystals of potassium permanganate (something always carried for testing the purity of water). I sliced at the wound with a razor blade till blood flowed, then rubbed in some crystals: it was already so painful that there was no additional pain.

There followed two days of throbbing discomfort, unable to walk: glands in my thigh knotted. Some people came to visit me in that drab rest-house, but I wrote no notes and, fortunately, this time is lost to memory. On the third day I hobbled to the car and we left on the final stage back to Rashad. By now it seemed possible that search parties would be out: I felt a form of guilt that two days had been wasted. Perhaps someone was waiting for me at home.

The car laboured up the last steep hill to the village in the middle of a hot afternoon when the whole population was asleep, even the dogs. At the back of the house we climbed stiffly from the car, shook the dust from our hair and looked about as if expecting something to happen. There was only peace – silence!

At Home

With some sense of foreboding I headed for the office where a smart salute from the village idiot did nothing to lighten my spirits. The heady days of freedom were over. From now on my actions would be subject to scrutiny.

I looked at the threatening pile of wires and letters on the desk, the accumulation from weeks of absence. My spirits sagged further – there was no mail from home. Part of the thrill and anxiety of returning had centred on the possibility of getting letters from Marion. She was serving in the forces in Ack-Ack Command, and anything could have happened in the long period since my last news of her. With a feeling of emptiness I stacked the papers in piles according to their dates and source, then settled into a chair to learn the worst.

First, from Alex, there were a number of telegrams all dealing with rather mundane topics – transport of crops, monthly reports, contracts, staff wages – but there was nothing that could be considered personal or even friendly. There was no 'welcome back to Rashad', not that such was in the least likely, but it would have eased my current humour. It occurred to me also that he made no reference to the subject of soil conservation in his correspondence. Was he really interested in tackling the erosion problem? Would my opinions matter in the slightest?

There was an instruction to return to trek again 'earliest possible', together with a list of work to be done in the mountains – well-digging for Nazir Zbeir; an urgent study of the Talodi Settlement Scheme for the Government to act on; and so on. At least it all had meaning for me now. I understood what was wanted, and it was better to be trekking than sitting in an office in Rashad.

Yet there was something lacking. In fact, I still needed to become accustomed to the isolation of life in the mountains. No one to share my problems with or to listen to my ideas. I would have to make do with Ibrahim and Mahomed, as far as company was concerned.

An important-looking letter caught my eye, and I was surprised to see it came from the province Governor in El Obeid. I read it over several times, trying to absorb its significance. ' . . . Please come to El Obeid on 15 April to speak to Province Council on subject of soil erosion.'

RASHAD ANNUAL REPORT

COVERING SEASON 43/44

SEASON.

Rainfall throughout Rashad district was average but generally, distribution was better than for previous years and the heavier late falls were of great benefit to the maturing crops.

Rainfall over a period of 5 years has been as follows (in mm.):-

	1939	1940	1941	1942	1943
Rashad	814.5	595.8	719.6	657.7	709.2
Um Berembeita	792.7	656.3	730.3	669.6	598.9
Abu Gubeiha	767.4	576.9	626.2	615.5	571.0
Abbassiya	730.3	693.0	713.4	744.6	624.4
Totals	3104.9	2522.0	2798.5	2687.4	2503.6

It is interesting to note that according to above figures there is a slight tendency for an annual decrease in rainfall; this may not be significant although there are regions in the Nuba mountains where the people speak of appreciable decrease in rainfall over a period.

Warning of rainfall decrease sent to Khartoum in 1944.

Well, presumably I could cope with this; there was plenty that could be said on the subject, though I wondered whether I would be required to speak in English or Arabic, and to whom. That could wait. Then I realised I would be trekking again for several weeks and this request was for one month ahead. Hmm!

Lastly, a letter from Khartoum from the Director! What could he be wanting? I tore it open and read it with a feeling of frustration. ' . . . Because of crop failures and famine in East Africa concentrate on producing maximum possible grain in the coming rains. Make sure sufficient seed is available throughout the mountains. Prepare for trekking by horse: I have discussed this with Alex Graves and he will be in touch with you.' Finally, as if in an afterthought, came the bleak information: 'Your Higher Arabic examination is on April 12th/13th in Khartoum: be sure and turn up.'

All this, and an examination for good measure!

My future was in the hands of three different people it seemed – Alex, the Governor, and the Director, and all of them had to be obeyed.

I wrote a long telegram to Alex saying I would leave on trek again as he had asked, and stating also the requests from the Governor and the Director – did these moves all meet with his approval? In fact, a reply came the next day with some further instructions, but approving my arrangements.

The village idiot took the telegram to the post office, and I walked slowly homewards to break the news to the boys.

There was a conflict of ideas in what was now being asked of me: it seemed quite unreasonable to request that more and more grain should be exported from the mountains in the face of the serious spread of erosion. What was the point of persuading people to move in opposite directions at the same time? Yet, if there was starvation in neighbouring countries where did the priority really lie? I had no answer to this, and could only do as I was directed.

This was a gloomy enough prospect: then there was that Arabic examination, of all things. On arrival in the Sudan I had been told that advancement in the Civil Service was conditional on passing Higher standard in Arabic, so I had no cause for complaint now that the time was coming. Yet it was only fifteen months since I had learned my first Arabic word – I could speak well enough, but the written script: I hadn't practised this in months!

Determined to share my gloom with others, I called the boys and told them we were leaving again in two days' time, so they had better get organised quickly.

Mahomed took it calmly. It always surprised me how well he had taken to trekking; after all, he wasn't exactly young, and it was no great source of pleasure to be bumped from place to place in the back of the car, then to improvise meals from the sparse food of the area. He really seemed to like the life and had never once complained.

Ibrahim took the news differently. He listened, then, unusual for him,

Bakhit at Rashad.

walked away in silence, probably in a sulk – something not too uncommon. Well, he could get on with it.

I called for Bakhit to be saddled and eased my humour by an hour of hard riding over little trails and wadis, until darkness forced me home.

After dinner, served in total silence by Ibrahim, he appeared beside me on the *mustaba*, wringing his hands and with his head bent down. He had the look of one seriously in trouble.

'Ibrahim, what is it you want?'

Still he hesitated, then out it poured. '*Jenabo*, I need your advice! I don't know what to do!'

'Carry on, Ibrahim,' I said encouragingly.

'I have met a woman I want to marry: she is a widow with three children. What is more, I *must* marry her!'

'Good for you, Ibrahim.' Then I thought: three children! And what about his young cousin with the red frock? 'You must have changed your mind very quickly.' It was less than a month since I had met the other candidate.

'I never really wanted to marry my young cousin; it was my uncle who put pressure on me to do so.'

'You must surely make you own mind up and marry the person you love?' I put this more as a question because I had learned from earlier discussions that Ibrahim did not believe in love, at least, not the kind of love indulged in by western society. To admit to being in love, in his opinion, was tantamount to confessing a ridiculous human failing.

'Why not marry the widow?' I persevered.

'In the name of Allah, it is not as easy as that. My parents died when I was young, and I was brought up by my uncle, so obviously he insists that I marry his daughter. He said that if I don't, I need never darken his door again!'

This complicated the issue, as no one wants to be cast out of the family. So I took the other tack.

'But why marry a widow who already has three children? You will not be able to support such a big family.' It seemed appropriate to stress this point as I had visions of being asked for a 'rise'.

'It is Allah's will that I marry the widow and help to look after the family.' If it was Allah's will, it was surely a compliment to my powers of mediation to be permitted to speculate on the Almighty's judgement.

'Ibrahim,' I said with an air of finality, 'if Allah has decreed in this matter you must obey, and leave your uncle to get on with it.'

'That's what I thought too! *Kater kherrak* (many thanks) for your advice!' He padded away, smiling at last. I was also smiling, realising that my troubles were not so bad after all; at least I did not have Ibrahim's worries – praise be to Allah!

Abu Anga

I was determined to have a rest day before setting out again for the south. With the scorpion sting healed and no longer causing inconvenience, the world looked a better place even the distant prospect of the examination in the city could not quell a feeling of optimism.

Ibrahim served breakfast on the *mustaba* and he, too, was full of the joys of life, obviously now that his mind was made up about his marriage, family problems had been brushed from his mind.

The sun was just breaking though a soft morning mist showing the hill-top Nuba houses as if they were floating in the sky. It was a day for some special adventure – what better than to ride to Abu Anga and perhaps even climb to its summit?

I ordered Bakhit to be saddled and was making ready to leave when a rider in Arab garb rode up to the front gate. I recognised the Omdah and invited him to the *mustaba* for a cup of coffee. We sat down to drink and he explained the purpose of his visit.

'*Jenabo*, I have come to discuss water with you. You will know the *hafirs* in Rashad often dry before the rains come.'

I felt rather pleased that he had thought fit to ask my advice. By now I knew efforts had been made to find an answer, but without success. We talked over the problem for a time. I asked him:

'Is it perhaps new wells or – larger *hafirs* that are needed?'

He shook his head. 'Wells are out of the question on this rocky hill, and *hafirs* need to be blasted out of the rock.'

Where then did the answer lie?

I told him that I was about to ride to Abu Anga and the horse was ready, but would be pleased to explore the area with him. We rode off together to examine the wadis and valleys in search of a place where a dam might be built, but the steep rocky terrain offered little feasibility of a solution. I told him that I was intending to climb to the top of Abu Anga and from that height perhaps I could see a possible dam-site. He shook his head. Never before had Abu Anga been climbed: in fact, no one had ever attempted it, it would be tempting providence to attack the rock: it would be a waste of time.

He told me the history of Rashad and Abu Anga as we rode slowly over the trails. Before roads were made to Rashad by the *hakooma* (Government), Rashad was almost inaccessible and easily defended against outside intruders. It held out for the Mahdi after other places had capitulated to British forces. A second Mahdi rose in this area so that the British had to lay siege until he was finally captured and taken to El Obeid, where his body was hung up for other potential rebels to see. Indeed, several punitive raids were made by British forces into the area to quell the continuing spirit of rebellion.

I asked the Omdah, 'Who was Abu Anga?'

He looked at me for a few seconds as if surprised that I should not know of a figure important in the Sudan's history.

'In the Mahidiya he led us to victory against the Turks.'

I learned that Abu Anga had been a slave who rose to become the Mahdi's greatest general. He had been a commander at Khartoum when General Gordon was killed, greatly feared because of his ruthlessness and yet possessing qualities which were respected alike by friend and foe. Abu Anga had lived for a time in Rashad and the tall, rocky peak outside the village bore his name.

He went on to describe the turbulent history of earlier years when there was often tribal unrest.

'At least, since the British came there has been no more fighting,' he said magnanimously. I knew that this was true, that the Sudan had known years of peace since British rule came to the country, something relatively rare in its history.

We found no solutions to the water problem, but agreed that when the DC returned, his support would be enlisted to find an answer, as well as investigate what Government funds were available for this purpose.

Afternoon, and I rode off alone towards Abu Anga, past one of the few village wells where the women were busily engaged in drawing water, and in gossip. 'The women gossip at the well, the men gossip in the suq.' I left behind the natural rock pillars guarding the village and after a short hour's ride came in sight of the mound-shaped hill with its great rock pinnacle perched on top, as if planted there by some giant.

Back in Rashad it had seemed a tempting prospect to climb Abu Anga, but as I drew closer it took on the appearance of an insurmountable core of rock, well beyond my skills in climbing. I had bravely told the boys of my intention so, at least, I must make the attempt.

I left the track and rode over old Nuba terraces towards the base of the hill. A little group of sweating half-naked men were threshing grain, and shouted their blessings: looking at the now gigantic rock I was beginning to think I would need them.

When it was no longer possible to ride owing to the jumble of broken rock at its base, I hitched Bakhit in the shade of a tree and set off on the climb.

From the start I was faced with a mass of tumbled rock with thorns and creepers growing in every crevice, a maze in which great slabs formed chasms and platforms, with the occasional dead end, which meant a search for another route. Only too soon, struggling for breath, I was questioning why inflict this agony upon myself; after all, I had had no climbing practice in years. Several hundred feet of this and a broad, rounded shoulder of rock stretched smoothly up and out of sight: the exposed core of the mountain. On all fours, fortunately my shoes had rubber soles, I crawled upwards maintaining a precarious balance and only too aware of my perilous position. My weight was supported on the point of toes and the palms of hands – then I realised it was becoming too steep, in fact unclimbable.

Rather late in the day I realised that I was doing everything wrong – balancing with aching legs in a situation of danger, and nobody at hand to pick up the pieces. There was only one way to go – sideways, where I could see a slight ledge beneath a vertical rock wall.

Foot by dangerous foot, I sidled towards the ledge with every muscle aching and sweat trickling from my nose. At last a seat, and I was forced to turn and gaze at the spectacle below, extending far north beyond the escarpment, and into the limitless plains.

It was hot, roasting hot, as I was sitting directly in the rays of the westering sun. I felt utterly dwarfed by the dimensions of this rock face and was suddenly gripped by a sensation of complete loneliness, as if I was the only living person in hundreds of miles – which was not too far from being the case.

My eye caught sight of a crack stretching upwards to the top of the cliff – somehow I reached it, and somehow, later, I was lying on this cliff top, exhausted, and peering outwards to an Africa both gigantic and minute at once.

I was on a broad rock shelf from which the mighty central core of Abu Anga tapered upwards like a gigantic cathedral spire. Blocks of rounded stone as big as a house balanced precariously, and looked ready to drop over the cliff at a touch. Some large slabs leaned against each other, forming deep, dark caverns.

The air was still. An intense silence pressed on the eardrums. Black shadows stretched across the rock floor. It was a place for the imagination to run riot. Walking round the base of the central rock – one colossal slab of stone had slipped outwards, forming a narrow black cavern eighty or ninety feet high. I entered timidly. Overhead, where the slab leaned against the mountain, little holes sent down fingers of light like beams from a torch, and far into the cavern, there was another side-crack apparently going into the mountain's heart.

Suddenly I remembered the Omdah's words about the curse of Abu Anga, and hurried without further delay to the fierce light beyond. There is something about solitude and the might of natural forces which combine to make one respect local superstitions; or rather, fear the worst!

Out in the sunshine I found a wide cleft stretching upwards and, without hesitation, started climbing. It was surprisingly easy for the first one hundred feet, until gradually I became aware, yet again, of the precariousness of my situation and, this time, stopped defeated, with courage melted away.

I was able to sit on a little ledge and view the spectacle beneath. The red westering sun burnished the scene with its flame. Blue smoke from a bush fire trailed upwards into the sky, and peaks of a distant mountain reached up to engulf the sun. Far below, the little white road seemed to turn and twist for no apparent reason, as if with no plan to go anywhere.

Suddenly a sharp band of reflected light from a neighbouring mountain caught my eye – the little waterfall which provided a means of irrigating the Rashad garden. Could that be the answer to Rashad's water problem? Could water be led the few miles to Rashad? Here was an idea!

I found an easier route down from Abu Anga and rode home, tired and thirsty, but well satisfied with my holiday. There was also just a possibility that the water question could be solved: yes, it had been a good day!

Back on the Trail

Next day I sent Alex the appropriate signals that I was leaving for the south once more and, after an early lunch, with the car loaded, and the boys crouching in their usual nest, we set off into shimmering heat – hotter than I had ever expected to find in the mountains. Perhaps because of this there were no potential fellow travellers, and our departure was as silent as the arrival of a few days before.

We drove through that same ocean of dead, golden grass on our way to Abu Gubeiha – not a drop of water in hundreds of square miles. Much of the soil was good and capable of bearing food crops, but without an enduring source of water to permit the establishment of communities of people, it was worthless to man. A great band of similar semi-arid land stretches the breadth of Africa, and only favoured areas support a population. These 'favoured areas' were suffering from over-cropping, over-grazing and de-forestation, causing desert to creep southwards towards the heart of Africa – I had seen this already, all too clearly.

People were able to survive at subsistence level provided the rains were average: a failure in the rains spelt disaster.

All the various ecological factors had been in equilibrium for centuries, but now a serious change was taking place: a change threatening the forest, other wildlife, the soil, and ultimately, man.

It was all so easy to see: even an idiot could read the signs, I thought. Why had nothing been done about it sooner, or rather, was it possible to do anything?

Far better to forget about it all and just leave it in the hands of Allah, as the people were prone to say. But no! I looked at the arid but fertile plain stretching to the horizon on every side – something could be done to reverse the cycle of change: in fact, failing this, there could come a day when the population of the Nuba Mountains would be decimated. Was I the only person in the Sudan wrestling with the problem of soil conservation? It seemed ridiculous!

Suddenly we stopped at the rest-house: I came out of a dream to the shrill, startling trill of female voices – there was something afoot, a wedding perhaps? I had still not learned the customs of the people to the point of being able to differentiate between the various sounds made by women when special happenings occur. The noises were coming from more than one quarter – Mahomed said to me with meaning:

'Death!'

I could see one man only, standing outside his house: I asked him what was wrong. He shook his head, held up his palms and said: 'Relapsing fever in the village: Allah save us!'

Relapsing fever! One of the most dreaded diseases; a disease brought about by water scarcity and bad hygiene: unwashed clothes harbour ticks and lice which inject a parasite into the body – a disease which can spread like wildfire and cause many deaths.

I was directed to the Nazir and found him in a huddle with some men of the tribe. 'When did this start, *ya* Nazir?' I asked, after a careless exchange of greeting.

'Yesterday! Three people have died but many are ill. It is the will of Allah.'

'It is not Allah's will,' I said. 'You must take action – have you sent a messenger to Rashad?'

'Not yet, there has not been time.'

'I will send my car at once and alert the medical service of the Government.' I didn't wait for an answer, but drafted a telegram to El Obeid and sent Jacoub off with the car with urgent instructions to dispatch it at once. This was a notifiable disease, and I knew that the moment such a disease was identified the medical services had to be alerted as soon as possible.

With relapsing fever action was ruthless. Heads and bodies were shorn of hair, great cauldrons of boiling water with sterilants were set in the centre of the village into which all clothing and bedding was plunged. Grass houses in the village would be razed to the ground and the bodies of the unfortunate villagers scrubbed under careful supervision. Everyone had to submit to this vigorous treatment – there could be no refusals. Only by action on this scale could the progress of the disease be arrested.

I had arrived at Abu Gubeiha intent on launching the new drive for grain production, and there was a question of wells to be dug and other matters, but Nazir Zbeir was not interested, he had other things on his mind. I returned to the rest-house knowing that there was little I could do to help, except keep out of the way.

The sad noises echoed throughout the village into the night: they came now from other houses, telling of further casualties.

The car returned and Jacoub said he had witnessed the message being tapped out within minutes of his arrival in Rashad. It was just possible that help would arrive the next day, so I decided to wait until then in case I could be of service to the Nazir.

That night, in bed, I lay for hours listening to the sounds of distress and wondering at the agonies of the people. I knew by now that such situations did not arise because they were inherently dirty or unhygienic; after all, what can one do when water is so absolutely scarce? I thought of a parallel event in any city with taps dried up and the population reduced to grovelling for water in muddy holes – unthinkable! But say it did come about? Soil, water and people! Yes, indeed, that's what my work was all about, and everything else was subsidiary.

Yet I still had to persuade the people to grow more and more grain. This was wrong, yes, very wrong! But I had been instructed to make this my priority.

The urgent call for help was acted upon at once in El Obeid. Early afternoon of the following day, vehicles rolled into the village and a group of native medical assistants set about their well-ordered routine. Two askaris came with them to ascertain that the village was sealed off, and to see that every single person underwent treatment.

In solemn mood I set off, late in the day, for Kologi. In the darkness it was difficult to follow the track and we occasionally lost sight of it and wandered into the bush. It was a relief to reach Kologi and settle into the rest-house, now quite familiar to us. The village was in silence but within minutes Nazir Mahomed walked over to find who had come to his village at this late hour. It was too late for talking so we made our plans for the following day, and I was left to think over the day's events in peace.

I had dinner and was on the point of going to bed when a figure approached out of the darkness, into the small circle of lamplight. The boys had settled down for the night. All was still, when this person sidled up close to my table and began to speak words I could not understand. I was further startled to see it was a woman, loosely clad in Arab-style robes. I noticed that she was quite young and good-looking, with colour applied to her lips and eyelids. There was a silver ring through a nostril: she was obviously from a well-to-do family.

I asked her what she wanted and who she was, but she continued to make strange guttural sounds, then squatted down on the ground at my feet. She looked up at me, pulling her robe belatedly over her face; I sensed there was something quite abnormal about her. Minutes passed and I was feeling uncomfortable – why should an Arab woman act like this?

I called softly for Ibrahim. He came from behind the rest-house and looked on in surprise as the woman continued her strange monologue. He went forward to speak to her, and then stopped as if shocked.

'*Hiya magnoon!*' (She is mad).

He stepped back as if determined to run away. I guessed he was afraid because he had previously told me that people's minds become abnormal because they have been possessed by a jinn, and even to see a jinn is enough to unhinge the mind. I had also learned that the people cared well for their mentally handicapped, and saw that they were never neglected: there was no need for mental hospitals in the mountains.

I was bending down to help the woman to her feet when Nazir Mahomed and another man approached. He apologised that I had been troubled, then spoke to her with kindness, asking her to come home – but she refused to budge. Peremptorily, the two men lifted her from the ground without a struggle, and she was carried away still talking in her strange language.

Illness of the body and of the mind: I had seen it all in the one day. The people did not have the remotest understanding of the causes of these conditions, but there was something very heart-warming in the way they supported one another, and shared each other's sufferings.

Revelations

As arranged, Nazir Mahomed turned up with his two donkeys and we set off together on our day's work. It was an uncomfortable day to take a long donkey-ride as there was a combination of burning heat and a dust-laden wind.

I explained to the Nazir the need for increased grain production, saying that the government would buy every ton that was brought to the suq. He apparently foresaw little difficulty in this, and thought it might be appropriate to bring everyone together in the evening so that the programme could be outlined to the cultivators.

We rode for hours, examining wells then riding over the cultivations which were, by now, parched and untended. The land for miles around presented an unhappy picture, showing classical signs of sheet erosion and a widespread network of little gulleys leading into wider channels. Millet had been cropped from this soil year after year, and the practice was likely to continue until it would crop no more.

Close to a low, rocky hill the land was more undulating with areas of red eroded gravel from which watercourses had erupted, gouging out wide channels. One of these had spewed torrents of water into a village which stood derelict, with houses in ruins, and thatch roofs tilted to the ground. It had happened in the last rains: I groaned inwardly when I saw that grain had been grown almost to the threshold of the village – and still, my instructions were to encourage these people to grow additional grain for export.

I dismounted to walk over the difficult terrain; some of the new water-courses were three-foot-deep gashes through the soil, and hard to cross. The soil was loose, and even as I watched, puffs of dust lifted up and were borne away in the wind. There was grit in our teeth, our skin was coated, and it was difficult to see. Some large 'dust devils' spiralled and twisted, causing us to watch warily as they whirled past.

The scene reminded me of a trench-scarred battlefield: indeed it was a battlefield where the stabilising forces of nature had been destroyed by man. Surely this land would never again be cultivated? I dug my toes into the soil – it consisted of broken-down particles, with no binding organic matter.

Why did men do this thing? The pressures of men and grazing animals on a sensitive ecological system: what was the answer?

All trees in the neighbourhood had been removed for fuel or for building. It was a certainty that no replacements had been planted.

I stopped in my tracks, and at that moment a thought struck me with visionary impact – I must make the people aware of this threat to their lives. Despite my orders from Khartoum to increase grain production I would give first place to soil conservation. I must develop an appropriate idiom to put over this message persuasively.

For some time I had stopped, silent and thoughtful: the Nazir eyed me in wonderment. How was he to know the change these last few minutes had brought? I had come as an observer, but I would leave to teach with all the power I could muster. In fact, that evening would give me an opportunity to put over the message for the first time. I called to the Nazir:

'Do bring the people together this evening, I have something important to tell them.'

Nazir Mahomed's face lit up, perhaps he thought it was an opportunity to hold another dance. I quickly quashed that idea:

'We shall meet for an hour only, and please make sure every cultivator turns up.'

In fact, from that day I took this new gospel of soil conservation wherever I went. I preached it many times and, by the time of the province meeting at El Obeid, the words rolled off the tongue with confidence.

But that was still in the future!

Later that evening a big crowd gathered in the centre of the village. It could well have been the self-same crowd of the dance a few weeks before. Probably they all expected another celebration: had they known what they were in for, they would not have come in such numbers.

A fire burned as on the earlier occasion, and the Nazir with his warrior consort arrived at the rest-house to escort me to the scene. I accepted a seat, and signalled for everyone to sit down also, so that in a moment I was looking at a sea of faces. Somehow, they did not have the bearing of cultivators eager to share in my revelation; rather it looked suspiciously as if they might be expecting the young inspector to provide some new entertainment – perhaps a solo dance or concert. Heads tilted expectantly to one side – I quickly got into my theme.

'*Ya nass*, (people) I have something very important to tell you . . .'

I told them I had toured their cultivations and I outlined my discoveries;

145

the theme took shape easily, even the technicalities of erosion and the means of arresting it poured out with much passion and waving of arms. Soon I was pacing the ground before them counting over the various points on my fingers. Carried away with my enthusiasm.

Mouths, by this time, hung open; an awed silence seemed suspended over the crowd. Eventually I dried up and sat down to await results. The silence continued. Normally, at this point in a meeting people had lots to contribute, but not on this occasion. It suddenly occurred to me that they were completely vague as to what I had been speaking about! I tried again, slowly and patiently, but it was useless – a waste of time. Only when the subject changed, and a little light-hearted humour crept in did they take part in the 'entertainment'.

That evening I lay awake, despondent. I had done all the wrong things – bad organisation, the wrong crowd with wrong expectations – how could I ever make the slightest impact on this vast territory with its different races? It was a ridiculous presumption on my part. But I had learned some important lessons – there were many more to follow.

To change people's traditions and practices of the years requires more than a few pep talks, particularly when given by someone from another culture – it requires education, resources, example and patience: but it can be done, even with such an intransigent problem as that of the spreading desert in the Sudan.

Two more days were spent in Kologi area performing the various tasks of an inspector of agriculture, and inevitably, the subject of increasing grain production had to be raised. This subject was easily understood by the cultivators, and it was easy for me to picture a vast ocean of millet around the village when the next rains came. A contribution to feeding the hungry people of East Africa would finally be made, but only at high cost to the mountains.

From Kologi I chose a little-used trail, westwards towards Heiban and the main mountain range. I had work to do at the Nuba villages there, and this was the direct way. On the map it looked a reasonably convincing route over a wide plain, crossed by large watercourses. It seemed a good risk!

We set off due west on a very indistinct trail, obviously seldom used, and for the first thirty miles experienced no difficulty – then the track apparently disappeared, lost in the dead grass. There was nothing for it but to keep going in the general direction o the mountains, just visible on the horizon.

It was like sailing through a golden ocean. Fortunately, when rocks stood in the way the grass thinned out in time to let us make a detour. I made a record of the various soil types for entering on a soil map I was planning. It was pleasing to find that there was still a lot of good, undamaged soil throughout this region, though how it could ever be used to feed people was another matter.

At last a deep gash in the ground, the first major dry watercourse, and a barrier to our progress. I decided to turn northwards in the hope of finding a crossing point, and at a shallower part of the wadi we crossed, but only after much digging and pushing on everybody's part.

This was a dangerous place in which to break down or get lost, as it was a totally uninhabited area due to the absence of water. Yet, failing the worst, it would be possible to retrace our steps to Kologi, following the broad swathe cut by the car.

It was time for a meal. The table and chair were set up beside the car in the burning midday heat. Mahomed produced cold, or at least, lukewarm soup, then a plateful of stringy goat flesh garnished with sweet potatoes. The boys crouched to their meal, still at a respectful distance behind the car. We all washed down our food with flat-tasting liquid from the goatskin.

I stood high on the car to look at the wide plain stretching in all directions as far as the horizon, apart from the rim of the Heiban Mountains: many hundreds of square miles without a single person. If this one stretch of land could be cropped using good husbandry, it would feed many thousands of hungry people. But that was just a pipe-dream.

We continued on our way, but ten miles further on were again stopped by a watercourse. I drove southwards this time, but without success; there was apparently no way over. Retracing our steps to a point beyond the starting point it came as a relief when there before our eyes was the track, running down and across the wadi.

This had taken time so, as the sun was lowering, I decided to set up camp for the night beside a small outcrop of rock. The boys set about their tasks cheerfully; after all, we had found the road again and would reach Heiban area after a short morning's drive.

The sun was setting into the mountains in brilliant red when we all jumped to our feet at the ominous thunder of some charging herd of animals. The sound drew rapidly closer: we were unable to see the creatures because of the tall grass and some scrub trees. Could it be buffalo, or even elephant? Then, the grass parted and a veritable deluge of ostrich raced diagonally past, missing us by perhaps thirty yards at the nearest point. It was as well we were not in their path, because they were running in panic, perhaps pursued by predators.

They rushed like an avalanche into the wadi then up the other steep bank, little wings flapping, necks stretched out, then, in as many seconds as it takes to tell, they disappeared, lost in a cloud of dust.

One little ostrich followed. Rather pathetically it flopped into the wadi, then disappeared likewise, along the path beaten down by its elders. There was no other sign of animals, no explanation for this rush in panic.

We looked at each other in amused relief and as might have been expected, Ibrahim raised his eyes heavenwards and said:

'Praise be to Allah!'

I spent three days among the Heiban villages, meeting the chiefs and speaking to the people about the two pressing subjects – grain and soil conservation. Only a few people spoke Arabic so that my words had to be interpreted, making explanations so much more difficult. In each village I was hospitably received and given little gifts of food or eggs, and occasionally meat.

Whenever possible, little groups of cultivators were gathered together. They stood patiently as I spoke of the devastation brought about by carelessly lit fires and over-cultivation but, generally, their faces registered lack of comprehension. Translation into Nuba was a slow tedious process and I questioned whether it was worthwhile using time in this way.

Occasionally a man spoke with some enthusiasm, saying that he had read the signs in his area, and agreeing that practices should be changed. But what next? Once I was away, things would continue as before.

On the Sunday I fulfilled a promise by visiting the Heiban Mission to attend a church service. I reached the little church at 7 a.m. where a little clanging bell was already ringing for morning prayers. It was like being in a different world, sitting there under a cool thatch with thirty or so Nuba, while the missionary conducted the service in their tongue which was incomprehensible to me. Hymns were sung in the rousing Negro manner with swaying bodies and clapping hands, and they all looked as if worship was a happy experience.

After the service people came forward to welcome me, and I was freely told 'May God bless you,' unlike the 'May Allah bless you!' to which I was accustomed.

I was asked to address the school pupils the following morning, to tell them of my work and my faith, in the Arabic language. To speak of work was easy, but to talk about faith was a more difficult exercise. After so long away from home and the company of Christians, the certainties of youth had faded: it was so easy just to drift on and to forget.

When the time arrived, I found the little school hall filled to overflowing with about one hundred people, not all of them pupils. I started to speak, but with less assurance than that which I had acquired at recent village gatherings. I told them of the good fortune they had in being among the few Nuba receiving an education. Then I gave an account of the importance of good husbandry in order to protect their land when they became farmers on leaving school.

I took the opportunity of asking how many of the pupils would be returning to the land when their education was finished. Not one of them! Unbelievably, each and every pupil had an aspiration to go to the city as a clerk or mechanic. There was something very wrong here!

I closed by saying that I felt God had brought me here for a purpose: I was slowly learning that purpose, and my only hope was that my service would be faithful.

That night I lay awake wondering at the words I had used about my 'faith': they had come out involuntarily but, yes indeed, they were true. They also gave me much room for thought in days to come.

It was a good school, where missionaries and their Nuba helpers did good work, but they were teaching the wrong things – how could it be they were teaching the youngsters away from their homes to head for the alien city: or was this too simple a view? Would the educated mind not be able to find fulfilment here in the mountains? What was education supposed to do for them if not to give them a fuller quality of life within their own culture?

Questions of this nature are not confined to Kordofan as I have learned since – they can be applied to 'education' worldwide!

Sibr

We moved on towards Talodi. I had the prime objective of getting that 'great social experiment' – so it had been described – 'The Dam Jamad Resettlement Project for Returning Soldiers' launched, in readiness for the coming rains.

The journey was leisurely and interesting enough and we were quite at peace with the world when, at a little village called Mandi, I noticed a great stir of people high on a raised piece of ground on the far side of a watercourse. Some ceremony was taking place under the hot morning sun. I told the driver to stop and went over to investigate.

A large crowd of naked Nuba waved spears and shields, apparently in full dance as I climbed the little hill towards them. At my approach they peeled off, then without any signs of welcome or recognition, danced round me in a circle. Their faces were solemn . . . feet pounded the earth in time with rapid drumbeats, voices chanted raucously on all sides. Suddenly, after the peace of my recent experiences, here was a bedlam of noise, deafening and all but frightening.

Still, no one made any move to welcome me. They stared glassily before them as if in a trance. I had to stand patiently if apprehensively until, with a final jump and deafening shout, the dance stopped. One warrior, apparently the chief, approached me, feathers in his hair and body daubed with a mixture of oil and clay. I was relieved to see him smile and reach out to shake my hand.

He spoke Arabic falteringly, but I could understand from him that this was a *Sibr*, an important celebration, and also that they regarded my visit as an honour.

In the time I spent there I was able to discover that a *Sibr* was a ceremony of initiation in which young men and women went through approved rituals over a three-day period, to test their suitability for acceptance as elders of the tribe. It happened only every third year, and was therefore quite a rare event.

Young men and women, their bodies shining with colour, strutted about as if knowing that the show depended on them and they were the centre of attraction. Indeed, they were virtually perfect in body and form, being

Nuba women in ceremonial dress.

Tribal body marks cut into the flesh.

perhaps between fourteen and eighteen years of age. Their elders sat around in a circle looking on them with critical eyes.

Apparently, during this day and the next two, they were to be put to the test, facing trials of courage and resource from which there must be no wavering – to fail in the *Sibr* would be followed by a lifetime of disgrace and scorn.

The ceremony was organised by the *kujur* (witch doctor), who sat on a crude dais with some of the impedimenta of his trade, such as gourds and bones, at his feet. He sat there, an impressive giant with apparently no interest in me, staring straight before him.

I had arrived after the completion of an anointing ceremony in which various coloured clays had been daubed on the novices. The chief left my side and a fresh dance started up.

A young girl chanted, the crowd took up the chorus and the dancers moved round me as before. With knees bent and arms reaching out before them, they alternately swung out chest then hips to the beat, while older natives lifted and lowered their spears in time. I was hemmed in by a mass of stuffy, perspiring bodies, occasionally uncomfortably so, and it was easy

Sibr test of womanhood.

to detect that, even as early as this, quantities of beer had been consumed. I had noticed that the chief spoke through the effects of it.

The sooner I got out of this the better! But before I could break out of the crowd, the witch-doctor stood up and shouted a command – as quick as lightning the young men and women rushed towards a larger hut, and all of them squeezed inside. For fully twenty minutes shouting and squeals of laughter emanated from the hut while the elders sat around discussing the affair with animation. What was going on in the hut is open to conjecture.

The chief explained, at least as much of his explanation as I was able to understand, that the dance would continue into the night, then on the following two days there would be trials in which men would battle with long wooden staffs, and the girls flail each other's bodies with deadly thonged lashes, like cat-o'-nine-tails. He said that blood would flow, but rarely was anyone killed. 'They must be brave and without fear,' he reiterated.

Suddenly, the young people rushed from the hut, formed into groups then went from hut to hut soliciting offerings of food, which were laid out in order close to where I stood.

I was led behind one of the huts and was fascinated to watch some older women busily engaged in cutting designs into the flesh of three girls. Intricate designs had been chalked round breasts, stomach and buttocks, and sharp little hooks were used to flick out little pricks of skin along the lines of the design. The sufferers stood there cheerfully talking while the red blood flowed. They appeared to be as relaxed as women in any beauty salon. The wounds would heal; then, like their elders, they would carry these designs for the rest of their lives.

The afternoon was wearing on. I suddenly realised it was time to move on, something often regretted since.

I left the scene with the boys who, unknown to me, had also come to witness the *Sibr*. In the car now, I pondered how such rites had survived, especially in the close vicinity of Christian missions. Should they yield to the advance of civilisation? Was it not right that such primitive backwaters should live on, or perhaps even be shielded from change?

My very presence here was disruptive to the old ways. To encourage order as the government interpreted it, to stimulate trade, to introduce medical services, even to protect life from famine – all of these brought inevitable change. The old culture would, in time, yield to the introduced culture that modern 'civilisation' imposes, with its mixture of good and evil.

Who is to say which is best, particularly for people such as the Nuba?

Settlement of Soldiers

At Talodi I was both surprised and disappointed to find another car drawn up at the rest-house. There had been no warning of visitors, but of course I had been on the road for some time now, and a message probably lay on the desk at Rashad.

Who could it be? It wasn't an agriculture vehicle – it was strange how the long period on my own had made me uncertain about 'white' company.

Inside the rest-house I found a man in mid-bath – a young engineer visiting the cotton ginnery, it turned out. For the next few hours we spoke, then shared a meal on the *mustaba*, but it was obvious we were equally uncomfortable in each other's company.

It was my intention to visit the Talodi club again so I suggested we both go. He replied, 'I see enough of the black b — s during the day, and I want a change at night!'

That did it as far as I was concerned. Without speaking another word, I left him and walked into Talodi. If he felt that way, why had he come to the country in the first place? I had known from the beginning that he had a chip on his shoulder and resented being away from the city. Better forget him.

The same noisy music sounded from the club. My friends were there, with, in addition, a Sudanese touring judge and a visiting nazir. The evening passed cheerfully as on the previous occasion, and I made a point of returning 'home' late. The engineer's bed was set up in the open, some distance from mine. Apparently he was sleeping. He was due to travel north in the morning and, with luck, I would perhaps not see him again.

I found Tahr Effendi busy at the Resettlement Scheme when I turned up there next morning. It was a pleasant meeting – he was a friendly, hard-working Arab from northern Sudan, quite at home in Talodi, and he was pleased to have me back again.

There had been progress in my absence. Some of the circular mud-brick houses already carried sweeping fresh thatch, and the village was taking shape. We surveyed the last of the holdings, decided on a location for the village well, and agreed where trees should be planted to increase the amenity of the village.

I gleaned all the information about the scheme and its costs, then set to work writing the report for the Director – he would not lack information, and perhaps – who knows? – communities such as this might be established throughout the mountains. But that was still a long way ahead.

Our intention was to interview potential cultivators so that they should be settled in their new houses by the time of the rains. Tahr had done the groundwork, circulating requests to the Native Administration and doing everything possible to encourage applications from suitable people.

On the appointed day, we sat at a little table beneath a tree as the cultivators-to-be, about twenty in number, were interviewed in turn. Quickly it became evident that most of them were hardly to be compared with young soldiers returning from war.

Four of them were old ex-soldiers, from which war in history was hard to judge; there were two very suitable applicants who had been casualties in the present fighting and had mainly recovered from their wounds. Several had remote connections in the past with government departments – others were from a mixed background, some of whom had worked in the city, but this group had the appearance of being unlikely farmers.

I was assured that these were the best that could be found, as most of the settled Nuba had no desire to leave their villages. We did what we could, selected the best of them, then took each to see his own holding. They were each allocated a house and their assistance was recruited to complete the building of the village.

When I took time to look at the new cultivators doubts began to creep in. Few of them would ever have been classed as A1. There was a preponderance of grey hair, stooped shoulders and bleary eyes. However, Tahr was a good man, he would keep them working, and the experiment must bear fruit.

Had I known the unpredictable variables which lay in the future – indolence (on the part of a few), monkeys (in abundance), alcohol (with some of them), not to mention a few deviations from the 'straight and narrow', I would have been less than optimistic!

The most pressing interest of some of them was what their pay was to be, and this after our long explanations on the short-term loans they were to get until they marketed their first crop. There seemed to be a vague feeling that they were re-enlisting for government service. Various affirmations of loyalty to the flag were declared, quite unsolicited on my part.

I left the village that day savouring my doubts!

I made one final visit to the scheme before heading away from the mountains to Khartoum for the Arabic examination (the realisation of its imminence made me shudder). An ex-soldier was given the role of agricultural sheikh of the village a smart young man, he was very intelligent and looked 'natural' for the job. Another was appointed to look after the plough-bulls, and another to start a little village shop.

Now I could leave with an easy mind! I said goodbye to Tahr and was climbing into the car when one of our select few staggered towards me, apparently in the twilight of alcoholic coma: he reached out to shake my hand then fell flat on his back!

Back to the City

I returned to Khartoum with some sense of distaste, and not in a frame of mind to enjoy it. The three-day journey from Talodi had seemed unending, and, temporarily, the country had lost its appeal as I stared at Arabic text-books, only too aware of my limitations. Finally, the books had been thrown into a case – it would be a matter of sink or swim: almost certainly the former.

At Khartoum I regarded the lounging residents at the Grand Hotel and their pink gins with scorn. At the Agriculture Department, office-wallahs were preoccupied with paper, as usual. As soon as I entered the office the Director questioned me about developments in the mountains, referring at times to a collection of wires from Alex spread out on his desk.

Dam Jamad Settlement Experiment: had I brought the progress report with me? Grain: what were the attitudes of the people about increasing output? – and so on. He made no reference to the matter of soil conservation. He was a new director; I ventured some remarks on the subject, but apparently it was not politic at the moment, and he showed no interest. A War Supply meeting was to take place after the Arabic examination. I was told to attend, and that the subject would be 'grain'.

Next day I went to the examination as a lamb to the slaughter. There were another twenty or so candidates; it cheered me just a little to find them equally pessimistic.

We sat in the bleak atmosphere of an examination hall and resigned ourselves to a three-hour struggle with a paper that bore little relationship to everyday life in the Nuba mountains.

'Translate the following using Arabic script –
1. Domestic Science is part of the curriculum.
2. Preservation of Harig grass is essential for good cotton establishment.
3. Be careful to insert valves into the correct socket.'

There was very little Domestic Science in the curricula of Nuba schools; for that matter, there were scarcely any schools!

Dead silence apart from a ceiling fan; the gimlet eyes of an invigilator – the usual alien setting sure to stifle the imagination.

One candidate rushed from the room to a cheer from the rest of us – a quarter of an hour and he had been defeated. I sat looking at the blue sky beyond the window and occasionally made a futile sally at the paper.

Time trailed its leaden heels, then it was over! To a man, everyone prophesied doom! The second day's paper was only slightly more inspiring. To forget our sorrows the entire body of candidates then went to the Blue Nile Cinema for the evening.

Now came the day of the oral part of the examination; at least I would show I could speak the language, then they could get on with it.

Three bearded Arabs sat on a low platform in a little classroom. Some white official sat with pen poised at the rear of the room. I was given a seat beside the Arabs: they spoke rather kindly to me, I thought. I felt myself on familiar ground at last.

'In Arabic, give an account of your life since coming to the Sudan,' they asked. This was too easy! I was asked questions on land tenure and other topics, about which I fortunately had some knowledge, then I steered them towards the problem of soil erosion in Kordofan Province. They were actually interested! Now, with a mounting feeling of excitement, I poured out some of my discoveries as rapt as a preacher converting the non-believer. They listened, silently, asking only the occasional question.

Half and hour, and it was over. I left the room in a wave of excitement, carried away by my enthusiasm. Had I made a fool of myself?

Only too soon excitement waned – I could only await the inevitable report of failure. One thing only mattered now – escape from the city, then on to El Obeid to address the province *jelsa* (meeting) on the same topic.

Then I remembered the War Supply meeting and this vexed issue of 'more and more grain'.

Next day I was ushered into a conference room where a large group of people sat in debate round a table. I saw the Director, a number of army officers – and, yes, the Civil Secretary who had met me on my arrival in the country. They looked up, waved recognition, and left me sitting in a chair behind them for some time.

Eventually they all turned towards me. A voice said:

'Can you grow, and deliver, an additional 1,500 tons of grain to Kaka before the rains?'

I thought of the words of the various sheikhs and nazirs in the mountains – 1,500 tons more seemed to be 'stretching it'; then, how could it be transported when all the camels in Kordofan were already hard at it?

I could only say, 'Yes'.

Then came a command –

'You are to be in the mountains during the rains – it will be necessary to grow every possible ton: make sure the people fully understand this. Grain will be needed next year as well.'

At this, I faltered. What about the soil? What about the irreversible damage caused by erosion? The words hovered on my lips, but I remained silent: this audience had no interest whatsoever in the subject. I took the coward's way out, but had I spoken would it have made any difference?

'You will get thirty captured Italian lorries to remove the grain before the rains come – they should reach the mountains in a fortnight.'

That should ease the transport question, but what had I committed myself to, rushing frantically from place to place persuading the people to bring more and more grain to the purchasing centres?

The Lecture

It was a relief to leave Khartoum behind.

I brooded alone in my compartment – I had been sent to Kordofan with a special remit to study this worrying problem of soil erosion, and now, without apology or explanation, I was being asked to further aggravate the situation by persuading people to grow ever more, irrespective of the soil's condition. Why had I not spoken up when I had the opportunity?

I talked over my troubles with Alex soon after arriving in El Obeid. He was fully versed in the situation and tried to ease my mind.

'You must take the long view: today there is a war and a famine – there can be nothing more pressing than this. We must produce our share of the food needed to help both situations; everything else has to wait.'

'But –' I began, rather lamely now.

Alex chipped in. 'In any case, I have promises from the Director that you will get as much support as he can give you to deal with the soil question. I expect him to send heavy excavation machinery into the mountains to see if we can provide permanent water stores in some of that new land you are finding.'

This was a bolt from the blue – machinery to dig large *hafirs* would be very useful indeed: it could be a start. The new Director was aware of the situation after all!

Alex said, 'Just keep this in the back of your mind until you hear from me again. If it comes off, I can assure you you will be kept busy!'

We went on to study plans for extracting all of the extra grain from the mountains – quotas from each tribal group, purchasing arrangements, and so on. Alex undertook to look after the Western Jebels (which I had not yet had time to visit), leaving me to concentrate on the Eastern Jebels.

He closed the topic by saying we would meet at Talodi in a few weeks' time and, in all probability, the Director would be with him to visit the Resettlement Scheme.

In all of this, the province *jelsa* had been pushed into the background. This annual assembly brought all the chiefs together with the Governor, to mull over the problems of the day. It was an important occasion for the 'flag';

indeed, for all involved, and it took place with full ceremony and attention to diplomacy.

For the agricultural session, Alex was to speak on the need for more grain, followed by my talk on soil conservation: and, of course, we had to speak in Arabic. Well, that should be easier than the previous day's examination!

About thirty people, most of them in dazzling white *jelibiyahs*, sat round a table in a hall decorated with tall palms, and with ceiling fans turning overhead. The Governor sat in some splendour on a mini-throne and rose to greet us, introducing us to the tribal leaders and officials. A few of them I recognised. Alex pointed out Mek Adam from the kingdom of Tegali, 'his old friend' from another part of my territory I had yet to visit.

This session was confined to agriculture and the land, and concerned matters important to everyone present, because they mainly came from the hills and plains of rural Kordofan.

Alex stood up to speak on the need for increased grain output. As in the past I admired his command of the language and the easy way in which he related to his audience. They all knew him well and listened carefully, as he outlined the way in which the province must respond to the needs of its neighbours. The army, too, had to be fed by their efforts – these were difficult times but Kordofan would meet the need.

They were nodding in agreement, and declarations of intent were called from each area. I was half listening, but also rehearsing in my mind what I would say to them about the encroaching desert, which affected everyone in the room. Again I realised it was anachronistic for them to be encouraged to grow still more crops on this fragile soil, then to be told about the damage resulting from their efforts.

Suddenly it was my turn.

I knew that the subject of soil conservation had not previously been brought to their attention. In fact, I knew they were all apparently blind to the dangers of soil erosion. But could I capture their interest?

I launched straight into the theme: '*Quasr el ard*', destruction of the soil by their own hands. Their beautiful land was being destroyed by ignorance: had they not seen the dust blow? Did the wadis not carry away their soil? What about the forests, what was happening to them?

They had seen it all! I spoke severely, but with that same enthusiasm for the subject – was it not Allah who had gifted them the land? The remedy was in their hands: failing that, disaster! Ten minutes of this then I closed by explaining the measures that could be taken to arrest the destruction, as I then saw it.

Then it was over, and, aware only of silence, I sat down.

It was Mek Adam who rose to acknowledge what I had said.

'It is true what the *moffetish* (inspector) is telling us: we have all seen the changes taking place. There is scarcely a tree left within miles of Abbasiya (his home town) and the land is suffering. This is something we must pay attention to or, as he says, we shall all suffer!'

There followed questions and discussion on the subject, but it was new to them and most, I could see, would forget about it when they returned home.

After the session Mek Adam approached me. I warmed to him at once, as he continued to talk on the theme. Finally, he told me about a gathering of the people of Tegali soon to take place – would I please attend in order to explain to his people what I had just said? I accepted with some sense of joy – was this a beginning? Could the people really be alerted to take practical steps to conserve their environment, or was this just wishful thinking?

But how could the repeated demand for additional crops be reconciled with preservation of the land? Did the answer perhaps lie in providing new permanent water sources on clay plains where erosion was not so pressing? Could a fresh start be made there in which the husbandries were carefully supervised?

There were so many questions. So much work needed to be done to even begin providing solutions.

Zikr

The boys had driven to El Obeid to collect me after my city days, and we returned straight to Rashad, where I found the flags up, and the District Commissioner returned from his period of absence. He came out to meet me and, after we had eyed each other for a second or two, we both relaxed realising that we were going to 'get on'. It was important we should agree because although trekking separately and performing our individual duties, it would be necessary to share a lot of the work. There were no other officers in the Eastern Jebels!

Neil had a sparkling sense of fun; a tall balding Scot who was seldom parted from a silver-topped cane which he toyed with continuously, he had a 'feeling' for the people of the mountains. He had many years of service behind him and I knew that his knowledge and understanding of the Jebels were just what I needed here in Rashad. On the other hand, as I soon learned, we were both loners and preferred to go our own ways separately.

I discovered that the Political Service was also being brought into the drive for grain – a reflection on the serious situation in East Africa. We spent a long evening sitting in the lamplight, and beneath a bright moon, talking over our work. I told him about Mek Adam's invitation to speak on conservation at the Tegali gathering – Neil was also going and he gave me something of this background.

The tribes of the area had broken from Tegali many years before. Gradually, they had come together again under Mek Adam. This gathering was to celebrate the return of the last tribe to the fold, the Hawazma. There was a serious side to the gathering, but there would also be tribal celebrations and dancing.

By chance, another event was about to take place next day in Rashad. Neil informed me that we were both invited to attend the last day of the Mulid, an annual celebration of the Prophet's birthday. He said it was a privilege to be invited as, until recently, Christians had been barred from such festivals.

When the time came, we dressed up for the occasion with an embellishment of black-silk cummerbunds and bow ties. After sunset, a police escort called at our houses: they formed a square then, in the light of a pressure lantern, paraded us to the festival at the far side of the village.

A broad strip of carpet had been laid in honour of the guests. We walked up this in some style through a large crowd and, at its end, joined a group of notables on a high dais. I sat between the Rashad Judge and a prominent khalifa; then, our host for the evening, the Rashad Omdah, served up refreshments.

We were looking down on two brightly-lit squares, each one of them surrounded by a large crowd. I was told that each represented a different sect of the Moslem faith.

The ceremony started when a group of white-robed men, possibly *fekii* (holy men) swung into the circle of light, to the accompaniment of rapid drum-beats. Their bodies gyrated wildly to the pulsing rhythm, then the entire crowd swayed in time, sagging knees then standing erect, their lips venting a loud wailing chant of the familiar protestation of faith, so often heard –

'There is no God but Allah and Mahomed is his prophet!'

The other crowd could have been competing, as they shouted some chanting response to the shrill voice of a leader.

The noise and beat was stirring – almost electrifying. Then, just below the dais, a man collapsed to the ground, his body twitching. He was ignored by his neighbours. Then another fell, and another – until throughout the crowd a number of people could be seen lying at the feet of the swaying crowd. I was told that this was a common outcome from such events: to be in a *zikr*, a form of religious frenzy or ecstasy, was something meritorious, and even a measure of zeal.

The evening continued with a sequence of similar energetic dances, interspersed with orations from the platform. The khalifa, at my side, gave one speech in a form of high Arabic which I could scarcely understand. The Judge told me that in fairly recent times and throughout history, the two religious groups had refused to celebrate side by side, and he was pleased to witness the signs of harmony between them

Neil and I sat through four hours of the ceremony until, exhausted by it all, we reeled home, surrounded again by our escort. It had been a pleasure for me to share this occasion with the DC and as I lay in the garden in the early morning hours with the hilltops still echoing to wild drum-beats, I felt there was a lot to look forward to in our work together in the Jebels.

Next morning we went our separate ways on the great grain quest. Day followed day of never-ending travel and talk. I visited every possible village accessible by car, occasionally over trails that had seldom, if ever, seen a car before. At meeting after meeting every inducement was given to cultivators to bring grain to the nearest market.

I looked at the evidence of erosion in many places and was constantly torn by the nagging tension of priorities but, for the present, one subject was necessarily in the ascendant.

This was also a bleak time for the boys as we pursued the life of rootless nomads, with unremitting labour, and with no time to enjoy the freedom of trek. Mahomed had a difficult time of it, encouraging me to eat the dreary food of the mountains: local grains, sour millet bread, sweet potatoes, cassava, and a morsel of string meat. All this taken with coffee, muddy-flavoured from the unappetising water in our goatskin, meant that I ate less than was good for health. Most of the time we had no sugar, as the allocated ration was minimal because of war conditions.

A week passed in this way, in which I worked gradually towards Talodi with the purpose of meeting Alex, as had been arranged at El Obeid.

We were bumping along a trail when a vehicle approached from the opposite direction – a rare event! The cars stopped, cab opposite cab, and through the window I shook hands with an English judge and his wife. They were from that rare group of people who made occasional sallies into the mountains in the course of duty.

It was midday so we shared a meal beside the track and discussed our respective jobs. They told me that, although nearing retirement age, they had not been long in the country: indeed, they were city types and wondered at my rugged way of life. Having visited the Nuba, they spoke enthusiastically of all they had seen.

The boys prepared a table with cloth, napkins and all the accessories for a three-course meal, then came the *pièce-de-résistance* from a wooden box – a tin of peas: unbelievable!

The meal took a leisurely two hours – I marvelled at the spacious luxury of it all, generated by a woman determined to take the rough edge out of trek. A siesta for all could have followed, but I was determined to press on.

In the course of conversation the wife said:

'We spent last night at a dreadful rest-house at Talodi: it was impossible to sleep because of the sounds. The boys were terrified; we left in a hurry!'

By the sound of it they had been just as afraid as their boys. They had been sleeping on the garden *mustaba* when voices came from inside, followed by what sounded like a fight. Looking through the windows into the house, they could see nothing.

The story sounded very convincing and they had all been startled by the event. Thinking of the grim rest-house I could well understand how the imagination runs riot. I smiled to myself: after all, they were from the town, what more could one expect?

We said our farewells, then continued working towards Talodi to arrive, exhausted, an hour after sunset. With the usual efficiency, a fire was lit in the cook-house and the furniture erected on the *mustaba*.

The night was unbearably hot and stuffy, making it an effort to breathe. I sat writing in my little circle of light, then, remembering what the judge and his wife had said, I felt persuaded to walk through the empty rooms, as we had done on our earlier visit. Of course, they were bare, there was nothing to see except my own exaggerated shadow on walls and ceiling.

I emerged into the open, smiling a little grimly at the fears of other people, but Ibrahim had seen the moving light and stood nervously in the garden.

'*Jenabo*, we were told there were jinns in the house last night: we don't want to stay here, can we spend the night in the town?'

'That is ridiculous, Ibrahim! These people on the trail were from Khartoum – people like that fear the countryside, they dream things!'

Mahomed came on the scene. '*Jenabo* is right, Ibrahim, we can't leave Mr Meki here on his own, can we? Come . . .' He pulled Ibrahim back to his quarters.

There was nothing to remain up for, so, earlier than usual, I climbed through the mosquito net and lay down on the hot sheets to sleep. The lack of air combined with an over-active mind kept me awake for a long time.

Then, a sudden, cool restless wind shook the net and I fell asleep. Perhaps two hours later I wakened, shivering with cold and pulled the sheet over me. A whispering voice at my ear said:

'There is someone in the house!'

I felt the hair prick on my scalp – I could just make out Ibrahim.

'What are you talking about?' I asked uncertainly.

'There is someone in the house,' he repeated. 'Listen!'

A sudden 'thwack' came from within, followed by a shuffling noise. The boys were all there now, looking wide-eyed towards the building. More noises sounding like loud footsteps – clop, clop, clop! It was on ny mind to say 'Well, do something!' but Jacoub had the car keys, and I had no doubt at all what they would do, so I stayed silent.

Minutes passed: the noises continued. I got Ibrahim to light the lamp then I moved towards the door of the house. I felt it would be futile to extend an invitation to the boys to accompany me.

The sounds quietened at my approach. I fumbled open the wire mosquito door, then slowly squeezed open the sagging inner door – a rush of cool air all but put out the light, but the dancing flame rekindled, playing patterns on the wall.

Peering inside – of course, the hall was empty. I walked gingerly in: a resounding knock came from the rear of the house. Holding my breath I tip-toed from room to room, but had only the dancing shadow for company. Suddenly, there came a report from above my head followed by others in succession – then, out of my surprise, the answer suddenly dawned. The ghost was exposed – the rest-house jinns would haunt no more!

I ran from the house in relief and shouted to the boys.

'You can come in now: your jinn won't trouble you!'

They wouldn't budge from the *mustaba*, so I took it in hand to explain the simple principles of science which had intimidated us all. The walls and roof of the house were steel-framed: there was no thatch on the roof, only corrugated iron. At this time of year, with fluctuating night temperatures, the twisted steel frame expanded or contracted, thus causing a shuffling of its members, particularly the roof cladding. Hence the many sounds!

This is what comes of listening to old wives' tales! We had arrived wondering about this jinn, and our imagination had discovered it. The boys were still sceptical but, at least, they returned to bed, as did I.

That is as it happened. I am quite certain of it, because it was the kind of night that is not readily lost to memory!

Next day, Alex drove into the rest-house garden bringing with him the Director of Agriculture. I had had a full day at the Resettlement Scheme getting things in order, because I regarded the coming visit as of considerable importance; after all, they were making a long journey to find out what was happening here. One of our new cultivators had melted into the bush and had not returned; one ex-soldier was never sober long enough to understand what was going on. Tahr Effendi had his problems!

The visitors unpacked in the exorcised rest-house then sat down to a dinner, which had caused Mahomed to scour the Talodi suq from end to end. If I had expected to be brainwashed about grain or perhaps the fine points of the Scheme, I was disappointed – the two men knew Nuba from past years and spent the entire evening reminiscing. They were enjoying being away from the office for a spell, so I was compelled, as a mere junior, to sit and listen until they had talked the moon down.

Next day, business started over the breakfast table. 'Yes, we shall get the extra 1,500 tons of grain!' 'Lorries will be despatched soon to deliver it,' and so on. Had I got horses for trek? Not yet! 'Talodi is the place to get them.' Was the Gathering in a month's time? Yes, I would arrive there in time to obtain six pack ponies. We talked on, then the Director stood up, tightened the belt on his bush-shirt and said, 'Now for your new Resettlement Scheme!'

He emphasised the 'your' as if it had been my idea in the first place. I drove them to Dam Gamad. Tahr was standing, waiting nervously: he had never had to contend with so many personalities before. The 'cultivators' stood around – some came forward, clicked their heels smartly and saluted. It was very impressive, they faintly resembled soldiers returned from the war. The drunken one, now doomed to be evicted, was lying on his back behind a hut. Things looked good! The Director walked smartly round the new village and paced some of the holdings with a large retinue trailing behind. Some of the men had worked well, others had done virtually nothing – but such is typical of the human state, and no disparaging comments were passed.

Apparently, the Government was regarding the problem of a returning army with some seriousness, and it was thought that this little experiment was going to show how it would be solved.

One could but live in hope!

They left, after lunch, on the route north. With pleasure, I watched the dust of their departure settling, then thought cheerfully of spending the evening at the club.

Athena (an idyll)

Several hard days later, Alex and I both pulled up again at the Talodi rest-house, covered with a day's trekking dust. Table unfolded, we were soon enjoying a welcome cup of tea. Alex had his liberally topped up with whisky, and drank it with a sigh of contentment.

A well-dressed *sufragi* (servant) came up the road from Talodi, saluted smartly and handed over an envelope. Alex fidgeted out his spectacles, scanned the document and read out:

'Please come to dinner and dance, 7 p.m. this evening (wife's birthday). Kosti.' A dinner dance in the deep Nuba Mountains? Unbelievable. Kosti was the local Greek merchant I occasionally met at the club, who by some miraculous accident of history had drifted to this isolated spot and opened shop. Greeks and also Armenians turned up in all sorts of unusual places; their nose for business and willingness to live almost native produced a formidable blend which defied mere hardship.

Kosti was no fool, because here in Talodi with its cotton ginnery the Nuba handed over their rain-grown cotton in exchange for money which only represented worth to them when passed over Kosti's rough wood counter. True, there were other shops of a kind, but it was Kosti's where the best coloured beads and the biggest miscellany of 'rare' oddments were to be purchased. Even lemonade on ice could be bought at a price. His emporium – a wooden shack with its heaped-up marvels – was a source of wonder to the local populace, who willingly parted with piastres and pounds for the meagre treasures he purveyed. Kosti did well.

So, Kosti had a wife! I had known nothing at all about him, outwith his swarthy moustachioed stoutness and his shop. He was hearty and welcoming, particularly at the prospect of a sale, but that was it. Alex, on the other hand, appeared to have some memories of Kosti's wife. He rubbed his hands with pleasurable anticipation and sent the boys scurrying – bath, white shirt and flannels, polished shoes . . . the lot.

I did not share his enthusiasm. To dress up after a hard day, then to listen to talking over drinks until the early-morning hours, was a daunting prospect and not my idea of a night's relaxation. Of course, the reference to a dance was a joke because we, and the Kosti family, were virtually the only Europeans in a hundred miles. Nuba dances were unlikely to be part of the programme, because, though attractive to watch, they were far beyond our skills, and no doubt the Kostis' also!

I reluctantly sat in my canvas bucket-bath, scraping off the mud and producing a shine suitable for a 'dance'. I climbed into the most appropriate clothes, looking meanwhile at the grey-whiteness of Ibrahim's laundering – it must be good enough for Kosti's party!

Ibrahim wound the ten feet of cummerbund round my waist then, like Alex, I was ready for the fray. Alex had two more whiskies – 'to fortify me for dancing with Mrs Kosti,' he said with a chuckle.

Off we went, walking the road to Talodi, trying to keep the dust off our shoes. It was already dark, but a crescent moon hung low over the hills, competing with sparkling fireflies to illuminate our path.

We walked into the little town past a rickle of huts then the more substantial mud houses of a few more affluent natives, and finally up to a high mud wall, topped with broken glass. A crackling gramophone already sounded beyond the wall, so the scene must be set for the evening's festivities.

Alex beat enthusiastically at a stout wooden door, then stepped back to await results. Our host himself, in full radiance, swung it open, bending low from the hips, and welcomed us to his '*beit amin*' (humble home).

We were 'flourished' into a tiled compound or rather, patio, where five basket chairs surrounded a circular drink-laden table.

Just as I expected, I thought; seats, drinks, an old gramophone – but who could the fifth chair be for? Possible grandma or a stout maiden aunt – what a prospect!

We sat down: Kosti clapped his hands and ordered drinks to be poured. The inevitable mild banter followed my request for lime juice, but we settled to our chosen refreshments and the evening's unending talk got under way.

Alex knew Kosti well, and the pair chattered on, leaving me to study the very attractive surroundings. The neat walled square had two attractive trees spreading from opposite corners: vines climbed the walls and gaudy bougain-villaea festooned the balcony beside our seats. The central feature, a concrete mustaba, had little plots of zinnia and petunia around it, suggesting the presence of a tender hand and green fingers in the Kosti family. A low moon and stars beautifully finished off what can only be termed a romantic scene.

Then out came Mrs Kosti with arms outstretched, like a prima donna about to burst into song. To describe her as stout would be an understatement, but somehow her considerable frame had squeezed into a gay cotton frock which at places was stretched, and overstretched. On top, however, a face beamed with smiles – a really jolly face.

At first Mrs Kosti did not see me: she went right up to Alex, tittering meanwhile like a safety-valve about to blow. He gallantly kissed both hands, and passed remarks which sent her into peals of laughter. Then she turned to welcome me. So, we were four in number and, amid no doubt scintillating conversation punctuated with merry laughter, we all settled for another round of drinks.

The servant wound up the gramophone as required and changed the records, which tended to be of an early vintage, but it played on, unheeded beneath the jovial banter and conversation. This, at least, was more cheerful – with patience the hours would pass until, I thought, the capacity for drink was exhausted and the moon was far down the sky.

But, there was Alex escorting her ladyship to the platform and, with unexpected grace, waltzing her around. They made an interesting couple – Alex small and lean and Mrs Kosti! This left her husband discussing the weather with me, and the price of camels.

Then it happened! Something twirled through my brain, affecting both eyes and breathing – stepping from the house and on to the verandah was an unbelievable girl, or was it a vision, dressed in a long shining white dress, and with features of a breathtaking beauty – or so it seemed to me as I staggered to my feet, almost knocking the chair over. She stretched out a hand soft as velvet. Her eyes smiled at me, and her mouth showed regular white teeth set in a smooth, sunburned complexion.

Athena! I had just heard the name. Athena – it sounded like music to my ears. I had the sense to sit her down, to join her, and then to search in my mind for words more original than those I had just shared with Kosti. The latter no longer existed for me, but I have a shrewd idea he tipped his chair back, rolled his fingers and stared at the two of us with some interest. But now we were five and it looked like being a most pleasant evening. After all, I had been in Africa for what seemed like an eternity as far as meeting attractive European girls was concerned. Who could have imagined such a girl in this remote outpost of Empire? Had Alex not known of Kosti's daughter?

At this point the dancers joined us. Alex expressed compliments to the proud parents on their beautiful daughter, and then the elders settled to another round of drinks.

This left me looking at Athena, and Athena looking at her fingers.

What was there to talk about? I was bereft of words and apparently she suffered the same affliction, because precious minutes raced by, and I was getting nowhere.

How could Mrs Kosti ever have produced such an offspring – did she once look like Athena? Ridiculous thought!

A record started playing and the two dancers were on the floor again. Nothing else for it but to stand, take her hand, lead her to the *mustaba* and to dance. The dancing as a mere act was unimportant. I was in some minor form of trance, her perfumed hair only an inch from my nose, her gentle form gliding beside my awkward frame. I could sense the pressure of her body – this was just not Africa with its heat and hardship – it had to be a dream!

But I was gradually returning to earth. I asked her about the flowers – she knew them and enjoyed their colours and perfumes. Did she live in Talodi all the time? No, she spent much of the year in Khartoum helping in her uncle's business. Did she enjoy Talodi? Not really, but she hoped to persuade the family to return to the city. Some hope, I thought. Kosti will stick here to extract the last brass farthing. Did she enjoy dancing? She loved it but seldom had the chance, even in the city.

I threw glances at Kosti, still happily parked on the wicker chair and watching us carefully. After this gentle conversation we returned to our seats while the senior members refuelled.

Music played up again. Alex whisked Athena to the floor from before my very nose, whereupon I looked tentatively at Mrs Kosti, apparently intent on doing the same with me. So it happened, and in a moment I was being twisted and turned: strangely, she danced well and I got the feeling I was doing likewise.

Mrs Kosti talked on about subjects now forgotten, but suddenly a question was slipped in:

'What do you think of my daughter?' – was it asked with a thoughtful narrowing of the eyes?

'She is very nice,' I ventured. Rather an understatement, but I felt it would be unsafe to enthuse. Middle East mothers require cautious handling. It occurred to my simple mind she might have some plan afoot – I was giving nothing away.

The dance ended and we followed the drinks through a wide French window and into a dining room, romantically lit with candles. We sat at a table, laden and almost sagging with its burden of food. This was not to be a meal, but a banquet. A heap of roast pigeons; something smaller, possibly sparrows; a huge joint of meat; vegetables for a regiment; crystallised whole fruits – guava, lemon and so many more. The memory fails!

All of this was topped up with cake, ice-cream, and black coffee. My appetite, no doubt shrunken through months of simple trek fare, permitted only small inroads to this gargantuan feast. Equally, Alex only toyed with little bits and pieces, but Mr and Mrs Kosti adequately compensated for our deficiencies. Athena, too, ate delicately and as the cheerful chatter continued, I found myself actually sharing in the fun and doing my share of talking.

The party was going very well – then my eyes caught Athena's and for a long second we looked directly at each other, time enough for some sign of mutual interest to flash – enough to silence me!

The feast over, the participants left the table and carefully edged their bodies back into the wicker chairs beside a fresh stack of bottles. For obvious reasons there was no dancing for some time. Athena and I sat, watched, and listened as the conversation, now with some alcoholic impetus, went brightly on.

Conversation darted from topic to topic each one of which gave our hostess some cause of amusement. But, time was passing: my nails dug into my palms as I wished for the ingenuity to say something inspiring, or, even better, to whisk Athena away to where we could study the novelty of being alone together.

There was no hope of this! In spite of mother's overflowing zest, a certain latent and invisible force emanated from her – a force that could well turn legs to jelly. I continued to sit, and exchanged only guarded smiles and words with Athena.

Food safely down, the faithful *sufragi* set the music in motion once more, and the evening proceeded, with mother and father Kosti still the imposing sentinels.

At last, weariness crept in and, in what instinctively I knew would be the last dance of the evening, I found myself on the floor, alone with Athena holding her closer than before. She lifted her face to say something and in what to me was the simplest of acts, I bent and kissed her soft, moist lips. Our hands pressed tightly . . . then the music ground to a halt. With heavy heart I returned her to her chair.

Our three seniors were in a state of passive somnolence but, unfortunately, sufficiently perceptive to know that the festivities had come to an end. Alex stood up briskly and surprisingly steadily to announce our imminent departure, and in a few moments we staggered our way back to the rest-house.

Later, under my mosquito net, I lay pondering over the evening's events and thinking of that fragrant flower fading from my life probably forever: but it had been a good dance.

Some time later, on trek to Talodi, this time 'alone', the boys clung on as I raced over the rough trail to the rest-house. In next to no time I washed, dressed and set off 'casually' for an iced drink at the emporium. Heart beating faster, I found Kosti standing in full splendour at the door. He clutched my hand, his usual beaming self, and invited me to his home for evening drinks, an invitation which I found myself able to accept. Amid the burst of talk on cotton, trade and other trivialities, I casually enquired, 'Is Mrs Kosti in good health?'

'The very best, she'll be pleased to see you.'

'And Athena, how is she?'

'Quite well, I think. She left for Khartoum several days ago.'

Probably my mouth fell open; certainly, my spirit sagged at these tidings. The evening at Kosti's has long been forgotten as is the remainder of that trek: just a blurred memory like many other travels at this time.

There is postscript to the tale of Athena.

About a year later I was heading for the Red Sea Hills by train, on local leave. It was time for evening meal so I walked to the small dining compartment further along the train. A lone lady, back to me, sat studying the scenery. She turned – Athena! Athena alone and on her way to Erkowit, my own destination!

In a moment we were shaking hands and exchanging words of greeting and reminiscence. She was almost the same person; slightly plumper, I had to admit to myself, but still the Athena of memory.

Had I paused to think, I might have spotted some reticence on her part and a slightly furtive look in her eye.

I talked cheerfully, enthusing about the coming holiday, when a rather fat, greasy-skinned man suddenly intruded his presence, so that I was obliged to accept him in the scheme of things. Athena looked at the objectionable intruder, pointed to each of us in turn, and said:

'Mr Mackie, meet my husband!'

Taken aback, I sprang up to shake hands with the owner of a pair of eyes which were regarding me with overt suspicion. Then along came father and mother-in-law, so, realising I was superfluous, I retreated to my corner and back into bachelor oblivion.

Virtuoso

Not very long after the Talodi dance of fond memory, I was getting on with the job when a jarring message was placed in my hand. 'Bishop Gwynn coming El Obeid 25th inst. please turn up to play organ – Governor.'

At first sight this document was bewildering – to travel from Talodi to El Obeid in three days time to play an organ? There must be a mistake! Never before in my life had I even touched an organ. I cast around in my mind for the reason for this summons. Then it clicked!

When invited to dinner at the Governor's house after the 'conservation' talk, I had admitted in a less guarded moment to playing the piano. No further details had been sought, or it could have been explained that my talent was limited to a few jingles on the black notes – essentially without reference to printed music.

Unguarded words: here was I in a situation of crisis through careless talk. Admittedly I had beaten out a few rhythms in college days and I played a reasonably correct version of Handel's Largo, but was that likely to be adequate for this rare visit of the one and only bishop of Egypt and the Sudan? I had visions of the little El Obeid church packed to the door with the entire British population of the province all standing, mouths open awaiting my brave efforts, before bursting into song. My nerves trembled at the prospect!

Yet this was virtually a royal summons, not to be carelessly disregarded. If only it had been a question of tribal wars or ginnery breakdowns, or such minor trivia, instead of this crisis.

Perhaps if I reached El Obeid with a day to spare I could learn to play the organ: perhaps, with luck, the car might break down in some vast unpopulated wilderness! There was no alternative but to go. The thought of letting down the side caused an involuntary shiver; I could well believe there was no other potential organist in the scattered British population – several could play the bagpipes, but that was hardly appropriate . . .

The very notion of the Bishop coming all the way from Egypt to sing without music – Heaven forbid! Nothing for it; 250 miles to El Obeid to play an organ.

I decided to stop everything and leave the following morning, after all, whose fault would it be if things went wrong in my absence?

With the box-car loaded and Mahomed and Ibrahim perched high, we set out over the Western Jebels route, one quite new to us. It was a glorious opportunity to discover fresh country and find out more about the Nuba, but the impending ordeal weighed too heavily – I was virtually blind to the tribesmen and the animal life we passed on the way. With relief, we reached the plains and churned our way over the sand into El Obeid.

There was no time to waste! I hunted out the church key and quickly surveyed the instrument in question. No ranks of silvered pipes climbed the church walls, only an innocent little pedal organ with a vase of flowers set on top. That was a relief – it had the look of a piano, but for its row of knobs.

The silence of the lovely little church was soon disturbed as 'Largo' trundled out falteringly followed by a string of hymns, on the black notes. There was no other key as far as I was concerned.

Sunday morning dawned and, in the course of events, I was introduced to the Bishop, a fine old Welshman with a twinkle in his eye. Belatedly it dawned on me that a simple Scottish background was poor preparation for the intricacies of an Anglican service: this occasioned us to reach a compromise with regard to the coming programme. He took this in good part, declaring that the majority of the congregation would be Scotsmen in any case.

The time arrived, and swallowing my fears, I found my way to the organ seat. The church was already filling with district commissioners, senior veterinary officers, inspectors of this and that, not to mention, where appropriate, their wives.

The first notes of Handel were pealing out when in came the Governor who, with a bit of luck, might not have an ear for music. His eye caught mine at an intricate part of the melody, producing a modification to the Handel theme, but his wink, next best thing to thumbs-up, set me off again with renewed vigour.

I was running out of tune and planning a re-run, when the Bishop made a stately entry, moving up close to the organ where he stood patiently for a few moments. Silence reigned: I was aware of him looking at me from the corner of his eye as if expecting something. Nothing was forthcoming, so he started to speak.

'I am happy to be here among you in El Obeid . . .' and so on: but my ears were deaf as I planned the first hymn – on the black notes. I got the 'nod', played a few bars, where upon the congregation stood up and let fly.

Things were going famously, the 'chosen' key must have been about right because the singing was strong enough to drown the organ. The second hymn passed in like manner. It would be wrong to claim that the organ lead was inspiring, but there was a majority of bass voices which sang on regardless.

I had noticed the word 'Voluntary' on the programme, to be played while the offering was being extracted; a bit of a problem as I felt the congregation would be amply satisfied with one rendering of Largo. My repertoire was limited, but happily I remembered a childhood jingle based on a Schubert melody. This transference from Handel to Schubert no doubt showed virtuosity. I noticed the Governor watching me thoughtfully.

Now came 'Guide Me, Oh Thou Great Jehovah', which went swimmingly, and had me singing in strong tenor. Then came the last hymn, the name by now forgotten. The singing started, but there were problems – some of the men seemed to be reaching up in high falsetto while the remainder groaned at low pitch, searching for notes.

There was no point in changing the key, as I only had one. The Governor was listening silently with a smile on his face. As for the Bishop, he seemed to be enjoying the choral efforts, head tilted to one side, eyes closed.

Like all good things, the service came to an end. Both Bishop and congregation filtered out leaving me in full command. To celebrate the end of the crisis, I played one and on, savouring freedom.

Before returning the long road to Talodi, the Bishop and the Governor praised me for my playing, but I rather think that when they did, they were still 'winking'.

Of Horses, Armour and a Sword

After the musical interlude, the prospect of escape to the mountains was glorious. That solitary trek table far from anywhere had, now, an overwhelming appeal.

Alex, however, kept me two days in El Obeid going over plans for the next few months. The rains were due in just over two months and much had yet to be accomplished before the roads broke up and the mountains got cut off by flooding watercourses. The Talodi horse meeting in a few days' time would give me the opportunity to purchase pack horses.

We talked over the subject of horse trekking and agreed on the goals to be achieved. The question of reaching our targets for grain output was also pressing as time was now limited, but Italian lorries were already arriving in the mountains to carry it to the river.

On the morning of departure for Talodi, Alex received a dramatic message from Khartoum: 'Excavation machinery being assembled for *hafir* digging Eastern Jebels, will advise despatch date. Make all preparation.'

The suddenness of this came as a surprise to both of us. Obviously reports I had written on the subject had been read by the Department. Alex said, 'It's up to you lad. It's your baby! The preparations are in your hands – you had better collect a 'dumpy-level' from stores to survey your sites, as well as any other things you may need.'

I had written about areas of virgin clay which could be opened up by mechanical aid, thus taking the pressure of population from deteriorating land. The hope was that large enough reservoirs could be built to provide a source of water through the dry season. If this proved successful, then an effort might be made to introduce good husbandry and, hopefully, reduce the spread of erosion. This exercise, I hoped, was to be considered as a conservation experiment – at least it was better than, fatalistically, doing nothing. Apparently all of this also had to be fitted in before the rains.

I had much to think over as we drove towards the blue ridge of the Western Jebels but, this time, I relished the journey through valley and forest and past hills covered with Nuba terraces. The people, tall and statuesque, usually stopped to wave as we drove past.

At Kadugli we met the first of many groups of Arab horsemen heading for the Talodi meeting, the first time I had seen much evidence of horses in the Jebels. It appeared that riders came long distances for this event, and it had the nature of a carnival as well as being a centre of horse trading.

The morning of the horse meeting dawned. It was cool, due to a thin high layer of cloud masking the sun. From daybreak, a large crowd of Arabs and Nuba gathered on a clearing near the town, and as I drove over the shoulder of the hill from the rest-house, a haze of dust stirred up by many hundreds of Arab horses masked the scene.

The horses were cause for admiration and pride, to both owners and spectators. They were beautifully groomed and many had brightly coloured harness. It made a splendid scene. Then, as I joined the crowd, my eyes picked our a number of riders dressed in chain mail and wearing spectacular helmets. They carried lances or swords in medieval style, and might have been heading for a tournament. Such dress is highly prized and it received admiring attention from the onlookers; its presence at Talodi is deeply rooted in the past and the armour is supposedly from the time of the crusades. The name of Saladin was spoken with reverence when I asked questions about the chain mail, indicating an awareness of history as far back as the crusades.

During the morning various parades of horses formed up in which riders demonstrated their equestrian skills by making the horses prance and cavort in front of the crowd. The more spectacular efforts received loud cheers. Then races started in which horses, a dozen at a time, thundered the length of the arena to the excitement of everyone.

There was even a form of tote, perhaps introduced to the mountains by soldiers in earlier times.

All of this was of great interest but I had come to the meeting for one purpose only – to buy six pack ponies. Small groups of people gathered at random were engaged in buying and selling. I watched and listened to the endless haggling over the price of horses – a sale without a lengthy argument in advance is a deprivation in the Sudan.

It quickly went the rounds that I was going to make some purchases and several potential sellers gathered round, each one intent on taking me to see his particular horse. I had taken the precaution of having with me a sergeant of the Sudan Defence Force, a resident in the small Talodi garrison, as an advisor and, perhaps, also as a protection against over-enthusiastic traders. He was an able authority on horses, and saw merits and/or defects in animals well beyond my ability to recognise.

A rather attractive, broad-backed pony caught our eyes. The sergeant examined its legs and teeth and he nodded knowingly – it would carry pack well. The owner's eyes shone optimistically – white men have money, here was his great chance!

The tussle started with an eulogy on the horse's merits, its remarkable pedigree and superior virtues. At the appropriate moment I interjected: 'Ten pounds!'

The man tugged at his beard and stared, aghast, as if mortally offended. A pause, then he said: 'Forty pounds and not one piastre less!'

It was my turn to throw my hands up in surprise and laugh at his suggestion. The eulogy started again: he lifted the horse's leg for me to inspect and I was instructed to pinch its smooth hide – time to increase my offer, with some show of reluctance. 'Twelve pounds and no more!' I declared. The sergeant at my elbow nodded his approval.

'Thirty pounds and I am giving it away at the price, and only because you are an inspector.'

More incredulity on my part, followed by ten minutes of argument in which I was told that I was a hard man and must be inexperienced not to recognise the worth of this horse. I knew that its worth was about fifteen pounds, so I offered this sum and got another refusal. With dramatic finality the owner declared:

'Twenty pounds — my final price, take it or leave it!'

We were getting closer now so I said, 'Sixteen pounds!' – waited a few seconds, then turned my back on him and made to walk away. He called me back, made some asides about my kinship to the Jewish race; and so we settled for sixteen pounds.

The deal complete, he blossomed into smiles; we shook hands on it and he moved off clutching the money.

I could see now that by the time this effort was repeated another five times, it was going to be a long, tiring day, but with some exercise of authority and ingenuity by the sergeant, the operation was somehow abbreviated, and by midday I owned six pack horses which, together with Bakhit and Gamr in Rashad, gave me my full establishment of eight.

The horses were delivered to the rest-house, and that evening I spent some hours admiring them and trying to decide on what to call them.

The local Mamur kindly offered me the services of two policemen to ride with them the long road to Rashad so I was free once more to move into the deep mountains and get on with the job.

Deep in the Nuba Mountains as late as the year 1940, there were parts rarely, if ever, visited by white administrators. The Meks of these areas had, for long, resisted the introduction of law imposed by a central government as this was liable to affect the powers vested in them under customary tribal law. Partly because of their isolation and inaccessibility, these areas were left virtually untouched, and it could be said that the people there were the original primitive Nuba whose lifestyle had remained unchanged for centuries.

Tribal law was administered by the Mek, supported by a *kujur* (translated – priest or witch-doctor) and, occasionally, by a group of tribal elders. These 'sensitive' areas were considered to need extra care and diplomacy on the part of the visitor.

I had been given a remit to visit such an area, roughly thirty miles from Talodi, so, not knowing what to expect, set off with Tahr Effendi and the usual crew, in search of the 'real' Nuba. Tahr had a smattering of the Nuba tongue which might prove useful. We took with us sufficient provisions for three or four days and carried a tent, as there were no rest-houses. The boys shared my excitement at visiting this area, because they knew there was an element of the unknown in what lay ahead.

The further we travelled from Talodi, the more evident were the signs of difference from most other Nuba I had seen. The customary friendly waves were replaced by shyness, with people standing uncertainly at a distance, as if nervous at the presence of a white man. Nearing our destination almost all of the men had their bodies coloured with clay, a uniform red and grey colour, and they carried weapons, usually very long spears. When the car stopped, no one approached and it was difficult to judge their attitudes.

At the first village I walked into the compound to ask for the chief. A man came forward and shook my hand in the Nuba style; gradually a few others gathered round – Tahr struggled with the language, trying to put over our message, and heads slowly nodded in understanding. The spontaneous friendliness we were accustomed to was lacking, and there was no offer of hospitality so we moved on to the next village.

At sunset, camp was pitched at the head of a valley where there were a few scattered houses. High on the skyline hundreds of little Nuba huts indicated a fairly high population and, as light failed, I could see numbers of people descending to the valley in our direction.

Mahomed lit his cook-fire, Ibrahim and the driver erected the tent, and

Tahr sat down with me at the trek table to discuss the day's events. We were both very aware that no one had come forward to meet us, but as we sat in the light of a pressure lantern, a crowd gathered looking at us from a distance. Ibrahim came to the table, obviously nervous at having a silent audience watching our every move. I told him to serve dinner as normal and to ignore them. Then a giant Nuba, at least six feet eight inches tall, pushed through the circle and came towards us. He alone in the crowd wore clothes; a full-flowing Arab *jelibiyah* topped with a *guftan*. I stood up to meet him and we shook hands: he spoke Arabic saying that he was Mek of the surrounding tribe. He was the very person I wanted to meet.

He asked our identity and the purpose of our visit. There was no sign of unfriendliness in his manner, and at my invitation he sat down on a trek chair, but pulled it back a few feet from the table. Ibrahim arrived with our meal, but he refused food, accepting only a drink of coffee.

By now the surrounding crowd had gathered closer to the table, and at a sign from the Mek all sat on the ground to listen and, perhaps, to wonder as we wielded knives and forks and performed other culinary antics quite new to them.

After the meal we kept on talking. A group of men had, by now, moved to the front of the crowd, and the Mek occasionally interpreted to them the substance of our discussion. Questions were asked about a source of good seed grain, and it was explained that a stock was available for them to collect from Talodi. I explained the need for them to grow additional grain to meet the hunger of other nations. The evening melted away and I had some sense of relief at the way the conversation was opening up once the ice was broken.

Throughout the proceedings a little group of children stood at my knee staring silently at my face, and occasionally daring to touch me, the first white man they had ever seen.

Then I remembered the gramophone at the back of the car and thought that a late-night concert would go down well with the crowd. They watched with some wonder as I wound up the box – a sequence of actions hitherto never seen. The music started. This was the pre-transistor radio age, and noises from a box were something far beyond their range of experience.

The children ran off in fear; adults stood silently, bemused – one man looked as if about to prod the box to see if it would squeal. Slowly they began to smile and shake their heads, then they settled to the music. Presumably the music, as such, was just 'noises' to them, but when I played 'The Funickle Man Who Had an Old Sow' their sense of humour was tickled (presumably at the sounds, not the words!) and they laughed, then asked for a replay.

They might have gone on listening into the small hours, but I felt that it was time to stop – the voice ground to a halt as the spring wound out and when they were told that the man in the box was tired, they accepted this explanation and gradually left to return to their villages. The chief said he would call again in the morning. Then we were left in peace!

The night was still, save for drum-beats from the hilltops. But for the evening's meeting behind us, the sounds would have seemed ominous: there was, however, no need for anxiety because the people of this valley were not 'rebels', they were just uncertain of strangers.

With the coming of dawn I wakened to the chattering of numerous people outside the tent. Ibrahim, sounding disgruntled, was apparently restraining visitors until I was up and dressed. The tent-flap opened and heads peered in and, somehow, an influx of people moved in to greet me and to find out what a tent really was.

The confined space became filled with chattering humanity apparently unconcerned at my lack of dress. Indeed, with only pyjama trousers, I was the best dressed person there, as the sum of clothing of the others amounted only to a few strings of beads and leather thongs.

I pulled on some clothes, as and when I could reach them, then they were persuaded to move outside where they watched with interest as I performed morning toilet. The exchange of interest was mutual – many of the women had ears, lips and nostrils stretched round metal rings: some rings piercing their lips were large, giving them the appearance of ducks.

I reached to examine these beauty features and they pulled at one another and giggled. The better-dressed women wore a ring of blue beads around the waist and a thin leather cord between their legs. Unmarried women wore neither. They lifted every portable object and passed it from hand to hand, but nothing was taken.

Ibrahim stood offended at this transgression of his authority, but I asked to leave them be, as their intentions were good-natured and innocent.

The Mek arrived now, and with a few words in Nuba quickly cleared the tent of people; he had with him several of his wives, and what might have been aunts and uncles as well. He invited me to his village and I spent the entire morning, much as on previous visits to Nuba homes, meeting people of all ages and entering their red clay and thatch homes.

Almost everyone who could came to shake my fingertips in the Nuba way, with the Nuba greeting 'Aafi!' accompanied by a fascist-style salute. In one home I met an old blind man who greeted me, then ran his hands over my face, clothes and body, as if to identify my uniqueness.

Several times people told me how wild buffalo, the only animal they feared, raided the valley cultivations during the rains – could I please help by destroying them? I told them that this was beyond my powers.

Little holes, hundreds of them, had been cut at regular intervals into the bare rock outside their homes and filled with soil brought up from the valley. Crops of tomatoes and tobacco grew in them, carefully tended, but these were dwarfed because of virus disease. Here was something with which I could help, by obtaining healthy seed in time for their next crop. The men smoked clay pipes with very long stems and apparently spent the entire day smoking and talking while women tended the cultivations.

We left this valley with some regret, being waved on our way by a considerable crowd. Again, the question rose in my mind – in what way could government improve the lives of these friendly people?

Several more communities were visited that day, testing the car springs as it jolted over tracks never meant to be used by vehicles. At sunset and after driving an almost un-negotiable track, we stopped at what amounted to the most isolated community of all. Darkness fell, and on this occasion no one came near, and the evening hours passed silently and undisturbed. There was an eeriness about this silence but after our earlier experience there seemed no cause for anxiety.

Morning came, soft and red. I looked out from the tent to a valley bathed in a special beauty, with its many little houses scattered over the mountainsides. The silence was complete, nothing moved – then I noticed a path in the distance leading upwards to a cleft where two hills came together. People like brown ants moved up this path, even as early as this, and they apparently disappeared into the hillside. Why this flow of people? I watched for some time, but there was no answer so I got on with the day's routine.

With breakfast over, I was on the point of leaving the camp with Tahr Effendi to find the local Mek, when a group of Nuba approached who stood motionless a short distance away. One of them wore some scraps of clothing and, as I moved towards them, he stepped forward. He appeared to regard us uncertainly as, without the slightest edge of a smile, we shook hands and exchanged the usual greetings.

He spoke in Nuba and, after much repetition, Tahr was able to make him understand the reasons for our visit which concerned the well-being of the people. At last, a smile came: he was joined by the others and there were handshakes all round. He was the Mek!

This day was different. There were fewer people about, although those we met were friendly. Various headmen came forward to meet us throughout the day, and it was only in the middle of the afternoon that Tahr discovered what was going on. Apparently a ceremony was taking place high on the hilltop path I had seen earlier. The ceremony involved a sword and *kujurs* (witch doctors), with people going to some special place to witness religious rites.

I asked Tahr to ask whether we could witness this ceremony. When, at last, the Mek understood, he shook his head indicating that our presence would be unacceptable: and why, after all, should I expect otherwise? The subject was dropped, but I noticed that the Mek sent one of his young followers off in the direction of the hill path. He went away with long, loping strides and I could see him climbing upwards and out of sight.

We returned to the car, having accomplished our mission in the valley. The boys loaded the gear in readiness for our next move and I indicated to the Mek that it was time for us to go – he shook his head in a manner that suggested he wanted us to wait.

We stood rather awkwardly in silence for some minutes, very aware of the communication barrier between us – then he pointed to the hill where figures could be seen running towards us. The messenger returned, accompanied by a man draped in a red robe – there was a rapid exchange of conversation with the Mek, then he smiled and waved towards the hill saying that I was invited to visit the 'place'.

Time was moving on, and I was anxious to travel to our next destination, but it seemed only fair to accept the invitation after the effort which had been made. I agreed, and was told that the invitation was for me alone – Tahr was excluded. The Mek cut a stick, a form of pilgrim's staff, for my use and I was requested to remove my socks and shoes. The prospect of climbing a stony path barefoot was a bit daunting, but we set off on our 'pilgrim' way, the Mek, the 'priest' and myself. The boys stood, side by side, watching us go, looking slightly unhappy, perhaps because I was going to witness some pagan ritual offensive to their Moslem scruples.

The sun lowered as we climbed the steep path which, by now, was thronged with people descending from the 'place'. The path, narrow in places, caused us to squeeze past the returning devotees. Each pilgrim carried a staff like my own. They apparently accepted my presence without surprise and most of them lined up to greet me, fondling the tips of my fingers in that unusual way.

One group of four tall young women lives in my memory – erect, of beautiful physique, and with bodies shining like polished mahogany. They went through the friendly greeting ritual, then moved on, deep in their private conversation as if foreign visitors were commonplace: something which was far from the case!

Soon we were high on the hillside; I could see the car far below. Then we came to a little bare piece of ground in front of a fifty-foot sheer cliff of red rock. A narrow cleft split the cliff face and through it people emerged as if from the mountain's heart.

There was room only to move in single file between steep rock walls. I entered, walking on a sandy floor and, almost immediately, had to squeeze tightly past people moving in the opposite direction. Twenty-five or so yards of this then, with dramatic finality, I entered into a flat sand clearing surrounded by cliffs of solid rock. The scene was breathtaking – a flat mountain-rimmed bowl about two hundred feet in diameter, with, on the west side, a break in the rock where the sun could be seen setting in a ball of flaming red. A natural rock platform just beneath the sun's orb was apparently the centre of interest: I could see red-robed *kujurs* as well as a small queue of people moving towards a central point.

The day's ceremonial must have been coming to an end, because there remained only about one hundred people in the arena. The setting was perfect for purposes of ritual, it could have been chiselled to an exact specification. The Mek walked with me to the end of the queue where we awaited our turn to climb up to the rock platform.

An old, bent and wizened woman clad in red came down from the rock and walked towards me, and beckoned with hooked finger for me to follow her on to the rock. The crowd watched silently as I was led to a point where a pile of votive offerings was heaped.

Then my eye caught the object of their devotions – the rusty remnants of a sword, plunged vertically into the rock, leaving about two feet of its length visible. I had watched the actions of other devotees and knew that it was necessary that I should behave in like manner so as not to offend the niceties of the *kujurs* who were watching carefully. I laid some coins on the heap, kneeled before the sword, and bent forward to touch my forehead on the rock, staring for some seconds at the sword but not daring to touch it – when and how did it become imbedded into the hard rock? Why was it considered as a focus for a religious cult which certainly held the surrounding tribes in its grip? There were no answers. The *kujurs* had the cult firmly under their control. I was ushered from the platform, but before climbing down, stopped to view the sheer vertical precipice just beyond the sword, lit by the final edge of the, by now, gigantic sun.

It was a place for worship, for sacrifice: a truly fearful place! I had learned another side of the Nuba character – its acceptance of the power and influence of witch-doctors.

My questions on the return journey remained unanswered, partly because of the difficulty imposed by language. We said our farewells and made our way in darkness over the almost impossible road. I had much to turn over in my mind in the days that followed . . . days spent among similar peoples. The haunting thought kept coming back – should these people not be left in peace to pursue their own ways without interference? How could civilising influences ever add to their contentment?

Happy Return

It was time to shake off the dust of Talodi and head north to arrive in time for the Tegali Gathering.

The topic of soil conservation had never been far from my mind in the Nuba hills although damage by erosion was less dramatic there. This was due to the seasonal rains extending over a longer period; also Nuba are hunters rather than farmers, and possess relatively few hard-grazing livestock. Their cultivations are more carefully managed as is shown by the hillside terraces, although, admittedly, many of these are no longer in use. All of these factors have lessened man's impact on the soil; but even in the Nuba hills, the signs were there to be seen. The forest had shrunk far from village communities, causing a parallel reduction in animal life.

Forests are demolished by cutting or burning, but no single tree is ever planted as a replacement: in time, the hills drain more quickly, rivers flood with dramatic suddenness and the processes of erosion are speeded up. Even here, in these tranquil hills, the ecological balance of past centuries had been upset – was it because the new stability exerted by central government, together with some reduction in past endemic diseases, was bringing about a population increase? A rise in population could affect the balance. In this region of Africa, with its erratic seasonal rainfall, man can create a desert out of a fertile paradise in a very few years then, sadly, as the forest diminishes, rainfall becomes even more erratic, and the disastrous spiral continues. This picture was clear as we drove the long trail northwards, and I searched in my mind for some way to stimulate the Tegali people into action so that their land might be preserved.

I had decided to follow a trail, one I had not previously travelled, and closer to the River Nile. The promised heavy machinery was due to arrive before long, and I wanted to ease my mind by having a quick look at the land where it could most gainfully be employed.

The evening's destination was the village of Terter where the people, Aulad Himeid, were under the rule of my shuffling friend, Nazir Zbeir of Abu Gubeiha. The people here, though black-skinned, are arabicised Nuba like many of the other northern tribes, and all of these peoples descend from the nomadic Buggara who still make seasonal journeys from the northern plains to the Nuba hills.

This interweaving of the tribes and races was slowly fitting into place in my mind, like pieces of a jigsaw puzzle. The picture was made more complex by the way various territories were at times inter-mixed with the boundaries obscure. It had been a situation where conflict was endemic before the arrival of British rule, although it must be admitted that the years of the Mahidiya had unified all the people for a period against a common enemy. It was helpful, indeed necessary, to remember the tribal origins of each community, because of their several differences!

After a long, hot journey we were within a few miles of Terter when a sequence of unusual events took place.

An Arab family, four in number, walked towards Terter. I offered them a lift. Ibrahim was annoyed, though Mahomed smiled placidly as the additional bodies broke up their 'nest' among the trek kit. Pieces had to be moved to make room, but soon we continued into the twilight.

A mile beyond this point, I noticed an animal in the centre of the track. We passed over it without doing harm, and I called a halt to investigate. The boys preoccupied as they were with their fellow passengers, had not seen the creature and possibly thought I was retiring for other reasons.

I walked back to find a large chameleon, over a foot long, walking shakily towards the bush. This animal, I knew, was harmless so I lifted it and placed it on my wrist, where it balanced while I returned to the car to show it to the boys. The mixed bag of passengers sat in glum silence when I presented my capture for their inspection.

Suddenly, pandemonium reigned!

To a man they went, nor did they hesitate about the manner of their going – they rolled to the ground and fled to the bush as if the devil himself had appeared. Even Mahomed, showing remarkable agility for his age, joined the panic. To make matters worse, Ibrahim's shirt-tail caught on a projection and he left to the accompaniment of a resounding tear.

There was apparently some antipathy where chameleons were concerned. I shouted after them:

'This is only a chameleon: it is quite harmless!'

A plaintive voice from the wilderness shouted:

'Get rid of the unmentionable creature before further evil befalls us!'

I realised that in order to complete the journey it would be necessary to dispose of the animal at an approved distance from the car. Only then did they crawl slowly from hiding. The family were a shade reluctant to risk further progress in the vehicle, but they did climb aboard. Ibrahim had a face like thunder.

'That creature – there is a curse on it! You risk our lives! It is too foolish of you!'

I had to take the ticking-off gracefully, and I had to admit that it is an unusual creature – what with its oscillating eyeballs and colour changes. After all, what normal creature would be able to do that? Ibrahim seemed a little mollified at my repentance, but he couldn't resist a final thrust.

'No good will come of this!'

We moved off again with Ibrahim nursing his torn shirt-tail, and had only travelled a short distance further when his prophecy of doom proved correct. It happened in seconds! There was still sufficient light to see the outlines of trees against the hard back-drop of the evening sky. This time we all saw 'it'.

It took shape of an eagle beating its way into the sky and looking gigantic in the half-light – dangling from its talons was a snake. The startled bird swept over the car, dropping the snake in its fright, which landed among the passengers and slithered to the floor.

Another sudden evacuation, though the car was still in motion — bodies landed in tumbled heaps on the dusty track. The driver went with them: I was close behind. The car rolled on, driverless, but fortunately with its gear disengaged, to stop among some bushes.

For a minute or two everyone was speechless: eyes no doubt wide with fear, although darkness prevented observation of this fact. Then Ibrahim found his voice.

'See! What did I tell you. We might all be dead!' He spat out the words. 'What are you going to do now?'

It was not merely a snake that was curled in the bottom of the car, it was a retribution for tempting fate!

I stood alone in this matter, even Mahomed looked at me with scorn – the family of four were already beating it hastily in the direction of Terter, without having offered a word of thanks for the lift! How to get a deadly snake from our clutter of baggage in the darkness in the face of a hostile audience?

I successfully unearthed a paraffin lamp and fumbled some matches from the dashboard: with its dim light, I pulled pieces over the open tail-board until the car was virtually empty. At last – there was the snake, ominously still. I jabbed it with a stick then levered it out, to discover it was headless. I might have known that an eagle would behead a snake before carrying it off!

The kit was re-loaded and we set off, with me the victim of utter and scornful silence. It took them several days to get over my ignorance. Ibrahim had the satisfaction of purchasing a new shirt at my expense!

By the time we returned wearily to Rashad my transgressions were forgiven. Days had been spent walking the bush to find possible sites where *hafirs* could be dug by the heavy machinery due to arrive soon. It had been a novel though exhausting experience identifying these sites where, it was to be hoped, new village communities would become established in the course of time.

Mek Adam of Tegali had shown interest in this project as the area chosen came within his tribal jurisdiction. Some concentration of effort was needed if a beginning was to be made in arresting the spread of erosion; if the effort was successful here, it could act as an example to be followed in other areas of the mountains – perhaps even of the Sudan.

If only I could attract the interest of the people at the Tegali Gathering and even involve some of them in the new project perhaps wheels would be set in motion. It was an exciting possibility!

Rashad looked as sleepy as ever. Nothing of special note ever happened here, after all it was just a little village chosen as administration centre because of its attractive environs. but there was some congestion at the rear of the house where the recently purchased horses were arriving from Talodi. An improvised stick-and-straw stable had been built for them, now numbering eight, and amounting to a full trek *hamla*. It became necessary to engage two additional young grooms so that the horses would be well exercised and trained to carrying pack.

But first things first!

Ibrahim stood before me, rather humbly now.

'*Jenabo*, I need a day off work as I have some business to see to,' he said.

'What is your business, Ibrahim?' Perhaps I should not have been so inquisitive.

'Well . . . I'm getting married.'

'Good!' I said. 'I expect your uncle will be happy now.'

'No, I'm marrying the widow,' he said, not very pleased.

I had forgotten that he had changed his mind.

'Oh, so that means that you will have a ready-made family of three children! What about your uncle and your young cousin?'

He shrugged. '*Alla keyfak!*' (I couldn't care less).

Ibrahim got his day off and I could but wonder at the effect this new addition would have on the 'establishment': I would soon have sufficient staff and camp-followers to require our own separate village.

Meanwhile, I was holding back, hesitating to go to the office for fear of finding the Arabic examination results on my desk. Finally I trudged there, expecting the worst.

Neil met me on the office steps, a smile on his face. He reached to shake my hand: 'Congratulations, you have passed!'

Passed what? What did he mean? It could not be the examination! I ran up to the desk: an opened telegram lay in front of a stack of mail (so much for postal confidentiality) – 'Congratulations on defeating examiners . . . Director.'

There must be something wrong. I still couldn't believe it. Another wire from Alex repeated the message, and another from the Governor – did the whole country know?

Then it sank in and I shouted with relief – no more study, no more examinations! Neil invited me to his home for a meal. When I was alone I looked at the mail, uncertain again – was there any news from home? At the bottom of the pile I found four air-mail letters – everything was going well at home.

What a return! What a Day!

Late into the night, Neil and I discussed our work and, for once, it was a pleasure to talk shop. He had just returned from a circuit of the Jebels and we had many experiences to share and tales to tell about the people and places we both knew well. Our work was very different and yet we shared a common thread, strengthened now by our joint efforts to produce more grain, a project which was going well and likely to achieve its target.

The coming gathering at Tegali was at the forefront of our minds. We were both involved, and it would be the first work in which we could actively co-operate. We talked over the history of the country and, particularly, about the significance of the coming event for the people of Tegali.

The Sudan's history, though not recorded in stone to the same degree as Egypt's, is equally ancient, going back thousands of years. Its earliest phases are subjects of conjecture, but from 700 BC on, several well-developed, even brilliant, civilisations were at the centre of the historical stage.

The Northern Kingdom of Kush, a dynasty of black Nubians, dominated much of the Sudan and Egypt from 700–300 BC. Hundreds of years before

Christ, when Europe was little more than a primitive backwater, Kush was a highly developed civilisation of black people. A migration of people from Kush could well have populated the area now known as the Nuba Mountains centuries BC, bringing their customs with them. It is also a probability that this people, as has happened to other ancient civilisations, ceased to develop and remained 'frozen' in time. The isolation of the Nuba Mountains in its geographical backwater kept 'civilising' influences at bay, so that the Nuba of my travels represented an ancient and living history.

After Kush, a new dynasty – Meroe (35 BC to 350 AD) – developed in northern Sudan, and exercised an important influence throughout Africa and southern Europe, exporting gold, iron, copper, and sandalwood. After this long period of dominance, Meroe was overrun by a new power from Ethiopia – the Christian kingdom of Axium. The Sudan remained largely Christian until the fourteenth century AD when followers of the Prophet filtered in from the north and the east to win the people for Islam.

In the fifteenth century AD a new power rose in central Sudan in the region of Kordofan and Blue Nile Province. This dynasty was known as the Funj, or Black Sultanate, composed of people of mixed Arab and Nilotic origin with skins as black as those of the people of Tegali today. The story goes that in the year 1505 the Funj united with a powerful tribe, the Quawasma or Hawazma, and together they defeated the last of the Christians to rule most of northern Sudan. The Funj was noted for a just rule and an advanced system of administration based on powerful central government, in which the tribes all had representation. The Funj was at its peak in the eighteenth century, and as late as the nineteenth century many of its sons were sent to Cairo for a university education.

There came a time of cruel oppression and disintegration in which the Hawazma went its own way, leaving a vacuum into which foreign power penetrated. Under the Ottoman Turks, oppression was rife until a rebellion was fomented in which tribes rallied round the Mahdi.

After the followers of the Mahdi were defeated by British forces, the Kingdom of Tegali, with its roots deep in the Funj, remained un-cooperative to the extent that government administrators hardly dared venture into the area. Punitive expeditions were sent to the mountains and, at about the time of the first Great War, the power of the Mek was broken. As late as 1930 flights of aeroplanes were sent to subdue rebellious tribes.

A new leader, Mek Adam Geili, was appointed and the Government made it a keystone of its policy to foster the regrowth of Tegali. Mek Adam earned the respect of all parties and his people, and he was eventually knighted in London. He resisted being called Sir Adam, because he considered the title Mek more ancient and noble.

Neil and I were about to attend the final reunification – that of the Hawazma, with the Kingdom of Tegali, an important event in the Sudan's history. To mark the occasion, the province Governor and Alex were also taking part: the year was 1944 and the Great Council, as it was called, was to last two days.

Tegali

Two days before the start of the Council, Neil and I drove to Abbasiya, capital of the 'Kingdom' of Tegali, to help prepare the ground, and receive the distinguished guests when they turned up. We shared the rest-house and our respective boys set up house while we went about our business. Neil spent the day with Mek Adam mulling over arrangements, and I was allocated a sheikh, Musa by name, to look into agricultural matters.

I quickly found that Sheikh Musa's interests stretched beyond the realms of agriculture. A devout Moslem with very black skin like most of the Tegali people, he started by questioning whether, in truth, I was a Christian, as if to be one was a matter of default. Having sorted this out, probably to his dissatisfaction, he seemed determined to show me the error of my ways, although still remaining polite. He asked me about my beliefs, shaking his head doubtfully, while constantly invoking the name of the Almighty. At the appropriate times our progress was stopped as he jumped to the ground to spread a mat and pray towards Mecca.

His devoutness was commendable as nothing was allowed to interfere with his religious disciplines. In the course of the day, Musa stopped at a village not far from Abassiya to show me a house where the Mahdi had once lived – the second ruined house of the Mahdi I had seen in the mountains.

'These were glorious days: the days of the Jihad, when the enemies of the Sudan were routed!' he said.

He took me to one place where he announced: 'English soldiers were once beheaded here!' and drew his hand dramatically over his throat.

He may have looked at me thoughtfully at that moment! I doubted his claim that the unfortunate soldiers were English, but I held my peace. Close by was a hollow in a rock face – a cave in embryo where the Mahdi had gone apart from his followers to pray.

I was grateful for the difference sixty years had made, because Musa would have been first in the field of conflict!

At one point a group of Tetal antelope were disturbed by our passing: he grabbed my arm lest I drive too close to them. 'He who hunts or chases the Tetal dies,' he explained. A religious man, he was also, apparently,

Sugar black-marketeer.

superstitious, as are indeed many people in the 'civilised' west, who read horoscopes or refrain from walking under ladders.

The land for many miles round Abbasiya looked like a miniature dust bowl. The relative wealth of the people, together with the absence of tsetse fly, had brought about large cattle herds which were grazing the heart out of the land. Here, the people's status and wealth was measured by the size of their herds. In addition, there were large flocks of sheep and goats. All of these were an important factor in the erosion equation – overcropping, over-grazing, destruction of the forest – progressively reducing the soil to dust, which in turn, was blown or washed away.

The Tegali Gathering, in due course, became a starting point in tackling these questions because, of course, there are solutions provided there is the political will, and resources are provided to meet the scale of the 'disaster'. Unfortunately, like many efforts to improve the lot of man, they were swallowed up in the politics of change.

That evening I sat in the lamplight with Neil talking over the day's work and working out with him how the question of the land and its needs should be tackled – could the people be encouraged to plant and conserve trees? Would a programme of mass livestock selection to improve the quality of cattle and, perhaps, reduce their number be adopted? Could a form of crop rotation be encouraged? These and many other ideas were exchanged that night. We both understood that any changes would only come about if the people were convinced of their value. Where better place to begin than here, under the auspices of Mek Adam Geili.

As if in recognition of our hopes, a remarkable event occurred as we were going to our beds – some raindrops pocked the dust at our feet, the first in many months. It was a pointed reminder that the rainy season approached and much work still remained to be done.

Next morning, important visitors poured into Abassiya for the Gathering. Neil and I joined Mek Adam in welcoming them – nazirs, omdahs and sheikhs, all in bright robes as they rode or drove into the little town. Some came on camel-back, some on donkeys; only a few arrived in motor vehicles, usually merchant's lorries.

Alex drove in with the governor at midday so that the little rest-house became congested with its four occupants and their complement of 'boys'. We each occupied a corner, and our four beds were lined outside in the open, objects of curiosity to the many passers-by.

That evening there was ample opportunity to talk over the various urgent matters which needed finalising before the rains. Neil was told to release me from any further work with grain, so that I would be able to prepare for the arrival of the fleet of excavating machines. The sites I had chosen would require another visit in order to survey them in detail, and to draw up plans. More dramatically came the news that the Governor General was coming to the Nuba Mountains in a few days time to attend a great gathering of the Nuba at Heiban. There was no argument that we would all have to attend that event.

This was my first year in the mountains, and I had little idea of how soon the roads would be broken up. It surprised me that so many happenings were being squeezed into a short period of time. In the course of discussion I learned that the rains came earlier to the Talodi reaches of the mountains than they did in the north, where one could still risk using vehicles for a few extra weeks.

Next day, at the Mek's modest palace, the great consummation took place. In a spirit of high good humour, accompanied by long dreary speeches, hands were shaken and documents signed. After the long gap of years, the tribes were united under Mek Adam, and welded into one administrative unit.

The day was taken up with a combination of political business and feasting involving the Governor, and Neil, as District Commissioner. Alex and I were merely spectators of this day's events: but we took over on the following morning when we were given the floor, much as had happened at El Obeid. There was a more relaxed air now, assisted by the knowledge that on that evening there was to be an inter-tribal celebration for the massive crowds who had, by now, poured into the town.

Alex spoke his 'party piece' with his usual command and authority, then it was my turn with my now familiar theme of soil conservation. It was an impassioned session, strongly supported by Mek Adam: it seemed to last for hours, after which a group of the most influential sheiks joined together in working out a campaign programme which would be taken to their own villages.

The blue-print which was drawn up then is just as valid today, over fifty years later.[1] Had it been acted on over the intervening years, and had the 'gospel' spread throughout the Sudan, many thousands of lives would have been saved from death by starvation.

Yes, it is easy enough to make plans, to appoint committees and to draft solutions. The difficult part is always seeing the action through. A beginning was made as a result of the Tegali meeting – tree-planting, a growing interest in improved agricultural methods leading to localised action, mass livestock selection, and the rest . . .

A start was made to capture the people's interest. Mek Adam with his new, strong native administration took up the theme and formed working groups among the various tribes, and in the years that followed some changes took place. But the Sudan is vast; it is a poor country; 'conservation' is low in the scale of priorities: most of these countries are preoccupied only with national survival in the short term, while the disaster of soil erosion continues to spread.

Even today, at the eleventh hour, there are solutions . . . solutions which will depend on governments giving up their primitive posturings and using their resources to conserve the land, as well as the people whose lives depend on it.

Here is the greatest challenge, both nationally and internationally, facing the people of the world today – to stop the cycle of destruction affecting the environments of countries worldwide. Success with this would send shock waves of prosperity to every country. If even one country – say the Sudan – could be taken in hand by the rich countries of the world uniting

---

1 See appendix

to give a mere quarter per cent of their 'income' in a great gesture of goodwill, a precedent would be set which, in time, would reverse the whole process. Sadly, the collective mind of governments does not work this way.

Alex and the Governor drove off to El Obeid once the agricultural session was finished, leaving only two of us to contend with the Mek's party.

Neil and I cheerfully anticipated the evening's entertainment. The population of Abassiya had swollen to enormous proportions, most of whom had already participated in field events and trials of strength during the time of the assembly. This final celebration had the promise of being memorable!

We dressed carefully for the occasion – Neil had unearthed his bow tie, and at the appointed hour we marched to the 'arena' to meet the assembled dignitaries. A long row of probably thirty chairs was occupied by the nazirs and other leaders. We walked along shaking each hand in turn, then returned to the middle to sit close to the Mek. Before us, in a wide circle, a great ocean of people waited expectantly for the fun to get under way.

There were bonfires and lanterns at various points providing as much illumination as it was possible to devise. Light refreshment was handed out to the guests – cheerful banter and laughter ran along the line: even the oldest grey-beard was set for a carefree night of fun. The Mek clapped his hands and the company settled back in their chairs. I looked along the line of faces – some with pointed beards, a few with heavy moustaches – eyes reflecting the light from the fires and looking expectantly to the arena.

Drums broke into the usual fiery rhythm and an orchestra of tubed and stringed instruments took up the beat – the same swelling Arab cadences which, at least initially, sound so strange to European ears. A large troupe of female dancers swayed into sight and each one went separately to different parts of the wide circle, then gathered together to dance as a group.

It was always remarkable how quickly the audience took up the spirit of the dance – bodies swaying, hands clapping and eyes alight with pleasure. Dance followed dance, sometimes accompanied by shrill singing, and loud whoops from the crowd and we had to rise, nazirs and inspectors alike, to perform the finger-clicking stamp I had learned previously at Kologi.

A new version cropped up! We learned that it was expected of us to press a piece of money on a dancing girl's forehead. She danced for a few seconds with the money in this position, then tilted her head so that the coin fell between her bare breasts into a fold of cloth round her waist. The dancers must have assumed that we were specially entertained by this action, as they kept returning until we were penniless.

Time went on and the dance became more lively – girls took our hands and led us out where, to the pleasure of all, we made some dancing sallies around the performers. Mek Adam and the others, age was no barrier, rose from their chairs to take their turn, so that we were all caught up in the spirit of the dance.

Neil tapped my shoulder and commanded, 'Follow me!'

Quite unsuspecting I went with him into the darkness beyond the crowd, where he stopped and said, 'Let's show them a British dance!'

I had scarcely ever danced before in my life, but protestations were swept aside as he continued:

'Hurry, it's quite easy: See? This is all we need to do.'

He had me on the go in a second.

'Half a minute Sailors' Hornpipe like this . . . then face each other, hands high – the Highland Fling: on to a circle waltz . . . then . . .'

Blissfully the details are forgotten. Two quick practices, then we returned to the ring. Neil told the Mek that we would perform if he so wished! He jumped up with delight, walked into the arena, raising his arms for silence and called out for all to hear –

'Their Excellencies are now going to demonstrate the 'Dance Englese'.'

I followed Neil into a basin lined with faces – he was actually laughing as if enjoying himself!

We stood in a new silence; face to face, hands on hips – up on toes, bow: arms folded, Hornpipe, etc., etc. I did the Polka when I should have done the Fling, but Neil shouted, 'Keep on jumping!' – which I did. It may have lasted five minutes: it could well have been five hours, but it finished and we returned to our seats.

A howl of acclamation rent the air. Sticks, guns, spears waved in all directions, to the danger of all and sundry. Mek Adam grasped our arms, his face full of admiration at our efforts: he led us back for an encore.

The second time round it was easy!

Well after midnight we undressed in the rest-house. It had been some dance! We chuckled over the events of the evening – it was as well the Governor had left before the dance, though who knows, he would probably have been on the floor as well!

Next morning the first Tegali Agricultural Committee was formally constituted, followed in later weeks by others.

We returned to Rashad. I was in expansive humour and the world looked good. Neil drove right on to El Obeid, leaving me to organise the next trek into the mountains, my last one by car, before the rains came. In the office I wrote up the minutes of the Tegali meetings and thought over the events of the past few days.

How easy it is to consider peasants of a rural economy as backward, even primitive, though they have lived successfully within that economy for centuries. The fact that their environment is deteriorating, albeit by their own acts, need not be cynically condemned by others, because there is scarcely an environment anywhere in the world that has escaped the ravages of man. Closer to home there is ample evidence of people's indifference to their environment. But for the favours endowed by nature, Europe would have become a desert centuries ago!

The interest of the people of Tegali are centred on their land and their animals, and their main concern centres on the security of their families, as one would expect. They have the potential to learn and to change like any other race, and the traditional practices of they years can be altered when understanding comes.

Change, in the Nuba Mountains, would be a painfully slow process perhaps it would come too late, but the signs were there: it could happen!

Entertaining Ladies

Ibrahim obviously noticed my good humour and he decided to put it to good advantage. He came into 'the presence' after lunch, stood smiling for a few seconds, and then announced:

'*Jenabo*, you never have visitors – I would like to bring my new wife and her mother to meet you again, perhaps with a cup of tea.'

This struck me as being unusual – to meet them with a cup of tea. It was not long since he had brought them to the house. But there are times in life when it is difficult to say no!

'Bring them along,' I graciously declared, and without thinking very deeply about the impending entertainment, went about my business.

Ibrahim said as I left, evidently with some feeling of gratitude at my acquiescence, 'I will decorate the house for the occasion, and you shall meet them this evening.'

If I thought at all about his parting remark, I probably pictured Ibrahim picking a vase full of flowers to decorate our sparse furnishings. The afternoon melted away and with work over for the day I returned, having forgotten all about the impending entertainment. I entered the living room to find Ibrahim standing with a beaming smile of welcome – then I looked beyond him: he had indeed decorated the house!

I stared at his artistry – magazines sent from home had been carefully dissected and pages were stuck at random over the walls: stuck down with flour paste. Row upon row, some upside down. I looked in horror, thinking of how interior decorators were non-existent in the mountains. Those lovely cream-coloured walls . . .

'Ibrahim, what have you done?' His face lengthened; sufficiently crestfallen to arrest wrath.

The 'pictures' were still there when the guests arrived – five guests in total: the children turned up too. Ibrahim, by now recomposed, buttled them in. They entered shyly, the older visitors shrouded in robes, with only eyes, fingers and toes visible, and a lovely little girl of perhaps six and two smaller boys. I said to Ibrahim:

'Get the folding trek chairs.'

But no, after we shook hands they sat on the floor, and Ibrahim brought in the tea. I suggested to him that he join us for a cup, but he shook his head energetically:

'*Ana khadim bus!*' (I am only a servant) – and he stood hovering in the background.

I struggled to find a subject to talk about. Nobody ever says 'It's a fine day!' in the Sudan. I amused the children with a few bits and pieces in the house then complimented the wife on her family, then conversation dried up! The tea party lasted a long twenty minutes, then they were all ushered speedily out, leaving me to survey the decorated room.

Follow-up was quite rapid. Within the hour, Ibrahim said:

'I have a big family now and I need a big pay to support them.'

I had known it was sure to come, but he was going to have to work for it.

'Ibrahim,' I said. 'Remove all these pictures and, provided the walls are as good as they were before, you will get your increase.'

He worked long and hard: the walls never looked the same, but he got his money!

Worms in the Bath

With the dry season almost at an end, water was 'tight'. It was brought to the house by prisoners with ankles chained, and with a rifle-carrying soldier in attendance. It was poured into a tank which, by miracles of plumbing, gravitated through several yards of pipe to a wash-hand basin, and a bath. The real miracle was the amount of mud carried by the water, and how it ever succeeded in arriving at the required place.

I bathed, some time after the tea party, lying in the mud and toying with the inevitable population of blood worms, when it entered into my mind again that steps must be taken to remedy the water situation in Rashad. Worms and mud in the bath would drive anyone to desperate acts.

The waterfall at the Rashad garden! I had often thought of the visit I paid to Abu Anga, with the sight of that high-trickling waterfall – was there an answer there?

The maps of Rashad area showed two possible routes to the top of the waterfall – the first one, a long horse ride round Gebel Nimr (Mountain of the Leopard) then up and over the top, to reach the water shed. The other looked very simple; namely a ride to the bottom of the fall, then a climb up the steep cliff at its side. Lying in the bath, a climb seemed easy enough, so a decision was made that almost cost me my life.

Next morning I rode Gamr to the garden, left him in the hands of the Arab gardener, then walked the mile or so into the valley close to the fall, where two steep mountains joined to form a 'V' of sheer rock.

I started to climb – first over tumbled rocks then, for some hundreds of feet through shrubs and trees which clung to rock crevices. Looking upwards, there were ample hand-holds. I threw caution to the winds and continued, enjoying the climb. It became very steep, but still quite climbable, then close to the top, a mass of rotten rock broke free from beneath my feet and I was left clinging, unable to move up or down. My fingers remained locked to hand-holds and, fortunately, my feet found a small ledge.

Stuck! This was it! Far below, almost vertically it seemed, the rocky valley bottom was ready to receive me should I let go. A frantic pattern of thought raced through my mind (thoughts still remembered today!). What a fool I had been: to let it all finish here!

How long I hung there is difficult to say – aching had turned to numbness, until it felt as if to let go would be an escape from pain. Then a voice came from below – looking down between my legs, a climbing figure – I was encouraged to keep my grip that bit longer. A panting, brown figure, the gardener, barefoot, was edging close to my side. 'This way!' – he reached out his hand to pull me towards the waterfall side of the cliff. I felt a shudder of fear at the thought of moving towards the sheer wet rock and signalled for him to approach from the other side. This he did. He stretched out a stick for me to grasp, and somehow my fingers held as I was swung towards a little tree which had found a root-hold in the weathered rock.

We got off that mountain, but only by helping each other hand after hand. Back at the garden I thanked him and tried to compensate him for the risk he had run on my behalf. He smiled, but refused to accept a reward, He said:

'You would have done the same for me.'

'But,' I replied, 'you saved my life!' – which was only too true.

He said: 'Praise be to Allah!' and the subject was closed.

I had failed in two attempts at mountain climbing in the Sudan. By now I had learned my lesson.

I could not forget what the gardener had done. Some time later I returned to see this man, who, I was convinced, had saved my life. I carried some small gift for his family – what it was has long been forgotten.

The man was bent over a plot of vegetables in a corner of the garden. He straightened his back, gave a welcoming smile and touched his forehead in salute. Once again I thanked him, then held out the gift. At first he refused to accept it, saying it was unnecessary for him to be rewarded. Then, slowly he reached out to take it, holding his head down as if this was cause for guilt. He said:

'Excellency, it is I who owe you a debt. Here I have work in the garden: I have a home and my family are fed.'

'That is not the point!' I answered. 'Your work earns you these things. I owe you gratitude because you came to my aid when I might have fallen to my death.'

'No!' he replied emphatically. 'Thanks is to Allah alone! It is the Almighty who caused me to see you on the high cliff; it is he alone who guided me to the place where you were; it is he who gave me strength.'

To this I added, 'And he alone brought us safely down!'

'Yes,' he said. 'Allah is generous: Allah is compassionate.' I agreed with him, because it seemed a miracle that I got off that mountain: in these conclusions there was nothing to divide us.

My God – his Allah: the one true god. We were united in this awareness. Once again I was troubled by the things which separated – and yet united – believing people. I thought for long after of the question of goodness – or is it Godliness – which is to be found in people of all races and creeds, something which is more enduring than that which separates.

Habibala's Party

There was urgent work to be done in Talodi so we travelled there in one long day's drive. I was beginning to sense the approach of the rains. One morning had brought a drop of temperature from 101°F to 65°F in a few hours, so that I shivered as if it was mid-winter. Cultivators were thinking of seed-time; rainmakers were preparing to invoke the spirits.

I could fit in two days at Talodi before the Nuba Gathering at Heiban then it would be a rush northwards again to prepare the ground for the arrival of the *hafir*-digging machinery. There would be no more time off for a very long time – every day counted!

We were settling in for the night when a figure appeared in the circle of the lamp. Quickly I recognised one of the club members, Habibala Younis by name, a senior clerk here at Talodi. He was easily recognised because of his portly figure and walrus moustache.

He gripped my hand. 'Allah is great!' he said. 'It is all over, it is all over! Praise be to Allah!'

I stood up – the war had ended? Hitler defeated? But no. . . He continued: 'I have a new son, praise be to the Almighty!'

I knew that the praise was much deserved because Habibala was by no means young, and he had a recent new young bride.

'Tomorrow I am entertaining guests to celebrate the birth: you must come.' My mind ranged over the workload and the potential effect of a party on its completion.

'I will come, but only after midday.' I knew that festivities in the mountains were by no means brief, and prone to last an entire day.

'You honour me.'

The die was cast – one moment an almost impossible work schedule, the next moment a party!

Dawn the following morning brought with it an unexpected announcement from Ibrahim.

'Sir, your hair is too long, you must get it cut.'

He had never said this before; perhaps the remark had been triggered by the two impending celebrations – Habibala's, and the Governor General's at Heiban.

Yes, now that he mentioned it, my hair *was* long!

Hair-cutting in the mountains was normally effected by a dagger, resulting in a style which might be termed 'billiard ball', and one that I considered inappropriate. Occasionally there was an ex-soldier who could wield scissors; it turned out there was one such in Talodi. The 'barber' in question owned a little coffee shop but, unfortunately, he was away for the duration of the rains. Another five months was too long to wait so I asked around, ever hopeful.

Did I not know that Mustafa the ginnery mechanic cuts hair? This sounded a possibility, so I moved on to the ginnery and explained my needs to Mustafa – a six-foot-six giant with hands like hams. He had never cut an inspector's hair before, but he would try! I sat in a chair amongst the ginning presses and waited while he searched for his tools. He returned with a smile of pleasure, together with a horse-sized pair of clippers and a six-inch dagger. There was still time to cancel the contract but, instead, I closed my eyes – perhaps I prayed.

The first few flicks of the clippers into my forelock removed a tuft by the roots. His big hand, despite howls of protest, seemed unstoppable. I grasped his fist and it sank in that something was wrong. Firmly, the clippers were relegated to a nearby table to join hammers, files and other blunt instruments. Reflection in a pane of glass showed me a white, hairless patch of skin just off centre. The operation was finished using the dagger, but to the accompaniment of detailed instruction from the chair.

Indeed, my hair was cut! It took months to recover, but in this part of the world the new hairstyle was as acceptable as any other.

In due course I arrived at Habibala's home, a square mud-built house with a flat roof and a surrounding courtyard. There were two rooms, both of which had been gutted of wife, child, and the larger furnishings, to accommodate husband and an already assembled crowd of almost fifty men.

They rose to a man to greet me – I noticed that some were Nuba, but most were Arabs. All of them had an Arab-style dress and apparently they belonged to a richer level of the Talodi population. When I spoke the words '*It fad'l*,' (be seated) they settled on to the floor and resumed their conversations. I noticed with some interest that the two races were intermingling, something fairly uncommon. A number of the guests came in turn to speak with me, taking the opportunity of my presence to raise issues on the coming season's grain campaign, the scarcity of sugar, price of cotton and as many other points.

One of the fattest men I had ever seen stood up to make a speech of congratulation to the happy father. This man, a celebrated camel contractor, Nazir Toomsah – *toomsah* is the Arabic word for hippopotamus – thoroughly deserved the name; presumably it was not his real one. He laughed at his own wit and it was of interest to all present to watch the rippling bulges of fat.

Then came an interlude with the call to prayer. Some members of the crowd carefully removed their sandals, then knelt in a row while one of them intoned words from the Koran. Others present continued with their noisy conversation, apparently careless of disturbing the devotions.

Prayers over, it was soon time for food. I was among the ten guests selected for the first sitting. We sat in circles round two large platters set on a dais and laden with food – a whole leg of mutton, rice, *kisra* (millet bread) and spicy sauces.

Fingers tore at the flesh and handfuls disappeared into hungry mouths. I did my bit by holding the leg firmly while they tore at the last vestiges of meat. All around were wet, sticky hands and mouths, smacking lips, the sound of eructations of wind. Somehow my appetite had gone! I did sample the fare, however; an essential courtesy on the part of a guest.

Other courses followed and the amount of food consumed was indeed remarkable. Finally the diners staggered to their feet to permit the next group to attack a fresh leg of mutton.

The party opened my eyes to an aspect of mountain life I had scarcely known existed. Even here, in the far remoteness of Talodi, there was an affluent, well-fed class apparently finding wealth amid a race of people living in poverty and very often at starvation level. It gave an elementary lesson on how the producer or peasant scratches a bare subsistence, while those who distribute, or own land, succeed in accumulating wealth. The 'simple' peasant carries the rich merchant or landowner on his shoulders.

Well wasn't this just business opportunism, something in modern terms to be praised? I left the party later that night just a little troubled that whatever might be done to improve the lot of the cultivators, there would be some who would glean the majority of the wealth for themselves.

The Nuba Gathering

I had been warned that rains started early in the southern mountains, yet the first storm came as a shock. There was an element of terror in it!

It was the night before the Nuba Gathering. I was alone at the Talodi rest-house, asleep in the garden, when it arrived with an almighty crash. Months of drought, then to waken to a crash of thunder with driving rain washing over my face. I staggered out of the wet mosquito-net, collected all the bedding and fought against a sudden gale to the shelter of the house.

Ibrahim turned up too late to be useful, then I lay on damp bedding in the now cold and draughty barn of a house – that dreadful house! Thunder echoed from the hills and rain hit the tin roof like a hundred kettle-drums.

The storm continued for an hour – then came a long continuous drip, drip from the eaves. I lay shivering – and very lonely. Even after two years from home, I was not beyond being homesick. The scant information that reached the mountains about the war gave the impression it could still go on for years. Leave, home to Scotland, was just an impossible dream. The storm – the house – whatever the cause, I lay awake all night, yet with sunrise and the appearance of Ibrahim with the morning cup, everything changed and I rose to the prospect of a day with the GG and the Nuba.

Approaching Heiban, it looked as if the entire population of the area was on the move, heading for the gathering. At 3 p.m. I parked the box-car behind the *Merkaz* (Administration Office) then set off on foot towards a prepared arena not far from the village. It was a perfect setting for an epic event: the blue backdrop of the mountains contrasted strongly with the iron-red soil, and all around milled a throng of naked or scantily-clothed people.

There was a little canvas-and-wood stand capable of seating thirty guests and, as I was the first white person to arrive, I made my way to the rear to sit beside some nazirs and meks. The crowd was being gathered together by native police to form a wide circle – a good-humoured crowd, like one at a football match, only happy and apparently non-partisan. There appeared to be every possible device for making noise – drums, guns, old bugles; indeed, there were hundreds of rifles on show. I had once heard that after the Mahdiya (in which many Nuba had taken part), 20,000 rifles

With Neil DC at Heiban mission station.

disappeared into Kordofan and the Nuba Mountains – as I looked around I could judge the story to be true. Rifles without a source of ammunition presented little threat, so authority tended to turn a blind eye.

Every few seconds a man ran into the arena, made extravagant gestures with his rifle, then fired at an invisible enemy. With homemade blank ammunition, when there was a loud bang, the crowd cheered; very often there was a gentle pop which raised laughter. It seemed a miracle that bodies were not dropping to the ground on all sides. Others darted out with shields, and club or spear, dodging or parrying the thrusts of invisible enemies. Hundreds of onlookers took their turn in a good-natured, spontaneous exhibition, though the real show had not yet started.

Other officials turned up and some army officers, missionaries and a visiting doctor; all there to witness the spectacle of the year.

At 4 p.m. the official car drove over the arena to the little stand. Throats cheered hoarsely, guns fired. The GG stepped out, resplendent in dress uniform and waving a fly whisk at the crowd. The Province Governor, with Neil, followed at his heels. We, in the stand, stood at respectful attention to be introduced in turn, then we returned to our seats as the show started with a vengeance.

A throaty yell rent the air at the far side of the arena, then a mass of painted 'savages' bearing the entire impedimenta of war set off in mad charge towards us. Fortunately, this was part of the programme. They drew

Nuba wrestling.

up only when we could see the whites of their eyes, and an accompanying dust-cloud settled over everyone.

Forty splendid giants in full regalia of paint and feathers, and with rattles strung round ankles and wrists, seemed to blot out the landscape.

Now began the war-dance – backwards, forwards in line, waving spears and shields to the accompaniment of raucous chanting and beating of drums. Pounding feet made the ground tremble, the heavy smell of bodies filled the air. It looked fierce, but always one could sense the rhythm and harmony of dance which is peculiarly African. Even giant warriors tire. Finally they retreated, walking backwards and bowing towards the guests.

It was the next event, inter-tribal wrestling, which had been most eagerly awaited by the crowd – it can be considered the 'national' sport of the Nuba. Pure man-to-man combat, primitive and genuine.

Representatives of two tribes adopted stances at either side of our dais. Murmurs ran round the crowd as the people discussed their champions. Each group performed a strutting dance like turkey-cocks building an appetite for battle. Two lines of combatants moved in parallel dancing in threat as if to inspire fear. Feet thumped the ground, hands slapped hips, then with a loud yell they jumped high from the ground.

Back in their corners, fighters were stripped for action until they wore only metal wrist bangles with the appearance of knuckle-dusters.

Now there is complete silence: two warriors step forward, then arms held high they let their chests come together; this courtesy over, they turn away for a few seconds then, crouching almost double, they circle warily round and round seeking the advantage.

An attempted strike with one of the bangles, then another – this is more than wrestling, because there is blood on the arm of one of the fighters; now a clutch, two great men almost equally matched. Taut muscles, streams of sweat and slowly one man is lifted bodily from the ground and flung on his back. The bout is won!

The victor's tribe roars acclamation and the victor struts triumphantly beating his chest and throwing back his head. Many bouts follow, all of them similar, but each one exciting. Sometimes faces are badly cut and a 'referee' separates the combatants, declaring the man who struck the blow, victor!

The entire display was impressive though brutal, yet, in the context of a warrior people like the Nuba, it was somehow acceptable.

There followed a hilltop race in which a large crowd of naked Nuba participated, then tribal dances, and various trials of strength. During the proceedings, an aide-de-camp ushered the guests in turn to a seat next to the GG. My turn came and the GG proved himself knowledgable about the Nuba and my work. He said: 'You know, you are getting a lot of machinery to dig *hafirs* in the mountains – they shall be arriving in a few days' time. I expect to come and see your handiwork later in the month. Do you think it will make any impact on the water situation?'

I enthused over the prospects. Later I asked him about modern slaving in the Sudan and he told me it still went on, with children being sold into bondage to become servants and concubines. This was a practice not easily stopped.

With my time allocation up, I returned to my seat as a fresh display of fighting got under way, this time with highly dangerous wooden staves which frequently drew blood.

The exhibition continued until twilight. The Governor rose to walk through the crowd followed by the occupants of the stand and to the accompaniment of noisy cheers; then the show was over and we went our separate ways.

There had been neither a breath nor a whisper of antagonism by the Nuba at the sight of the 'flag'. The event could not have been more splendid; past suspicions were apparently forgotten. Would the future change this peaceful state? Presumably it could not continue like this forever.

Excavations

The parties were over. It was time to get back to serious business; back into the bush and away from the crowds.

We were home again at Rashad and faced with a future of living in tents, with excavating machines churning the virgin soils of the mountains. I called the boys together to explain our future programme; at least three weeks digging *hafirs*, then off on horseback when the rains started. For me the prospect was exciting, but Ibrahim had a different view.

'That means we shall be away for months: that is no way to live!'

Here was the first sign of wavering on the part of my fellow-travellers, but he probably had good reason as he had scarcely had a day with his new bride and family since the wedding. Then I piled on the agony:

'We are travelling in the Merkaz lorry instead of the box-car as I will need it to carry equipment for the machines.'

Even Mahomed winced at this prospect. The steel-bodied, sturdy little lorry was not built for passenger comfort, particularly when travellers had to sit in the rear. Add to that the fact that in some areas there would be no roads, as we were breaking ground in this attempt to establish new communities far from the existing eroded village areas: it would be hard going!

I told Mahomed to take food with us for a month. Considering the dry fare of the mountains that should be easy enough – a sack of grain, one of pulses, our sugar allocation, salt, fruit from the garden to last as long as possible, and that was about it. Perhaps we might buy some meat at a village with luck. There were more important things to consider than food, which rated low in the scale of priorities then.

Neil, meanwhile, had left to trek the Western Jebels, and it was open to question whether we would meet again in the next six months, as he was leaving for the north to miss the rains. In a few weeks' time I would have the Nuba Mountains all to myself (as far as white skin was concerned) apart from the few missionaries who stayed and weathered it out.

With the lorry loaded and the boys sitting gloomily in the rear beside a large square water tank and a full load of trek gear and equipment, we bumped out of Rashad on the long road to Terter, and the first excavation site. Ten miles further on a tyre burst!

Jacoub, who had transferred from driving the car, got out to change the wheel which he brought for my inspection – it was almost threadbare. Circles of canvas showed where tread should have been. The other tyres were little better. This was not uncommon in the Sudan where, because of the war, new tyres were unobtainable.

It did not augur well for our coming expedition, but there was no point in returning to Rashad; we would have to make the best of it. We reached Terter in the evening, tired, but in reasonable spirits considering the many discomforts en route. An elderly white-bearded sheikh, Babikr by name, was expecting our arrival as he had been forewarned during my earlier visit to the village. Local knowledge would be invaluable.

The tent was erected beside the village, Mahomed set to preparing the evening meal, and Babikr and I peered at some rudimentary maps of the area. There were to be five sites in all, roughly in a line, and each approximately ten miles apart. From the map, I chose the first district to be examined: about twenty miles east of Terter, on virgin soil, and at a distance from the eroded plateau around the village. Later that night I listened to Sheikh Babikr as he told the tales of his people, their involvement with the Mahdi and of the cruel days before the uprising. A natural storyteller, he spoke on with a gently modulating voice, spinning romance out of old histories. He spoke frankly about British rule – 'just and honest, but cold and impersonal'. What did the British really know about the Sudan and the needs of its people? I ventured that our present mission to build large *hafirs* must be a benefit to the people.

'That is good,' he said. 'We of the *Aulad Himeid* could never do such things by ourselves – may Allah bless your efforts!'

Next morning, with the rising sun, we left on our search – Babikr, the driver and myself. The lorry was virtually empty now and it bounced uncomfortably over a rutted drove track which led eastwards in the direction of the Nile, probably eighty or ninety miles away.

The warm sun shone straight into our eyes as we left behind the low hills of Terter and entered an interminable, sparsely-vegetated plain. Apart from scattered rock outcrops there was nothing at all to relieve the scene. Could people ever be encouraged to live in this expanse of nothingness? Yet, with good soil and adequate water the primary ingredients for life are there, and the people with their nomadic instincts would not be slow to take advantage of it.

The vehicle appeared to sit down with a groan – a spike of wood had penetrated the tyre. I helped Jacoub to jack up the lorry and screw on the rather weary-looking replacement. The sun, already high, brought out beads of perspiration; gratefully we settled to continue the journey. One mile further, and the 'new' spare gave out.

I exchanged meaningful glances with the driver. We climbed down to renew the struggle while Babikr sat back patiently in the cab, no doubt conjecturing on the greater reliability of camels.

By the time patches were slipped between tyre and tube and the puncture mended, knuckles had parted with skin and my mouth was caked with salt. The milky-white fluid in the goatskin tasted more abominable than usual, but somehow it was 'good'!

A further five miles, then another blow-out. Were these tyres going to prejudice the entire operation? I groaned with frustration, but Babikr came to the rescue. 'See!' he pointed to a knoll, about a mile ahead. 'That is a suitable place to dig, as a watercourse passes close by!'

We went on foot, leaving the driver with the tyre problem. All around, the soil was fertile, heavy clay with wide drought cracks, excellent soil for cropping millet, or even cotton for that matter. The mound, a mixture of gravel and sand, seemed a perfect place to found a new village; the surrounding networks of dry *khors* would provide an ample water flow to fill a large *hafir*.

The more I examined the site, the better it looked. It should not be difficult to design a suitable water store: the great imponderable was whether it would be large enough for the water to span the dry season. I looked across the interminable plain, a shimmering landscape devoid of human habitation – could this be changed so that it supported a population, or was it an impertinence even to try?

I spent two hours making drawings – the mound was a perfect base for the machinery once it got as far as this. Babikr sat patiently on a fallen tree-trunk occasionally making suggestions – then everything changed dramatically. A black swarm of angry bees literally landed on top of us. They arrived from nowhere and became entangled in hair and clothes before we could escape – a mad dash followed to the shelter of the lorry: even Babikr showed a fine turn of speed.

In the cab we counted our wounds – I had three stings, but the Sheikh must have been of choicer stuff as it took quite a time to extract stings from arms, neck and other parts.

The *hafirs* were being bought at a price!

With the tyre by now repaired, we eased the lorry gently back towards Terter and somehow arrived without further mishap.

In the same way, four other sites were investigated, close to tumbledown villages at Mishatnat, Wakera, Gir-Gir and another nameless spot precisely in the middle of nowhere.

In due course another vehicle arrived with more dependable tyres, then, thankfully, the Rashad lorry headed for home.

On a hot afternoon in Abbasiya, Mek Adam's village, a crowd gathered looking towards the north where a cloud of dust was to be seen approaching from the far distant railway station. I stood with the Mek and a group of sheikhs; we had waited some hours for this event, the arrival of the machines. The people were familiar with donkeys, camels and the occasional vehicle, but roaring diesel engines – no!

The dust cloud arrived. From out of its midst emerged a flotilla of gigantic yellow caterpillar tractors, five in number, and each trailing a 'carryall' excavator, then, bringing up the rear, a smaller machine equipped as a bulldozer. In seconds, the sleepy mud-brick town became transformed into something resembling the bustling confusion of a frontier boom-town. They had done me proud in Khartoum! I shared some of the villagers' awe at this invasion. People leaned on their sticks at a safe distance; village pye-dogs skulked out of sight.

The Mek welcomed the black drivers and quickly identified their leader who, as it turned out, had originally left the Nuba Mountains twenty years before. Then a solitary support truck turned up bearing with it stocks of fuel, a five-hundred-gallon tank, and what looked like a workbench, with a sketchy collection of nuts, bolts, and spanners.

To celebrate the event an assembly was called for the evening to launch the campaign with appropriate speeches, and to provide a 'feast' for the visitors.

The entire community turned out for the occasion. The gaping population lined the roads as an impressive procession moved through the town. Memory easily retains the image of Mek Adam clutching tightly to his seat in the leading machine, while his sheikhs sat equally uncomfortably in those that followed.

Never before had there been anything like this influx of technology: it was an occasion the seers and story-tellers would recount for years to come.

The machines finally gathered in a wide circle as crowds circulated around, trying to imagine what they did and why they had come; then the speeches flowed.

'. . . Life in Tegali will be transformed as monstrous *hafirs* are excavated. There shall be water where previously there was only drought!'

If anything, the speeches erred on the optimistic side: it might be successful, it might not – time would tell.

By the late evening a slight cloud appeared on the horizon: because of the villagers' generous hospitality, several of the drivers were drunk. It was as well that work was about to be executed far in the wilderness, beyond the reach of local vice!

Early the following morning I drove off to Gir-Gir, the first site to be excavated, with Sheikh Babikr still in close support. He had lasted the pace well and seemed determined to follow the work through to its conclusion.

On arrival, the boys set up camp and I struggled with a dumpy-level, charting the area, and completing the design of the *hafir*. At the first glance the site looked no different from the surrounding plain, but there were slight undulations in the ground at suitable places, with a good-sized *khor* running through, big enough to feed the *hafir*. Close by stood a low hill which could be a desirable feature in the rains when flat clay becomes a quagmire of mud. As for soil, there were tens of thousands of good acres stretching far and wide on all sides.

With pegs knocked in to the ground at appropriate points as a guide to the tractor men, everything was finally in order for an early morning start on the following day. In retrospect, and by the time it was finished, the entire operation was notable for its simplicity: no civil engineers visited the scene or were ever consulted, presumably budgetary procedures were of the simplest, designs were worked out by an inspector who used a 'level' for the first time in his life and the supply line for spares was hundreds of miles long. The very mechanics on the tractors had no one who could be termed a foreman.

Everyone just got on with the job, and it worked!

By evening the machines were arranged in a neat row with the drivers, obviously well trained, fuelling and greasing, ready for an early start. A wood fire lighted the surrounding scrub sending sparks high into the sky. The 'engineers' played cards far into the night: Mahomed and Ibrahim kept their distance from them!

Despite the array of powerful machines with their oily smells, the air reverberated as always with the noise of crickets, and the vastness of starry space reduced everything to perspective.

Soon after dawn an almighty roar of diesel engines shattered the peace, and the first deep sliver of soil was gouged out and deposited where the earth walls of the *hafir* were due to rise.

The native drivers handled their machines with skill so that before our eyes, a transformation came about. Two days later I could look down from high earth walls to an excavation with a base larger than half the size of a football pitch. Long arms of soil stretched out to receive the waters when the *khor* flooded. Nine feet below original soil level, there was still the same impermeable clay.

Meanwhile, I had moved on to plan the next site at Wakera, ready for when the machines turned up after the first *hafir* was completed.

That evening the supply truck delivered a telegram from Alex. 'Meet GG and self at Rahad p.m. on Monday. Visiting hafirs.'

The expected visit of the Governor General and his staff – and it was the very next day! I was gripped by some slight sense of panic – would they approve of the work done on the first *hafir*? Was the design correct? Would it hold water? Were the levels correct? All sorts of uncertainties came to mind, and I was persuaded to hurry back to Gir-Gir to make sure that the work done would match the occasion of the GG's visit.

At the site the sun was setting. Impressive earth walls rose higher than the flat-topped thorn trees – I clambered up to look, thrilled at an excavation which, by now, was simply immense. The machines, still scraping and digging, looked tiny in the depression. The GG must be satisfied!

That night before going to bed, Ibrahim said mysteriously 'Have you seen up there in the sky . . .?'

Seen what? I looked upwards but saw nothing unusual.

'Look, there at the moon!'

Following his pointing finger, there was something I had never seen before – Venus, the evening star, radiantly bright, was so close to the points of a young moon as to appear to be within its circle.

By now, the drivers were also staring and wondering. Ibrahim said:

'It must be a portent, for *el Zohar* ('the flower' – the name for Venus) to sit there: perhaps it is wrong to disturb this old land!' He shook his head: 'After all, the land is Raboonah's (the Creator's) and man has no right to tear it apart.'

The drivers listened with some interest – could it be that they were tempting providence by their actions? Then they laughed, which came as a relief. They were from the city and less likely to be influenced by such superstitions, so the subject was closed.

Yet it was an unusual sight, and who could tell . . .?

Next morning Babikr decided to accompany me on the journey to pick up the GG. It seemed appropriate to give him this trip after his patient help over recent days, and in any case, I quite enjoyed his company. Unlike other Arabs, he never carried a donkey stick or a staff, but invariably took with him a rather antiquated rifle which, since I had met him, had never been fired. I had thought that it was probably just a prestige symbol carried for show.

We were bowling along at a good speed when a solitary ostrich took it into its head to challenge us to a race, running probably 20 yards from the car. Babikr lifted the rifle and took aim: it seemed he was merely amusing himself and pretending to fire, so I paid no heed and drove on; after all, the rifle was just an 'ornament'.

There came a sudden, sharp crack and the ostrich dropped dead! Amazed and shocked, I stopped and grabbed Babikr's arm – too late now! Ostriches are protected creatures and one of my duties was to further that protection. I had virtually condoned the crime by letting it happen – and the GG would return this way in a few hours' time.

I berated the rather self-satisfied Sheikh, then we went to look at the large bird – a male. Babikr began to pluck out tail feathers – never! I was not going to be caught with incriminating evidence in the car! We moved on.

Later, a procession of four cars left the station to drive towards Abbasiya and the new *hafir*. I drove the lead car with the GG at my side; Alex and the Governor sat behind – lesser fry followed in the other vehicles. At Abbasiya, Mek Adam joined the party and we drove on towards Gir-Gir. This was no mean occasion, it appeared.

I held my breath as the place where the ostrich had been shot drew near – how could a newly shot ostrich be explained away? Unbelievably it was shrouded in vultures, so many as to totally obscure the remains: it might have been anything, and no comments were passed.

At the *hafir* I took them to a selected point where the view was most impressive; we climbed the steep earth walls. The tractors were making their final passes before moving on to the next site. It made a splendid picture. One hour later, having toured the entire excavation area, we all sat to a sumptuous picnic which had come with the party.

The *hafir* was 'just what was needed! Impressive! Most interesting!' Then they all left and, once again, I was alone with my thoughts.

Four *hafirs* were completed in like manner. Many difficulties arose, sufficient to show that the drivers were also worthy of the name of engineers. When breakdowns occurred, as they did frequently on the hard clay soil, clever repairs and improvisations quickly set the excavators in motion again. In one *hafir*, machines dug through the clay and into a layer of sand which required replacement of some of the clay and an alteration in design. Then the skies became heavy with the threat of rain and I considered it expedient to stop operations before the final *hafir* was finished, in case the equipment became trapped in the mountains. In the short period of work at Tegali a score of four out of five was quite satisfactory. Perhaps others could be dug in the next dry season once their value was proved and the people were seen to benefit.

On the very last evening before saying goodbye to the drivers and their machines, we were camped close to Mushatnat village – it was scarcely a village, more a collection of dilapidated stick-and-straw huts: as poor a habitation as it is possible to imagine. The only water source was a miserable mud hole used by animals as well as man, and could be smelled at a distance.

Now, the village boasted one of the largest *hafirs* in the country, a reservoir which should fill up in a matter of weeks and completely change the quality of life of the people.

Occasional lightning flashes reminded me forcibly of the coming storms. I should have been home in Rashad by now, trying out the *hamla* (trek animals) and preparing for the coming travels through the mountains.

A loneliness gripped me. I could hear the drivers laughing over a game of cards, in high spirits because of their imminent return to Khartoum. The boys crouched round a fire in earnest conversation, equally pleased at the prospect of movement once more.

This life of trek had its high moments, but who to share them with? I looked back to the time when a solitary life of trek seemed the perfect life, but it had been impossible to anticipate the effect of solitude. The boys were company after a fashion, but there were limits to the ways in which they could meet such a need. Alex darted in and out of my life like a will-o'-the-wisp! There was no one else.

Introspection did not grip me often; perhaps it was the prospect of change once more. Travelling by horse in the rains, what would it really be like? Head sunk on my chest I walked slowly into the bush until the halo of light from the fire was far in the distance. Dead grass crackled beneath my feet – the world was empty. There sounded a crash in the bush, followed by a short squeal not many yards away: an animal had made a kill, though what kind of animal I could not guess.

A cool breeze moved the grass making me shiver involuntarily. A few more steps, then my ears picked up another sound. Hastily now, I retraced my steps to the camp, anxious to return to the security of the fire, when I saw a stationary figure in the shadows, silhouetted against the light. It was certainly not one of the camp personnel – I moved up as silently as I could, then called out: 'What do you want? Who are you?'

Only silence – the figure looked as if about to run off.

I called: 'Stop! Tell me what you are doing there!'

There came now almost in a whisper:

'Allah bless you, *Jenabo*!'

It sounded like a woman's voice – but how could it be? I returned a greeting and said:

'Follow me, let me speak with you.'

Only very slowly she followed me to the trek table where I sat down, and she stood a few yards away, head bent in silence.

'Tell me please why you have come here. Is there anything I can do?'

Then the voice – it was indeed female – spoke almost in a whisper:

'You are a government man: you are bringing water to my village . . .'

'Yes' I said. 'Do you think the new *hafir* will be big enough for you?'

She ignored the question. 'I just wanted to see you. I have been listening to the noise of the great machines and I heard that the work is finished, and tomorrow you are leaving.'

'Yes, I have to move on to other work. But have you come here just to look at me?'

'Goodbye, I must return to my home.' She made to move off.

I was still puzzled at her answers, so I called out: 'No, stay! Tell me about yourself and your family.'

She hesitated. 'My name is Zohar. I wanted to see you because my mother's father was *Englesi*.'

She moved off into the darkness. Her grandfather an Englishman! And her name Zohar (the flower) that of Venus, the evening star which only a few nights before had assumed that unusual position in the moon's circle.

My mood was transformed, I could but marvel at life and its continuous gift of the unexpected.

Horse Trek

By now there was a feeling of excitement in Rashad that was difficult to define. It could be seen in the actions of the people staring anxiously at the sky, and turning frequently to sniff the wind, as if they expected some cataclysmic event to take place.

The ground, still parched from months of drought, was cracked and dead, with trees reduced to the appearance of lifeless skeletons, so that it came as a surprise to find buds poised to open with the very first shower. Water-holes were virtually dry and yielding minute quantities, which were patiently collected and carried away on the heads of the carriers. Wind, which for months had carried the dust of erosion and the smoke of forest fires, was edging to the west, and bringing with it the dank smell of new wet soil. Rains were cruelly slow in coming this year. Grass, by now, should have sprung, with starved cattle eating their fill again, but both man and animals still suffered patiently.

The rains might fail or at least be poor – that had happened in the past. Everyone knew that it depended on the 'spirits'. Rainmakers had exacted their usual levies from the anxious cultivators, but the angry spirits were demanding a second, even a third tribute. Still, it remained dry.

The prospect of being cut off from the outside world for several months had no bearing on the people's anxiety; after all, this was home ground: only inspectors and merchants normally scuttled away to healthier places in the north, leaving the tribes to pursue their ages-old way of life undisturbed.

Some eyebrows were no doubt raised that the Inspector of Agriculture was staying behind – the Rashad people, for some weeks now, had witnessed his *hamla* of eight horses exercising on trails around the village, making ready for the time when watercourses flooded and trails were broken up – there must be something afoot!

With *hafir*-digging over for the season, I was sharing in the exercises. Hundreds of miles on horseback over the coming weeks required greater stamina than riding in a box-car. It also required detailed planning. The grooms, and the boys, Mahomed and Ibrahim, had to know all that was expected of them, and there was that little matter of being certain of my own objectives. This kind of trekking was no game to be taken lightly: it could well be dangerous, it would certainly be hard.

We had to be self-contained, carrying everything needed for life-support, from tanks of water to a mere bandage. Two of the horses would be carrying water tanks, hitched to special wooden-framed saddles: four would carry trek gear with the boys and grooms riding on top. That left the two larger horses – Bakhit and Gamr, to be ridden by the head groom and myself.

Various facts about trekking had become clear since coming to Rashad. These were jotted down for later use – for example:

HORSES drink up to 5 gallons of water per day
HORSES eat up to 9–10 lbs of grain per day
FANTAS (saddle tank) holds 5 gallons – weight full is 76 lbs.
HORSES carry 150–180 lbs on trek (camel carries twice as much)

Carry the following drugs etc. when on trek

> Chlorodyne
> Quinine
> Aspirin
> Calomel
> Epsom Salts
> Castor Oil
> Tinct. of iodine
> Solution of 1% picric acid
> Boric acid powder
> Zinc ointment
> Permanganate of Potash
> Lint wool and gauze
> Bandages
> Jaconet
> Eye Bath
> Forceps
> Scissors

There was other good advice –

BITES OF WILD ANIMALS – paint thoroughly with tincture of iodine. Do not attempt to wash.

BITES OF SNAKE OR SCORPION – Suck wound, apply tourniquet, incise over the bite freely and then rub in permanganate of potash. There is no virtue in excessive doses of alcohol.

ULCERS – treat with hot fomentations, then apply boracic or zinc ointment on lint.

BROKEN LIMBS – cut away clothes: paint wound with tincture of iodine and apply a dressing. Straighten the broken limb and compare it with the other side. Place bones end to end: use rifle or any available stick as splint.

HEAT STROKE – get the temperature down quickly by using 'ice' packs or wet sheets. Evaporate by fanning.

In fact, there was information for action to take in every possible emergency. It had to be hoped that it would be unnecessary to apply any of the above, but if the worst came to the worst in coming weeks, I would need to be my own doctor.

The route I would take was partly over uncharted country, uninhabited due to the lack of permanent water: there would be an opportunity to examine soils, with the continuing hope that areas of potential development might be found. The greatest risk of trekking in such country was the absence of water-holes or, conversely, the flooding of clay plains, when blind watercourses spilled their torrents over wide stretches of country. From a health point of view, the rains magnified the risk of disease, as insect 'carriers' multiplied: extra precautions would have to be taken because to be ill in the bush far from doctors or hospitals, in fact, beyond their reach, was a risk to be taken seriously.

From an agricultural viewpoint it was the right time to be in the Nuba Mountains: it was the time when 'everything' happened – crops were sown, erosion brought about by storms could be witnessed; in fact, it was the time to be among the people and to show the 'flag'.

One important decision remained – when to set out. With the rains being late, roads were still intact, and it seemed ridiculous to be setting out on horse when a car would have served; there was also the risk of water-holes being dry. But the 'signs' had become so obvious that I sent off a last wire to Alex, and made up my mind to leave the following morning.

Insects of every kind had appeared as from nowhere, including a new arrival, Dud el Matar – the rain bug which could be seen in numbers crawling over the soil. More picturesquely, the stubby grotesque poison tree had become transformed within hours into a beautiful pillar of pink flowers.

In the evening, with everything ready for an early departure, I sat on the *mustaba* sensing the thrill of approaching storm. Drums throbbed incessantly in the village accompanied by occasional cries, as if the spirits were being invoked. An electric storm flashed overhead, lighting up the hilltops. A wave of cool air moved the branches of trees, sending a shiver through my body, and the soft hiss of the pressure lamp changed to protesting splutters, as wind ruffled the flame.

The stars were by now swallowed up by inky blackness – there was a taste of wetness in the air; then, with a violent crash of thunder, the first raindrops fell, singly at first, then with a violence which lifted spume into the air. After several minutes, sufficient to send little rivulets of water tearing over the surface of the ground, it stopped again, suddenly, as if orchestrated, leaving only the sound of drips from the house thatch.

From inside the house, I noticed that drums were now stilled, leaving only a brooding silence. I slept indoors, if sleep it could be called because of stifling humidity, and the occasional rumbles of thunder echoing in the hills.

By first light the house was astir, the boys carrying boxes to be laid out for my inspection, and the grooms lining up horses for a final examination before being saddled. To my surprise, dry soil had sopped up the night's rain, and the ground was drying even as I looked.

I had deliberately organised an easy first day of 30 miles down the familiar road to Abu Gubeiha: an opportunity for a 'shake down', by both men and animals. There was no real hurry to depart.

The horses stood patiently with their respective loads and riders, beside them. The two taller horses, Bakhit and Gamr, carried with them an air of superiority, not being required to carry clumsy loads like the others; smoothly groomed and saddled, they might have been entering a point-to-point.

The new names of the pack animals were by now well established, and their idiosyncrasies known to the grooms.

Nugta – (Spot) a black horse with a white flank patch, was assigned the job of carrying my personal kit, with Ibrahim seated on top.

Bortugan – (Orange) was Mahomed's mount. It was going to be carrying two steel boxes containing kitchen and table gear. A collection of pots and a few bags of food would complete his load.

Amir – (Prince) and Fantas – (name for a water container) would carry no riders as they were the strongest of the pack animals and were thought most able to carry the heavy water tanks. It was planned that as the water was gradually consumed, loads would be redistributed to ease the other animals.

Barmel – (Barrel) was to carry a full load of tents and furniture, together with one of the grooms.

Flash (so called after a horse from my early days on the farm) was booked to carry all the remaining furnishings and oddments, such as valise and mosquito nets. He too would carry a groom.

Part of the arrangement was that a Nuba guide would accompany us, riding a donkey, and also a native policeman, acting as a mounted escort for the first stages of the trek.

It took an hour or two to saddle up and settle all of the loads into place – this day was more or less a rehearsal, and we were as well to take it easily and enjoy ourselves in the process. The boys laughed and chattered with excitement, making it sound like the start of a holiday jaunt; obviously Ibrahim had easily reconciled himself to a separation from his new family.

Then it was time to go! In single file, as we were to trek in coming days, we rode out of the village, with the Nuba in the lead, and the askari bringing up the rear. A small crowd had watched our preparations then cheered us on our way.

For the first few miles dry roads showed little sign of the previous night's rain, then a transition took place as we rode into an area where there had been more rainfall than at Rashad. Grass was springing on every side, transforming land which had seemed sterile and barren into a green carpet with all the promise of life replenished. In patches, a miraculous blossoming of multi-coloured flowers looked breathtakingly beautiful, flowers which had apparently sprung into bloom overnight. Now, our first flowing water-course: it was an experience to see a real stream after so many months; it was even more comforting to see that this small flow of water had carved into the road making it impassable to motor vehicles. One could almost see the trees bursting into leaf; some already carried a green canopy. Nature was not wasting time: the rains lasted a few months only and each day counted.

Halfway to our destination we stopped for our first meal, sitting in a circle on the road. The horses relished the young grass, to the point that I thought that a sudden rich diet would injure them: fortunately, it had little effect on their health except to cause a prodigious rumbling within their stomachs.

No rain fell that day, which was just as well because man and horse alike were weary by the time Abu Gubeiha came into view. My body ached from contact with the saddle. The boys were silent by now, each one suffering from his own particular sores. Obviously a lot of toughening-up was needed before we reached difficult country.

We used the rest-house that first night, and soon after arriving, the Nazir turned up to welcome us. His village was recovering from the attack of relapsing fever in which a total of eight people had died. This total would have been much higher but for the quick arrival of the government medical team.

People were out in their cultivations sowing millet although the soil in the neighbourhood was still too dry to assure a good germination. The risk in this practice was that birds and insects would consume the seed before it had a chance to germinate – very often there was no seed in reserve to sow a second time, and the crop could be lost. When I spoke my fears to the Nazir he shrugged and said:

'Allah is generous; it is all in his hands.'

It troubled me to have to tell him to make sure that as much grain as possible was sown, and yet the erosion problem was not so severe here as in most other areas. There was a chance the village might escape damage.

Some more rain fell that night, giving the crops the prospect of a better start, so I slept with an easier mind.

Seseiban

We were all up and saddling by the time the sun topped the hills. The village was quiet and there were few witnesses as we left. This was the comfortable time before the heat of the day, when the boys were cheerful and horses made good speed, so it was important to take full advantage of it.

It was time to move away from familiar territory and turn westwards, over a narrow twisting trail leading to Seseiban, an isolated village rarely visited by outsiders. The track was unsuitable for motor vehicles and it was questionable when, if ever, an inspector had travelled this way before.

The route twisted through mile after mile of dense thorn scrub, where vicious hooks tore at limbs and branches threatened to unseat the riders. By now the horses were walking comfortably in file so that the riders could sit, half-asleep, leaving each one to follow its neighbour.

We rode over a small clearing where a group of about 15 ostriches took fright at our approach, leaving behind a little prickly baby, only 18 inches high. Ibrahim jumped to the ground to pick it up and show it to me: it seemed remarkable that such a defenceless creature could escape predators.

We came to the first real hazard, a fast-flowing watercourse with steep banks of red clay. I eased Bakhit into the current but the muddy water was little more than stirrup-high, and everyone crossed safely.

By mid afternoon, Bakhit was pulling at his reins as if impatient at the slowness of the *hamla*, so I decided to give him his head and, with the policeman for company, we trotted the remaining six miles to the village.

Seseiban was indeed a poor village scarcely worth a place on the map. It consisted of about 40 little straw huts set at the base of a low rock hill. At our approach, people appeared sleepily at doors, no doubt just a little bit alarmed at the appearance of an askari and a white man on horseback.

We dismounted in the village, then, hesitantly, people emerged to stand in silence, as if waiting to see what we were going to do. One man, dressed like the others in a ragged *gufian*, slowly moved forward to shake my hand. After a few words of greeting and explanation he beckoned to the other villagers, until what could have been the entire population of about 100 came forward. Soon we were shaking hands all around and with the ice broken they were now at their ease and chattering away with smiles on their faces.

I told the village headman that the *hamla* was approaching and we required a site to set up camp nearby. He led me to a possible place, but like most small villages, it was ringed with the bones of dead animals, some of them too recently dead for comfort, so I decided on an area a further distance away. The *hamla* arrived, and within minutes 50 clumsy assistants began helping unload the animals. Half an hour of spirited confusion produced a tidy camp, and a fire where Mahomed was already squatting with his pots.

The village people were arabicised Nuba fairly similar to the people of Rashad. Their crude village was set amid thousands of acres of excellent virgin soil, its poverty no doubt due to poor water sources. Not far from the tents a stream flowed gently, yet once the dry season returned it would become, once more, a dry gash on the earth's surface.

I was washing inside the tent when Ibrahim called, '*Jenabo*, you have visitors.'

I looked out to find the village sheikh and several other men standing there with a sheep – as I had often seen before, they were about to kill it as a token of welcome and hospitality. I protested, realising how poor they were, but they merely smiled and went through the rites of slaughter, offering it to me.

I thanked them and exchanged the blessings, '*Allah yasallamak!*' (The blessing of Allah rest with you) then retreated into the tent to write up the day's report.

'So much good soil, and little evidence of erosion as the population is small . . .'

Had this region a potential for future development and settlement? It would depend on whether sufficient water could be stored over the long dry season, and it was worth spending a full day here to find out. I was feeling at ease; after all, the trek had started well and men and animals alike were hardening to the work. I looked at the map and realised that before long the day's travel would need to be increased, particularly when crossing unpopulated areas where there might be no water-holes.

A voice called from outside the tent: '*Jenabo, ta'al hinne!*' (Sir, come here!)

I looked out to find the head groom looking rather anxious.

'It's Barmel, he's sick. You had better come and see.'

A sick horse! It had never occurred to me to bring a spare animal in case of accidents.

I crossed to the line of horses and saw at once the animal was fevered, its head drooping almost to the ground. There were areas in the mountains where tsetse fly attacked horses, causing a form of sleeping sickness. These areas were far from Seseiban; I had taken care to memorise their localities, as they were marked on the map. However, Barmel's condition could not be so serious – perhaps a day of rest might help. The groom provided a comfortable straw bed, then fed a light millet mash; there was nothing else we could do.

Suddenly I felt very tired: the outlook could change so quickly!

I knew it would be expected of me to talk to the villagers but my mood had gone. I found the Sheikh and told him I would meet with them all on the following evening, and asked him to take me to his wells and cultivations next morning. He was obviously disappointed at postponing an evening's session of talk – the rare event of an inspector's visit obviously had deep significance to the people.

The Sheikh rode Gamr and we set off next morning on an inspection of the area. The village got its water from deep wells close to the hill: obviously the water-table was low in the ground. It was unlikely to be different elsewhere in the area. Two large mounds caught my eye with a watercourse running between – a possible area for an earth dam.

We searched the area and afterwards I prepared some charts showing possible means of storing water. Obviously this large area of good land could be opened up: if the new *hafirs* in Tegali held water and were proved a success, here also was a place with potential. In what better way could a government use its resources than by opening up new land in a controlled way, followed by education in the husbandries to suit the local ecology? I thought of the miserable conditions of the people of Seseiban and places like it and tried to picture the transformation that would be brought about by providing durable stocks of water. It would be a miracle to them!

Areas of virgin forest had been cut and burned and millet-planting was proceeding round the still-smouldering stumps. Older cultivations were already planted with yet another grain crop; the same careless practice that led ultimately to erosion. I spoke to the sheikh about this danger. He listened and agreed, but mainly out of politeness: how could I ever expect him to understand, and to act?

That evening the promised 'session' took place in the village. A string bed acted as a seat for me and every single person, from the youngest child in its mother's arms to the oldest grandmother, gathered round and sat on the ground. I started on the subject of grain.

'The government wants you to grow as much as you possibly can, because . . .'

They listened silently as I explained how well they would be paid for their crop; money was of little use to them, so there was very little incentive for them to grow more. A few questions: then I started on the subject of using crop rotation in order to avoid erosion. The two subjects, as ever, were poor companions – grow more but conserve your land. Probably it was a waste of breath.

A question came from out of the crowd:

'Nomadic Buggara graze over our land in the dry season with their big herds – they eat all our *Gussab* (straw)! Can you please stop them, because there are too many for us to deal with!'

This touched a raw nerve and a babble of voices joined in – the meeting became alive. I could only say that the DC would be told when next I met him.

'By Allah's name, there is not a grain of sugar in the village . . .' – the meeting continued into the night on topics of importance to the villagers.

A little boy with a hugely distended belly stood in the crowd. I brought him forward and he stood reluctantly while I explained how deficiencies in a child's diet caused this deformity. They listened patiently, but at the suggestion of widening their diet to include meat and vegetables there was cynical laughter – 'Where can we get these luxuries?' Any improvement in diet could only come from finding a solution to the water situation. There were no short cuts!

I was finding that travel in the mountains made little reference to time. One hour was as good as another, and the sun provided a sufficiently accurate timepiece: at night, time was judged by the size of a yawn. I stood up and yawned hugely: everyone accepted the hint and we all dispersed to our homes.

In my private world inside the tent I lay, conscious of aching muscles and a sense of complete tiredness. I had found gifts in the corner of the tent – a little heap of eggs, some lentils, and a gourd containing milk. How is it, I wondered, that people who have so little can be so generous?

Out of the silence came the voice of an Arab woman singing a gentle eastern song. I held my breath and listened. Here was a moment in life when time stood still: a moment when memory is lastingly etched.

After a restless night Ibrahim wakened me with the usual morning cup. I quickly dressed and went to see whether Barmel had recovered sufficiently for the trek to continue. He looked much better, standing erect, eyes brighter. We agreed that it would be possible to travel after noon, provided he travelled light. It would mean arriving at our next stop – Abu Adam village about twenty miles away – after dark, which might cause problems, but we would just have to take a chance on this.

No rain had fallen in the previous twenty-four hours and the nearby stream had dried up, leaving only a few muddy pools. The main rains had evidently not arrived yet and local cloudbursts caused plants to burst into leaf, whereas only a few miles distant ground remained parched. To have horses carrying tanks of water was a necessary insurance in such conditions!

We loaded the *hamla* after a midday meal and went on our way, with the entire village population waving their farewells. It was the wrong time to set out with the sun still violently hot overhead, but as we rode on into the evening, increasing coolness cheered the party up and shouts of laughter sounded along the column. Ibrahim was the main topic, with bawdy comments being shouted at his newly-married state.

The trail led upwards to rougher land, red and sandy in nature and completely unpopulated. Grass showed green tips through the ground, with trees throwing out their first leaves, and probably because of this new bounty, a sudden abundance of wild animal life attracted everyone's attention. First of all a lynx, not far from the horses' feet and showing very little sign of fear at our passage, then a large group of ostrich watching us suspiciously from a distance. Two separate groups of giraffe looked at us carefully, their heads high above the flat-topped acacia trees, but they continued grazing as if we provided no cause for alarm.

A low irregular line of hills showed in the west. According to the map, our destination, Abu Adam, nestled at the base of these hills.

Rather than have the entire *hamla* descend on the village, I decided to ride on ahead with the askari, leaving the *hamla* to plod on at its own pace. I noticed that Barmel was travelling well, having apparently recovered from his illness.

Riding through bush country of this nature it was necessary to pluck ticks from our clothing. Sometimes they were bigger than a thumbnail and fat with blood. They also clung to the horses, and each night a careful search had to be made, particularly in loose folds of skin, because if missed, a suppurating sore quickly developed. It was common to find the ears and other parts of wild animals packed with ticks.

We were halfway to Abu Adam when a group of travellers on camels approached from the opposite direction. This was a rare enough occurrence and I was exchanging greetings with them, when to my surprise, the askari pointed his rifle at one of the men and told him to dismount. When the camel was on the ground, an examination of its load revealed sacks of sugar – black-market sugar! The askari had recognised the rider and had guessed at his load. Two camels carried sugar, and they, together with the black-marketeer, were forced to accompany us to Abu Adam; the other riders were sent on their way.

Topping a rise I passed a group of cultivators working on a newly-cleared holding. They dropped their implements and ran to greet me, curious as to who the unexpected visitor was. The path led upwards towards the village and I rode into a ramshackle collection of houses just as the sun was dipping behind the hills. By this time what must have been the entire population had come out to witness our arrival.

A little grey-bearded man with bandy legs came forward to introduce himself as the village sheikh. His *guftan* was tossed over his arm. He welcomed me with a broad smile and shook my hand, then the villagers squeezed forward to do the same. This was a more welcoming group than the shy people of Seseiban! They were not intimidated by the arrival of a white stranger so late in the day.

The people were apparently a mixture of Fallata and Nuba. Most were clad in Arab style and spoke Arabic. On the tops of the neighbouring hills I had seen some Nuba houses, so the two ethnic groups lived close together as in other parts of the mountains.

The askari stepped forward to question the Sheikh whether he had been dealing in black-market sugar, as the camels had been found close to his village. In a rather comical manner he protested his innocence, although a meaningful look flashed towards the 'prisoner'. It was agreed that the askari would return to Rashad on the following day, taking the black-marketeer and his cargo with him.

I selected a campsite on a low hillock close to the village near a gently flowing watercourse, and within an hour a confusion of volunteers gave a helping hand to erect the tents; in fact, I was surprised to find people from such a remote spot reacting so spontaneously to our visit. I was still more surprised when the Sheikh said:

'You are Mr Meki from Rashad. I saw you at the Tegali Gathering – you must dance for us while you are in my village.

My reputation had apparently gone ahead of me! The Sheikh was a widely travelled man and had even been as far as Omdurman. He was indeed remarkable, because he insisted in having erected, for my sole use, a stick-and-grass lavatory: if only to reward him for his efforts, I must at least use it once!

Mahomed was already preparing dinner and Ibrahim had bath and fresh clothes ready. The Sheikh insisted, however, that I go immediately to his house for refreshments where I found a table already prepared with a range of drinks all of which I would have to sample – thick coffee, scented tea and a sweet drink: Tamerahind. The threat of dysentery from taking drinks made from unboiled water is always present, yet how difficult it was to refuse such ardent hospitality.

Women moved about the little house in a way which showed a lessening of Moslem influence. They spoke to me cheerfully without attempting to conceal their faces or their limbs.

I suddenly remembered that with so much water about, there was an acute danger from malaria-carrying mosquitoes, so I made my apologies and hurried home to bath, then don mosquito boots and a long-sleeved shirt. Now that the malaria season was here it was essential to take regular dosage of prophylactic mepacrin, a chemical which had the undesirable effect of staining the skin yellow.

On this occasion there would be no avoiding the evening 'meeting' with the usual talkative crowd round about. The men of the village boasted skill in the use of the bow when hunting. Some straw dummies suspended from a tree were used to demonstrate this skill, which was indeed precise, despite the crudeness of the weapons. When, finally, I could settle everyone to talking business, we went over the same themes as on so many other occasions. They listened carefully on the subject of erosion; apparently they had experienced its effects.

Discussion was, by now, becoming impossible. The air throbbed with the sound of frogs. Back at the tent I was beginning to realise that the campsite was far from perfect, with insects in clouds and the roar of frogs guaranteed to destroy sleep. There were always new lessons. I would choose more carefully in future.

Out in the open I was climbing through the mosquito net, resigned to the worst, when yet another noise tore at the air – an antelope burst out of the sparse scrub, and rushed straight towards the tent, followed immediately by dogs. It tripped over the guy-ropes and was picking itself up when they pounced at its throat. Nuba hunters now rushed on the scene and a spear plunged deep into the animal's body – all this a few yards from my bed.

I was shocked at the suddenness of the event: it was hard to believe that its nearness was a chance accident. The Nuba now approached me, shook my hand in the Nuba way and spoke words I could not understand. Eventually, the animal was carried off to the Nuba village, leaving me with all prospects of sleep gone.

A tremendous mist, '*ratuba*', settled on the village and everything was soaked in dew; large wet beads coalesced on the net and trickled to the ground. Water could almost be squeezed out of the air – it was too stuffy to move into the tent. The dreary hours passed.

According to arrangement, the Sheikh arrived at dawn. We rode off to examine the area. Mist reduced visibility but, almost at once, we were confronted by the spectre of soil erosion close to the village margin. A new gash through the ground showed where, with one more violent rain storm, a torrent of water could spew into the village destroying more homes and creating new waste land. Every tree and shrub had been cut in the neighbourhood so that the banks of the *khor* were no longer anchored, leaving floods free to tear the land to shreds. I spoke earnestly to the chief about this danger, and he nodded as if in understanding – why did men let this happen? How could people wait passively until their homes were washed away? Was it fatalism? Were they totally dependent on the will of Allah to the extent that they took no action to protect themselves? I felt a sense of frustration, even anger, that this should be. How long would it take for the healing hand of the Tegali agricultural groups to reach places such as Abu Adam? Perhaps never.

In fact, I returned to this village the following year to find a deep canyon running where the village had stood. It was wide enough and deep enough to hide a bus, and it ran for over a mile, with masses of tributary gulleys feeding into it. The people had simply built new huts beyond the destroyed area, and were starting the process all over again.

Solemnly I continued the morning's ride, and I felt wearily unsympathetic towards the cultivators who left their work to speak with me. Here, sowing grain was a family operation, with the men plunging a 12-foot-long pole into the unploughed soil, then the wife and children dropping seed into each hole, then covering it, using their feet.

We rode through a *babynos* (ebony) forest - I broke a stem to see the black heart-wood - then on over a wide area of good land. There were many heart-nosed monkeys above our heads, and in one place the chief pointed to giraffe in the distance. He said:

'Giraffe make good sport when hunted on horseback. It takes a good horseman to kill a giraffe!' Giraffe, of course, are protected animals.

'Do you hunt the giraffe?' I asked.

'I would, but we are too poor to own horses, and you can't chase them on donkey-back.'

Mahomed had lunch ready on our return. I invited the chief to share the meal but he refused, saying that he could not use my tools in any case, so he went to his house with the promise of another evening's meeting. Having seen their cultivations I was now determined to shake them into appreciating the error of their ways.

Lunch that day consisted of peanut soup, followed by mutton with sweet potato and cassava, and finally the last Rashad grapefruit. It was a good meal, had I only been in a humour to enjoy it. Then Ibrahim came forward with his troubles:

'Sir, I can't see, my eye is swollen. Can you cure it?'

I might have proposed that he search out the local witch-doctor, but instead I looked through the medical box to find a cure for swollen eyes. The almost universal panacea – Beecham's Pills – were there in abundance, but their container made no reference to eyes. A bottle marked 'sal volatile' looked more hopeful. I dabbed the offending organ, following up with some ointment, and he reported himself cured next morning.

The afternoon was unusually cool, as the sun remained obscured by a mist haze, so it occurred to me that the best way to overcome low spirits was to attack them. Some mischievous imp made me propose a game of cricket. Needless to say the villagers had never heard of field sports, far less cricket, but once they were wakened from their afternoon siesta two 'teams' – namely Trekkers v Abu Adam – stood ready on the village 'green.'

The people were totally without comprehension as to what was about to happen, but they stood docilely while I explained the rudiments of the sport. I chose the Sheikh as captain of the home team – an office which he took in his stride – a Doleib nut was wrapped round with a rag and a bat was shaped out of a branch.

A boundary of women and children was 'erected'; wickets were planted, and I asked Ibrahim to throw the first ball – my first problem; Ibrahim couldn't throw a ball! Mahomed took over and operations slowly started. When the ball was actually hit, the boundary laughed and cheered: at one point the Sheikh took two quick runs before the ball had even left the bowler's hand, and he still got a cheer! By ignoring the finer points of the rule book the game proceeded for the best part of two hours – it was actually enjoyed, although at the game's end few of the players were much the wiser as to what had been going on.

At sunset we were all taken aback when several Nuba, naked and dust-covered, approached carrying the body of a small dik-dik antelope. They walked straight up to me through the gathered villagers, each one solemnly shook my hand, then they laid the animal at my feet. With scarcely a spoken word they moved on towards the path which led to their hilltop houses. The Abu Adam villagers stood silently while this event took place and no comment was made about it afterwards. There was a strange quality in the relationship of two quite distinct races living so close together, but somehow ignoring each other. In my eyes they had little in common, except that both were generous in being prepared to part with the little that they possessed.

The evening's meeting, the last before leaving, was attended by the entire population of the village. I took them to task vigorously on their cultivation practices, keeping them on the theme even when they tried to introduce other topics. This time it seemed that the message was getting through . . . that they really understood that land was something precious, to be conserved; and by them! Yet, as I have already written, part of the village was washed away one year later!

There was still time for other matters – a father brought his son forward, indicating that his stomach was '*aiyan*' (sick). The boy was in tears, his stomach distended through eating the simple bulky diet of the area. This time, the Beecham's Pills were dispensed with some prospect of success – I had long since learned, as most doctors do, that to hand over a 'healing' pill with an air of confidence can bring about remarkable cures. The father and the boy went away satisfied! Saddest was the number of people present whose lives were burdened by cataract of the eyes – one of Africa's scourges.

I said goodbye to the villagers, as my plan was to leave on trek long before dawn. The next stage of the journey was likely to be long and perhaps without any water sources. It would be necessary to travel in the cool hours, mainly in the dark and this time more than 30 miles per day would need to be covered.

The boys had everything shipshape and ready for striking camp. I lay in bed listening to Nuba drums speaking from the nearby hills: were they talking about me, or was some celebration taking place?

Problems of Water

Two a.m. and I found it surprisingly easy to rise and superintend the break-up of camp. Drums were now quiet and the villagers asleep: only frogs heralded our departure with their never-ending chorus.

Saddling and loading was now routine and we went through the operations without speaking a word. Cold was intense, with the riders draped in blankets, old great-coats and every available piece of clothing to shield them from the dampness and low temperature. This damp chill would become bitter cold to heat-accustomed bodies, and to ride cold would be utter misery.

In the rekindled firelight we drank tea, then the cups were packed and loads adjusted. Still without conversation, we moved forward, and were just leaving the village when the barefooted Sheikh came shivering from his hut to bless us on our journey. I felt touched at his consideration and left with the promise that I would return. He said he would call on me at Rashad, so we parted on the best of terms.

Trekking now started in earnest, and so followed dreary cold hours in almost complete darkness, where the horse immediately in front was scarcely visible. Cold, in spite of our wrappings, became a torture, and we huddled tight in the saddle as best we could, with heads sunk deep into our coats. There was nothing remotely glamorous in this half world, where the only awareness of our surroundings, was the sound of hooves on the varying soils, and the different movements, which corresponded to the prevailing terrain.

After leaving the village the horses moved at first over sand, and then over flinty stones, as the trail gradually ascended the range of hills. There were apparently no serious obstacles for several miles, with the guide having little difficulty in identifying the route.

I followed after the Nuba guide, mounted on Gamr. The head groom was on Bakhit, then came the long string of heavily-laden pack animals nose to tail. Barmel was, by now, fully recovered and carrying a full load of water.

Chill numbed the mind. The sheer inactivity of sitting on the slowly rocking saddle was soporific. Soon, like most of the others, I was asleep or, perhaps half-asleep, because some corners of the mind were accepting signals. Then the path grew steeper and we were all jogged out of our stupor. The horses laboured up a rough rock staircase between high walls of stone suddenly commanding our full attention. It became necessary to dismount and lead them for the next half-mile; exercise welcome because of our stiffened limbs. Soon, like the horses, we were all gasping for breath, until the path levelled once more and the riders huddled down to another cold stretch.

For me, at least, there was no more sleep. The Nuba guide shouted warning of an overhanging branch. We all ducked, except Mahomed Omer, the cook, perched high on his kitchen gear, who was obviously in sound sleep. There followed a loud thud, a rattle of pots and a cry of anguish from Mahomed. He scrambled up, fortunately none the worse and was heartily cheered by the rest of the party.

The horses splashed through an 'invisible' stream, then into another black gulley. A thorn whipped across my cheek drawing blood, but there were no more mishaps.

Suddenly I could see the faint outline of trees against the sky. The rider in front assumed a definite form then, very slowly, pale light spread over the eastern horizon, lifting a curtain from the landscape. The horses were cresting a ridge and there before us to the west stretched an interminable plain, still banded with the gloom of night. The horizon slowly took form, a straight line without break.

We now started a descent towards the plain, over a broken surface of shifting stone. The horses felt cautiously for the surest footing, but there was no need to dismount and progress continued fairly rapidly.

Six a.m. and I decided we had covered a sufficient distance to permit a stop for breakfast. A spreading zaan tree provided a suitable place, and in minutes a fire was lit with the inevitable pot of tea brewing. I ate boiled eggs and millet bread; the other trekkers shared a bowl of millet porridge. Everyone was in good spirits, and it was tempting to rest for a time, but I was perplexed to find the watercourses dry at this side of the hill, and not a single blade of grass. It was like stepping back into the past. Before us, to the horizon, stretched a completely arid plain. There was no time to waste, with our limited provision of water, and the day becoming hotter!

We mounted again to follow a scarcely visible path, obviously rarely used. From the position of the sun I could see we were now heading south-west. The guide was apparently confident about our route.

Down on the plain a sequence of eroded gulleys slowed our progress as the horses struggled over and through a succession of obstacles. So much for that straight dotted line on the map! How many extra miles would terrain such as this add to the journey? This parched hot wilderness depressed us all!

I questioned the Nuba again about water prospects ahead. He shrugged, admitting disappointment that the rains had not yet reached the area.

'Failing anything else, there is a water-hole close to El Azraq where I have often watered my animals,' he said.

El Azraq, according to the map, was 45 miles as the crow flies: how many miles would that mean on the ground? A minimum of two long, hard days depending on our own water stocks – four saddle tanks to supply the needs of nine horses and seven men.

A wide, spreading blotch on the landscape right across our path turned out to be a forest of bamboo many miles wide. It looked an impassable barrier but the Nuba rode straight towards it and entered into the semi-darkness by means of a dry watercourse. The horses shied a little then felt their way uncertainly over the sandy bottom. The transition from harsh sunlight was dramatic, and the cool air made me shiver. It was like riding through the vaults of a crypt with bamboo stems arching 20 feet above our heads.

Hooves sank deep into the sand, and this, together with the heavy baggage, was proving too arduous for the animals, so the passengers were compelled to walk. The *khor* turned and twisted, sometimes almost doubling back on itself and always adding to the journey's length. Had the *khor* been in flood it would have meant a wait until the waters subsided sufficiently to permit passage: at least there would then be no shortage of water! Every few yards, dead canes straddled the *khor*, some of them brittle, and collapsing to dust as we pushed through. Others had to be pulled aside laboriously. Horses and riders were, by now, dust-covered – tempers were getting short.

I called a halt at a little rocky clearing where numbers of many-coloured lizards scuttled away on our arrival. For the first time on our trek a saddle water-tank was tapped and each rider had a single cup of tepid water. The horses were given a little drink from a gourd.

As quickly as possible I had everyone mounted, and we moved on in that same uncomfortable progress. Would the bamboo never end? I was beginning to despair when, suddenly, we were through and into fierce daylight again.

The sun was high. By now we had been on trek seven hours – a long, hard trek for the horses, but it was necessary still to press on before halting for the remainder of the day. Looking behind, the hills of Abu Adam were disappointingly near, although so much ground had been covered since cresting the ridge.

Now that we were in the open again all of the horses were moving smartly without sign of stress in spite of once more carrying their full load of riders and kit. We were entering a charred, desolate landscape, burned by a recent fire. I was writing a brief record of the soils, as well as any outstanding features of interest as we travelled, but this was an inhospitable, eroded area of poor land, with nothing to recommend it.

At intervals bleached animal bones lay scattered, mainly cattle and sheep with occasionally the remains of a camel. Some were partially covered with the blown dust of years, other were more recent and still with traces of hair and hide.

The nomadic Buggara would probably graze over this area while there were still water-holes to sustain life. I rode back along the *hamla* to 'cheer up' the riders who were now noticeably silent and nursing aches from their uncomfortable positions.

'Where are you taking us?' Ibrahim asked. 'Is it not time to stop? My back is breaking!'

His position on top of boxes looked particularly uncomfortable. Mahomed smiled wanly but said nothing. In comparison to their discomfort, my ride on saddleback was luxury!

On every side there were 'lake' mirages, something I had not expected to see in the rains. Sweat froth was showing beneath the saddles – a danger sign, as heat and friction can raise blisters on horses' skin; a precursor of saddle-sores. I told the riders to dismount and lead their horses over the last stretch, something which raised no cheers from the weary travellers.

Fortunately there came a diversion which started the party into earnest conversation. A faintly discernable branch-track split off northwards, and at the point of division, an ancient gnarled thorn tree stood, festooned with little scraps of cloth and oddments – little cups, glasses, pipes and even an ancient rusty knife – squeezed into every crevice, so that it was a marvel that the tree could survive.

In a moment the trekkers added their own contributions: they made sure that I did likewise so I pressed a small coin into the bark. 'A cajoor tree,' Ibrahim said, where propitiation had to be made to the spirits of the trail. No one could ever risk passing such a tree without making an offering. With this duty accomplished there was evident haste to escape from the scene – a jinn might be seen: they now needed no further encouragement to travel on and leave the tree far behind.

At last, an outcrop of wind-eroded rock – time to stop! We rode over, found a reasonable overhang which gave some shade then, thankfully, the gear was unloaded and everyone busied themselves. Smiles returned!

It was midday, with the sun directly overhead beating down on the still-parched soil and making shade blissful. The horses were rubbed down carefully, ticks picked off, and skin pressed to identify whether saddles had caused any tenderness. Fortunately, there were no ill effects. Mahomed had the job of superintending the distribution of water: the horses drank thirstily, the men had one more cupful each. This made considerable inroads to the water stocks, as could only be expected.

We all gathered in a ring after a sparse midday meal to discuss the day's events and to plan the next stage of the trek. It was agreed that a start should be made soon after midnight to make the best of the cool night hours. I estimated that we had only travelled 28 miles so there was still a long waterless route ahead. There was no sign of rain; the sky was brassy and cloudless, so there was no occasion to erect tents for the night and the boys prepared to stretch out in a row at the base of the rock.

I felt that I had work to do: after all, who had ever come this way before? It had certainly never been mapped. The top of the rock hill offered a vantage point from which to observe a wide area of country. Some tips of mountains were just visible on the skyline – among them, the merest edge of the Heiban ridge – at least it was possible to see where water was to be found.

I pencilled as much information as could be determined from the scene, and made some record of the soils we had traversed – they had been largely of inferior quality from an agricultural point of view. Over wide areas, trees had been gnarled and dwarfed through some soil mineral deficiency: one stretch was a mass of two-foot-deep pot-holes, for reasons I could not understand. One area of clay bearing a stand of good acacia trees was evidently a flood plain when the storms came, with drift, consisting of small twigs and grass, interwoven in high branches. Even when travelling in darkness it had proved possible to form some judgement of the soil beneath the horses' hooves.

By now any semblance of a track had been lost: night-time guidance must come from the stars.

Before sunset we had another light meal then everyone settled to sleep. I lay down on the trek bed, sensing aches in every limb. I looked at my lean frame, with its covering of yellow-stained skin, the result of taking the anti-malarial tablets – grotesque! This trekking life had its high moments: it was always alive with interest, but in the end it had to achieve something. That was the question – would anything ever come out of these hard days that might improve the lot of the people of the mountains? My overactive mind ranged over what might have been. Yet, here I was in the middle of a great wilderness looking for – what?

To be so tired and yet not to sleep; the hours trailed by.

I must have gone over, because it was 12.30 a.m. when I wakened to the rattle of harness. My one urge now was to sleep on . . . and on. A fire was already flickering, but I closed my eyes fervidly hoping that it was a dream. The next instant Ibrahim was there with a lamp. He whispered kindly: '*Jenabo*, waken up: it's morning!'

It was barely morning, but there was nothing for it but to rise. The night was impenetrably black; the stars mere hard points of light. I sat for some moments filled with gloom at the bleakness of the moment: more long hours of night riding to cover as much ground as possible before the blistering heat of the day.

Everything was covered with dew, my shirt and shorts wet and limp. I crowded on all the clothes I could find and draped a blanket over my shoulders. People were stamping about for warmth. Mahomed's cup of tea made some difference, but few words were spoken. This time there was no frog noise, only the chirrup of crickets.

Firelight flickered on the rock wall which had been our shelter from the heat. In a drowsy state it was easy to conjure up thoughts of jinns and the cajoor tree not very far away. I could sense that others had similar thoughts in their minds. Saddling and loading went on rapidly with the boys speaking almost in whispers. Only the horses seemed unaffected as they stood patiently flicking their tails and occasionally tossing their heads as bands were tightened.

We mounted and set off at a good pace without looking back. There was no path now, or if there was it was quickly lost in the darkness. The leading horse pushed through dead waist-high grass, with a constant crackling noise, avoiding the scattered sparse thorn trees and shrubs which were ever present, even on the poorest land. Stars shone clearly overhead and provided us with a sense of direction. I remained aware of the North Star 'close' to my right shoulder and saw that it seldom strayed from that position.

As on the previous day, each horse followed the leader with its rider huddled down in a chilled torpor. My hair was running wet with dew and the horse's back as damp as in a rain storm. Even under a blanket, chill shivers jerked through my body.

Time lost meaning: I could only register the ongoing discomforts of the moment. Probably the other riders were sleeping, but some hard uncomfortable barrier in my brain kept me awake. At about 3 a.m. an electric storm flashed continuously to the south, with an occasional rumble of distant thunder, but no rain fell. The edge of a late moon rose behind us giving a pale, cold light, sufficient to open out our world just a little.

Since setting off we had ridden in silence, but this new light encouraged me to ask the guide about our route, and any likely obstacles before us.

'There is a deep watercourse not far ahead. It is as well that it will be dry, otherwise there would be difficulty in the darkness.' He was aware of my interest in soil, and added: 'We are crossing a wide area of heavy soil – it is good soil and can graze many animals.'

I had thought by the sound of the hoof-beats that there had been a consistent firm beat, as if there was clay underfoot which was likely to be fertile. In fact, this must be a very large area indeed. The Nuba tried to describe its size but his units of area and distance were unknown to me. Here, in one of the remotest regions of the entire Nuba Mountains, the same rule applied as anywhere else – 'good soil, plus permanent water produces settled communities of people and animals.'

The guide shouted a warning and everyone was jolted into wakefulness – it was the vertical cut into the deep watercourse which he had been anticipating. It was as well he was alert, although by now I had confidence in the sure-footed awareness of the horses. The guide turned south to find a way across, but it took what seemed like a long time before we were able to enter the *khor* by means of a shallower tributary. The other bank was gradual, so at last the trek continued westward.

I dozed off completely yet somehow managing to stay upright in the saddle; for how long, it was impossible to say, but the palest shiver of dawn was fanning out from the east when suddenly Bakhit feinted to one side, tossing at the reins and all but throwing me to the ground. The lines jerked from my hands and I found myself clinging to the horse's neck, and only in time managing to recover balance. Cries of alarm and thuds from behind told me that the others were also in a state of confusion.

There was a crashing noise in the bush, slowly receding into the distance.

We had ridden into some wild animal herd with the horses caught unawares. Remarkably, Flash alone shed part of its load, though several of the trekkers nursed bruises.

The sky was alight when, with straps adjusted, we got under way again. There was no more sleep that night as my mind was kept in rapture at the unfolding dawn.

A wave of gold dust rose from the Abu Adam hills and appeared to fan out as if by a mighty wind, to glisten on the flecks of morning cloud. Slowly, the sky became a soft blue with stars, pinpricks of light. The drab clothes of the riders looked like mantles of gold. It was so brilliant that the delays and frustrations of the morning were forgotten, and there arose an unwitting sense of victory that the dark hours were behind.

With the first edge of the rising sun – 5.30 a.m. – we stopped gratefully for 'breakfast'. The riders slid stiffly to the ground to enjoy the absolute pleasure of the sun's first warm rays. We stood like statues absorbing its comfort with feelings akin to ecstasy, then slowly everyone slipped into the rhythms of watering and feeding the animals, and ourselves – Mahomed presided over our diminishing water stock.

It had been a long stretch since that early morning start, with probably as much as 18 miles covered in spite of the frustrating delays on the way. The horses were carefully groomed and examined, then covered to prevent their backs chilling. Fantas had a slight swelling where the saddle gripped, which would mean some redistribution of weight; the water tanks he carried were, by now, nearly empty so that presented no problem. Surprisingly, Bakhit too, had a tender spot which, when pressed, caused his hide to jerk and his ears to twitch. Things could have been worse. Obviously we would have to rest over the hottest hours around midday.

A rocky ridge obscured our view towards the west and the Heiban Mountains, so the Nuba scaled the tallest tree at hand to check our progress. He pointed, shouting that we had travelled too far to the south in the dark hours which would add extra miles to our journey: a depressing prospect!

By now the sun was gathering heat, so there was little time to waste. We quickly reloaded and the *hamla* set off at a smart pace – I sat gingerly on the carefully padded saddle trying to ease the pressure on Bakhit's tender back.

With our water stocks low, I looked forward keenly to reaching the promised water-hole in the evening. The electric storm of the night had gone without trace, with the ground as dry as ever.

Soil, which had looked fertile over long distances, was now becoming broken and uneven as we approached the ridge which had obscured our view. It became so steep that everyone had to dismount to scramble through a gulley with dangerous loose stones at its base. Then, on reaching the crest, we looked towards mountains coloured with tones of brightest blue – but, even more dramatic, there were patches of green at their base, as if the forest was in leaf. At last there was some prospect of leaving this arid plain for good and finding water. Surely to trek with sufficient water would be more leisurely and enjoyable than the experience of the past few days.

The guide pointed excitedly to a sharp rock reaching vertically from the plain and quite isolated; possibly 12 miles away. 'The water-hole is close to that rock and the village of Fariq is an hour's ride beyond it,' he said. The Nuba was returning to his people, where he would remain, while the trek continued. It had been a fortunate coincidence that he had planned to take the same route as the *hamla*, after having spent some time as a labourer in the city.

I sent the *hamla* on so as to take advantage of this good viewpoint and draw up some record of the surrounding country. With Bakhit hitched to a tree, I sat on the highest rock with notepad out – much of the land appeared to be good, though still covered with dead grass and leafless acacia trees. Several rock needles and jumbled heaps of stone set on the flat plain told of centuries of weathering: it was just possible to follow the lines of *khors* because trees grew taller close to their banks. In the distance giraffe strolled leisurely through the bush; once new grass came, a migration of wild animal herds would take place from the Nile and other favoured areas.

I heard a whinny from Bakhit and saw that he was moving restlessly, tearing at his halter. The cause was only too apparent: only 50 yards away, a pair of leopards watched us with some interest. I quickly mounted and he went off in a rush, scrambling down from the ridge in a hurry to reach the security of the *hamla*.

Mile after mile followed over good land, with the heat almost unbearable; yet, still, there was no awakening of the land. Any rain that may have dropped had been insufficient to germinate grass.

It was time to stop because the horses were beginning to suffer. Their heads hung low: some of them needed persuasion to keep up with the *hamla*. Bakhit kept slowing down and wanted to shy from the slightest obstacle in his path: apparently his feet were tender, and yet there was still some distance to go to reach the water-hole.

We stopped beside a small bamboo grove which offered the best promise of shade, and, once again, unloaded the tired animals. By the time water was distributed the tanks were virtually empty, and still both animal and man could willingly have drunk more. A few of the horses had tender areas on their backs: with hindsight it was easy to tell that they had not been hardened sufficiently for this kind of work. Neither had the men for that matter, as everyone nursed aches, and to a man they groaned at the prospect of further riding that day.

It is difficult to judge distance in shimmering heat; we were learning these things to our cost! That was the trouble with being a beginner: we were all beginners and had to learn the hard way, but I had the small consolation of knowing that even an experienced trekker would have been unable to predict the lateness of the rains that year.

The bamboo thicket offered broken shade, but lying there and resting, a dusty, untidy group, the heat was stifling. Even with this discomfort most of the party slept, and I wakened with surprise some time later, to find the shadows lengthening. It was time to go.

The animals were saddled again and carefully loaded, and with water containers almost empty, each horse had a reduced load to carry than earlier in the trek. The dead grass, burnished red with the evening sun, was thicker and higher than ever before in our journey, proving the soil excellent, but I had lost interest. I had only one obsession: namely, to reach water.

Darkness came suddenly. With the last grey light the Nuba called back with excitement that he recognised the locality and the water-hole was near at hand – yet, still we continued, now over stones. Bakhit was suffering discomfort – I dismounted to lead him over this last stretch. There was a different smell in the air by this time; a voice from further back in the line shouted: 'Grass!' I bent down to touch the earth; true enough I could just feel the tips of young grass breaking through the ground.

Spirits lifted at once and voices shouted out along the column. The Nuba told us to look ahead where a tall rock pillar showed dark against the stars.

The water-hole! Everyone jumped to the ground and moved towards the rock, where the Nuba was apparently wading in. Our feet sunk into mud – it was only a skinning quagmire of foul-smelling mud!

Ibrahim lit the lamp and we gazed in dejection at the mess of clay and animal droppings. Mahomed called:

'We can't drink this – even the horses can't drink this!'

Indeed, there was nothing to drink! If recent rain had filled the hole, it had dried again – another effect of the late season. What next? We could only travel on to the village of El Azraq – the Nuba had said 'perhaps one hour from here.'

Dejectedly now we continued our way with everyone walking beside his horse. Never before had this hole been dry so late in the season: normally there was some little water right through the dry season; the guide was disappointed like everyone else that his prediction had proved wrong.

Strangely now the horses seemed to be speeding up, making the boys hold them back – was it the prospect of grass — perhaps even the scent of water?

A sound of barking dogs! Through the trees, the glow of a wood fire. We rode into a completely ramshackle collection of huts from which people looked with fear.

The horses meanwhile pulled over to a little stream of flowing water. We had arrived!

The villagers made no move to approach us and waited in their huts, perhaps through fear of the invaders. It was scarcely to be wondered that they were afraid at the arrival of so many people in the darkness. I approached the door of one hut and called out a greeting in Arabic: it was answered in the same language.

At last a man walked towards me from a different hut. He had a twisted cloth round his waist and only hesitatingly put out his hand for me to shake. Who were we? Why had we arrived in the night? Where were we going? I reassured him that we were friends, then slowly people emerged from their huts and gathered round in silence.

I told him we had come a very long way and would be camping overnight close to his village. I learned that the people were Fallata who moved with their cattle, making Fariq their headquarters during the rains. They had only arrived a week before. Perhaps this explained the impoverished state of the village.

That night, to have a thorough wash in an overflowing canvas bath was absolute luxury. The boys in their own tent sounded in high spirits, laughing and teasing as if they were on a holiday jaunt. Later they all lined outside in earnest prayer towards Mecca, an act which they had neglected for some time. Perhaps they were expressing gratitude that there was now good water to drink.

I had promised them a rest day before moving on into Nuba territory – a prospect which interested all of us.

The people of the village still were reluctant to come towards the camp which was unusual and, I thought, due to our unexpected arrival. The sky was cloudy, and we were going to sleep under canvas in case of storm: I was about to climb through the mosquito net when Ibrahim's voice called: '*Jenabo*, the headman wants to speak with you. There is trouble here!'

There was a loud crack of thunder overhead, even as the man entered the tent, and heavy raindrops pocked the canvas. He stood silently for a few seconds.

'*Salaam Aleckum*, is there something I can do?'

'*Ya haderatak*, our cattle are dying, they have Abu Dimea, I thought you should be told now.'

Rinderpest, one of Africa's deadliest cattle plagues, a disease which might well kill their entire herd, and leave them impoverished. It was a disease which struck so suddenly and with such devastating effect, that little action was possible to halt its spread.

'Wait, I shall come with you and take a light to see the animals.'

I quickly dressed and together we walked through beating rain and vivid lightning flashes to the place beyond the village where the herd was standing, head down in the storm. In a minute I counted 15 carcasses all recently dead: there were others lying as if on the point of death. Live animals stood among the dead as no attempt had been made to separate them. Even in this storm the smell of decaying flesh hung heavily.

'Why have you not separated the living from the dead?' I asked.

He shrugged. 'It is in the hands of Allah, the almighty one!' he answered.

One body had been recently butchered – for the village, I was told! Scraps of the carcass had been scattered around by wild animals or dogs.

'We must do something,' I said. 'Tomorrow we shall drive the living to other pastures and try to do something about the dead bodies.'

Again he shrugged, probably as aware as I was that it was too late and a waste of effort.

I lay in the tent unable to find sleep – at one point a vivid flash was followed instantly by a fearful thunder crash which seemed to leave an acrid smell in the nostrils, then the storm rolled away leaving the new sound of the rushing stream, not far from the tent.

The following morning it was a different world. Large pools of water filled every hollow, and the watercourse had become a river of chocolate-coloured water. Sounds had a hollow, booming quality which made voices sound closer than they really were. People were slow to stir as the storm had prevented sleep: probably the leaking roofs with their broken thatch had soaked all of the occupants.

The village headman arrived and I asked him to bring all of the men together to discuss with them what action should be taken. A ragged group of about 12 boys and men collected beside the tent. It was time for deeds, but I struggled to explain that diseases such as Abu Dimea were caused by very small organisms which had been studied by men, and that a sick animal should always be separated from others in the herd. The traditional fatalism in which people bowed to the 'inevitable' was quite apparent, but these were cattle men with cattle their wealth and inspiration, so some of them must have taken heed.

During that day the live cattle were driven far beyond the village; a *zariba* (thorn compound) was built to isolate the sick, but they could not be prevailed upon to gather the dead bodies together, and these were left to be picked by vultures.

So was that day of rest spent! In the evening I sat to speak with the people and reinforce what had been said earlier about disease and simple hygiene. They said very little because their troubles weighed heavily on their minds. I had in my saddle box some little trinkets which, at my request, had been sent out from home: these I gave to children who looked on them with wonder, small as the gifts were.

In spite of their many difficulties they gave me a gourd containing eggs, which I knew it was the right thing to accept. There is a level of poverty at which any further hardship is accepted as an inevitability, without demur, but I knew that their resilience was such that they would recover in time and continue to follow their age-old migrations.

Rain poured again that night. I brought the Nuba guide to the tent to discuss the next stage of the trek – to El Azraq, his home village, where we were due to part company. As far as I could judge from his description, it was only 12 miles away – a pleasant saunter for the horses! Watercourses might be in flood, but otherwise there was not likely to be any difficulty getting there.

I told him: 'We shall stay the morning here then leave for El Azraq after midday so that the horses are really rested before leaving.'

'*Jenabo*,' he replied, 'I am returning to my home after a long absence, so I shall leave on my own at dawn.'

It was natural that he should be impatient to go, so I thanked him for his help and asked him to warn his village of our coming, and in particular, to tell the Mek that I was looking forward to the visit. He left the tent, and I sat down to write up the day's events with rain drumming on the canvas.

El Azraq, I thought – the 'black place' as the name implied: a fitting one for our first Nuba village. It was good that the guide should go ahead and prepare the way for our arrival.

Rain fell most of the night: I could hear it splashing, as into a lake. By dawn, there was silence, apart from the sound of the flooded watercourses and the discordant booming of frogs. No one stirred in the village, and the boys too were catching up on lost sleep. I lay still: a new experience to lie in with the sun rising and the tent becoming hot.

When at last I opened the flaps, a steaming mist blotted out the landscape, though mist curls were already being sucked up by the hot sun, revealing a quagmire of mud which would obviously restrict any movement for a time. A child came out of a hut but sank into the clay and quickly returned.

I waited until, perhaps an hour later, Ibrahim came over, grinning his apologies for being so late. Already, in such a short period of time the surface clay was skinning over and people were emerging from their huts.

The groom came to report on the condition of the horses – Bortogan had a slight saddle-sore which would mean him riding light later in the day. Surprisingly, Bakhit had two little raised blisters which would require careful watching. Over a short stretch of 12 miles we could take turns in walking to spare the horses as much as possible.

Tribal Troubles

According to plan, we rode out of Fariq soon after noon, and settled to a steady walk through country now vastly different. The sparse thorn scrub was changing into thick forest with many strong fleshy-leaved trees. In places, grass had grown more than 12 inches tall, resembling a meadow filled with nutritious vegetation for hungry animals. We had moved out of a desert into a paradise where the hollows were often filled with flowers which resembled cornflowers and marigolds. Nature was not wasting a moment. Birds of every conceivable colour were part of the frenzy of life, filling trees with their song and displaying plumage to best advantage.

We were all cheerful and I enjoyed walking at the head of the column and wading the occasional stream. Two miles on our way we were halted by a fast-flowing river 15 feet in width: I waded into the muddy water and was almost swept away by the current which piled against me, chest-high. Ropes had been brought, because it was easy to foresee a situation such as this: once one was attached to trees at each side of the river, men and horses slowly shuttled over without event – that is, apart from Fantas carrying empty water tanks. The buoyant tanks floated him downstream but the situation was easily recovered and he was brought to dry land – another lesson learned!

The *hamla* was lining up again, when Mahomed pointed to a little rocky knoll at one side.

'*Shuf* (see), *Jenabo*: Nuba watching us!' A group of armed Nuba, bodies stained red with clay, looked down at us without moving.

I shouted the Nuba greeting '*Aafi*!' and waved to them, but surprisingly there was no response, and they turned away out of sight behind the knoll. It could have been a hunting party, surprised at our arrival, and keen to get on with the chase.

Rain began to fall, gently at first, and then a steady downpour which soaked us through. I stripped to the waist: it was surprisingly cold. I was riding again and as the saddle became wet and sticky I could feel skin being lifted from the inside of my legs until the discomfort became unbearable. In this hot climate, riding was done mainly in short trousers – obviously not suitable for wet conditions!

I was contending with this problem when a group of Arabs ran up in a state of high excitement, talking at such a rate that I could not understand them. They gathered round the horse, pulling at me so that Mahomed yelled: '*Imshe* (clear out), leave *Jenubo* . . . stop it!'

More Arabs arrived and I was surrounded by a rabble with eyes flashing: it was hard to grasp that events could change so rapidly. The normally quiet Mahomed rode up as if to protect me from any violence.

'*Iskut*! (silence!) stand back, and then say what you have to say!' he shouted.

I was beginning to understand, but Mahomed interpreted for me:

'They say they have been attacked by Nuba: people have been killed and they expect to be attacked again.'

There was some order now, though the people were restless and fiery, determined to show their grievance.

'Tell me now!' I shouted. 'Why should Nuba attack you – what happened?'

A voice said:

'We were doing nothing – they killed some of our cattle then they pounced on us. This is our land, our fathers grazed their animals here as we do.'

Now, it was quite clear – an ages-old problem of grazing over country which Nuba regarded as their own hunting ground. This was the flashpoint of the two races, in which wandering tribes occasionally moved close to Nuba ground. With the new rains, and the arrival of wild animals from the south, the Nuba were angered at the encroachment of the cattle people.

These Arabs were similar to the people of Fariq, returning to a traditional stopping place on the arrival of fresh grass. I could only go with them to their village and learn the worst.

I rode ahead of the *hamla* with a numerous running escort a distance of roughly two miles north of the track. Here was another broken-down collection of huts. Before I could dismount, a crowd gathered and, to my surprise, women clutched at my legs crying out in shrill voices. I tried to shake them off but, fortunately, one of the running men pushed them aside with apparent anger and shouted:

'Stand back, the *mofetish* has come to help us!'

A clearly understood voice said deliberately, 'Revenge on my dead husband!'

Another said, 'They outnumber us: kill the slaves!'

'*Ta'al hinne!*' one woman said (follow me!). I went to her little hut. A covered body lay on the ground.

There were two dead Arabs in the village: several other men had blood-stained cloth wrapped round wounds.

Meanwhile, it was still raining and I was still half naked, though the people were too incensed to notice. The *hamla* rode in. I knew I would have to sit this out. I called on the boys to prepare a campsite, then asked the men of the village to sit down and talk the situation over, which they were not disposed to do. They were now shouting: 'Revenge on the Nuba! Lead us to the Nuba!' (something which I was certainly not disposed to do).

They became tired of shouting, and suddenly decided to sit as I had suggested.

'Where did the Nuba come from?' I asked.

'They are slaves from El Azraq!' came the answer.

This was an interesting turn – that was the home of our guide! I told them: 'Sit here while I go for my books.' I hoped that this would sound significant to them and that they would leave me for a minute or two with the boys.

I left them arguing among themselves and hurried to where the tents were being grudgingly erected. I called the boys together and urgently told them my plans.

'Mahomed, ride at once to El Azraq and tell the guide to make certain no one leaves the village until we arrive in a day or two.'

I told the head groom: 'Ride as quickly as you can to Heiban – tell the sergeant of police to come here as quickly as he can with as many askaris as he can bring!'

They understood at once. I got Ibrahim to bring a dry shirt from a box then returned to the village men with my diary. Heiban must be about 28 miles away – it would be a long wait.

An Arab stuck his blood-covered arm into my face – the blood was dry and caked.

'This must be avenged!'

Aggressive attitudes were something I hadn't previously experienced. I searched for words.

'You say the Nuba outnumber us: it will be futile for so few to go against so many. I am sending to Heiban for help, then armed soldiers can come to our aid.'

This could only sound cowardly: one man swore loudly.

'In the name of Allah, I will go and fight them by myself!'

Fortunately it was only histrionics, and gradually they became assured that my proposition was the correct action to take. I was weary of the discussion, which went on and on, but was nervous of leaving them in case their wrath flared again.

The women were all moving in a wide circle at the fringes of the village, their voices ululating in the death-wail. Ibrahim had a fire lit and was standing beside the tent, watching. I signalled to him to prepare coffee and said to the men:

'You must share my hospitality – come and have coffee at my tent.'

This was an improbable proposal as there were at least 15 Arabs, but it touched a chord.

'No: it is we who should be hospitable.'

At last the tension eased a little. We drank thick black coffee and the talk continued, until, I could return to the tent and be alone at last.

That night and the day that followed were long hours of protracted misery. The dead were buried. Much of the wrath had cooled and people kept to themselves, but in the evening I sat with them for some time beside a fire and talked. I learned about the precarious life of the nomad and of their poverty, although they did not appear to be aware that they were unusually poor. The people who, 24 hours before, had been aggressive and threatening, were as gentle now as people in any other community I had visited.

It was very late when, at last, there came the sound of hooves. People came out of their huts to look. A weight lifted from my mind at the splendid sight of six soldiers – no, there were five: the sixth person was the administration omdah of Heiban in plain clothes.

I spoke my gratitude to the Omdah for having come with his men so quickly. The exercise of law was his province and it was with great relief the burden was placed on his able shoulders. He held a meeting resembling an impromptu court, then, after long, tedious discussion I slipped into bed in a state of utter exhaustion.

In the course of time, the leaders of both tribes were taken to Heiban where a full court was held, and appropriate judgements made. My presence was not required, so we were free to continue our trek into Nuba country – at last!

El Azraq

The progression from the village to El Azraq was like an escape into Paradise. The trekkers were all quiet and solemn, no doubt tasting their escape, just as I was.

The path led through a verdant jungle moving with life – monkeys, gazelles, a solitary Tetal antelope – and steaming like a tropical forest. Watercourses flowed gently between leafy banks: the change was bewildering! This was the kind of country the Abri missionaries had come to in the years before the onslaught of erosion. If erosion continued its progression south, this beautiful forest was also likely to be engulfed within a matter of years.

The *hamla* approached a grove of tall durot trees. Between their trunks I saw the first houses of a mud and thatch village: unbelievably, we had already reached El Azraq.

We rode into a tidy circle of huts where people were standing at the doors as if awaiting our arrival. Whoops and cries came from houses as if the news was being spread, and soon a crowd of cheerful people surrounded the *hamla*. They did not look at all warlike. Their eyes seemed to shine with innocence, and yet two days before some of them had engaged in bloody fighting.

Our old friend the Nuba guide came forward to welcome us, but first of all I had to ask him about the fighting.

'Were people from your village involved in fights with the Fariq people?'

'El Azraq is a wide-scattered village, but no one here was fighting. We know about it because Mahomed came and spoke with us. You had better talk to the Mek when he returns: he has been away today.'

I could get no further information and set the boys to building camp a little distance from the village. The distance was mainly decreed by the presence of numerous black pigs, animals which the boys, as good Moslems, were unable to tolerate.

Unlike the temporary villages we had recently seen, El Azraq showed every sign of permanence. My first thought was this must arise from the manner in which they were able to live in balance with their environment: there were no great plantations of millet or herds of goats and cattle, so there was less evidence of the land being exploited. They cultivated small patches of land with a greater range of crops which included maize, tobacco and even tomatoes. But they are by instinct hunters, with the husbandry of crops and livestock providing a lesser part in their diet, and this usually performed by the women.

While Mahomed prepared a meal, I walked through the village and could not but admire the attractive little houses. Inside and out they were elaborately decorated with bright traditional designs depicting plants and animals, commonly snakes, quite unlike other Nuba houses I had seen, and showing a variation in tradition throughout the mountains.

Everyone greeted me with the word '*Aafi*'. The menfolk were all completely naked apart from circlets of plaited straw round ankles and wrists; single women were also naked, though married women wore a decorated leather waistband with a thin leather thong between their legs. Most women had pierced and stretched earlobes holding circular metal rings, sometimes six inches in diameter, and their hair was puddled into little balls with red clay. Most pleasing was the way men and women alike shared in the conversation.

In one house I sat down amid a crowd of village elders, all engaged in smoking home-cured tobacco in finely made clay pipes. Some old women also sat naked and cross-legged, puffing away contentedly: presumably this was how the old people passed the time of day. The houses contained rough wood furniture with, occasionally, room partitions. There was even a form of central heating in which a carefully contrived clay flue conducted smoke and heat at an angle to a chimney.

The Nuba of El Azraq were perhaps naked, but they were not necessarily primitive!

A crowd gathered to watch as I ate lunch beside the tent. They were silent, as none spoke Arabic, but by now, I was accustomed to an audience at mealtime.

After the meal, two young 'giants' walked with me round the cultivations; their bodies had been first dabbed with clay then polished with oil and they sported black and white feathers on their heads making them seem taller than ever. (Never once did I see Nuba with their bodies painted with intricate patterns as is shown in modern literature. This is a recent art form for the benefit of tourists!)

I felt dwarfed by the men and, as they knew only a few words of Arabic, they answered my questions with grunts. It was easy to imagine how a few men such as this could spell havoc to the neighbouring Arabs if they were so inclined. Once again, I marvelled that such as these had ever been considered as slaves!

On closer examination the little plots, resembling kitchen gardens, contained an even wider range of crops, which included egg-plant, peppers and a range of podded legumes. This variety I could only attribute to the influence of the Heiban mission, because it was unusual. We passed a crystal-clear spring of water, bubbling from a sandy bed: I had to stop and drink from this rarity – and it was good!

Late evening, I was sitting engrossed with writing as usual, when a visitor, dressed in dazzling white, rode up on a donkey. He slipped his leg over the donkey's head, walked over with a smile and, in Arabic, introduced himself as the Mek.

'Sorry to have been away – I have been looking into a matter at Fariq village, these are bad people and sometimes they fight us,' he said.

This time I got the story from the other side – the Arabs with their cattle spoiling their traditional hunting grounds, and so on. Obviously, it occurred to me neither party had the monopoly of blame. If two irreconcilable groups such as the Nuba and Arab continue to lead separate existences, yet so close to one another, there will always be flashpoints.

Thunder gave warning of a coming storm so he left with the promise to visit me in the morning. That night there was more than rain and frogs to disturb the camp, as pigs discovered the tent and were enjoying the novelty of rubbing their backs on guy-ropes – they just would not stay away! Apparently Nuba pigs slept by day, then foraged and knocked tents down by night!

The village cockerels, of which there were apparently many, gave a good hour's notice of the coming of dawn. Pigs joined in the chorus and with first light, people were awake and setting about their daily chores.

Ibrahim brought in an early breakfast, then, in company with the Mek, I was out among the cultivations in the early red morning light.

Women and children were hard at work in the plots hoeing weeds and drawing up little terraces to hold water and thus minimise the eroding effects of heavy rainstorms. These simple steps of protecting their land caused me to speak to many of the women with the help of the Mek who translated patiently. They replied that this was their custom, as if to say, 'there is no other way'.

I asked why the men were not out helping with the work. He replied, 'Growing food is woman's work!'

I thought that this was rather hard on the women.

'But what do the men do? Is it not right that they should help to feed their families?'

He looked thoughtful for a minute as if this possibility had never occurred to him. 'But men hunt for food and they discuss the affairs of the people!'

This was rather a weak explanation as hunting seldom took place in full daylight. I asked, 'Where are the men just now?'

He answered, 'They are most likely sleeping, as it is early.'

Early for the men, but not for the women!

Unlike in western society, it was the women who were the main providers and it was the men who spent most effort in colouring their bodies and demonstrating their physique. I noticed one heavily pregnant girl wielding a long-shafted hoe. She was perhaps 12 or 13 years of age, an early age to be pressured by life, and amply demonstrating a woman's lot in the mountains.

The Mek was no ordinary tribesman, as I discovered during our morning travels. He had retired from the Sudan Defence Force with the rank of sergeant; in fact, before the war he had been in London on some ceremonial occasion. On receiving a wound when engaged in fighting the Italians in Eritrea, he had reluctantly been invalided out of the forces. This was one Nuba who had successfully returned to his native village.

I asked him whether the many Nuba soldiers would return to the mountains after the war. He shook his head.

'Few of them have interest in the land, and hunting is not what it used to be. They shall want to make money, and it is not easy to do that here.'

I mentioned to him the Settlement Scheme for returning soldiers.

'That will work,' he said with a laugh, 'provided there is plenty of beer and entertainment for the men!'

That did not sound particularly hopeful: there was certainly no government provision for a beer 'den' at Talodi! This disruption of tribal life brought about by the war was certain to break down old communities and increase the size of the few cities in the country.

He took me proudly to a little citrus plantation, with oranges and lemons already showing fruit, the first evidence of private initiative of this kind that I had found. There was obviously potential for a high quality of life in areas such as this – if only the people had the will to settle to creating it.

This man, with his experience and skills, could be an example and 'growth point' for this area of the mountains, if the people from surrounding tribes were predisposed to follow the example of a neighbour.

It was only at the end of our morning travels that the Mek surprised me by saying: 'I am a Christian and was educated at the Heiban Mission.'

Here was another 'first' for me. He expressed a desire to accompany me to Heiban when we left El Azraq the next morning.

The Python

In common with the boys and the villagers I enjoyed the novelty of an afternoon siesta, to catch up on sleep after so many disturbed nights. Ibrahim let me lie, and it was surprising to find the sun low in the west when at last I looked from the tent. An afternoon's sleep is seldom comfortable to the body and there now came an urge to do something energetic.

Close to the village a weathered rocky hill 200 to 300 feet high stood up sharply from the plain. It was a typical feature of the area, resembling at a gigantic level a tower of blocks built by a child. Hills such as this reared from the forest floor, and consisted mainly of bare rock except where an occasional tree found a foothold. I decided to climb it and study the surrounding country from the vantage point it offered.

Equipped with notebook and pencil I struggled up and over the jumble of rock, until, just short of the top, I was stopped by one large cube of stone which marked the summit. It seemed a pity not to surmount this last obstacle, difficult as it was, and only after some effort and risk I succeeded in getting to the top to sit down on a dead flat surface about the size of a kitchen table. Looking over the edge I discovered that three of the sides were precipitous, with the route I had climbed the only means of ascending or descending.

The sun looked set to drop behind the Heiban range. On every side stood virtually unbroken forest, concealing the land, except where other rocky hillocks peeped up. I enjoyed the colour of the scene and the feeling of coolness which this slight altitude provided then I turned to jump down from the high rock.

Just in time, my eyes picked out a movement – a python slipping between fissures in the stones towards me: it was fully 6 inches in diameter, with the length of its great body not yet fully in sight. I moved back beyond the snake's range of vision and waited entranced, expecting to see the squat head with black and yellow body appear over the edge of the rock. Should it appear, I was trapped!

Minutes passed and nothing happened. I peered down and saw the animal coiled at the base of the platform as if completely unaware of my presence.

The camp was clearly in view below, so I waved time and again, to attract the attention of the boys, but no one was watching.

There was only one action to take: namely jump and land on the small rock platform beside the resting python. Holding my breath I eased my body outwards and flopped down, a foot from the python's head. Presumably it was more startled than me, but I was up and rushing down the hill before it knew the cause of the disturbance.

I ran to the camp in some excitement to tell the boys of my 'narrow' escape – at least I regarded it so at that time. Ibrahim listened, then, to my surprise, began a 'halloo!', whooping loudly for the entire village to hear – some primitive blood-lust had stirred within him. A few 'warriors' from the village soon arrived with spears and quickly scaled the hill with Ibrahim well in the van. I struggled up behind, but on reaching the spot, the animal was already in its death throes. Had it been a small wriggling snake, Ibrahim and the others would never have gone close, but a great slow-moving python was apparently no reason for fear.

The 18-foot body was carried to the village where, no doubt, it was eaten. I watched them removing the skin, which I was given as a present after the rains, several months later. Without proper curing, however, it is hard and of little use! Python-skins were commonly used for personal adornment or for decorating weapons and shields: they could be purchased for a few pence in any market place.

Next morning we left the village in the company of the Mek, destined for Heiban and the mission station. I looked forward to meeting the family there and they were sure to welcome my visit now that the rains had isolated them. Tucked away in one of the trek-boxes were a number of items of mail for the missionaries and their children. At the time of packing this had seemed a disproportionate load to carry, but now that Heiban was so close I looked forward to handing them over.

During the day's trek the Mek spoke about the beliefs of his people: the importance of witch-doctors. Birds and trees had their own special folklore – one large black and white bird – '. . .don't make it fly if you see the underside of its wings leaving the ground, it will mean death,' – and so on. There was a great web of superstition surrounding natural things, all of which he apparently believed, at least in part.

Suddenly the path led into an open space and I was both surprised and pleased to recognise the motor track, already quite familiar on treks from Talodi. We had completed a traverse of the district!

In the distance a small group of people walked towards us, although we were still about two miles from the station. I recognised the missionary in the middle of the group, and as they came near, it was easy to see his delight at having visitors during the rains, something seldom experienced in the past.

Then a Heiban askari rode up to escort us in. He was one of those who had ridden 'to the rescue' at Fariq village. This unexpected welcoming surprised us all, and we rode into Heiban with some vain feeling of accomplishment that we had covered at least a quarter of the trek without mishap.

I was invited to stay in the mission house 'for as long as possible', but with the entire *hamla* to think of the offer was refused, and instead we took over the Heiban rest-house. Tea was, however, brewing and even before I could remove the day's grime I joined the missionaries for a typical afternoon-tea (with scones) in their lovely home. It was absolute pleasure to escape from water problems, saddle-sores and sick horses, for a short period.

The mission house was the best-designed, and coolest, I found in my entire stay in the Sudan, yet it was made only of the same materials as are used by the natives, namely mud brick and thatch. A structure of fairly irregular tree trunks supported a sweeping thatch reaching almost to the ground. The walls and room divisions, all relatively low, left a wide gap for air to circulate. Reflected light got into the house through the space between outside walls and eaves. It was my first experience of 'open-plan': it was always cool and airy: it was ahead of its time! It was also a reminder that local building methods and materials are very often superior to 'foreign' alternatives. The most uncomfortable buildings in the mountains were of red brick and sheet iron!

If the mission house was outstanding in design, it was as nothing compared to the rest-house lavatory. Indeed, the rest-house lavatory out-splendoured any other building in Heiban. It must have been built by some contractor in earlier years who either had undue reverence for his white brothers, or a wry sense of humour. Were it possible to transfer this edifice *en bloc* to the British Museum it would provide one of the most splendid mementoes of 'empire'. It is remembered with awe!

It consisted of another large thatched building. On stooping to enter, the urgent visitor was confronted by an ascending pyramid of beautifully painted steps leading to the throne – literally a throne! To sit up there when duty called, left one in no doubt as to the importance of the occasion. The Arabs, accustomed as they are to wide open spaces, use the words '*beit el adab*' (house of the proud) meaning a lavatory – an appropriate name for the Heiban edifice!

The village resounded to a continuous whirring sound as of a flight of propellered aeroplanes about to take off – caused by young people, busily employed whirling pieces of wood round and round on the end of a six-foot length of cord, which produced a monotonous drone. The missionary complacently said that it was a traditional 'rain-maker's' device to ensure good rains: some competition to the efficacy of prayer!

The rest-house *mustaba*, surrounded as it was with frangipani in full exotic bloom, provided an uncomfortable sleep due to the overpowering fragrance of the flowers.

Two days were spent using Heiban as a base for touring the neighbouring Nuba villages. On this occasion the missionary shared my travels and acted as interpreter at a number of cultivators' meetings. He was able to visit his surrounding Christian cells at the same time so we both gained from each other's company. I was able, also, to witness the work of healing in the little hospital and could but marvel at the hard work and dedication of the staff there; after all, they were giving in effect almost voluntarily, what government had failed to provide. The Nuba had very little experience of medical care, or schools, or craft training, apart from that which was provided by the missions.

The Nuba in their isolation were a race apart from the rest of the Sudan. They had no concept of the idea of nation in the wider sense. To speak to them of the national need for grain or of government policy, would be met with blank stares. If there was a government beyond the rule of the tribe, they could well think, what did it do for them? What did it provide that improved their conditions? The answer was inevitably, very little, apart from maintaining 'the peace'. Yet, to travel among them during the rains I had to emphasise the presence and the role of government, for what it amounted to. Even to introduce cash as an inducement to grow additional crops, had only limited and localised effect.

The pity is that so much good could have been done there, had the resources been applied, but, sadly, the practice with overseas territories was for resources to flow out of, rather than into a territory.

In spite of all these qualifications as to the value of rule from overseas, it is probable that unbiased observers, if such ever exist, could well judge the years of British rule in the Sudan as being a period of benefit to the people of that country. One thing is beyond question – the majority of the British staff who served there, did so with high ideals and a large measure of compassion.

Deep Nuba

By the time I had done all that was required of me in the Heiban area, the horses were well rested, and we were keen to get on the move again.

The overall route for this horse-trek was in the shape of a figure-eight with Heiban the crossing point on both the outward and the return journey. Our next step was into the high mountains west and south of Heiban, with Talodi the furthest point of the trek. This region, deep in pure Nuba country, was where I had made various short journeys by car in past months, and it promised adventure of a special kind, giving an opportunity to spend more time with the hilltop communities there.

According to the cloth map, which had a little more detail on it of this area than that we had previously traversed, the path climbed steeply from the plain and looked far from easy. The Mek assured me it was negotiable by horse and we should have little difficulty; after all, he had done it several times on donkey back.

Early in a morning we loaded up and left amid the good wishes of our friends, including a gathering of children determined to give us a send-off. There had been no rain for the past days, so it was necessary to have the water tanks full, as it was impossible to predict what lay ahead on the rocky trail.

The first few miles were a pleasant walk through leafy glades, except where forest fires had exacted their toll. The horses could not resist pausing for the occasional nibble of young grass and had to be prodded on constantly. Gradually the climb started, with the path becoming stony, reducing our pace to a crawl. The valley floor was filled with scree and massive rocks as they had tumbled from the steep mountain before us. Soon each man led his horse. Rocks leaned together making narrow chasms and occasional tunnels, so that the wide packs stuck, and we all had to push and manoeuvre to get the animals through. The Mek could well have done this stretch by donkey, but pack-animals were proving another proposition as early as this in the journey.

We were quickly sweat-soaked and gasping for breath. Horse and man alike were coated with red dust and, finally, in desperation, I called a halt in the shade of a cliff to enjoy some liquid, and to rest until the hot hours passed. There was a long way to go to reach the top, but already, looking back, the vast plain we had recently trekked stretched out to the distant horizon and showed clearly many of the rocky features we had passed by on the way to Heiban.

Occasionally, Nuba, singly or in groups, but all on foot, passed by, with everyone carrying a little cloth pack and a spear. I was beginning to doubt the wisdom of bringing loaded animals on such a difficult track, particularly when they had very little experience of hill work.

Two hours later we moved on and, almost at once, arrived at a rock staircase with some steps so high they might have been rock walls marking the end of the route. I went ahead several hundred yards by foot to get assurance that this really was the path, before tackling the 'steps' – yes, it did ease off eventually!

There was only one answer. The loads were all untied and manhandled to the top: that was the easy part compared to the difficulty of persuading the horses to lift their forelegs and make the spring to the next step – eight of them in turn! We pulled and pushed, were sent spinning as animals swung off balance, and at times looked at each other in despair wondering what to do next. It took all of three hours to clear this stretch with everyone sore and exhausted and determined to go no further that day. In the last light of day we were able to see the path ahead of us crossing a short stony escarpment, towards a final climb to the mountain tops.

We had stopped on a broad ledge devoid of living things without even grass for the horses, save in a few sparse hollows. The stars showed clear, with no indication of rain, so there was no point in unpacking tents. We eventually lay in a row to sleep, with our heads to the rock wall, and feet pointing to what looked like infinity.

It was easy to see that this high rocky perch unsettled the boys, unaccustomed as they were to mountain life. They gathered in careful formation to pray earnestly towards the east, and even when I lay down to find sleep, I could hear voices monotonously intoning words of the Koran in half-whispers.

The morning sunrise was perfect. The sun, impossibly large and oval, shone straight into our eyes, so that we all lay for some little time in rapt admiration of the scene. I was reluctant to move. Like the boys, perched as we were on this high ledge I had a feeling of disassociation from everyday experience, as if life was quite free from care. This had to be a holiday: almost a dream, an escape world to enjoy without end. How difficult it became to return to reality and normal anxiety, because, even here high in the Nuba Mountains achieving a lifetime's ideal, there were worries, true or imagined, to spoil the thrill of fulfilment. Thus do we lessen our moments of greatest joy!

And so at last we all stirred and voices broke the spell, as on any ordinary day. Within the hour the horses were loaded and, as usual, moved in single file along a mile or so of easier terrain, until the final steep climb to the top. This last stage would have been considered difficult by horsemen anywhere, but after the struggle of the previous day, the horses took it in their stride and, at last, we arrived on more level mountain tops, and at our first high Nuba village.

People looked on us with wonder at this sudden invasion: they hesitated to come forward, uncertain as to the purpose of our visit. We stopped to picnic and slowly a little crowd gathered round in silence as we ate. I spoke in Arabic to them, but there were no answers until, at last, a man who had been watching for some time suddenly ventured: '*Salaam aleckum!*'

There was at least one person who knew the language! I asked him where the Mek of the village was, but he knew very few words; instead, he pointed into the distance and sent a boy running, no doubt to fetch the Mek. The village was perched, like so many others, on the bare rock of the mountain top. It was close to a precipice and I had to marvel at the way children from their earliest days could play without injury in such dangerous surroundings. Presumably to start life in places such as this, children develop confidence and a sense of balance which keep them out of danger. Probably the converse is also true that children over-protected by parents may never develop this type of confidence, and then say in later years – 'I have no head for heights!'

I watched the smallest toddlers sitting dangling their legs in space, and no Nuba called 'Keep back from the edge!' – yet they survived!

In time, the Mek turned up. Surprisingly, he too was clothed like the Heiban Mek. Apparently, the Arab *jelibiyah* was considered a robe of office! And he spoke Arabic well, and thus was able to contribute to our stay on the high tops.

Every possible inch was carrying crops – green salad, tomato or tobacco and occasionally a form of bean. The plots were more like plant containers because, with the top being virgin rock, every depression or crevice contained imported soil. On every hand, houses were surrounded by these miniature gardens, all of them carefully tended by the women. There was a lesson here for any visitor from the outside world: a lesson which taught what can actually be achieved with minimal resources. It was also a lesson in survival. People such as the hilltop Nuba will survive unaccountable hardship provided one condition is fulfilled – that there is permanently available water. This is more than can be said for many other peoples I had seen!

As in other Nuba areas they suffered one great handicap – many of their crops were riddled with virus diseases: but this can easily be put right by a caring government.

Before arriving in Kordofan from the Gezira, it had been said to me on several occasions that the Nuba were among the world's most primitive races. This is a superficial opinion, one which I hotly oppose: depending, of course, on how the word 'primitive' is defined. Primitiveness, like intelligence, has many facets. Few people, worldwide, will have the intelligence to survive successfully as the Nuba have done on their bare hilltops.

After making these commendations about this striking race, I then have to say that there is another, not so attractive feature, as was demonstrated during that first day on the hilltops. The Mek took me to his gaily coloured home – outside a neighbour's little house there sat a woman, badly beaten up by her husband with her body bruised and blood-smeared. I was encouraged to take no notice of her, as indeed everybody else ignored her injured state. Apparently the husband had had good cause to 'reprimand' her. But, here again, no race can virtuously condemn the Nuba in realms of wife-beating, such primitiveness occurs in 'civilised' realms.

We set up camp in the village of Kongrei, a few miles further into the hills. The Mek had agreed to accompany us, so he brought his pack with him and stayed with us for the next few days, an arrangement which suited me well. The boys, usually so indifferent to the Nuba, accepted him into their fellowship too, perhaps because of his ability to speak Arabic.

There was still an hour or two before sunset and I was keen to see all that I could before dark. The Mek said in answer to a question:

'We have a very powerful witch-doctor here: she is also a powerful rain-maker.'

So far, I had kept out of the way of witch-doctors: I had seen a few, but had had no need of their good offices. A 'she' witch-doctor sounded particularly interesting and I could not resist asking:

'Is it possible to meet your female witch-doctor, to give me a chance to speak with her about her work?'

He looked aghast for a second, as if there was an element of danger implied in this proposal.

'The *kujur* will speak with no one, but she will cure sickness if it is necessary.'

Later, after I had explained this to the boys, they were also intrigued that a witch-doctor could be female. Being Moslems, they abhorred that people could be so superstitious. Somehow their minds were able to accommodate 'jinns', but not witch-doctors, whom they regarded with contempt. Then Mahomed came forward with a brave proposal, one which might permit us all to see this woman.

'Tell the Mek I have a *batn aiyan* (pain in my stomach) and say that I want it healed by the witch-doctor.'

Such acts of courage were what I had come to expect from Mahomed. He was even prepared to risk a witch-doctor's ministrations to satisfy my curiosity!

Without hesitation, as soon as he was told of Mahomed's sad state, the Mek walked over a crest, to return some minutes later and beckon us to follow him. We followed him to a sub-village, with one house, the witch-doctor's, set apart from the others. We were asked to sit on the ground some 50 yards from the house, easily identifiable by the many bits and pieces which hung from its eaves.

In a conspiratorial manner, the Mek whispered in my ear: 'Don't forget, it will cost you money!'

My first thought was that it was going to be an expensive evening, but further explanation assured me that 10 piastres was a sufficient payment.

An interested crowd of spectators gathered round to sit beside us on the ground, just as if this was the normal practice when the *kujur* got down to the job. A suitable delay followed, enough to make us wonder, then out came a strange female figure: she was virtually naked and unadorned, but she had a gross deformity of the right leg and foot – Elephantiasis – a condition not uncommon in tropical countries where limbs swell several times their normal size. If I had come to criticise or even scorn acts of witchcraft, I could now only pity the perpetrator of these acts. Yet, it was easy to see that she held the spectators in awe, as she trailed, with her disfigured limb, to a place in front of Mahomed, where a spear, a little black-metal pot and some small containers with unknown contents, were neatly laid in the dust.

She completely ignored me, as if the presence of that most rare creature, a white man, held no interest for her.

Mahomed looked at me appealingly as if to say 'is there no possibility of cancelling the operation?' – his courage was waning: and no wonder!

Now, quite leisurely, she reached forward and parted Mahomed's garments to reveal the supposed offending organ – his stomach. Turning her back on us she kindled a fire of dry twigs and put the little pot securely amid the flames, then emptied in some contents from the other containers.

There was absolute silence; I was almost sharing the superstitious awe of the other onlookers, watching a sequence of rites, as the concoction began to boil. Then, with unexpected speed, she picked up the spear and plunged it into Mahomed's stomach – or so it seemed! A gasp went round the crowd: Mahomed must have thought it was his last! But, on closer scrutiny, the fingers of her left hand arrested the point of the spear, which she now waggled about to give the impression of prodding Mahomed's internals.

In a flash the spear was thrown to the ground and she bent, apparently to suck the 'wound'. There came a grunt and she jerked back her head to show what could well have been a fragment of rusty iron in her mouth. This was held up for everyone to see. Down with her head again and Mahomed was now minus a fair-sized pebble. To complete the operation, a wad of cotton lint was dipped into the hot brew then wiped over the 'wound'. With the operation over, he was left with a red stain resembling blood on his flesh which he eyed distastefully. The *kujur* took the money, collected her implements, and, without ever having spoken a word, limped back to her hut.

We returned to the camp. Mahomed was particularly thoughtful!

Without question, the Nuba were convinced by all that had taken place, as they no doubt were if and when they were the patients. Whether it be a 'civilised' doctor or a witch-doctor, provided healing skills are practised with authority, the patient is closer to a cure!

Two more days were spent in the Tira Hills as we continued the trek south. They were days like others I had spent with the Nuba, rich with event and experience. If my meetings with the people, in which I attempted to explain the role of government and further its objectives, were fruitful, that is incidental to the fact that I was there, because, though the trek through their country will long be forgotten by them, it has left me with many fond memories.

Then, we left the 'tops' and returned to lower ground by the side of the large Tira Mundi watercourse. In a normal season it would have been a fast-flowing river, lipping steep banks; instead, it was running a mere foot of water, which the *hamla* waded across with ease.

There remained one final goal before trekking south the remaining miles to Talodi. In the Limon Hills west of the road lies the mysterious valley of Kinderma, mountain-locked and remote. I had no reason to go there, apart from curiosity. On the map it is contoured to resemble the plan of a vast football stadium – shut in by steep cliffs and with only one narrow entrance point.

Outside the valley, a little Nuba hut, serving as a rest-house, provided our last night's lodging before reaching Talodi. The valley was a source of wonder; wading a shallow stream between steep walls then suddenly entering into this enclosed valley – a perfect redoubt where a group of determined warriors might repel an army. The valley, though terraced and with signs of earlier habitations, was unpopulated at this time. It is a valley with a history – it must have, but it was a history I never learned.

Troubled Times at Talodi

A tired and untidy group trekked into Talodi at sunset next day. We were all jaded including the horses. They had the prospect of several days' rest before returning northwards again. Not for me, however! For some time I had been anxious about the 'Resettlement Experiment for Returning Soldiers', because I knew only too well of the Government's interest in its outcome. To be unable to influence its progress for such long periods was a source of unease. If the scheme was a failure, there was no doubt who would be accountable.

Talodi in the rainy season was the same uncomfortable place. But the rains here had been sparse, to the extent that on all sides, millet crops were wilting with the heat. Trees were in leaf, giving some welcome shade, so that the town had a more pleasant feel about it.

On this occasion there was no alternative but to live inside the rest-house, as rain had the habit of dropping unannounced. It was well the ghosts were 'laid'! A thin carpet of dust covered the tiled floors: the place had the feel of a mortuary.

A messenger came to the door with a letter: of all things, it was from Alex. Apparently mail for Talodi had been brought across country from El Obeid; possibly by horse or by camel. What could Alex be wanting? I tore it open, and read:

'Hope the trek is going well. This letter is to warn you that you have been booked for leave to Uganda by river steamer on 20th inst. Be sure and get out of the mountains in good time. The road north should remain open until then, but don't take any chances. You will be needing a break by now. Hope there is plenty of grain being sown in the mountains. I look forward to getting your reports and to seeing you again when you return from leave. Have a good time. Alex.'

My heart almost missed a beat: the sight of the letter had made me fear the worst. I had thought that it might be news from home, perhaps bad news. Perhaps . . . Instead, it was telling me I was to go south on leave! It was slowly sinking in. Because of the war, arrangements for leave were a matter of improvisation. Without question, I could do with a break. The prospect of once again travelling for weeks on end on the Nile had little appeal, when my one interest where leave was concerned was to return to Marion in Scotland. That, however, was still very far in the future.

I would have to make do with a journey to Central Africa – and yet, that would be an opportunity to visit new places – perhaps the Congo, or Kenya again. The prospect was not so bleak after all.

That left me with 17 days to complete this trek and join the sailing at Kosti. An unexpected turn of events, yet it did leave sufficient time to do what had to be done, and get back to Rashad.

I drafted a reply for the messenger to despatch back to Alex, though he too could already be off on leave. Now I would be working within a time framework: each day would count and there was no time to waste.

Early next morning I rode to Dam Gamad to the Resettlement Experiment, and quickly discovered a snag – whereas the six or seven miles to the site was an easy drive, to travel by horse wasted a lot of time. Bakhit was slightly lame and needed a thorough rest, so I rode Gamr through groves of leafy trees and over a gently flowing watercourse.

I approached the cultivations with trepidation – crops should be through the ground, and the new cultivators hard at work. I swallowed hard as I rode past holdings with crops almost fighting a losing battle with weeds. There was no one in sight! What was going on? Thankfully, there were several good holdings close to the new village. Probably I was expecting too much.

For once, the bush telegraph had not worked. I found Tahr Effendi the agriculturalist drinking coffee with the new village sheikh. They offered me a cup, but I was too impatient to drink.

'Where are the cultivators? Why are they not dealing with the weeds?'

Tahr, rather nervously, reeled off an account of human ailments which would have kept a witch-doctor busy for months: the selected tenants, on the whole, were apparently a frail bunch.

I wasn't having it! With Tahr at my heels, and swallowing my wrath, I went from house to house calling out the cultivators until a broken-down group of men stood before me. I said my piece: none of it specially complimentary, although the few good cultivators were singled out for praise. Then I learned we had a dissident on our hands. An ex-soldier minus an eye and with a mouthful of broken teeth said in a sulky voice:

'The Government will take our crops from us – why should we work for them? It is not worth the effort.'

This was contrary to everything that had been explained to them at the start, and I knew that it was a cloak for indolence. Now indeed I spoke some home truths – I laid into him verbally so as to leave no doubt about the Government's real intentions. The others took it all in.

My tirade finished and I shouted:

'Give me your hoe; give me your hoe! You have not got sufficient strength, I will do your work for you!'

A chorus started up from the group in general:

'No, no, no! The *mofetish* must not do such work. We *are* strong! We shall get our tools and we shall finish the job!'

With this newly awakened enthusiasm they made a sally towards their various cultivations and attacked the soil with a fervour which I knew only too well would quickly dissipate. Still, perhaps it would be the turn of the tide!

In the next day or two I hovered in the background like an overseer of slaves, minus a whip, and the scene gradually changed so that the crops began to flourish. But there were also the good cultivations. The agricultural Sheikh proudly showed me his crops: if returning soldiers at the end of the day were like him, a new age would dawn in Nuba!

There were, of course, technical problems which could scarcely have been blamed on the cultivators. Swarms of monkeys had raided the plots and might well have spoiled the entire venture. Tahr had a gun, and dead monkeys hung from bamboo poles on each holding. Sparrows had come from miles to feed on the seed grain and harig grass.

Harig grass was an important innovation, where an attempt was being made to establish grass as a crop for grazing and for manuring the ground – eventually to be part of the cropping rotation – an idea quite novel in the mountains.

Apart from millet, which occupied the biggest area in each holding, there were plots of cotton to provide a cash income with, in addition, plots of sesame and earth nuts to widen the diet of the cultivators' families. A few cultivators had even planted some salad crops.

Now that I took time to think about it, the experiment was not progressing too badly; after all, this was a social experiment, not a model farm, and the more I interfered, less true would be the outcome.

Another innovation at Dam Gamad was a community holding. The idea was to encourage co-operation, where the cultivators might grow the crops they wished, and use the income for mutual good. This idea was rather pious (as it might well be anywhere in the world) but, surprisingly, this holding was among the best in the scheme, largely due to the enthusiasm of the Sheikh.

A little shop called the 'canteen' had also been established with each cultivator having a 30-piastre share, paid out of his advance. There had been one visitor to the 'till' at one stage, but apparently it was working, and selling several simple commodities.

Tahr was doing a good job. At the end of the second day at Talodi I returned to the rest-house, looking forward to a restful evening writing up the day's report.

But it was not to be!

The sun had set, I was newly bathed and laundered, and settling to the inevitable bowl of earth-nut soup, when, to my acute surprise, the beat of an internal combustion engine made me sit up. A motor vehicle, in the rains! What was it: where had it come from?

An ancient Ford lorry drew up to the rest-house: it might well have been an original Henry Ford T-Model, with its square vertical windscreen and narrow wheels. It was laden with furniture and boxes. A white driver sat at the wheel. He stepped to the ground and I abandoned the soup in order to greet him. The boys gathered round, wondering: after all, they had laboriously ridden to Talodi on horseback and here was a lorry – if it could be so called.

I shook his hand, we exchanged greetings.

'This is a surprise – where on earth have you come from? I thought all the roads were closed,' I called out.

'I am heading for Kauda Mission Station, to my new job there.' He stretched himself luxuriously, then continued, 'I have driven up from the river on transfer. Do you know Kauda?'

'Wait a minute,' I said, 'no one drives here in the rains, yet you have come more than 100 miles. How did you do it?'

'Well, it was not easy: I needed a push occasionally, but this old bus takes some stopping!'

'Do you know the risk you have taken . . .?' I went on about the treacherous situations when watercourses are in flood: it had just been a chance that there was a lull in the rains at that time, and roads from the south were just passable. He had travelled in ignorance of the conditions and, apparently, without any advice from anyone who was familiar with the Nuba Mountains. His luck had held, yet, if he was to get to Kauda his problems were by no means over.

'What kind of station is Kauda? Are the Nuba good to work with?' he went on.

After settling in for the night and sharing the soup and other items of the evening meal with him, I spent hours answering his questions, and warning him that he might have some difficulty reaching Kauda, as we had just ridden down through flowing watercourses. He pointed to his vehicle, which would not have looked out of place with the Keystone Cops.

'She will get through all right. She's tough!'

His faith was touching, and he almost convinced me. Then I had another thought.

'You know, rain is most liable to fall after noon, so you had better get moving first thing in the morning.'

He listened, but perhaps it did not register, because next morning he showed a marked reluctance to rise, and I was on the move long before him. Prior to leaving for Talodi to begin the day's work, I suddenly had the inspiration of lending him Ibrahim as guide and companion for the journey, because the next day we would be heading north in that direction and could pick him up on the way. Ibrahim was happy to escape a spell on horseback and readily agreed to go with the missionary, so I left them with a final imprecation for haste.

This last day before leaving Talodi I had intended to spend at the cotton ginnery, tidying up office work there and saying my farewells, because with taking leave, it would be months before I saw Talodi again. I walked into town and was soon sufficiently busy to forget about missionaries and their problems. Hours passed smoothly, then it was noon and suddenly from the north, low rumbles of thunder echoed into the ginnery office: I could only presume that by this time the travellers had safely covered the 40 or so miles to Kauda.

Not long after, a violent rainstorm beat down, the first for a week. It would be a welcome relief to the crops in the area. Mid-afternoon and the desk was tidy: now I could close the door and return to the rest-house for some food. Rain was still falling. I stood at the ginnery door, chilled by a wave of cold air, and waiting for a lull in the storm. The town looked gloomy; hilltops were hidden beneath heavy cloud. The ginnery compound ran with water, tearing at its loose surface and leaving behind a net of runnels. Were the mountains to be deluged now, and would the trek north be impeded by flooded watercourses? Perhaps we could be stuck somewhere in the road north: perhaps, even, I would miss the river steamer and my leave south!

I shivered, then started walking and immediately was soaked to the skin. At the rest-house Mahomed was having a busy time doing Ibrahim's work as well as his usual kitchen duties – he was also preparing for our early departure from Talodi the following morning. He got me dry clothes, and served a belated lunch, so that it was a pleasure to feel warm once more.

The grooms had the horses ready for inspection; I did my rounds. They were in good shape and Bakhit looked ready for the road again. Darkness fell earlier than usual. Rain had stopped by now and I could think of nothing else to do – nothing to read; I was not in the mood to write. I wandered restlessly through the dark grounds. The rain had brought fresh clouds of insects; fireflies sparkled.

I paused beside the garden gravestones – they carried no marks of identification – just whitened stones. Why had it not been thought necessary to mark the stones? I sat on one of them conjecturing on the story of the long-dead person beneath. He would have been an army officer, perhaps here to deal with the unrest of 50 or 60 years before. How had he died? Was there anyone back home to remember him? Such a sad end to be left here, forgotten!

A new sound caught my ears: someone was running down the road to the house – I could see a figure dressed in white entering the lamplight – whoever it was called my name. Ibrahim . . . it couldn't be! He was at Kauda with the missionary! But there was no mistaking the figure leaning on the table and gasping for breath.

I approached him hurriedly. 'Ibrahim, what is wrong? Why are you here?'

He stared at me, panting, then: 'We were turned over at a watercourse. The lorry stuck in the sand, and a wall of water rushed down at us.' He held his hand head-high to demonstrate the height of the wall. 'I was washed away but managed to struggle to dry land.' He paused for breath.

'Where is the *gesiss* (missionary)?' I asked with sudden fear.

'I can't say,' he almost groaned. 'When I came back to the lorry there was no sign of him – I waited, then thought I must run back and tell you what happened.'

'But did you not search for him – was he still in the lorry?'

'I couldn't see: the lorry was under water!'

The worst had happened! Why had I let him go? I was to blame, and should have known better. The danger from flash floods was well known in the country. When sudden storms burst on the hills, it was healthy to stand clear.

It would take too long to reach the river by horse – I knew the place well, fully 15 miles from Talodi. No wonder Ibrahim was panting! There had to be another way – could there be a motor vehicle in the town? Yes, there was, at the Merkaz: the administration lorry remained at Talodi during the rains. I knew the Omdah well, and had visited his house on one occasion – he would help at once.

Fortunately the Omdah was at home when I ran into town. He did not hesitate, and said, 'Follow me!'

We hurried to the store where the lorry was kept. The vehicle, old-fashioned with half-sides of sheet iron, was set up on wooden blocks for the duration of the rains. I checked oil and put in petrol while the Omdah went in search of the driver.

He was a long time gone. I waited at the door impatiently until, fully a half-hour afterwards, he returned with a number of men – in prison garb.

'The driver is not in town so I have brought prisoners to help find the *gesiss*,' he said.

There was also an askari, complete with rifle: a sergeant! He took command at once, telling the blue-clad prisoners to lift the lorry off the blocks. This they did with ease, putting it firmly on the ground, then they piled unceremoniously into the back. I got behind the wheel – the battery was dead, but in seconds, half a dozen strong Nuba prisoners went behind and pushed until the engine sparked into life.

We made our cautious way along the wet trail, through large puddles, and rattling over ruts left by the afternoon storm. The vehicle lights were faint and it was a strain to see any hazards ahead, but rounding the Talodi hills the ground was stony and firm, and several miles passed uneventfully. The prisoners sang lustily in the rear, enjoying their temporary freedom and apparently unconcerned at the serious purpose of the journey.

Inevitably, the going became soft as the soil turned from sand to clay. The engine laboured, wheels spun in ruts, then suddenly, it became virtually impossible to steer in a straight line – the surface was as slippery as black ice. The lorry slipped to the side at the least camber then, gently, it tipped into a shallow ditch and emptied the passengers into the mud.

Apparently no offence was taken; they scrambled up and quickly set the machine on four wheels again, and we continued on our way. With passengers such as those I had aboard that day, nothing would have stopped our progress. We came to our first small watercourse – 10 feet wide and in full flood. A prisoner waded in – there was at least two feet depth of water. I drove in, landing in the middle with a spectacular splash, then willing hands pushed us safely through to the 'distant' shore.

Feeling apprehensive and with nerves ragged, I drew up to the scene of the accident, fanning the headlights, poor as they were, over the frothing river. There was nothing to be seen – just water in furious motion. Then the Omdah pointed to an area of spume – it was a box or a case: by the water leaping round it, evidently the missionary's lorry was underneath.

We were all looking in silence; even the prisoners were quiet, fearing the worst, when, unbelievably, a figure came out of the darkness – bedraggled, but a white man. He had survived! I could hardly believe my eyes. A happy crowd of prisoners gathered round – they were delighted and shouted out their pleasure.

The young missionary was tired and dejected, almost in tears. 'My furniture; my clothes!' he groaned, as if that were his only concern.

'Don't worry; you have your life. You are lucky to get out of this alive!'

He had been washed by the current far down the river and had only just struggled ashore.

I was making to turn the lorry round for the homeward journey when he gripped my arm. 'We can't leave all my possessions – the lorry is still over there. Can we not do anything to get it out?'

There seemed little prospect of fishing anything out of the flood and I said as much, yet still he pleaded.

'Look, the cases containing my clothes are there.' He pointed to the black object in the river which had caught our eyes on arrival. 'Can we not, at least, rescue these?'

The Omdah spoke sufficient English to understand his meaning and he turned to talk to the prisoners in the Nuba tongue. They listened, then nodded enthusiastically, making signs that it would be no problem to them to collect the cases.

A rope from the Merkaz lorry was tied round the waist of one keen volunteer, then it was paid out from the bank as he plunged into the water. Two attempts were made, but on both occasions he was swept past the submerged vehicle, only to be pulled in again to the bank. The sergeant of police now took over, instructing the swimmer to launch out holding a piece of wood from farther up the river than previously. This he did, just as the lights faded on the lorry, and we were all left in darkness. His head was only faintly visible, but we were able to judge by the movement of the rope that he had reached the vehicle.

This time, when he was pulled in, he was clinging to the wood, with, in his grasp, a large attaché-case. Nothing else could be achieved. To repeat the swim again, in darkness, was risking another life, so without further discussion, everyone climbed aboard for the return journey. The missionary sat disconsolately beside his sodden case, and we set off on the difficult road home.

My sense of relief was so great that I could not resist stealing glances towards him, as if afraid it had been a dream and he might vanish. The mountains had taught yet another lesson; namely that to survive in this hard, little-understood environment, absolutely nothing can be left to chance.

On arrival at Talodi, Mahomed quickly provided a hot drink and dry clothes – Ibrahim was in bed, worn out after his exhausting run.

With the case opened on the rest-house floor, the stained contents were transferred to a bath and I went, thankfully, to bed, leaving my guest gloomily tramping the mud out of his clothes.

Next morning the Omdah drove into the rest-house grounds before our departure. He collected the missionary and they drove north towards the river with the same complement of prisoners. By the time we had ridden the 15 miles over drier roads, and watercourses with much reduced flow, the lorry with its muddy furniture was safe on dry ground. It had been dug out of a mud bank, and the sheer strength of the Nuba prisoners achieved what, in other circumstances, would have required a powerful tractor.

It was well for the *hamla* that the flood had passed, otherwise it would have been necessary to wait, perhaps for days, until it subsided. Now, I felt there was no time to waste on the long road north.

By late afternoon of that same day the *hamla* was making good progress on the road towards Kauda and the north. I took a winding trail to the east of the road in order to have the opportunity of visiting Kalkudda, an isolated Nuba village.

For some time I had felt unwell, but when shivers began to rack my body, I knew it must be malaria again. I was angry with myself: how had I let it happen when there was such need to make good speed homewards? Talodi with its swarms of mosquitos had struck again!

Miserably, I told the boys, and there was nothing that could be done other than set up camp where we were. The tent was put up and within minutes I lay on the camp-bed shivering so that it shook, my limbs jerking with the violent malarial spasms. Both Mahomed and Ibrahim looked in to see if there was anything they could do, then I was left alone for long hours to sweat it out. They both knew it was just a case of letting the illness run its course.

The sweat came soon enough and I lost all account of time and place, lying amid a torment of wild dreams. How long this phase lasted was impossible to tell, but it was dark when I surfaced sufficiently to call for Ibrahim. Probably he bathed me and changed the bedding, but there came another time when it was daylight and I had a raging thirst.

Night again, but I scarcely cared what time it was. There was no medicine, not even an aspirin – just the flat-tasting water. At one point a wild thunderstorm broke into my dreams, and I was aware of rain beating on the canvas, but this also passed.

Once I awoke just as daylight was breaking and I knew that I was in the real world again. That was the day I took some thin soup, and, as it was so hot in the tent, my bed was carried out into the shade of a tree. Sweats and shivers still alternated, but with lessening severity, and slowly I took a renewed interest in the surroundings.

I had been conscious of a visitor during the illness: he came several times and on one occasion I had wakened to find him sitting close to the bed. When at last I was sitting up, in the tent once more because of the heavy mist, the visitor came, bringing with him a gift of milk and eggs. Ibrahim was annoyed at the way he entered the tent without his authority, but I let him stay because he was my one visitor, and his intentions were kind.

He was a Nuba; as far as I could judge he had no position of authority in his village, but had travelled in his lifetime and spoke Arabic. We talked about his people, of his several wives, and surprisingly he showed contempt for witch-doctors and their craft. After a time he stood up and said:

'When you are strong, you will visit my home, then I will show you the rocks of the ancient people.' Then he continued: 'I will be back soon; I have something to show you!'

Lying back on my pillow, I wondered what he would bring to the tent next – then the flap opened and he pushed two naked young women through the door, followed them in, and the three sat in a row beside the bed.

'My daughters!' he said.

They were young teenagers, probably between 14 and 16 years of age, and were attractive in any language.

By this time I was sitting up again. Some conversation took place while the girls giggled to themselves, then abruptly he rose and left the tent, with the young ladies seated as before. He never returned that day – what were his motives? Well, perhaps he had thought that female company would speed up my recovery! Perhaps this was another gift, like the milk and eggs he had brought previously.

For some time I enjoyed the gift to the extent that I showed them a mirror, which highly amused them, and other everyday items from a trek-box. Their laughter brought Ibrahim to the tent. He tut-tutted as a good moraliser should, then stood with arms folded watching their antics until we all became tired and they went home to father.

I was strong enough next morning to walk the short distance to the village, where my friend showed me round. The scene was typical, with the women at work and men at rest. Strips of bark cut from a Tabeldi tree were being pounded into a cloth-like material resembling felt. It surprised me to see an old woman with a high pointed skull, caused by the heavy pressure exerted over a period of time by carrying heavy loads on the head. A circlet of cloth on which the load sits had altered the shape of her head.

He took me to the 'rocks of the ancient people' – at the base of a high rock cliff a great slab leaned against the parent to a height possibly of 50 feet. The inner walls were painted with ancient bushmen's art and, because of being sheltered from the weather, were well preserved.

The people had some reverence for this place: it could well have been a temple and had the air of being regularly visited. It was a place worthy of deeper investigation but, by now, I was impatient to move on once more.

Our trek took us past Kauda where the missionary was now established, and his ancient vehicle looked ready for another phase in its long career. There were the usual calls at villages to say what I had to say, and it was markedly noticeable that the further north we progressed, the more were the signs of erosion.

Day followed day – rise at midnight – trek through the night cold, then sleep and work in the afternoon or evening. I had, by this time, written masses of data and information, enough to provide months of work in the future.

Bakhit had tender feet so that more frequent stops were needed than previously; some of the horses had minor back sores, but it was necessary to maintain progress. A crisis grew at one village when two grooms broke the rule by becoming drunk on local beer, something which I could not tolerate, but somehow the miles passed at reasonable speed.

North of Heiban I took a minor trail, and rode through a valley which provided unexpected surprises. One deep gulley was made of perfect sheet slate. The ground had the appearance of a devastated builder's yard and large sheets of slate were prised easily from the walls of the gulley. This material could have been used for building purposes, but I found no evidence that it was so used by the Nuba.

A valley of small broken hills had interesting geological features; I was told that gold had been found in the area. Rocks were streaked with green and red, as if a variety of minerals could be found. More dramatically we rode over an area of soft black 'stone' which immediately excited my curiosity. I found the material almost slippery to touch – graphite! Half a mile from our route, a low hill proved to be completely of this mineral. When a thin coating of vegetation was removed, the rock beneath was entirely graphite.

This discovery excited me – was I the first person to discover this valuable mineral here? I collected a sample of the material which was sent, in due course, to Cairo for testing: the report came back that it was comparable with, if not better quality than, Madagascar graphite (a resource which is exported to many countries). Did this mean that large mineral resources existed in Nuba, waiting to be tapped? No answer to this question ever reached my ears. Presumably any reports I sent in were carefully filed, then forgotten.

It is hypothetical whether opening up mineral resources in the Nuba Mountains would add to or detract from the quality of living there. To think of the Nuba as miners is anathema. Even worse would be the prospect of others growing fat on their labours!

Now we had come to tsetse fly country where certain areas of rocky hillocks had to be given a wide berth. It was known to be fatal to the horses to go within miles of these hills. This entailed camping at a distance, then walking to villages on foot. At one village an Arab merchant entertained me rather splendidly, and I bought cheaply a number of fine hair carpets – carpets which stood the test of time and looked as good as new 20 years later.

In past days rain had fallen intermittently, with watercourses in quite heavy flow. A stop was made at a little rest-house south of Berembeita, where part of the building had been washed away by a recent flood, leaving a large gap in the roof. Because of steady rain it was considered unsuitable to erect tents, and we all squeezed into dry corners of the damaged building. A violent thunderstorm gave the feeling that it all might be washed into a neighbouring river at any moment. These hours were bleak, depressing – we were all needing to get 'home' and back into some state of comfort again. The journey now had little novelty left. We were, for the present, sated with travel: we had all had enough!

The sun came out and I was tempted to plunge into the muddy waters of the river, and, for an hour, basked in cool flowing water, my first swim since the Christmas plunge into the Nile, seemingly so long ago. The effect was restorative; I tried to encourage the boys to follow my example, but swimming was not for them!

One valuable memory of that rest-house was of 'instant-forest'. Poles eight feet in length had been dug into the ground to provide a boundary fence: every one had taken root. Here was another possible way to arrest erosion. There must be many suitable places where trees such as this could quickly bind the soil and, in the long term, provide fuel or supply other domestic needs. An ecological survey of areas such as this might bring some valuable answers to help solve the problem of damaged Africa.

The final stretch home to Rashad was an anti-climax. There was no work left to do except get home, and as soon as possible. A watercourse close to Um Berembeita was in flood, which occasioned a 24-hour wait before the crossing could be risked. Finally, with the help of ropes strung between the banks, the other side was safely reached and we were able to continue the long wearisome miles to Rashad.

It was dark when we straggled into the village. As usual, the place was still, with not a single living creature in sight.

The Flood

By now I had had just about enough. After months of trekking, the prospect of a long leave and rest was blissful. It was not to be leave as I would have liked it, but it would break the unending cycle of work, and permit me to return to the mountains refreshed.

Rashad, now that the rains were established, had a special beauty. The trees and many-coloured shrubs with, high above, a ring of hilltops, gave it a character of its own. It could have served as a holiday centre for people from the north, but I was past enjoying it; my one thought for the present was to escape.

The appointed date for leaving was still three days away and after the recent trek there was office work to do before I could go with an easy mind. An occasional motor vehicle still came to Rashad from the railway as, at this end of the mountains, trails were rocky with less likelihood of getting stuck in soft, wet clay. It seemed remarkable that rains just north of the mountains were later in arriving, and lasted for a much shorter period. I had been assured that the roads would remain open long enough to let me escape.

To sit at an office desk after restless months of trek was proving an ordeal – reports, grain deliveries, cotton movement, staff lists. I tipped my chair back and looked at the pile of papers without enthusiasm. My mind kept wandering to the journey ahead. I would be driven to the railway, then an overnight train journey to the Nile, followed by that long, lazy river trip to Uganda.

The 'village idiot' disturbed my thoughts with his usual military display – click of heels and sweeping salute – and handed me a radio message: 'To confirm your booking Nile Passage leaving Kosti 20th.'

I had thought it as well to get confirmation, just in case!

The heat was enervating. My shirt stuck to my flesh like a wet rag. Outside in the deserted compound there was a stillness as of death. The bray of a donkey sawed at the stale hot air: why were people so sure the trail would stay open and let me away in time? Heat like this usually meant a storm.

I started writing again, but the pen moved sluggishly over sweat-dimpled paper. The sun was dead overhead; even the fan boy hardly had energy to pull the cord. Time had stopped still.

To write was futile – I pushed the chair aside and resolved to give up until it became cooler. That afternoon I rode the familiar trails round the village, and enjoyed seeing the transformation the rains had brought.

By the next afternoon, the pile of papers was getting smaller and a burden was slowly lifting from my mind. A mist veil obscured the sun and at one point I had been alerted by distant peals of thunder, but I had decided to stick it out; one more full day, then escape!

By previous arrangement, the Rashad Omdah came to the office. We discussed plans for the district during my absence and he invited me to a farewell tea party at his home on the following afternoon before I left, then he said:

'That is, if you ever get away, because there is a storm coming.'

'I have been told there is no danger, yet. Surely the roads will stay open one more day?' I pleaded.

'It depends on the Abu Habl beyond the mountains: it depends on whether it will let you past.'

That Abu Habl watercourse kept cropping up, with its jinns and its threat. But I had decided to stick it out until the appointed time for my leave to start.

Night came and drums started beating. I was sitting in the garden writing a last letter home, when there came an almighty crash of thunder, and I was driven into the house as rain came with a severity I had only known in the mountains.

There was very little sleep that night. Beneath the mosquito net was like being in a stuffy airless cellar. The ominous words of the Omdah kept throbbing in my mind – 'It depends on whether the Abu Habl will let you past . . . let you past . . . let you past.' Was it malaria again? I had to escape, and at once! Get out of the mountains . . . away!

Yet, with the first slanting rays of the sun and Ibrahim's cheerful greeting, it all changed, and Rashad was beautiful again. The morning sky looked innocent and clear, and I felt well and keen to work the day out. Late in the afternoon, before closing the office door with some sense of ceremony, I sent my last message – this time to Rahad, to warn them I would be travelling there in the morning: the usual warning in case of accidents. If I arrived midday it would give a margin of time before catching the night train.

One thing only remained – the tea party. I could have well left for the railway once the office door was closed, but the hospitality of a farewell party was a significant social custom which would provide an ideal start to my leave. A circle of white-robed notables gathered for the occasion and we sat round an unusual delicacy, a large fruit cake, somehow baked in my honour.

There followed ardent discussion on the theme of the moment – the propriety of a woman teacher being appointed to the local school. Woman indeed! Modern city ideas had to be kept out of Rashad!

At one point, lightning danced along the mountaintops and wind gusts whirled dust in our eyes, but the party continued to its happy termination and I left the company with an effusion of good wishes echoing in my ears.

Free! I returned to the house to find packing done by the boys and everything in good order.

The storms did hold off! At that time it seemed a miracle.

Next morning, before first light, the entire household was on the move. Jacoub had the car ticking over: my kit in the rear looked meagre, after the heavy loads in our recent travels. There was no time for breakfast, I was so keen to escape.

The boys stood in solemn row to wish me well on my travels: probably they doubted my ability to survive without them. Ibrahim would enjoy a lazy spell to get on with his marriage and as for Mahomed, he had a family somewhere far away, because I knew he regularly posted money out of the mountains. Once we had gone they would all settle to months of blissful idleness but, they too, had earned a rest. The grooms were warned to keep the horses well exercised.

Then we were off!

The village was still asleep and the first cocks were crowing as we drove past the silent houses. I felt my every muscle knot in an ecstasy of relief. We drove through steep rock walls beyond the village and it was a comfort to find the watercourse flowing gently as if recent floods had dissipated.

At the edge of the escarpment a huge sun was lipping the distant horizon, sending up spokes of light like child art. The plain below, stretching northwards to the infinity of the Sahara, had the purple tint of heather. It was a scene beyond description and I was in a mood to enjoy it. I stretched my limbs in sheer pleasure, savouring freedom from cares and responsibilities.

Jacoub drove the dangerous track, down and over the bare rock, like a master, so that the plain seemed to rush up to meet us and before long, we were free of the mountains and heading at speed towards the railway.

Some time later with a good part of the journey over, I decided to stop under a Haraz tree for a rest and some food. The sun was high, we were making good progress, and, in any case, the train would not reach Rahad until long after dark, so there was plenty of time to spare.

But, here, the land was still dry and covered by yellow dead grass from the previous rains. Buds in the thorn trees were beginning to spring – it was like stepping back into the past after the lush green of the mountains.

I stretched on a bare rock for a time recapturing the feeling of being a new arrival in a strange land – mile after mile to the far horizon of good soil, yet virtually unpopulated. The shame of it that the people here should be living at a bare subsistence level in a land with such potential – if only . . .! My mind roamed over recent events – had I really achieved anything during this first spell in Kordofan? Probably nothing at all! Things were continuing as they had always done since time immemorial, yet there were the new *hafirs*, and the Settlement Scheme for Returning Soldiers and the Agricultural Committees of Mek Adam, though that was the merest beginning. Yes it was a start to build on after returning from leave.

The sun's heat reminded me that it was time to go. We set off again at speed, leaving a long cloud of dust fanning out behind. We passed a string of camels laden with household possessions and passengers of all ages with a herd of cattle and sheep being driven before them. The nomadic Buggara were on the move; that ages-old migration from the mountains during the rains. They would return once the watercourses dried and the water-holes were replenished and in a position to see them through the dry season.

Now, more Buggara – several groups, all heading in the same direction with women and children riding on bulls.

By now Jebel Daier, that splendid rock peak rising from the flat plain was right before us, obscuring the view to the north. Not far beyond it lay the Abu Habl and the railway. The people would be anxious to cross the Abu Habl before floods came down from the mountains to cut them off.

The well in front of Sidra village was surrounded by a dense crowd of people and their animals, all waiting their turn to drink. The way twisted and turned through forest and rock outcrops and, by now, we were part of the migratory stream as, every few yards, family groups shepherded on their stock. It was an interesting and pleasant stretch which I was enjoying to the full, when my eye caught a change of scene: the soil was greening on all sides – there must have been a local shower here!

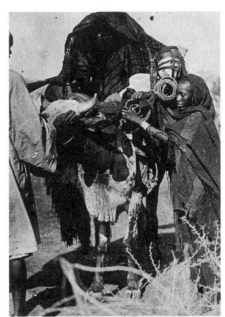

Nomadic Buggara.

A group of Arabs waved. Were they merely waving or beckoning me to stop? I turned, but already they were out of sight among the trees. Now the dust was laid and this made travelling more pleasant. Another corner, and now a few shallow puddles on the track, but the ground was firm for the car wheels.

Here was a new situation. Water on clay and the car would sink to the running boards – also the great watercourse was close by now. There must have been a heavy rainfall to account for this water. The way ahead was blocked by a herd of cattle which made us slow to a crawl – then we were through, and the wheels splashed into a shallow sheet of water.

I was sorting out this new development in my mind when an Arab splashed towards us, waving for us to stop.

'Go back; the floods have come. The way is blocked!'

I told Jacoub to keep moving forward. Had the worst happened? This was no local flood. Yet there was still a mile or two to the Abu Habl – surely it could not flood to this extent? I was relieved to see dry land ahead where there was a slight elevation, but this feeling was short-lived as a gathering of Buggara with all their animals milled around the water's edge. They were stranded: this was little more than an island!

An old greybeard approached the car with an expression which spoke all too clearly of the finality of the situation.

'The Abu Habl, the evil one, has trapped us. There is water ahead as far as the eye can see.'

He threw his *guftan* over his shoulder and asked me to follow him to the highest point. We pushed our way through the animals, and a few seconds later, viewed a vast expanse of water, miles wide. It might have stretched to infinity as its further extremities were hidden by tree-tops which stretched above the water's surface. From here, it might have been a vast lake instead of a flooded watercourse, as the water seemed stationary. No doubt, far in the distance water was in fast flood.

The floods I had witnessed far south in the mountains had fed into the tributaries of the Abu Habl – so much for official statistics and departmental advice. I should have listened to the Rashad Omdah, or even the witch-doctors. To think I had been attending a tea party while this was happening! I felt a sense of hopelessness; and yet the Buggara had been caught out too, so this particular flood must have reached Rahad earlier than in past years.

The water was still rising and in the short time since reaching the island it had gained inches. The car could well be trapped by now: my mind had to accept the fact that there was no retreat. There was no possible way round this flood, the only way was to go forward.

I looked around at the collection of animals and people all standing dejectedly. The confusion of animal noises and human voices was in time with the confusion in my mind. A holiday trip had become a disaster in a matter of minutes: there had to be an answer! The flood might continue to rise and engulf us all.

The people were beginning to gather round me. It seemed they were all talking at once. I realised that they regarded my arrival as providential – Allah, alone, could have spirited up a white man at such a time. The greybeard who led the group called for silence then addressed me politely:

'We are happy that you have come: *Allah karim* (Allah is generous). We must move forward, for to remain here is death. What is it that you intend?'

Fortunately, at that moment, a shout came from the driver, making us rush to the car which was sinking deeper into the flood – this, at least, gave me some time to think. There was only one way across water, and that was with boats!

The men pushed the car out of the water to a higher part of the little island. I had time to look around at the marooned creatures – a miscellaneous collection of camels, cattle, sheep and goats, not to mention the important human contingent of a wide age-span, from old grandmothers to little children. In addition there were all their other earthly possessions – sticks, pots, rolls of cloth and packs of all shapes.

Boats! Yes, that was the only way. I looked at the available materials on the island, the twisted trunks of thorn trees and nothing else. With luck, there might be sufficient material to make rafts!

I put a marker at the water's edge to check the flood level. This was no river pouring into a sea; it just spread itself over a flood plain until soil and the hot sun sopped up the entire flood. Another rush of water could pour from the mountains at any time, or perhaps the existing level might represent a peak: there was no way to tell. The highest point of our island was, say, 20 feet above the water level, surely high enough to escape drowning.

Then I remembered – my leave on the Nile Passage. The train would go from Rahad that night! I might as well forget about it – it would be sufficient to be able to get out of this alive.

The men gathered round again and I spoke of rafts and the need of every rope they had with them. The subject was discussed for some time and heads nodded in agreement but, before we could take any steps, a dramatic change took place. A bar of black cloud approached at awesome speed as if to engulf the little island. Lightning flashes danced from its edges: it looked like a jagged crown of thorns, and with it came wind and rain, a confusion of natural forces which stunned the senses. Darkness, too, had been falling so that in a matter of minutes the world closed in around us. A frenzy of human forms rushed from place to place erecting impromptu shelters. Rapid lightning flashes gave forms a jerky motion as in the early days of cinema and wet, half-naked bodies reflected the flashes in an unreal way.

Out of the chaos came some order and, as in a dream, I found myself huddled in one of the dripping shelters with some of the men. We squatted in a tight fetid mass with trickles of water running between us. My sandals were settling into saturated clay. Pounding rain and the constant explosion of thunder made speech impossible; we crouched there in utter dejection. It was easy to both sense and sympathise with the fatalistic mood of my fellows, a mood in which it was possible only to yield to the caprice of the spirits of the Abu Habl – Ibrahim had been right about the jinns!

How impotent is man before the powers of the supernatural: he is as a straw in the current. But no – I had to shake my head to remove a cloud settling on my mind: such thoughts were surely ridiculous!

Slowly the thunder echoed into the distance, leaving only the pounding rain: at least, speech was now possible. Everyone spoke, releasing pent-up fears – 'We shall be drowned . . . this storm must wash the island away . . . it is Allah's will!'

We emerged into the rain, gradually becoming more confident now that the storm was lessening. The marker showed that the water had risen only an inch or two so we settled to serious talk about rafts, axes and ropes – now I was merely one of the group with everyone resolved that it was better to make an effort rather than await the outcome of fate.

In teams of three we set about cutting, carrying and roping the twisted acacia stems, and now that they were working with a purpose, the mood changed so that they chattered and even laughed at their predicament. The women stayed apart in another shelter, and as for the children, they could well have been asleep because their life in any case was one of constant change, adequately supervised by their elders.

The island was a squelching ooze of mud and, like the others, I was quickly covered from head to foot. A few lamps had been lit and my own pressure lantern cast a fitful light over the scene.

After midnight, eight rafts of sorts were complete and as ready for launching as they could be, made as they were from such primitive resources. They were judiciously left on the higher part of the island and everyone settled down for a few hours' rest with the intention of leaving in the first light.

Jacoub had set up my folding bed and net beside the car, and I flopped down, clay and all, on the damp bed-covers. I struggled for sleep beneath a sky now bright with stars. The noise of frogs beat at my ears in wild crescendoes. This, together with humidity, made resting a form of torture. I could hear water entering cracks in the soil but my mind was blind with regard to the dangers ahead. Sleep! It finally came as a heavy weight pressing on the eyes, then the ears and finally on the brain.

With the first red lip of dawn I wakened to a wild cry coming out of some nightmare. In a daze I searched for reality, then, with an awakening fear, discovered the bed was in an 'ocean'. Without thinking I jolted up and the movement caused the bed to tip over into six inches of bitter cold water. I struggled with net and bedding, now tangled in the muddy water, and found my way to dry land again.

In the pale light I could see the driver peering from the car which had water half way up its sides, its wheels sunk deep into the clay. The Arab who had seen our predicament splashed out from the hillock which was all that remained of the island. The Buggara had had the foresight to keep to the high ground, but its area was now so small that it was congested with the variety of marooned creatures all jostled together.

Men put their shoulders to the car a second time till it was once more out of immediate danger. And there was yet another danger . . . snakes, scorpions and myriads of other small creatures had come to our island. Some pathetic little jerboa hopped among the animals' feet.

There was no reason to delay now that light was growing as the sun neared the horizon. We ate a few bites of food, probably all we would get that day, then the rafts were loaded with gear first of all, then with the smaller children and the old women.

I had adopted one raft to which the steel box containing my holiday kit was securely tied. There was still buoyancy so it was decided to crew it with two little girls, a dog and a tightly secured collection of live chickens. At first the girls refused to stay, but they were reassured when their father agreed to accompany the raft during the journey.

Jacoub was obliged to remain with the car, to return to Rashad when the flood receded. This he was only too happy to do. He shook his head doubtfully when I said my farewells to him . . . doubts which arose not from his prospects, but rather from the possibility of the rafts ever crossing the flood. I left him most of our food: he would not want for water! My last instructions to him were on the art of drying and airing wet bedding.

From the high point on the island a desolate scene presented itself. Trees stuck up from the water, sometimes only showing their topmost branches, while wide treeless areas indicated where they were totally submerged. These were places to avoid if at all possible. There were shallower stretches with grass tips showing. Tree-tops reduced the field of visibility to less than a mile, but it was at least cheering to see the edges of red sand dunes far beyond the flood.

There was nothing else for it but to set out. The other voyagers apparently were waiting for a signal so, with a dramatic wave, I set the flotilla in motion. The rafts, now floated, were hitched to animals which had been selected to tow the ungainly craft with their motley cargoes. It had been my intention to use the camels with their long legs for this purpose, but the Buggara had other ideas. They had no faith in the camel's ability to keep its footing on clay, and they also made the point that they were poor swimmers and would need their strength merely to survive. How right they were! In the first short stretch they slipped and floundered – if camels could swear they had every provocation, as humps continually submerged and reappeared.

Instead, two bulls were hitched in parallel to each raft. As cattle were accustomed to being beasts of burden, they bent to the task and I was forced, in time to admire their endurance. They looked half-starved with hide clinging to their bones, yet in the end, it was these which saved the day.

The Arab accompanying my raft was called Abdulahi (slave of Allah). He led our bulls into the water and soon a long string of rafts followed in single file behind. At waist depth, with the rafts buoyant, we waded beside them while, instinctively, the other animals clustered round, some wading while smaller ones were already swimming. A new-born camel was tied on one raft: two dogs swam nearby, still finding strength to bark noisily.

The women, forgetting their scruples, forsook their robes like their menfolk and, stripped to the waist, clung to the rafts. I was merely one of the group. At least for the present there was no awareness of race difference – no prejudice, no barriers – and I warmed to them as everyone concerted to the effort.

The rafts seemed to be intact, and for half an hour some progress was made over water of varied depth, but never deeper than chest level: then a raft splayed out, spewing its cargo into the water. Repairs were quickly made. The rough thorn trees were poor for that purpose and projecting branches seemed to catch on every conceivable object, taxing patience and strength. Furthermore, the coarse twisted ropes left much to be desired, so that to think of rough waters to come was frightening: how could the rafts survive? Fortunately, we were too preoccupied with the moment to worry about it.

A large snake was twined round the branches of a tree; the sun beat down on the voyagers warming the water, and ripples sent back mesmeric flashes to the eye. Drift, gathered on branches, crawled with scorpions and insects of many kinds. The water was like a placid mill pond, without any current. Half a mile at least passed in this way with some shallower areas where the sheep were able to rest, then inevitably it became deeper and there was nothing for it but to swim.

Talking ceased as man and woman alike kicked out with all their strength to assist the animals. Camels struggled with their heads high from the water, twisting their necks querulously from side to side; the bulls strained with the effort, and sheep and goats rapidly tired, bobbing along at the fringes. The dogs were already aboard a raft, standing legs wide with wagging tails, as if relishing the sufferings of their fellow creatures. The children clung on in rapture, overawed at their experience – in fact, there was absolute silence apart from splashing sounds as all concentrated to the effort.

I felt as in a dream. A camel rubbed hard against my shoulder and I tried to grip its flank to get what assistance I could, but my hand slipped off its wet hide. Then, with relief, I felt it rising higher in the water: its legs were on the bottom. Tips of grass showed ahead and in a few moments all were clambering on to a bank covered only by twelve inches of water. The camels almost reached full stature; smaller animals stood panting, their flanks heaving. It was interesting to see how kind sought kind. There were no wanderers; the animals had kept close together and, so far, all had survived.

Released from tension, children splashed in the water having a game while their elders rested. Here, there were whole families in it together, literally up to the neck, with everything at risk, yet they laughed and chattered as if long accustomed to journeys of this nature.

So far things were going well, and when all had regained their wind we set off again into what was to prove an exhausting and heartbreaking stretch of shallows, in which the coarse rafts jarred at every obstacle. There was no way round, and we were forced to heave and pull through the chocolate mud until finally everyone stopped to stare at each other in perplexity. There was only one possible action – the gear was taken off the rafts and loaded onto the animals. Children and adults alike waded on as the bulls tugged and stumbled with such unfair burdens.

Tempers became frayed for the first time and a climax came when one raft became inextricably caught in a tree-stump so that it had to be painfully untied then rebuilt, wasting fully an hour. But at last the water inevitably deepened, and it seemed strange that deeper water was preferable after that long wearisome struggle.

The rafts were loaded again and, wading on, lending my strength to the motion, I could feel the water creeping higher on my body. Sheep and goats were again swimming, and speed was regulated to suit them – these were fewer in number and I knew that if a situation of choice arose, they would be sacrificed for the safety of the others, because it was cattle and camels which were all-important.

We waded at a comfortable depth for some time and spent much effort pulling in exhausted sheep and tying their heads to the rafts; otherwise they would have drowned. A short distance ahead a little knoll stood out of the water with several quite large trees . . . it would give an opportunity to examine the best approach to the watercourse which by now could not be far off. Soon we were all safe on this muddy bank, but several of the smaller animals were too weak to bear their own weight. The children now employed themselves bringing them to the rafts and securing as many as possible.

It was tempting to sit still and rest but, reluctantly, I set myself to climb a tree and was shocked to find that my legs refused to make the effort: only by dint of heaving from below I found myself stupidly perched on a lower branch but, fortunately, able to see into the distance through a gap in the trees.

It would be a long swim now. And the current was increasing! There was a wide stretch of unbroken water, then, peering through the thin shimmering haze, I could just see white water – the main track of the watercourse. How could these frail craft now so heavily loaded ever survive over this distance? – it was hopeless!

Then I caught sight of a low brown line trailing out of sight behind the trees – an island, and at this side of the main current! If this could be reached it would mean rest before the final dangerous plunge. The island was right before us but, on second thoughts, it seemed obvious that the increasing current could sweep us past and into a situation where there could be many casualties.

There was only one answer – travel upstream at a comfortable depth, then head for the island at an angle: with luck, the current would aid us.

Looking backwards, it was comforting to see Jebel Daier and the Nuba Mountains in the distance: a big part of the journey was behind us, but the worst remained.

I was locked to my perch, muscles refused to work: it was a relief to be lifted down and, then, to find the support of the water. The entire group gathered round, men and women, to discuss the problem and it was agreed to go upstream to a point considered suitable, then to launch out.

There was no reason to delay further as men and animals alike were suffering. At least, all had regained 'wind'.

Already it was after midday. Hours of plodding and swimming without rest or food, and using muscles in unaccustomed ways, would have taxed fit men, but after malaria and the strains of trek, I was far from fit. My legs moved machine-like as if independent of the mind – then, there was cramp which was difficult to fight, and which jabbed mercilessly from time to time.

Several hundred yards we moved upstream, the sluggish current carrying away streams of little bubbles behind us. Each animal moved at its most comfortable depth, but there came a short bar of thorn shrubs which almost broke the spirit even of the Buggara, whose perseverance, by now, I had every cause to admire. Further shallows must be avoided or everyone would stop – dead!

Then, there came a point where we could go no further, and there was only one thing left to do. Without pondering the consequences, the long string of animals and rafts swung independently towards the island, each unit depending on its own resources for survival. With heads tied close to the logs, even the small animals kicked out gamely. Bulls, with their remarkable strength, tugged at the ropes and snorted heavily as nostrils were jerked below the surface. It seemed remarkable that the clumsy rafts moved at all, but there was movement and slight ripples trailed out behind.

Camels, with erratic jumping motion, kept up with the rest and for some distance touched the bottom; then they too were swimming. There was silence now apart from the occasional grunt as muscles strained and breath was forced through taut throats. Abdulahi swam close to me with one hand on the raft, his dark beard jutting out, his face a grim mask.

Then, disaster! A raft close to ours struck some submerged branch – the bulls floundered and went under in their efforts to struggle on. Two child passengers stood up on all fours and the two attendant men clung on bewildered. It was Abdulahi who reacted quickly . . . I saw he had conjured a bared knife into his mouth, and was heading to sever the tow ropes as the raft was breaking up. I, too, plunged towards the raft and in seconds there was a confusion of splashing and waving arms. A child clutched me, then I kicked out frantically towards my own raft, several yards ahead by now. Water closed in around me. I kicked desperately in the direction of the black trek-box, still high above the water. I seemed to lose the way to the surface, with ears roaring and blood-red lights flashing in my head, then air entered my lungs again.

The child, fortunately, had gripped my shorts, as I was beyond giving assistance. I splashed out, then arms were gripping me and pulling me to the raft where I clutched desperately, abandoning myself to fate, my legs swilling in the eddies as the bulls struggled on. When at last I could collect my wits, it was a relief to see all of the children aboard, and the other men clinging safely to the raft. All around, bits and pieces of their possessions were drifting in the current.

Abdulahi looked towards me with what could have been a grin on his face – he was shouting to the bulls as if to encourage them.

I could now see animals and rafts scattered widely, but all making their independent efforts to reach the island. It was possible to judge by reference to the few tree-tops in view that the current was increasing – a hundred yards to go; strength must be almost expended.

We were furthest down the current: if we made it, the others would be safe. I kicked out again in a last despairing effort to get to dry ground. The first camel reached safety and stood shaking itself, indifferent to the fate of the others. The heads of a few animals were visible drifting downstream, beyond help.

There was a cry: the first raft had reached safety, and the men were making efforts to assist the others, throwing ropes and clutching at the drifting animals. We were moving silently and helplessly past, and it seemed nothing could save us, when it became evident that the bulls' feet were churning the muddy bottom, partially gripping, while the raft swung, turning the animals with it. Men from the island waded towards us and reached out for the halter ropes.

The animals were exhausted: I could only look on helplessly, but Abdulahi fought his way to the head and soon a human chain was pulling us to safety. In seconds the raft was aground, and men and animals alike lay prostrate on warm dry ground at last.

The island was littered with worn, panting bodies. For some time I lay, face down, and for the present, unable to think or take part in any further action. But others must have been equally exhausted because I was left undisturbed for a long time. It was a woman's voice muttering a prayer of thanks that brought me round.

I sat up. Bulls lay with legs stretched out, their sharp bones prominent beneath lean hides; only camels were standing, grazing the thorns on the few trees. Men were beginning to move, sorting out the small animals – how many were missing was impossible to tell: this subject was never discussed. Abdulahi came to sit beside me. All of the people were safe: he offered me a piece of *kisra* (millet bread) which I ate gladly.

I tried to stand but my legs would not carry me, but the heat was restorative and eventually, like an old man, I crippled to my feet and walked to look at the steel trunk. It was as dry as when the journey started. My skin, dimpled and soft through long immersion, was crisping in the heat so that my cheeks cracked painfully.

The island, if it was worthy of the name, was merely a narrow sliver of soil just extending above the water's surface. Drift lay a few inches above water level showing that the flood was receding, but this could be temporary and, at any moment, another surge might drown the island.

The main watercourse still had to be crossed. I went with Abdulahi to the other side of the island, stepping over prostrate bodies and bundles which, for some reason, had been taken from rafts as if the people were thinking of spending a night on the island: something too dangerous to contemplate. We looked at a raging torrent 40 or 50 yards wide with, beyond it, the familiar slack water and trees stretching into the distance, although the sand dunes at the far side of the valley were clearly in view.

Was it a hallucination? There at the other side of the swift river, a native policeman with animals . . . in fact, two camels and a horse. The man was waving! The other Arabs had seen him and a cry of excitement went from man to man, then they stood waving back, almost jumping with relief. He was standing waist-deep, apparently shouting words which were lost in the sounds of the river.

He had been given my radio signal and had splashed this distance to meet us. No doubt he had witnessed our approach from the distant dunes. There must be one more mile of water but at least it was obviously shallow beyond the main stream.

It remained only to cross 50 yards of violent waters, then my troubles were over! The policeman was signalling, then swinging a weighted rope round his head – obviously he was wanting a rope to be thrown out from the island.

The solution was obvious!

Soon the rafts were being dismantled and the Buggara were working with a will recovering every possible piece of cord and rope. A stone was tied to a light cord – it sailed far into the stream but the weight of the cord pulled it up short.

Then I realised this was not the way . . . the cord should be floating! Now a length of stick flew into mid stream. Abdulahi carefully paid out the cord. It bobbed in the water; the policeman threw a weighted rope but the lines failed to cross.

Again we tried – on the third attempt, the stone fell behind our line so that he was able to draw in our cord.

The policeman had a length of heavy rope with him – obviously he had foreknowledge of Abu Habl floods; this was not the first time people had been trapped, and he had come prepared. It did not take long to pull the rope over and, in minutes, it was securely tied to trees at each side. It spanned the water in an immense arc, dragged out by the current and making a trail of froth as it tore the surface.

Evening had come, with the sun already westering in a dull red glow. It would be long after dark before it was all over and I saw the last of the Abu Habl. The roar of water dulled the senses – I felt myself getting more sluggish: it could only be the effects of this hard environment – Talodi, malaria, inadequate food; all taking their toll: or was I only making excuses?

The Buggara were getting on without my help, building one substantial raft out of the dismantled 'fleet'. I watched as it was lowered into the water and looped to the main rope. This was to be our bridge – shuttling people and possessions over the river to the shallower water beyond.

Whether out of courtesy or a need to experiment, my box was loaded for the first trip. The raft was eased into the current where the water whipped it into midstream, down the arc of the rope, till, with a judder, it stopped nose tilted down. But there it remained, adjusting to the eddies – the box still dry!

Now my turn. A rope was tied round my waist, then I went into the water clutching with all my strength to the 'bridge'. Immediately my legs were pulled out horizontally by the current: water piled against my chin, it was an effort to keep head above water. Hand over hand, down the rope – now I clutched the raft, hair in my eyes blinding me. The raft vibrated like a living thing as I tied my free rope so that eventually it could be pulled to the other side.

It must have been exhaustion – there is a nightmarish memory of fingers that could conceivably have lost their grip, but I edged round the raft to twist my legs round the rope and struggle to the other side of the river. Water in nose, eyes, ears and mouth – the distance, could it be as far as this? Where was I going and what was I doing? My brain seemed dead. Then hands were clutching at my shoulders, and with a groan of relief I felt myself dragged out of the current.

The policeman took the free rope from me and fixed it to his horse-saddle to pull the raft over. I could only watch. The current was too strong and the horse floundered unavailingly. Two Buggara crossed hand over hand to lend their strength, and now the raft moved slowly over; soon my trek-box was safely in the branches of a tree above the water level. Night had closed in to add to the difficulty, but this first trip being successfully over, the others should make it, given time.

The raft was pulled back round the arc of the rope and, in time, it returned with a number of passengers. Children were lifted on trees because the water was too deep for them to stand; and so started a slow, careful shuttle of people and their goods, until a routine was established in which some of the men kept repeating the crossing without outward signs of tiredness. If, in the past, the Buggara had appeared to be an indolent people, that idea was long since dispelled, and to think it had taken an emergency such as this for me to begin to understand them!

I waited with the policeman while it was all going on, although he had come with the sole purpose of seeing me safely to the station. The station! My leave . . . I had forgotten about leave: where would I head for now? I mentioned to the policeman that I had missed the river steamer south. He looked at me and laughed.

'You know, *Jenabo*, you have not missed the steamer: a wire has been sent to Kosti and they are holding the sailing back for you. You get a train at 4 a.m. and we shall get to Rahad station in time to catch it.'

I could hardly take it in. After all that had happened, I was actually going to get my weeks of glorious rest in the luxury of a Nile steamer! That the Sudan should do all this for me was beyond belief.

Finally, with the people and their goods safely over, it remained only for the animals to cross. Only vaguely in the darkness we were aware of them being driven into the water – they would swim over, and the men had spread downstream to intercept them. It seemed probable that most of them would reach safety.

Slowly the people returned. I had an unbearable longing to get out of water, and could wait no longer. Willing hands loaded my box onto a camel together with my other bits and pieces, and I mounted the horse, grateful to have a seat at last. Men and women, they all wished me a safe journey and blessed me on my way. I could not but feel, as I shook Abdulahi's hand, that some indefinable bridge had been built between us, something new to us both . . . a bridge neither would forget.

We moved away; then, at the eleventh hour, disaster! The camel with my baggage lost its footing and slipped sideways under five feet of muddy water.

I was stupefied. Camel's legs flailed the surface – once more, into the water with the policeman to free the load from the camel's back. It struggled up, panting and nervous, then sprang away so that it took several Arabs to catch its head-rope. A line of bubbles marked the position of my earthly possessions. The box may have been white ant-proof – I quickly discovered it was not waterproof! It took the strength of a group of men to lift it from the water and, once more, put it in a tree, this time to drain out the water.

My passport, wrist watch, best clothes, photographs of Marion; all soaked with brown water! Why had I not learned the lesson about camels in water – I had thought only of having a comfortable ride: but the damage was done, it was too late now.

I mounted now on the camel and, careless of whether it would fall again, we set off, splashing through the darkness too weary to speak. Two Buggara came with us, supporting the box on the pony's back. Soaked and despondent, I suffered agonies in the now-bitter cold which was the conquering pain of the moment. It cut like little knives into my wet, soft flesh – there seemed no end to this night of torture.

But the water was lessening. An Arab shouted that it was below his waist: then I could hear the animals wading over shallows. Another half-mile, and the first dry land – to save my life I had to get down and walk to restore circulation.

At what must have been 2 a.m. the weary group crossed the railway line to stop, at last, close to the silent village. I thanked my friends, the Buggara, who were still faced with the journey back to their people, then settled to opening the box and surveying the damage.

The policeman had lit a fire, and item by item my possessions were heaped on the sand so that I could empty out the last of the water. Even in the flickering light they presented a sorry spectacle.

The warmth of the fire was blissful. I lay flat out on the sand. There was something splendid about the Sudan – yes, it was larger than life! I had crossed the Abu Habl despite the flood, and even Ibrahim's jinns: I smiled to myself – 'a long, restful sail to Uganda!'

The policeman pulled me awake – the train was approaching, its headlight clear in the distance. We quickly pushed the stuff into the box and I was standing waiting when the train thundered in.

Another farewell, to the policeman, then I was aboard in my own reserved compartment. A bed was ready; I lay down without undressing and was soon oblivious to everything while the train swayed its way down the side of the Abu Habl valley.

Part III – Abu Habl

The Nile steamer beat its way southwards on the long journey to Uganda. For 24 hours I slept or tossed restlessly on a bunk, exhausted from long months of trek. It must have been fever, as my mind churned over and over again nightmarish thoughts of mountains stripped of soil, while people starved.

Missionary families were part of this torment. How could they go on living there year after year, isolated from the outside world with the whole of nature disintegrating around them? Yes! they had a message to give and they loved the Nuba people, but what if the land was no longer able to support them.

Where did God fit in? For that matter, where did the Sudan Government fit in? The people tended to say it was Allah's will, as if the damage was inevitable and outwith their responsibility. My own Agricultural Department was bleeding the mountains in its hunger for grain, and as for the tribes, were they not destroying their own habitat? The Government paid the people for grain and cotton; this new wealth resulted in larger herds of cattle and goats which grazed the land bare: even improved treatment of disease among the people meant an increase in population as the delicate natural balance of the centuries was lost and erosion set in.

All this was no 'act of God!'

Somehow this cycle of events must be reversed before the mountains died. I had been groping for a whole year without really understanding what was going on. There had been little time for clear thinking; action had followed action like sticking a finger in a crumbling dyke, or rather like planting footsteps on the ground to stop a few square inches of soil blowing away – so many reports written to El Obeid and Khartoum, what use were they after all?

These were lonely hours. The boat vibrated to the beat of its stern-paddles: a fan whirred overhead; there was nothing else but heat and sweat. On the second morning an Arab steward brought water and the offer of food, and slowly a more optimistic feeling filtered into my mind. Yes, good things had happened – the new *hafirs* with their water stores might help to provide settled communities where erosion could be held at bay; also Mek Adam and his people, they were starting to take some action. The Dam

304

Gamad scheme for returning soldiers was an opportunity for new thinking, perhaps cattle herds could be controlled; and as for trees . . .

I shook off the feeling of gloom and rose to meet my fellow passengers. I joined them for dinner – there was just a handful of Europeans and they too were seeking an escape after years without leave due to the war. From the beginning they tried to make me feel at ease, and I became caught up in a spirit of fun which drove away thoughts of the mountains. Two passengers turned out to be chorus girls from the Khartoum cabaret I had once visited. To be truthful they were not exactly girls, but they knew the choruses of the day. We sang, danced, played games for hours on end, and each evening before retiring to our bunks we took shot about at telling stories. It was a time when every life was a story, shaped by war and hardship even here in the heart of Africa.

One girl, a Jewess, told of her close escape from Hitler's Germany and the twist of fate which brought her to the Sudan. One passenger told of the battles against Italians in Eritrea; about journeys by camel and the agonies of war. When it came to my turn they asked about trek among the Nuba, and on one occasion I spoke about the old missionary couple at Abri and an event I remembered well.

A Tale of the Mountains

James Mills removed his spectacles to rub his tired, bloodshot eyes. He pushed away the Bible and papers which had occupied his complete attention for the last four hours. His wife Janet looked across the table to him, pleased that at long last he was giving it up for another day. She shook her head as she looked at the stooped, frail body of her husband, wondering yet again whether she would ever get him out of the mountains alive.

He remained bent over the table, starting unseeingly before him. His excited mind raced with the thought patterns of the last few hours, like a wheel continuing to revolve until its momentum is spent. James was a man possessed! The great ambition of his life was, at last, within reach: but time was short. It required only a few more chapters of Revelations to complete his translation of the Bible into the Nuba tongue; the first time this had ever been done. This marathon task he had started years before, and there had been many occasions when he had despaired of ever completing it, because of the multifarious duties of the mission station.

Thirty years as a missionary in the mountains had sapped his strength. Never-ending toil and tropical illness had left him so weak at the age of 64 that each day became a trial. It was a matter of conjecture whether he would last out the remaining months until his retirement. It really was a race against time.

For a number of years reports of his failing health had filtered to headquarters in Australia and, not being without compassion, the mission 'chairman' had repeatedly invited him to retire; after all, no white man had ever endured so many years in the inhospitable mountains, particularly through the rainy seasons when disease was rife. James had indeed resigned himself to the fact that the end was near. He could see it only as the end because, after such a long period, Nuba was his real home, and Australia a foreign land which he could not understand. To die beside his beloved little church was all he could have wished for.

But Janet had other views. As the translation commanded more of his time, Janet had taken over even more of the work. To her, Brisbane had always been home, and if she had anything to do with it they would be on their way long before the rains shut them in again.

Janet was a few years younger than her husband, and being the stronger of the two, still retained a little fresh colour in her cheeks. She was small, on the stout side, and with wisps of white hair constantly falling over her eyes. She was a Martha, a constant doer; in fact, the complete missionary's wife. Her early training had been as a nurse but since then she had become teacher, preacher, cook, gardener, and even joiner when necessary, because James was not a practical man. In her missionary years she had turned her hands to everything the mountains could require of her, yet, in addition, she still found time to be a devoted wife.

Life had been difficult for them from the beginning. Not only had they been faced with the problem of converting the heathen, because the pagan Nuba had been, and still were, slow to accept a white man's God; but they had found two alien forces in their path. One was the encroachment of Moslem influence from the north; the other was the Government. The Government was alien in the sense that many of its servants were indifferent to the struggles of the missionaries – not hostile, just generally indifferent. After all, the predominant influences within the country were exerted by the Arab north and it was not part of the role of government to proselytise for the Christian faith. For years, this had shown itself by the passage of government visitors through the district, who drove past the mission station without calling in. In many respects the missionaries were the poor whites with scant resources, who drove about in ancient motor-cars, and who offered tea, when drinks would have been more welcome. But there were also exceptions. Some government inspectors did all within their powers to co-operate with the work of the missions.

Isolation affects people in many different ways. It can breed nervousness of company, suspicion, or merely eccentricity. In the case of the Mills', they were no doubt old-fashioned and fussy, but they accepted callers in the only way they knew, with warmth and hospitality. On the arrival of a visitor, the kettle was on, the table-cloth spread, and a genteel tea party followed.

With the Mills partnership, he was father of the flock, the saintly dreamer: Janet was both manager and labourer. It had worked well through the years. The missionary society had had its 'pound of flesh'.

James vaguely hoped that the idea of leaving the mountains was a dream. There was so much still to do! How could he ever leave his beloved friends of these many years? Meanwhile, Janet was surreptitiously stuffing bits and pieces into tea-chests, logging all the outstanding jobs, and carefully ticking them off as they were attended to.

It was bedtime. The pressure lantern hissed on top of the low mud wall, the only division between the living quarters and the bedroom, all of which were under the bare sweeping thatch of the roof. After prayers and scripture-reading were finished, they climbed into bed. Janet was quickly asleep, as usual; James stared sightlessly at the roof still thinking over the words of the translation.

Five miles away from the mission station on a mountaintop, a strange scene was being enacted; at least, strange to western eyes. In the blaze of a log fire, a group of naked Nuba were gathered round the recumbent body of a girl, heavily pregnant and stretched out on a litter. One painted form was performing some ritual over the girl while her eyes followed every move with abject fear.

The onlookers, crouched on the ground, watched silently while the witch-doctor performed the necessary fertility rites over the girl who, herself, was little more than a child. The girl, whose name was Jila, was daughter of Ngala, the chief of a little Nuba tribe. She was a favourite daughter, being the only child from Ngala's second wife who had died while the child was still young. This was the second time the witch-doctor's services had been called on, because everything was not right. The women said the baby was overdue and Jila herself was showing signs of acute distress.

Jila had been married off to a young warrior at the age of 13, a practice which was not uncommon. To be pregnant at 14 was a common occurrence. Ngala could easily be picked out from the silent group. He was almost a giant in stature and his body, smothered in oil, shone in the firelight. He had no idea of his age, which must have been more than 60, but only his white hair and slightly stooped body spoke his years.

In a little pot on a separate fire some concoction was being brewed while the witch-doctor completed his ritual of adjusting patterns of bones on the dust and mumbling words over the girl's body. The potion was finally cooled with water from a gourd and smeared over the girl's belly. This ceremony complete, the witch-doctor collected his bits and pieces and, without a word, moved into his hut a short distance away, leaving the family to bear the child to her home.

Silently the party dispersed and Ngala, with one of his sons, placed the litter down in the chief's compound, high on a cliff face, and overlooking the mission station on the plains far below. Jila was fevered and she groaned at every jolt. They lifted her onto a string bed in a little thatched hut and with a display of affection, unusual in this hard country, the chief caressed his daughter's hand, mopped her forehead, then walked slowly out into the cool night air.

His mind was in a turmoil. Ngala was not given to introspection and he had long learned to live with suffering, believing that the outcome rested with the spirits, but in truth, he doubted the power of the witch-doctor. Running through his mind was the fact that many of his people had spoken of the healing powers of *Jenabo* Mills, the missionary. Indeed, on several occasions through the years he had listened to stories about the power of the missionary's own God. Some of the stories he knew quite well by now, but they were only stories, which had little meaning for him or his people. Yet, perhaps this God might succeed where the witch-doctor had failed! He hesitated for a few seconds then shaking his head, left for his own huts where his wives and children were already settled for sleep.

In one of the little string beds a girl of 16 lay, staring with wide eyes through the doorway of her hut to the bright stars beyond. Tamra was Ngala's youngest wife. Close by her side on a little pallet lay her year-old child. Tamra's hands reached out to clutch the sides of her bed as she remembered with horror the evening's events. She had locked within her an additional burden of guilt; a secret she would never have revealed to her husband. She had listened to the words of *Jenabo* Mills and secretly she believed them. A god of love was a concept she had struggled with for a long time, but it had come to have real meaning for her.

In this hard land the fact of love was never discussed. Perhaps it was taken for granted, but was never spoken about. The people knew they had to be mutually caring and protective just to survive, and this was merely a fact of life. But Tamra had grown up close to Jila, and occasionally, and in secret, they had gone to the mission station to listen with wonder at what the missionary had to say. She also knew that in the little dispensary Mr and Mrs Mills occasionally performed miracles of healing. Because of this she had become dissatisfied in her mind with many of the old ways. This night, after having seen Jila's sufferings, she knew that she loved her, and also that she must do something about it.

Another hour passed; then with fearful resolve she decided to go to the mission station at once to seek help for her friend. Silently she left her baby, moved out of the hut and across the compound to the cliff's edge where a rough ledge led down to the plain below. She had never done this before in darkness, and a jumble of fears all but broke her resolve, so that she pressed her back to the rock face as if frozen to the spot. She stood, eyes closed for many minutes until her returning courage, together with the memory of her friend's agony, gave her strength to continue down the steep and dangerous path. Two hours later a little figure crept to the door of the mission house when at first in little more than a whisper, then gradually in despair, she called '*Gesiss!*' (missionary) time after time.

It was Janet who first heard the call at the door. She was not afraid, because it occasionally happened that help was needed at the most inconvenient hours. Who was there to be afraid of among the peaceable Nuba in any case? In her long cotton nightdress she moved over to the door, opened it and looked at Tamra's cowering figure on the step. She lit a lantern and quickly recognised her visitor: both she and James in the past had had hopes that Jila and her friend Tamra might take the Christian message to the hilltop tribe, given time.

'What do you want, Tamra?' Janet asked kindly as she encouraged her into the room. James came through the bedroom door rubbing his eyes then stopped in surprise at sight of the diminutive visitor.

'Why, this is Tamra, wife of Ngala, is it not?'

'Jila is very ill; you must come and help her!'

Slowly Tamra told of her friend's trouble and of how the witch-doctor had failed to cure her. The story was scarcely out when James said, 'I must go!' He could have well gone at once in his nightgown, without ever even considering the steep climb and the darkness, but Janet cautioned him. She reminded him that he could never climb the mountain now in his state of health. His protests were brushed aside, and Janet said she would travel herself in the morning.

'Please, please do not say that I have come to speak with you!' Tamra pleaded. Her face was a picture of fear at the prospect of her husband discovering what she had done. Running and stumbling in the darkness the young Nuba girl rushed back to her home, desperate to arrive before the village awakened. With pounding heart she finally crept into her hut: all was still, just as she had left it, except that a village dog barked loudly and the first crows of the morning cocks cracked the still air. Thankfully her baby was still asleep. She could only await developments now.

It was just before midday that a hot, dishevelled Janet stumbled into the village, partly supported by two Nuba from the mission. Ngala was surprised at this rare visit. He knew well and respected Janet Mills, although for long he had resisted the Christian message she so willingly dispensed.

'I am honoured at this visit,' Ngala said as he walked over to shake her hand in welcome.

Janet wasted no time in explanation. 'I must see Jila at once, she is very ill!'

Ngala was taken by surprise, and after hesitating a moment, said: 'How did you learn of this?'

Janet was prepared for the question. 'I learn of these things!' – she looked inscrutable, leaving it to Ngala to conjecture from which mystic or divine source her knowledge had come. There was no holding Janet back once her mind was resolved.

Ngala led her to Jila's hut and in a minute she was examining the sweat-lathered body of the half-conscious girl.

'She must be taken to the dispensary at once, or she shall surely die!' Janet spoke with such determination there could be no argument. 'Even now it is probably too late!'

That evening James and Janet performed a Caesarian operation on the little girl. It was a difficult and distressing experience for both of them, because they both really knew that it was too late. Outside the dispensary door Ngala, and the larger family of the chief, sat crouched and silent. Tamra had her eyes tightly closed; perhaps she was praying.

One hour later the door opened and a tired James looked out, shaking his head from side to side. The people went inside. Janet was holding Jila's wrist, sensing the weak pulse which was the only indication that she was still alive. In complete silence the family squatted on the floor and sat still, simply waiting. Twenty minutes passed in this way, and then with a loud sob and with tears flowing down her cheeks Janet said: 'The poor child, she is dead.'

For some minutes there was complete stillness in the room then slowly the family rose and filed out. Tamra was sobbing quietly but on the faces of the others there was little expression to indicate what their emotions were. Soon only James and Janet were left. They looked bleakly at one another. Would it have been better not to have interfered? Should they have left the call for help unanswered? Even Tamra had left them without a word. This was indeed failure. God had not answered their prayers. Ngala and his people must be alienated for all time.

The next two days were sad, difficult days for both of them. Even the translation was put aside. Yet again, James questioned the purpose of his life and whether he had really achieved anything at all in God's name.

It was the third day after the operation that a group of Nuba came down to the mission station. James saw Ngala in the fore, and he wondered what could possibly be in store for him. Then he saw Tamra and she had a broad smile on her face. Ngala took James' frail hand in his own, a smile spread over his face. He said: 'Your God was not strong enough to save my daughter but he must be a good God to make you do what you have done for my people.'

James stood still gathering his thoughts then he breathed softly, 'Yes, my God, he is a good God!'

The company listened patiently while I told this story. It was more than just a story, because I had arrived at the mission station on the night of the operation. In fact, I had seen the Nuba family returning silently to their village. I told the story with feeling and even emotion, because I remembered all too clearly the patient faithful service of the old missionary couple.

Our route was by Lake Kioga into Uganda; long hot weeks of travel on water, and through tropical forest. At Kampala I left my friends to pursue my own interests, which related to the land and its vegetation. The others travelled on to Kenya.

After the threadbare hardness of Kordofan, Uganda seemed a paradise. There were no signs of erosion here as every square foot of ground supported a tangle of vegetation. Climatic factors caused some of the differences, but there was obviously more to it. The soil of Kordofan was commonly light and sandy and, therefore, vulnerable to changes in husbandry – yet there were areas in the Nuba Hills where land of this type was terraced and farmed with care, and showing no signs of erosion. On the other hand, where slash-and-burn was practised and large herds of animals exploited the land, erosion was most serious.

I walked through many of the little farms around the capital; they were carefully tended by settled communities. Was there an answer in this – establish settled villages with resources to outlive the dry season on good land? But that was what I had been working towards! I knew that in the Sudan, to provide security of land tenure, the laws of inheritance would need careful scrutiny. Yet it worked here in Uganda! The issue was complicated, involving so many things – people, governments, animals, trees, rain, law – an almost endless list of agents, yet all interlinked.

The streets of Kampala were colourful, the people happy-looking. In spite of the war, Uganda looked prosperous. It was a country under British Colonial rule, but it was common knowledge that beneath the air of peace there was an underlying problem of relationships between the tribes of the country.

Once again I visited plantations, some of the largest and most prosperous in Africa. There were no answers here for Kordofan. The Nuba Mountains could not stand the sledgehammer approach of plantation cropping; rather, it must be the fine-tuning of individual farmers with their own plots of land.

I moved on to join my new 'river-steamer' friends in the Kenya highlands where mist-covered hills made me think it was so very like Scotland. We sat round blazing log fires on cool evenings, singing and telling tales as before, and with the goodness of the rest seeping into our beings.

Two weeks of this and I was restless to move on. Alone, I set out for the Belgian Congo with a notion of visiting pygmy country, but malaria struck when I was within reach of my goal and all urges to explore evaporated. I set out on the return journey to the Sudan with crates full of White Leghorn poultry purchased in Kenya. My latest ambition was to improve the Nuba Mountain hens, where eggs were bantam size. The unfortunate birds sweated their way across the Equator and down the River Nile, placed on the bow of the steamer to catch the least puff of air. The passengers almost killed them with kindness. I did, in fact, get them all safely to Kordofan but, within weeks of their arrival, a wild predator killed them. But it was not in vain, as little white chickens began to show up among the drab local hens.

Back into Harness

At Rahad station the car and driver were waiting. Both had safely emerged from the Abu Habl flood and were by now dry and in good shape. We set off over the familiar trail home to Rashad, crossing the now dry watercourse. The only traces of the flood was drift material clinging high on tree-tops. I travelled with a mixture of emotions, organising my thoughts for another period of lonely months of trek. There would be the usual discomfort and, of course, targets of some kind to achieve. Then there was the question of mail – a three-month accumulation; some of it home-mail. There was always a nagging anxiety about what might be happening at home as the war made everything unpredictable. Marion: how would she be? We had been separated for years now! Such long periods without any news made life that little bit harder.

Rashad was the same dusty place high on its hilltop. The boys gathered at the door to greet me. They looked smart in their white robes and turbans, and were eager to help me feel welcome. Their smiling faces warmed me to home-coming in a way I had not expected. There were so many things they wanted to tell me – the DC had left on trek two days before but there was a message from him – the Omdah had taken another wife – the new school-teacher, a woman, had started work – a leopard had been in the garden, and so on.

Yes, it was good to be back again and, with regard to the post someone had thoughtfully brought Scottish mail from the office: a pile of letters and parcels waited my attention. Mahomed hurried to prepare the evening meal; Ibrahim stood at my elbow anxious to please as I settled to opening letters.

The sun set on a happy little community.

Late into the night I read and read then dropped into bed at peace with the world.

It was a different story next morning. I trudged apprehensively along the dusty path and was met at the door by the 'village idiot'. He bowed me up to the office, then went to find a fan-boy to stir the stale air. A fine coat of dust covered my desk, but my mind was set on the bundles of letters, cloth-bound parcels and an intimidating little pile of telegrams. Clerks came in to welcome me back, then the door closed and I was left to unravel the business of the mountains: that which had taken place in recent months, and that which lay in the future.

It was the future that most concerned me. I tore open the telegrams anxiously – from Alex, the province Governor, and one from the Director of Agriculture. The Director was asking urgently about the cropping situation since the rains: a number of reports from outstations in the mountains should give some kind of estimate – so that should be easy to deal with!

Alex said in his wire, as blunt as ever: 'Check on the new *hafirs* then come El Obeid earliest possible.'

The Governor was less peremptory though equally demanding: 'Your presence requested El Obeid on . . . to discuss new project. Hope you had good leave.' The date given was just one week ahead!

There were no great surprises in these instructions: Alex would likely want to hear about the horse trek and discuss my findings. There was a great deal to tell him. I had seen villages almost washed away; there were large areas of good soil which could be developed as part of an erosion-control project and, once I checked on the new *hafirs*, I would have a great deal of information to pass on. Presumably the Governor was also keen to have this information; it was he who had really started me working on erosion: but then he mentioned a new project in his telegram – what could it be?

I easily dealt with the rest of the mail but it took most of that day. Telegrams were sent off with my replies. confirming my trek to visit the *hafirs* and my attendance at the coming El Obeid meeting. Throughout the day it became ever more clear to me that by taking large quantities of grain and cotton from the mountains, I would be exporting the fertility of the land and hurrying on the work of erosion – that depressing paradox! Some very hard decisions were required to be taken.

Next morning, with the car loaded and the boys perched high on top, we set off to examine the *hafirs*. I looked through the rear-cab window: the boys were swathed in cotton cloth to protect them from the hot wind and dust. They had been cheerful, as if keenly anticipating another hard season of travel, yet, what was there in it for them? Their one duty was my well-being, nothing else. It was a mystery that they could endure the discomforts for so little reward – a few pounds per month and their keep! On many occasions their advice was important, their knowledge of the country more valuable than textbooks: without the willing co-operation of people like them the administrative system in the Sudan would have collapsed. They were at heart nomads and thought nothing of setting out for weeks on end, leaving their families behind.

Trees were bare, as it was long since the rains had stopped and tall grass, golden and brittle, stretched like an unending ocean to the horizon; fuel for the next bush fire.

The opiate of freedom seeped into my being. Solitude; the emptiness of nature; starlit nights beside a camp-fire; these were a heady mix suited to the time. Perhaps this feeling would change when the war finished and home leave became a nearer prospect.

The *hafirs* were all that I had expected: at least, most of them! There were some lakes of muddy water where previously there had been only dry barren clay. One *hafir* was damaged by a violent flash-flood which had ripped through its boundary wall: remedial action would be necessary here, but there was a solution. Another was quite empty, perhaps because on its base a stratum of sand had been exposed – this too could be cured. The others still held stores of water, while nearby little broken-down villages provided testimony that people were prepared to settle if water was provided.

I spent a time at one little home, as poor a home as it is possible to imagine. An old shrunken man blinded with cataract of the eye sat cross-legged on the bare soil with two little children playing at his feet. The cultivator, for such he was because some millet had been harvested nearby, came to shake my hand.

'Are you prepared to remain on this ground?' I asked.

'Yes, this is a good place and by Allah's will my family will stay, provided there is water to sustain us until the rains.' They had come from eroded land where their wells were dry. 'We should all have died at that place!' he declared vehemently, waving his arms with emotion.

To call this a 'good place' was relevant to the state of human need. It had good land and water but nothing else to recommend it.

There were three generations represented in this one family, the root and the seed of permanence!

It was a moving experience to see again how people could be content with such elemental needs – no shops, no doctors, no schools; just soil and water. Surely it was a basic government responsibility to continue work of this type, providing water reserves. Perhaps villages would grow up in time to provide some wider range of amenity. To dig large holes in the ground was just a beginning. It would need to be followed by terracing, tree-planting and some degree of communal resource in which the villagers could participate.

These *hafirs* were the first major effort of the kind in the Nuba Mountains, and the results of the experiment were encouraging.

By this time I had obtained enough information to fill a comprehensive report, so it was time to return and head towards the province meeting at El Obeid. In course of time we drove up to Alex's office where he welcomed me with his usual grin.

'Good to have you back! Had a good leave?'

Barely waiting for an answer, it was a case of straight into work. Alex seldom wasted time on pleasantries, but I knew him well and took no offence. Almost at once I found his interest was not centred on *hafirs* or horse-treks, he had other things on his mind. My reports would just have to wait for the present.

I sat facing him at his desk. He stared at me, his square jaw projecting, eyes sparkling with enthusiasm as they always did. 'You are going to be busy, there are new plans afoot!'

I waited silently though a little impatiently because I had had to deal with his plans several times in the past. Alex was seldom short of ideas.

'Several things were decided in your absence. Something has to be done about the problems caused by overgrazing in Kordofan; cattle herds are getting bigger and the land can't support them.' I agreed absolutely with this. He continued:

'I have arranged with the vets that we shall start dealing with this by having a livestock improvement programme at Tegali: Mek Adam has agreed to participate. You know the idea: we collect the herds together and castrate nine-tenths of the bulls, leaving the good ones entire to breed.'

'Will that make much difference to numbers of animals?' I asked.

'No,' Alex said, 'but it can be a starting-point. You know as well as I do that cattle are left to breed at any age – they leave it to nature, so that the herds are full of scrub cattle.'

I agreed with him that it would probably be worth a trial; perhaps it was a necessary part of the overall control of erosion in the mountains.

'You will be making a start on this after the province meeting.'

He rushed straight on to the next scheme: 'Khartoum is wanting more grain out of Kordofan because of the war. We have decided to tap the early floods of the Abu Habl by building a small dam and spreading the water over the valley by means of canals. It will be a major project and I want you to live on the scheme and see it through.'

The Abu Habl! To dam the Abu Habl? 'But Alex!' I interrupted, 'I was nearly drowned in the thing – the entire valley was filled with water when I went on leave, and I was lucky to get across safely!'

'Oh.' Alex paused. 'Well – then we must tame the Abu Habl, mustn't we? A dam and canal banks will also provide a route from the mountains in the rains so you will not have that problem again.'

Now, I was expected to move to the Abu Habl and set up camp – of all places!

'What of my work in the mountains? What about *hafirs* and all the other plans; there is so much to do there . . .'

'Yes, I know.' His eyes had a steely glint. 'Food is the priority; everything else has to wait. You know we are short of inspectors, we have to do the best we can, but you will still have the opportunity to go to the mountains later; the new Settlement Scheme for Soldiers at Talodi has to be kept going among other things.'

This change of direction was difficult to understand, and I said lamely, 'What of my horse-trek – my findings about the erosion question, is nothing to happen there?'

'It all takes time, lad; you have made a beginning. It will maybe need the war to finish before more resources will be provided.'

I felt sick at heart. Was he even interested? He rubbed salt into the wound:

'By the way, the Governor is going to the mountains soon. I would like some kind of a show put on for him. What about organising an Agricultural Show at Talodi – it doesn't need to be a big affair. We will get the native administration to bring the chiefs together to meet him. What do you say, lad?'

There was little I could say, his mind was already made up.

I lay awake that night thinking over the new twists in my fate. I was free to make decisions on trek, but here in the town I had but to listen and obey, only a small cog in the Government's machine. Of all things, to stay on the Abu Habl making an irrigation scheme! It seemed a very bleak prospect. The sharp clanking of wagons being shunted at the nearby terminus jarred me to sleep.

I knew only too well from past experience that a province meeting was no small affair. Anyone that mattered would be there!

Our arrival was timed for when political matters had been dealt with, so people were seated in anticipation of our entering. I looked around at faces by now quite familiar – the Governor, District Commissioners and a number of white-robed figures.

Business started at once. I was given a paper headed 'Abu Habl Scheme' and discussion became centred on how the new project could be accomplished. A lot of thinking had been done already – engineers were drawing up plans and money was laid aside for the work. The sheikhs were asked about sources of labour – over 1000 men would be needed, and their advice was asked on contractors to supply vehicles, food, and a wide range of other materials. As the afternoon progressed my role in co-ordinating the project became clear: contractors, labour, machinery – noise, confusion; in fact, the complete opposite to all my other Sudan experience. Obviously someone had to do it. Why had I been chosen?

It was late in the afternoon before the next item of business was introduced, namely the Tegali Livestock Improvement Scheme. Alex took up the theme, explaining what was intended and inviting the sheikhs to co-operate. They nodded vaguely at his promptings, although it seemed questionable whether they knew what he was talking about.

The subject of soil conservation was not even mentioned. Apparently it had been shelved for the duration, another casualty of the war!

With the meeting over and the chamber emptying, the Governor came over to speak.

'I know what you are thinking – no reference made to erosion in the mountains. I feel, as you do, a bit disappointed that for the present we have to change tack. It is unbelievable the pressure to produce more food. We just have to give it all we have got.'

I asked him, 'The village improvement work, the *hafirs* and all the rest – does that just stop?'

'Keep an eye on the mountains as best you can meanwhile: we shall get back to all this in the future.'

The boys stood before me disconsolate with the news that before long we would be living on the Abu Habl. Apart from its reputation for trapping the unwary traveller, and the capricious behaviour of its jinns, a superstitious lore hovered over the area. It was here that a large army had been wiped out by the Mahdi only 60 years before that time. General Hicks and 10,000 men had marched from Khartoum, but after getting lost on the way and being overcome by disease, they were destroyed by the Mahdist forces.

Mahomed and Ibrahim had cause for their gloom. In fact, I shared it and, like me, they had to accept their fate. There was no alternative. Fortunately there remained a few weeks of adventure in the mountains before transplanting ourselves there.

We made a quick visit home to Rashad then headed to Abbasiya to prepare the ground for the Livestock Improvement Scheme – something never tried before in the area. We drove past many large herds of cattle all apparently intent in pounding the soil into dust. For miles around Abbasiya ground was grazed bare of any signs of vegetation, while the animals ranged ever further afield to find food. Soon they would resemble walking skeletons as the dry season advanced. I warmed a little to the project. Something did require doing urgently.

Mek Adam was expecting me, and together we visited the main herdsmen in the area to enlist their support for the scheme. 'Your herds will improve if the poor-quality animals are prevented from breeding: it is good husbandry . . .' The story was repeated time after time. The herdsmen listened and nodded as if in agreement, then when the significance of the plan dawned they shook their heads doubtfully – the Almighty after all had provided male creatures with testicles for a purpose; it must be wrong to obstruct their use.

The will of Allah on this point was widely debated. The village Agricultural Committees were then enlisted but it soon became obvious that their enthusiasm could not be made to encompass castration. It began to look as if the campaign was doomed to failure, but I went through all the motions in the hope that the people might see the light. A stockade was prepared close to the village, and the evening before the 'campaign' was due to start I sat in the rest-house expecting the worst.

A car-load of vets turned up with their gear and moved into the rest-house beside me. 'Where are all the cattle?' I could but shrug and tell them that all was in the hands of Allah. Morning came: that same air of peacefulness prevailed. The Mek turned up throwing his black bony arms to the wind and giving loud opinions of the reluctant herdsmen.

'Fools, idiots! – they don't know what is good for them. They are all blind!'

We all agreed with him. Then he sent his aides to scour the countryside to rope in the offenders.

At the chosen site 50 or 60 of the Mek's animals stood flicking flies with their tails, with what could have been an air of resignation. The senior vet, a ruddy-faced Scot, laid his tools in a row then proceeded to roll up his sleeves ready for immediate action. An attempt was made by the herdsmen to drive a few scrub animals into the stockade, but it appeared they also were predisposed against the campaign. They snorted, pawed the ground and turned to left and right. Perhaps the sight of a white man waving powerful pliers in the air was a discouragement to them.

Spears were now prodded into reluctant hides and there began a stampede into the stockade. The vet saw the danger and took to his heels; which was as well! The animals knocked over everything in sight including the stockade and headed into the far beyond.

The watching audience stood bemused, perhaps thinking it was part of the plan. The vet was not amused however. He berated his assistants at length then instructed them to rope and upend the nearest bull. It was an unfortunate choice – a rather large Zebu-type animal with fire in its eye.

Try as they might, they were unable to restrain it. Impatiently the vet grabbed the rope, slipped it over a horn – but the animal was not having this; it set off at a trot pulling the vet in its wake. He held on gamely but the race went to the strong; he tripped and landed ignominiously in the dust where he lay nursing bruises and gathering breath.

His wrath now was a spectacle to behold. I kept well out of the way. In time, the assistants were persuaded to rope a lesser animal which was safely dealt with – and so the campaign got under way.

By nightfall the score was 9 or 10 animals. The spectators had all melted away so we called it a day. The 'campaign' lasted only two days, then the vets packed up and escaped back to the big city.

Livestock selection by methods such as this is an essential thing, but Tegali was not ready for it. The practices of a lifetime cannot be changed in a few days! The massive herds of Tegali continued to pulverise the land as if the vets had just stayed at home.

With the campaign safely over there followed a period of trek in the old style as our route took us towards Talodi and the 'Agricultural Show'.

It was a journey through familiar territory like a homecoming. Every corner, every forest held some reminder of how much I had become part of the mountains. The Um Tarag Tarag tree threw out long tattered streamers of bark like welcoming arms: the mountain peaks shimmering in their blue haze were like milestones by the wayside. We all savoured the pleasure of it.

I stopped at Kologi in the full knowledge that Nazir Mahomed would welcome me with open arms, and most likely arrange a dance. So it happened! Anything that resembled work was quickly dealt with and the village organised itself for the occasion. The great fire was lit and the processional ritual got under way with the arrival of the armour-bearer and his supporting multitude. We danced as on past occasions and received the same plaudits for our efforts: I felt I was beginning to get to know the girl dancers and they had no hesitation in making their advances.

Long after moonfall I was escorted back to my waiting trek bed to where it sat in the open nearby. Then the crowd melted away leaving behind them only the smouldering remnants of the fire.

I lay awake, chuckling to myself that I was actually paid for this kind of 'work' – dancing, enjoying hospitality and moving through a wonderful land! Was there any other job like it?

Even as I lay drowsily looking at the stars there came a murmur of prayer from the boys. I looked over, they were sitting side by side, cross-legged, their bodies rocking gently in unison, their eyes closed: Ibrahim was running his prayer beads through his fingers. They were creatures of nature, inseparable from the harmony of bush and space.

I listened entranced. Here was a harmony of which I was part, a spiritual harmony without discord, with God very close. I longed that this mood would last – and last – and last, but the disharmony lay not far ahead, months of anxious labouring on a new irrigation scheme.

Grain, more grain – while the mountains bled and died.

At Talodi we put up again at the grim old house resting beneath its towering mountain, a fitting mausoleum to the soldiers buried in its grounds. I walked to the club and found the members playing games and drinking coffee as usual.

There were handshakes all round. Kosti, my old friend from the emporium, rose to greet me.

'Welcome back, my good friend. I hope you stay longer. I am going to be a grandfather soon!'

'Not Athena?' I asked.

'Yes, who else. You must visit us again. Mrs Kosti shall be pleased to welcome you, and Athena too.'

'How kind . . . but . . .' My earlier enthusiasm for Athena's company had waned a little. '. . . There is so much work to do,' I pleaded.

I went on to tell the club that there was going to be an Agricultural Show in Talodi and that the province Governor was coming to attend it. There was, for once, silence. 'An Agricultural Show, what was that?'

They listened to my explanations about classes of livestock and produce, and demonstrations of this and that: 'But what for? Why?' was the next question. This was not easily dealt with – why indeed? That it was one of Alex's ideas was not the answer to give.

I then spoke of prizes, and this brought about a show of interest – prizes for the best animals and produce: brows became puckered in thought. 'You mean prizes for cattle, goats, grain . . .?' someone ventured. 'Wives?' There was laughter at this proposal: rather impractical, it was thought, as the community were a mixture of Arabs and Nuba. Judging would be difficult!

As well as the excitements of the Agricultural Shows and Stock Improvement Programmes there was always the routine ongoing work of the mountains to attend to. The Talodi agriculturalist watched over cotton transport, grain purchase and a host of attendant matters, all of which required checking. Important among this work was the Resettlement Scheme for Returning Soldiers. Khartoum required a flow of progress reports. With the rains over and the first cropping season finished this was an important visit. Anything could have happened in the intervening months: perhaps the cultivators had deserted and the experiment had folded up.

It is difficult today to picture the isolation imposed by lack of means of communication in earlier times. The mountains, cut off for months by flooding watercourses, relied on messages tapped out by wire. Talodi alone in the southern mountains had this facility, but the information it conveyed was sparse.

The native agriculturalist took me over the experiment and my mind was set at ease. Several holdings looked spick and span though as in all walks of life, some were better than others. Lamentable tales were told of raiding monkeys, alcohol problems, flooding and other hazards, yet on studying the books and talking things over with the farmers, things might have been worse. The little community had apparently jelled, in spite of the cultivators' diverse origins. The conclusion to the first year of work as written in the report[1] from this visit shows that an independent race of people, when uprooted for whatever reason, can be settled to form a new and stable community. Initial encouragement is important, not to mention patience, and a sense of humour. Peoples uprooted by the tragedy of soil erosion could find new hope in such schemes, provided they were treated with compassion and not with a sledgehammer.

It was the Agricultural Show, however, which gave me most cause for concern. After all, the Governor and Alex were expecting a show and no one here had either interest or knowledge of what was required. The new community of cultivators rallied to the call, and under the leadership of Tahr Effendi, the agriculturalist, things slowly began to happen.

On the outskirts of Talodi a clearing was made in the forest, and slowly a collection of stick and thatch huts took shape. As befits an agricultural show, stock pens and a ring were built. Throughout the area notices advertising the event were pinned up but, as the populace virtually to a man could not read, their value was questionable. Some press-ganging of chiefs followed:

'Bring your best animals . . . bring grain . . . bring vegetables – there shall be prizes!'

They all nodded vaguely in turn, a little bewildered as to what it was all about. Then there was that matter of the 'evil eye' which tended to act with malice when creature were singled out for attention. Thoughts, if there were any, took the following form: '. . . Better please them, particularly if the Governor is coming to see cattle and vegetables.'

There were several proposals made in the area of practical demonstration for the show ground – blacksmithing, although iron was a scarce material; carpentry; hygiene; a Rural Institute-type exhibit with home baking would have gone down well but, regrettably, this was a part of the world without cookers or 'hot and cold'.

The administration Mamur came to the rescue. 'What about the Talodi brass band?' he suggested.

---

1 Report in Appendix.

'The what?' I was taken aback – a brass band here in Talodi? I would never have guessed there was such a thing.

'Yes, the Nuba soldiers have brought brass music to the mountains over the years, and there is also the Junior Fife and Drum Band.'

This was laying it on thick! 'Bring them all: the more the merrier!' – but he wasn't finished yet.

'We can put on a play in English: we have been rehearsing at the club for some time!'

I could have embraced him there and then.

'Leave it to me!' he said. 'I will see that there is a programme to support the show.'

The day prior to the show arrived with things looking more optimistic – there would be something to look at, at least, and with luck, some people would turn up to watch. Then that all-too-familiar sense of unease began to settle on me like a cloud, because Talodi was carrying on in its usual medieval way quite careless that history was in the making. An occasional passing herdsman paused to lean on his spear in wonderment at the activity. No questions were asked. They probably thought a new suburb was being added to the town.

Rather frantically now I toured the area to drum up enthusiasm and was received with smiles and offers of refreshment, but little show of comprehension. They had no sense of one-upmanship – 'Why should our cattle be judged? What is the Government up to?'

I gave up and returned to furnish my own exhibit on the topic of Soil Conservation. I had gathered sheaves of the local grasses; also seeds, to show how they could be employed to regenerate soil. There were specimens of trees, hedges and everything I could invent to illustrate the theme. The samples of soil before and after erosion clearly demonstrated the problem – at least, they demonstrated it to me!

I stood back rather self-satisfied. There would be one good stand – but no! The cultivators from the experimental plots outshone my efforts with a demonstration on 'rural co-operation'.

'Good!' I thought. 'That will satisfy the Governor!'

Time and tide wait for no man; the day of the show dawned and I made my way to the ground. The field looked bare and deserted. I swallowed hard. I could picture Alex and the Governor having their morning shave preparatory to setting out for the first Talodi Agricultural Show, and then looking on this bare field. It was too late to do more than bury myself in my own exhibit and wait for fate to take its course. I wrote clear pithy labels on the various items – the locals would not comprehend but perhaps the Governor might be enlightened.

By the middle of the morning a slow infiltration of animals took place: a miscellany of living creatures all shapes and sizes but, fortunately, still plump from the rains. All were welcome! Cattle, sheep, goats were put in appropriate pens. Some cultivators appeared with little sacks of grain, beans, millet heads, tomatoes. I could hardly believe my eyes. The agriculturalist displayed the produce on benches. At last, I could heave a sigh of relief: it looked like a showground.

Then came the people! True, not a throng of eager farmers bent on enlightenment, but bodies giving the place a sense of purpose. There were little knots of naked Nuba sucking thoughtful twigs, Arab merchants and a number of in-between types – cultivators, herdsmen or simply hunters.

The native agriculturalist was a tower of strength. Together we prodded on the various events – some chiefs began to judge the animals. Their criteria of judgement were obscure, with heated argument, but prize tickets were handed to the victors who looked at them with wonder. What were they for?

Craftsmen began to demonstrate the skills of Talodi – then a box-car flying the flag drove on to the ground exactly on time. At a signal, the brass band struck up giving a sense of festival. The visitors stepped out, more than I had expected – apparently some visiting foreign dignitaries, but not the Governor! After all the work and preparation, merely the Deputy Governor of the province to witness this brave effort! But there was, at least, a show of a kind in progress and what with the crowd, the music and the backdrop of the mountains, it must look good.

The Deputy Governor apologised for the absence of the Governor and Alex gave me a nod, presumably of approval, then a handful of local dignitaries lined up for the purpose were introduced in turn. The official party moved round the field, surrounded by a jostling crowd who patently regarded the Deputy Governor as the prize exhibit. It all helped: it looked busy and I kept my fingers crossed.

In its turn, the Soil Conservation exhibit received attention. The notices were studied, then – 'Can this be done? Is this possible?' For a short time at least, conservation was back on the agenda.

'Village co-operation! Ah, that's interesting . . .' – the soldier-cultivators, past sins forgiven, did themselves proud.

The first day of the show finished at sunset with the Nuba still leaning thoughtfully on their spears wondering what had been going on. Herdsmen led their animals away clutching prize tickets and the few piastres earned as prize money: then Talodi reverted to its normal torpor.

There was room at the rest-house for the entire company. We dressed for dinner and afterwards settled for drinks and conversation. The Deputy Governor had obviously gained from having attended the show. The subjects for the evening alternated between grain production and erosion and he too was very aware of the paradox. Like me, he was a cog in the wheel of government, though a larger one, and we were both subject to other and to higher authority. There was agreement all round that erosion could and should be tackled immediately, but . . .

Apparently the Deputy Governor and Alex had a good agricultural show, but for the Nuba, it was open to question!

A row of beds covered by mosquito nets overflowed the *mustaba* on to the garden. Before settling to sleep I was invited to attend a very special ceremony at Delami in a few days' time, where some ancient tribal practices were going to be changed by consent of the people. It sounded intriguing, and Alex agreed to my going even though it was a matter only for the 'Political' service. Next morning we went our separate ways and I was left to get on with grain work, prior to going to the Abu Habl Irrigation Project.

The rains had been good, and heavy crops of cotton and grain were on their way north. Long strings of camels threaded their way towards the railway. Still more grain had to be persuaded from the cultivators to meet the requirements of the Government, so I travelled among the tribes with the same old message: 'We shall buy all the grain you can spare!' But money was of little interest to them. The Nuba are not a trading people and very quickly it was sure to filter into the hands of merchants. The wrong people got the wealth. Payment of money did very little for the Nuba. The land was dry and it was easy to see that with each passing week grazing animals became thinner as they fed only on parched vegetation. The air smelled heavily of smoke as a new generation of bush fires struck, apparently at random. There were places where the scars of erosion looked more marked than in the previous year. I still preached the gospel of soil conservation, but some of the edge had gone out of my efforts because of the shift of priorities. I knew now what it was to be a 'lone voice crying in the wilderness'.

On the appointed day I drove to Delami to take part in the ceremony which I had by then discovered was a gathering of great moment to the Aulad Himeid tribe. A branch of this people, the Hawazma, had marriage laws which were badly in need of review. Fighting and even murder were happening because of the injustices imposed by traditional practice. When a husband negotiated for a wife in marriage, custom made him pay separate 'bride-gifts' before he was able to remove the bride to his own home. It was like paying by instalments, because a young male did not have sufficient wealth to satisfy the total demands of the girl's parents at one go. Elders sat tirelessly arguing bride-price until a deal was struck and agreement resulted. The four parts of the price involved numbers of animals, traditional silver bangles, money and various items of adornment. A husband was considered to be married when the first instalment was met, but there was usually a long time lag before the remainder were paid up and parents parted with their daughters. It was fertile ground for unrest and violence.

A Mamur had been working on the problem for some time and this tribal gathering had been called to complete a resolution which was due to be accepted by the entire tribe. This resolution declared that, in future, brides would cost the husbands £6 only (divorcees half-price at £3). The 'administration' hoped that this simplification would bring about improvements in law and order among the Hawazma people, as well as a greater degree of marital bliss.

I reached Delami and joined the Governor and Neil, whose district it was, in time for lunch. The edge of the village was crowded with camels and donkeys, some of them richly dressed and hitched to every available corner. Groups of natives crouched in the shade of shop awnings arguing the business of the day, waiting for us to appear from the little rest-house.

At the appointed time we emerged into the bright sunlight. A group of greybeards welcomed us and we all gathered in a circle in the shade of Neem trees where there were only four chairs for the three white men and the Mamur. The sheikhs squatted on the ground, as was their traditional practice. Beyond, standing in the hot sun, tribesmen gathered round completely filling the village square. The Mamur signalled for everyone to be seated and a great bustle followed as people jostled for space so that in the end there seemed to be a forest of crossed legs, with sticks and spears standing up into the air before they all settled down.

No discussion can start before village hospitality is expressed. Drinks were placed before us on little tables and only then did the business get under way. The Mamur introduced the problem and gradually greybeards entered the discussion, illustrating their arguments with sweeping gestures. The proposals were resisted by two sheikhs who became quite angry and looked towards the crowd for moral support.

'The old way has served the people well: in any case, the proposed new bride-price is too small; older people will suffer!'

'It is unfair to our young men that they have so much difficulty getting wives: by Allah's name some of them already have children and are unable to build homes of their own.'

The pros and cons of the argument continued for some time, but the Mamur skilfully led them to a vote in which most of the sheikhs signalled their support for the change. A murmur of approval ran through the crowd.

The Mamur stood up, summarised the outcome for all present to hear, then called for a small table carrying at least 10 copies of the Koran, to be brought into the circle. We stood and moved to surround this little table. The Korans were built into a vertical pile, the judge placed his hand on top then each sheikh placed his palm on top in turn until there was a circle of sheikhs all looking into the centre. To my surprise I was asked to place my hand above the others – it took some effort to squeeze into the ring.

Now a solemn oath was spoken by the Mamur then repeated phrase by phrase binding the people to the new agreement. The ceremony concluded with handshakes and oft repeated 'May Allah bless us all and the new plan as well.'

Thus were new marriage arrangements accepted by the Hawazma, by democratic discussion and vote. The Mamur, who was the travelling judge in the area, could look forward to a quieter future and was overjoyed with the results of his efforts. He stood to address the crowd again, announcing that in the early evening there would be a mass wedding of all the couples caught up in the problem, to be followed by a tribal dance and feast. A cry of acclamation rippled through the crowd, which now slowly dispersed until the time of the ceremony. Later in the evening a great fire set the square into patterns of flickering colour and every available lamp created a festive air as the crowd assembled in high spirits to enjoy the wedding ceremony. Guns fired into the air, drum-beats throbbed incessantly and amid the noise and excitement we were escorted to our seats in the middle of a wide ring of expectant faces.

Once we were settled a string of young people was lined to form a row nearby: male and female paired off, and stood side by side often affecting great shyness at this sudden prominence.

The Hawazma, being so close to Nuba territory, had no strict purdah, and even though they were Moslems the women boldly showed arms and face for all to see.

The Nazir of the tribe mounted a little platform to address the crowd, which he did in a high form of classical Arabic which was difficult to follow. Most people also did not understand what was being said, but they listened quietly, appreciating the flow of words as much as the substance of the talk.

After a too lengthy speech, the first couple came forward arm in arm; the Nazir shook hands with them and blessed them, then the people cheered, waving spears, sticks and guns in the air. This was repeated until each couple was given similar treatment, after which we, the white visitors, and the Mamur walked along the line greeting each person in turn.

Everyone was in high spirits; noise deafening with drums beating louder than ever, and people swaying to the rhythm. Now came the feast. The newly-weds sat in a circle fed with bowls of cooked meat and vegetables, followed by fruit and gourds full of drink. We too had our refreshments at a long table from which the Nazir and many greybeards took their food then sat on the ground to eat. Circles of people, all enjoying the meal, filled the entire square.

At this point, the Governor called the Nazir over and suggested that before the dance started a beauty queen should be selected from the brides. This took some explanation, with the Nazir trying to comprehend what was meant by a beauty 'competition'. It dawned, and he broke into gusts of laughter, explaining what was meant to the other elders who, in turn, regarded the idea as a source of merriment.

Food was cleared. The Nazir announced the coming event and the brides were lined up, in absolute ignorance of what was about to take place. As the crowd watched in mystified silence, the Governor with the Nazir walked along the column of unsuspecting beauties – tall, short, fat, thin or nicely plump – looking them up and down and exchanging opinions.

The winner was chosen. Afterwards I learned the bride in question was one of the Nazir's own relatives. Perhaps judgement was subject to bias, but it was well received and the guns and drums started up again. The bride was given a money prize still wondering what it was all about, then everything in the square was cleared for the dance.

There followed a welter of tribal dancing and music, hour after hour until we were exhausted from the burden merely of watching it all.

The new law held! The people changed custom, although many fond mothers of brides must have regretted the day, as their daughters slipped so easily from their grasp.

KHARTOUM

Agriculture Show At Talodi

From a Correspondent

El Obeid, February 15.

Many distinguished guests attended the Agricultural show in Talodi on February 5 and 6. Among them were the Deputy Governor Kordofan, Mr. E.J.N. Wallis, the Senior Inspector of Agriculture Mr. H. A. Graves, Mr. R. Harrison, D.C. Dilling, Mr. N. Innes, D.C. Rashad, Mr. Reed, Agricultural Officer from Nigeria, Mohammed El Lowan of the Agricultural Department, Nigeria, Mek Adam Geili from El Abbasiya, Nazir Radi Kambal of the Owled Hamid, and Heads, of the Nuba tribes.

TWO SECTIONS

The show was set up in two sections: the exhibition of the Department of Agriculture and Forests and exhibits of Nuba and Arab cultivators.

The set up of the department included the following exhibits : agricultural crops, plant breeding section, trees, garden produce, Harig grasses, entomological section agricultural machinery, Veterinary Department, animal exhibits, ..., for animals, poultry, and soil conservation. The show was a most impressive sight and drew large crowds on both days. Mr. J.H. Mackie, Inspector for the Eastern Jebels, was responsible for the exhibits of his department.

LOCAL EXHIBITS

The Nuba and Arab cultivators were competing for prizes in their products of cotton, dura, simsim, groundnuts, lubia, dukhn, maize, kirkadei, vegetables, fruit, live-stock, poultry and transport bulls. The excellent standard of these exhibits reflect great credit on the labours of the Agriculture Department and the co-operation of the Nubas and Arabs.

ARABIC PLAY

There was also a good display of native handicrafts and an exhibition of modelling by the Talodi Boys School. The Talodi brass band and the boy's fife and drum band gave several concerts. On the second day of the exhibition, an Arabic play was given by Sudanese officials for the benefit of the basic English night classes. This raised £E. 80. On Wednesday February 7, there was a race meeting which drew large crowds. Over 2,000 people attended the exhibition and races.

The Well

In a well-fed society it is impossible to conceive of life at starvation level. At the period when these events were taking place, a few handfuls of grain together with a little pulse-seed and a little goat's milk when available, provided the average diet of the people. Only rarely was there any meat protein. An inspector's diet then, resembled that of the people except that there was more of it, and it got the occasional benefit of fruit from the experimental gardens. Mahomed the cook could juggle with these simple ingredients to make palatable meals, but they provided an uninteresting diet and eating became a tedium. This, in addition to constant exposure to the diseases endemic to the mountains, inevitably heightened the dangers to health.

A trekker in the mountains might occasionally have a sufficiently robust constitution to stay healthy, but in the end, most succumbed in some degree to the perils of the mountains. Stomach upsets were just a fact of life, but malaria sapped both body and will – and there was no medical service at hand to ease the fever.

After the Hawazma wedding ceremony a gap occurs in the trek records, for an easily understood reason: at a bleak rest-house somewhere in the bush, malaria struck again. I had taken the precautions – Mepacrin tablets, sleeping nets, protective clothing at nightfall – but an anopheles mosquito found its mark. Now, with raging fever and in a state of absolute weakness I lay for days inside a stifling sand-fly net with my mind disorientated, and nothing to ease the feeling of gloom. Only Mahomed, Ibrahim and the driver were there, no doubt patiently talking the hours away between their times of prayer. At long last I could sit up in a canvas chair staring at the hut wall, unable to walk a step. Every 'traveller' if honest, can tell of bleak and unheroic times; times which add nothing to the sense of adventure: I had ample time now to consider my destiny and to recollect stories of British inspectors and administrators virtually carried out of the mountains.

The events that followed this illness were influenced for me by a slow faltering return to health: there never was time for recuperation in Nuba, one just moved on as soon as the body could carry one's weight. There never was a 'rule book' for trekking – perhaps a thoughtful government might have prescribed – 'Take one week's complete rest!' – but presumably no one ever thought of this!

Inevitably, I was able to stagger to the car to head for Abu Gubeiha where work awaited with Nazir Zbeir, who, by this time had long overcome the relapsing fever outbreak among his people.

The car drove into the village at twilight. I was immediately aware of deep silence – a contrast to the turmoil of our earlier visit when death was in the air. The Nazir walked over to welcome me. On hearing of my malaria he left me to lie and rest, postponing our work till the following day. With a feeling of relief I lay down to sleep in the rest-house – but it was not to be. Minutes afterwards, there was commotion in the village with people crying out: and then – once more, that eerie trill of female voices which, at least in my experience, usually signalled tragedy.

I lay listening and wondering, then footsteps approached. The voice of the Nazir came: 'Call *Jenabo*, there has been a dreadful accident!' I jumped out of bed, felt for my sandals and stumbled from the hut. A group of people were gathering in the darkness. A tumult of voices confused my senses – then I heard ' . . . a well! . . . collapse of a well, with men trapped below ground!'

The old Nazir spoke up. 'You must come at once: some of my people are trapped. The new well we arranged to dig – scaffolding has collapsed deep down: my men may be killed! We must go at once with your car and take rope.'

Any weakness resulting from the malaria illness had to be brushed aside. I dressed and drove down to the agricultural stores to get ropes, pressure lantern, spades and whatever else might be needed. I knew only too well about the progress of this well-digging. It was one of the several government-funded projects designed to bring improved water supplies to marginal communities. The village of Hilawe, twenty miles from Abu Gubeiha, was shrivelling out of existence as local water sources disappeared. By digging deeper than hitherto it had been hoped that a subterranean water table might be tapped – indeed, a water diviner had been used to find the best site. Good well-diggers were scarce in the mountains and a group of men had gone out from Abu Gubeiha to undertake the work: presumably their skills had proved inadequate to the task.

With the car springs sagging beneath a weight of people the driver set out into the bush – there was no discernable track. Nazir Zbeir shared the front seat with me and guided the driver, using local knowledge in a way quite incomprehensible to the European, as each bush merely resembled its neighbour.

Headlights fanned out as the car twisted through the undergrowth. A memory seared itself into a still-fevered brain. Illness, turmoil, the proximity of death – the Sudan? It could have been a journey through hell! I clutched the vehicle's sides: my body swayed with the movement. It was well the Nazir was there to support me. Then, at one point darker than the rest the vehicle lurched to a stop. A spot of yellow light nearby intensified that darkness – then I could see figures in movement. The awful wailing trill of female voices seemed to pierce the brain from every side – then I could see the perpetrators of this sound walking in restless line at the fringes of the lamplight.

At the edge of the excavation a huddle of men rose to shake our hands in greeting, but with words softly spoken of invocation to Allah, and with shrugs of hopelessness. It was clear that any chance of men being alive in the depths of the well was minimal. They had listened carefully but no answers had come to their shouts – there were three men down there, and they were probably dead.

I lit the powerful lantern from the car, tied it to a rope, then, slowly, it was lowered into the depths. Down, down it went, the circle of yellow getting ever smaller and more distant till, finally, it reached the bottom and was in danger of tilting over and going out. There were heavy boards, almost tree trunks, making a cross over the well top, which was all of 8 feet in diameter, and looking into the depths from these it was possible to see earth slipping down from the damaged walls, so that the whole structure seemed in danger of collapse. Some of the helpers were persuaded to go back from the well-head as their movement was putting all in danger.

I peered into the depth till my eyes hurt. A jumble of wooden beams could be seen, then – dimly, what looked like a human head and arm, motionless. The Nazir confirmed this sighting – it must be a body: but could the others be alive and trapped beneath the debris? We stared in silence, then called others to look.

What was to be done? A heated discussion started. some advocated filling in the well as it was, but Nazir Zbeir was not alone in saying it would be on everyone's conscience if no effort was made to recover those below. I listened to the muted, though heated argument, passively not taking part: it seemed obvious that to be lowered into that crumbling hole would be tempting providence too far. Even had I been fit and well! – the thought made me shudder.

Then the Nazir waved his arms about, scorning the younger men present. 'I will go down – help me knot a rope.' He grabbed a heavier coil of rope, but others were restraining him – 'he was too old – it was for a younger man to try – !'

At length a man from Hilawe village bravely came forward, casting off his *jelibiyah* and twining the rope between his legs and around his waist. Within seconds he was seated on the timbers as others took the strain – in silence now, he slipped from view into the well and foot by foot the rope was paid out.

I could see him descending ever deeper, with the light still beneath to silhouette his body – which began to spin slowly – round and round. He touched the side to steady the movement: slower now we lowered him until his shape almost obscured the light. A muffled cry came from below – what it must be like to be down there amid crumbling walls of earth and wood! Motion stopped now: we waited – he was apparently reaching out to grasp what could be the arm we had first seen – then suddenly the light went out; a muffled rumbling came from below. A second's hesitation: a sudden cracking noise, then everyone jumped clear. A heavy tug came at the rope. Backwards the rope men tripped and fell though somehow pulling – another hard jerk as some obstruction caught at the man beneath, then, on again until at length a head, then shoulders appeared. Carefully now a body was eased over the edge of the collapsed diggings. Fortunately the rope had been thick and the pullers strong enough to overcome the general collapse down below.

The pathetic body of the courageous villager lay crumpled on the ground. It was possible to see part of his scalp hanging from his bloody head: in places, gouges of blood welled out of wounds. Another victim of the tragedy: an unnecessary victim – I should have forbidden any rescue attempt! My own bodily weakness seemed overpowering: with legs no longer able to carry my body – then the man moved. He was not dead! Everything else forgotten now, his wounds were tenderly bathed by the villagers, he was lifted carefully into the car and in the course of time we left Hilawe on the journey back to Abu Gubeiha.

Thankfully I crept into bed once more, an hour or two before dawn. Business with the Omdah was quickly done the following morning and we returned to Rashad where the wounds of the victim were properly dressed, and he was consigned to the one 'hospital' bed in the village.

All traces of the well-digging at Hilawe were effaced in the days that

335

followed, leaving the diggers in a very deep grave. The village without a new water source died a natural death, and the people moved on in search of another area which could support them: a process which must increase the pressure on other fully stretched communities. I met the injured man some months later. He greeted me cheerfully and it was interesting to see that half of his scalp, where new flesh had grown, was now white, as were the various wound regions of his body – all of which he justifiably revealed with pride.

The Nurse

A few days of rest and recuperation seemed called for, so on the day after the well accident I resolved to stay away from the office: rather, only to sleep and sleep, seemed a pleasing prospect. The boys were warned to leave me in peace until nightfall. But yet again, other plans were afoot over which I had no control.

Ibrahim came in with a telegram, marked urgent, brought to the door by the village idiot. I read it with some anxiety, but then with a sense of anger. It read: 'Nurse arriving a.m. today, please oblige by taking her to Abbasiya for two days. Mek Adam expects you – ZIRAA.' The word *Ziraa*, Arabic for agriculture, indicated that this was an order from Alex in El Obeid. I looked at the message for some time trying to sort out its meaning. A nurse coming here? What had I to do with a nurse? Why should Alex expect me to take her to Abbasiya! Then the name of Mek Adam triggered a memory. I had heard that he wanted a children's clinic at Abbasiya. This might not sound very remarkable to 'civilised' ears, but such a development in the mountains would make a considerable advance. The children of the tribes suffered all the many health problems endemic to Africa. The Mek had travelled widely in his lifetime. He had seen a lot, and he, Sir Adam Geili, was the person who could bring about lasting improvement to the people's condition. Yes, a clinic for children was a great idea, to be encouraged at all cost.

As for the nurse, probably arriving by the post lorry and having no transport of her own – she could well be coming to launch the whole initiative. I read the message again and suddenly the word *today* penetrated. All I wanted of *today* was to lie down, to rest, and to shake off the still lingering effects of malaria.

She would soon arrive and would need a meal, and there was likely to be very little food in the house, and the place was coated with dust. Wearily I called the boys – Ibrahim to stir up the dust, Mahomed to scour the suq for something worth eating. At the news of another departure, to Abbasiya now, they groaned in unison, sharing my disgust at the enforced change of plan, because they too had expected some rest days. Why should such random events intrude into my life? I shrugged in despondency, and gloomily set off walking to the office to meet this nurse when she arrived.

337

Female company had no appeal, in fact company of any kind was un-welcome: then, to have to head for Abbasiya! Why did Alex Graves do these things? A nurse? She must be hard as nails with a voice like a rasp! But on the other hand it would take some resolve to travel alone into the mountains – not that there was any positive menace in Nuba, but women just never trekked alone. I climbed slowly up the office stairs, flopped wearily into the swivel chair and waited. The papers needing attention on the desk were swept to the side impatiently.

The drone of an engine eventually echoed into the office from the Rashad hills as the lorry approached. On its arrival in the compound I moved to peer at the action beneath. One passenger stepped down. To my mild surprise it was no hardened matron, rather a girl, probably my own age. Reddish-brown hair, the usual khaki clothes – slender: the details quickly registered. I sat down again determined just to wait. I felt no welcoming urge; in addition to the effects of illness my pride was a little hurt that Alex should consider escorting a nurse a priority over my work.

At last steps sounded on the stairs. A Ziraa clerk ushered her in, then left us. The welcome she got was less than enthusiastic. In perverse mood, my voice sounded flat to my ears. Obviously she would see at once her arrival was inconvenient as far as I was concerned.

I indicated to her to sit down, asked her about her journey and plans. She confirmed that a child clinic was planned for Abbasiya. I led her to the wall map – pointed out the area of Tegali for which the proposed clinic would serve; but still could not warm to the theme.

Finally she said, 'Look, it is not my fault I had to come here. As far as I know there is a need and someone must think I can answer that need – I can go alone to Abbasiya if there is transport.'

This was reprimand enough: I rose to express my intention of going with her.

'Good,' she said. 'My name is Catherine – tell me yours, we may as well be on first-name terms!'

At this the cloud lifted just a little and we set off home for lunch, to find that Mahomed had discovered something resembling mutton around which to build an adequate meal.

We sat across the table and conversation of course had to flow. I tried to excuse my manner by telling her of the malaria attack. She was no stranger to the after-effects of illness and her smile told me that I was forgiven.

'What is your plan for Abbasiya?' I asked.

'I have been told to build on what I find there,' she replied. 'Failing anything being on the ground, I will take back an "action" report. I know the Governor is keen to develop something quickly.'

We talked about the diseases children were forced to endure. I told her of my own observations – dietary problems leading to deformity, and perhaps worst of all, eye troubles caused by poor hygiene and flies. 'These difficulties can be overcome when the people are encouraged to take steps for themselves, with the aid of simple medicines and the presence of a trained nurse,' she said.

I knew a little of what was already happening in Abbasiya. 'There is a medical assistant, doing basic healthcare.'

'I know that,' she said, 'but what is needed is a nurse coming from their own people. I think such a person is being trained for the post.'

Any lingering truculence on my part was by now gone. Here was a really valuable project. It would be good to play a minor part in its establishment. I called the boys to load up and to be ready for departure, not forgetting the nurse's gear. By mid-afternoon we were on our way.

She watched the passing scene with wide-eyed interest. Like myself not so many months before, she had grown used to the flat northern plains. This was a new world to her, and a major adventure in which animals, vegetation and people all drew excited comment. The track led through deep gulleys and forest; it rounded piles of rock fallen from the steep mountainside then it issued from the mountains proper as our destination drew closer, because Abbasiya with its jumble of mud-built houses stands in the middle of a wide plain of clay soil.

I stole a sidelong glance. Her neck was freckled. Her head jutted forward as she drank in the passing scene. I felt pleasure at being able to show her the territory which I regarded as in part my responsibility.

The rest-house at Abbasiya was a cut above the usual, consisting of a large single square room with thatch sweeping almost to the ground. It was surrounded by a *zareeba*, and tall water *zeers* stood apart in a little cool shed. An attendant looked after the visitors' special needs, and kept it well swept. All this was in keeping with the status of the Mek, who received a constant supply of visitors.

With the kit lying in heaps on the ground I was aware of Ibrahim and Mahomed having an argument. They normally, on arrival, went about the task of setting up house without a word.

Ibrahim came over and asked, 'Will the *Satta sitt* (honourable lady) share

339

your bed?' He made this highly improbable suggestion with a show of teeth, and a glint in his eye!

'Will she *what*?' I thought I had misheard him, knowing his sense of propriety! 'Well,' Ibrahim said, 'she has no bed with her, only a valise of bedding – will I then lay it on the ground?' To come into Nuba without the appropriate gear was virtually unknown: someone in El Obeid had slipped up.

Catherine was listening but obviously not understanding what was said. I gave her the full story – 'Ibrahim is asking whether you will share my bed as you evidently don't have one of your own.' She took this in her stride, questioning more in her mind how she could be in default.

'But are there no beds in rest-houses?' she asked. The obvious dawned on me – of course there were string beds, but no one ever used them because it was anyone's guess who or what had slept in them in the past. I explained this to her.

She shook her head. 'Let me look at the bed.' We examined it and turned it over. 'It looks almost new,' she said. 'I will take a chance on it.' With this issue settled the trek bath was set up in the hut and we took it in turns to wash and dress. With tea ready on a little brick platform outside in the compound, we sat down just as the sun set in crimson glory. Ibrahim served tea. In honour of the guest he wore his whitest robes and the green cummerbund normally only displayed on home ground; he was obviously entering into the spirit of the occasion. It occurred to me that I was enjoying the evening, malaria forgotten at last.

There was now plenty to talk about and an hour passed easily. A messenger from the palace came with an invitation to meet the Mek as soon as convenient. With a lantern in his hand, he led us the short distance to where the Mek himself was awaiting us on the palace steps.

Mek Adam stepped forward to greet us. Here was the great 'King' of the Aulad Himeid; a commanding black figure though stooped a little with the years. apart from the striking whiteness of his robes in contrast to his black skin, he dressed no differently from any other sheikh; but his presence quickly showed in the regality of his movements and the confidence with which he expressed himself. A widely travelled man, he was truly a bridge between government and tribe, respected by all in Kordofan Province.

His eyes were alight, welcoming and hospitable. This was a visit he had expected: at last, a project planned some time before could get under way. It required only encouragement from the Government in the shape of advice and, no doubt, also a supply of funds channelled via the province Governor.

Then came an honour rare in the Sudan – the Mek's wife appeared, holding a white veil to her eyes which after initial greetings she let fall, showing a strong face, much younger than Mek Adam's though with hair greying at the temples. The party settled on a wide verandah in lavish ottomans, where we sank deep, with legs folded. I looked around at the building – it was scarcely a palace though so called: in the light of the many lamps on the verandah I could see down into a wide square of mud-built houses. There was little to indicate unusual wealth or anything that was different from other little towns in the mountains; it probably showed that he was a man of the people, living in the same style as those around him. Refreshments were served on small individual tables and an animated conversation struck up, in which the wife took a significant part. It became quickly apparent that she was the main advocate for the new clinic. This was a pleasing discovery because it seldom happened that women initiated change in the Sudan, or at least if they did, it took place out of sight and behind closed doors. Catherine and the Mek's wife talked on, although neither spoke the other's language well, and they needed constant prompting from the Mek or myself.

It was quite late, with a descending moon low in the sky, when at last we walked back to the rest-house. There was nothing to keep us up any longer so in a short time we slipped into our separate beds, which were set up side by side on the little platform. Shut within our nets we talked for a short spell. It was a novel experience to have a sleeping partner so close, but my body ached for rest and I was asleep in minutes.

How long after is difficult to tell, but a sharp cry wakened me with a start. In the darkness I was aware of Catherine jumping up. 'Help me!' she shouted loudly. I bounded from bed, bewildered – she was tearing at her nightclothes until they lay at her feet in a heap. She stepped off the platform and stood shaking her hair and beating at her body.

'What has happened?' I called, mystified at the performance.

'I am bitten all over: get me some water and a towel!'

Ibrahim and Mahomed as well as the driver rushed to the scene bearing a light; if the sight of an unclothed female body troubled their Moslem scruples they showed no signs of distress. Her flesh was already pocked all over with flea-bites: the creatures must have crept out of the bed *en masse*. Water was quickly brought. All we could do was douse her completely; then she ran into the rest-house where, with powerful disinfectant and presumably meticulous care, she worked away to remove the last parasite.

There may be an element of the ridiculous where fleas are concerned, but an attack such as this in the middle of sleep must be the ultimate in discomfort.

I waited for what seemed a very long time till she completed her toilet – then she emerged wearing a frock, and with ample evidence of the attack on her face. She was actually laughing at her predicament only a short time before. This was a relief, because I had been pacing the compound with feelings of guilt at having let her sleep in that awful bed.

Now, she had to be persuaded to use my bed, an offer which was finally accepted. I improvised one out of trek-chairs and table. The night by now was well through, but I managed to doze uncomfortably for a spell. The first light of dawn was a welcome visitor. I dressed, then took a walk through the empty streets as the morning light unfolded.

For most of that day arrangements for the new work went afoot. There was an appropriate small building close to the palace which, though it stood absolutely empty without furnishings or a water supply or sanitation of any kind, represented a centre on which to build. Catherine and the Mek as well as other interested people talked over plans, so that by early afternoon with the work completed we were able to say farewell and head back to Rashad.

That evening, seated on the garden *mustaba*, Rashad looked its brilliant best. The hills were bathed in gold and orange: drum-beats sounded from the distance. We sat drinking it all in with little need to speak. A sharp tilted edge of the nearly-new moon moved slowly down to the west, increasing its light as day faded into night. Catherine said, 'I could stay in this place. You are lucky to be stationed here – and with such good people to share your life.' I could but answer, 'Yes!'

Next morning she left on her return journey to El Obeid but, as in many fleeting friendships in the Sudan, we never met again.

Domestic Duties

With the effects of malaria forgotten and the decision made to have two rest days, I decided that this was a suitable time to hold a tea party. I thought over possible guests. There was the Rashad Omdah, and the school teacher; also the chief clerk; perhaps also Sheikh Ahmed from the suq who had the main shop there. Four guests were sufficient to stretch the available resources – sufficient cups and saucers would present a problem – but Mahomed would conjure up something.

I called the boys and they agreed this was an appropriate thing to do, as little effort had been made so far in the realm of entertainment; in fact they both showed enthusiasm for the venture. Mahomed suggested that a cake could be baked. Ibrahim proposed it would be politic to hold the party indoors rather than on the *mustaba*, as opening one's home was a better expression of hospitality. It was agreed that invitations would be sent for the next afternoon. By then I looked forward to the event. With spending so much time on trek there had been very little contact with Rashad itself – not that there was much to the place; it was little more than an overgrown village with houses scrambled amid the jumble of surrounding hills. It was a cut above the average village in the mountains as far as affluence is concerned, due to the presence and influence of government, but high on the hilltops there were also poor outlying communities unchanged in centuries.

The guests arrived: first the Omdah on horseback as usual. He entered in his usual exuberant manner, white robes billowing widely so that he appeared to occupy a major part of the room. Indeed he was earlier than expected, but it became evident, as I might have known, he had an eye for business – did I want a horse? No! Perhaps some sheep: they were still plump and would keep me going in meat until the rains? No again! The topic was dropped. Then I ventured onto the subject of the community because he was a form of councillor. 'The people here have all they need except a reliable water source – as you know,' he said. 'Is it beyond the powers of government to send experts to solve this matter? The years go by and it is always the same.'

This was I knew from experience the main difficulty here. Rashad, a lovely spot, admired by all travellers, a sought-after work station – yet singularly lacking in life-giving water! But I had already tried to find an answer – I had risked my life in the attempt. To have built a community high amid rocky hills was probably an error – yet with difficulty it did manage to survive the long period between rains. There had to be an answer! Moncy could provide it but I had by now realised that administration of the Sudan was done on a shoestring. The country had so many areas where investment could benefit the people – water sources, hospitals, schools, transport – that available resources were spread too thinly to have enough effect, and were concentrated on the cities. The Omdah's was a voice worth listening to; he was of the people and not merely a tool of administration. Should there be discontent or need, he would be the one to bring the news.

The chief clerk arrived next – a stout complacent gentleman and a product of Khartoum education. He settled into his chair with a cultivated air of deference often found in administrative people. There was little to be learned from him. He was a nice person to deal with in business but his knowledge of the community was likely to be remote. As with so many of the British staff, his pleasure was in talking shop – about government people and policies – about abstract means of control rather than about people as such. Still, it was politic to have invited him.

The remaining two guests arrived at the same time. People more dis-similar would be difficult to imagine, and the only apparent thing they shared was their nationality. The market sheikh, an old and wizened Arab, stood hesitating at the doorway, as if to indicate he was in unaccustomed territory. His discoloured *jelibiyah* showed an indifference to appearance. He wore oversized sandals which flapped noisily on the floor. The fact that he had come at all was remarkable, and by way of being an honour to me. Sheikh Ahmed carried about his body the smell of his wares, a robust blending of spices, herbs and camels. The proffered chair was almost refused. His practice was to sit cross-legged on a piece of carpet in his shop, and being upright on a chair would be a discomfort.

The teacher, immaculate in khaki shorts and carrying a fly-whisk, walked with straight back and a display of assurance the other lacked. He gave off a strong smell of perfume; he carried with him a whiff also of college training which might well bear some resentment at British rule of his country. A polite man, it was difficult to penetrate this mannered veneer, leaving an uncertainty as to what lay beneath. He would provide little information about the people or their needs, because in effect he was more remote from them than I was. Even though teaching the village children, he carried with him pride in his status and some show of contempt for the unlettered people around him, which surfaced readily as the situation arose. He sat down in the remaining empty chair, laid his fly-whisk on his knees and crossed his legs languidly, nodding in turn to the others.

For the short time involved, it probably did not matter that they were an ill-matched group with little to say in common, but I quickly sensed an uncomfortable silence, something rare when Arabs meet. I gave a few verbal prods but topics quickly dried up. There were apparently undercurrents: were these between the merchant and the teacher? No; the Omdah was unusually quiet! The clerk sat blandly in silence, not at all prepared to help out.

Time passed slowly and heavily and it came as a relief when Ibrahim turned up with refreshments. I had not expected this outcome, and though a tea party may be a slight happening, in the course of events it triggered off deep questions in the mind, questions which would remain to nag for a long time.

With hindsight, bringing such a group together was done without any consideration for those involved: with no thought of their feelings. It had been done to satisfy a whim on my part. It was surely patronising and presumptuous to expect them to meet my requirements and to be automatically at ease in each other's company and mine. In Europe a similar random group would most likely have had little in common to share. A good host should give first place to the feelings of his guests.

Did this in an oh-so-small way point to the fault of one culture trying to rule over another? — that unwillingness or inability of the ruler to interpret the mind and needs of the ruled. There could be only one word to describe this — arrogance! Where, now, stood my right to be there at all?

Thoughts of the above nature were formed only gradually, and reinforced themselves from time to time in the developing circumstances. But life had to go on, and crowded events in days ahead pushed them into the background. Meanwhile my guests drank the refreshments provided, ate Mahomed's cake, then left, expressing carefully chosen words of appreciation. That night I lay for long trying to resolve questions which I could barely shape in my mind.

Next morning the mail lorry trundled in from the railway with its usual load of goods, passengers, animals and a sack or two of mail. There were no letters from home but instead, a bundle of British newspapers sent by the family, much out of date and carrying news of Rommel's defeat in Africa; more than this, there was conjecture about opening up a second front in Europe. My spirits rose as I thought of the growing probability that leave to the UK might be possible some day soon.

I called in the boys to tell them Hitler would be defeated before long then the supply of sugar in the market would improve. They smiled broadly at the news, not only because of the prospect of more sugar, but because even here the name Hitler was regarded with contempt. Ibrahim said, after a bit of thought: '*Satta sitt* (the honourable lady) will be coming out to join us soon. You must improve the furnishings before she comes.'

Ibrahim was right, of course! The few scraps which I found adequate – canvas armchairs, a string bed, bookshelves and the like – were indeed rudimentary. He added:

'We must begin to furnish the house so that a lady will find comfort in Rashad. I know an excellent carpenter who will make anything you need.'

I had not known that Rashad boasted a carpenter so I was immediately interested and asked Ibrahim to lead me to his workshop. When we got there it was hardly a workshop, though there was a saw and several other rather primitive tools inside a rickety shack with the 'carpenter' employed shaping some rough poles at the doorway. Rather doubtfully I asked:

'Can you make furniture for my house?'

'Yes, your excellency, I can make anything you desire.'

'A wardrobe?' I asked – at least I did not know an Arabic word for wardrobe so I drew one with my sandal in the dust.

'Yes, I can make that out of zaan wood,' – this was the local mahogany-type wood. I gave him an order for this and several other items, then went away pondering in my mind whether the carpenter's confidence in himself was justified.

He started working on the furniture at once. In fact, so quickly that I was taken by surprise when two days later he stood smiling on the doorstep.

'The wardrobe is finished. I will need help to bring it to your home.'

I got the box-car out and we drove to the shop to collect it where I stood amazed at the creation – never before can there have been such a splendid piece of furniture made out of boards nailed together, and almost large enough to act as a spare room. Obviously his ideas of measurements and size did not coincide with mine. Still, beggars can't be choosers! With our joint efforts it was lifted into the car and driven home where a problem presented itself – there was no way it could be levered into the house.

The carpenter was not upset. 'I will soon get it in, it's not difficult.'

He proceeded to dismantle it board by board and soon joined it together in the bedroom where it forcibly established its presence. In due course the house was furnished to Ibrahim's satisfaction and everything made ready for that great day when 'the excellent lady' would be brought to Rashad.

Taming the Abu Habl

Unexpected instructions from Alex came over the wire. In a sense they were welcome because it meant another short trek before heading north to the Abu Habl scheme – they read: 'Visitors arriving Rashad re Ground Nuts. Take them for quick tour of mountains before coming north . . .'

This message could have been a puzzle but for my having been told previously that the British Government intended growing thousands of acres of ground nuts in Africa to supply the demand for vegetable oils when the war finished. Some office wallah in Khartoum had thought the Nuba Mountains would meet the requirement, because ground nuts actually were exported in small quantities, but I was against the idea. If Britain needed vegetable oils in bulk these should not be got at the expense of the Mountains. However, I had my orders and it would be necessary to go through the motions.

Next day a well-dressed 'city gent' arrived, with a young woman perhaps 20 years of age sitting at his side. His white hair and moustache told his years while the girl, most attractive and sophisticated-looking, might have stepped out of a London fashion show. She was introduced as secretary to the ground nut expert; I found that, in fact, she was French, and she had a great gift of silence. They proved to be unusual trek companions but I quickly learned their relationship was closer than the term 'secretary' implied, so matters were simplified! The expert quickly explained that any developments in the mountains would involve use of heavy tractors and clearance of thousands of acres before a project could be made economic. This episode demonstrated the Sudan Government's confusion where policy for land was concerned: first had come plans for soil conservation; then more and more grain; now ground nuts!

We set off in two vehicles to travel hundreds of miles looking at the soil and arguing about peanuts, a journey I knew was a waste of time. They visited Nuba villages, studied interesting rock formations and enjoyed a good tour. For me, the best moment was when I introduced them to the stately 'toilet' at Heiban; it amused me to think of the secretary climbing the steps to the throne. Even of this experience (and it was an experience!) not a word was spoken. Throughout the trek the French secretary remained impassive and immaculate. Her carefully manicured nails, hairstyle and attention to matters of appearance defied the sweaty dirt of a mountain trek, but they kept her busily occupied throughout.

At the end of the trip they left to investigate other lands and as far as Nuba was concerned the matter was dropped.

By now there was no other way of postponing our descent to the Abu Habl valley. There were messages on the table which said things like:

'Heavy equipment arriving Rahad . . .'

'Engineers leaving Khartoum on . . . please meet them at Um Ruaba station . . .'

There were good reasons for our reluctance to leave the mountains: the work was an unknown quantity and had for me neither appeal nor relevance. I had had one bad experience on the Abu Habl, and as for the boys, there existed that dread for the place with its jinns and its inhospitable environment. Even Mahomed, who was always quiet and co-operative, looked miserable.

The box-car was fully loaded with tent, sacks of grain and other food to last a long stay, perhaps of three or four months, and every available piece of gear which could add to our comfort was stowed aboard. We trundled out of Rashad then down the mountainside to the plain as we had often done before. Not a word was spoken throughout the journey until approaching Jebel Sidra close to the watercourse, when Ibrahim reached round the cab and pointed to the western sky where a grey haze was forming. A storm cloud in the middle of the dry season? What could it be? The cloud continued to gather. I kept an eye on it as I drove. We began to grind our way over the sands close to the Abu Habl when a few locusts crossed our path – the advance of a great swarm. It could not have been better timed – the Abu Habl again! Why did things always happen here?

Now they came in a dark mass striking the car and forming a continuous carpet on the ground. We continued up the far bank of the watercourse, with the creatures rising in a brown curtain at our approach. They poured into the open sides of the car, covering the pedals and clothing us in layers of struggling creatures which tangled in hair and found their way inside shirt and shorts. The boys hid under a cover, already pressed around them by the mass of locusts.

It became impossible to drive. The track was hidden by the swarm: even thorn trees were turned into ropes of insects. We stopped and waited. The sun seemed to come out again as the swarm settled, showing a drab yellow-brown world of locusts as far as the eye could reach. The boys surfaced. Ibrahim gave me a look, shaking his head and saying only, 'Abu Habl.' For half an hour we waited and watched until a sharp whirring noise started and the entire swarm flew off eastwards leaving only a bare desert with gaunt skeleton trees stripped of everything green.

A thorn compound stood in the middle of the wilderness that was the Abu Habl valley. It contained some items of equipment; the first arrivals. A watchman slept in a little grass hut nearby, rising and stretching himself at our approach.

For some minutes we sat still wondering where to begin, then Mahomed moved to find a place, any place to set up 'home'. Ibrahim threw the kit to the ground with exaggerated movements, venting spleen on all that he touched.

I left them to sort things out and walked some distance through sparse thorn scrub towards the setting sun. A soft orange glow cloaked the harsh landscape with beauty so that I began to feel more hopeful for what lay ahead. Beauty and hope are close neighbours: perhaps it would not be so bad after all!

In coming days this wilderness was due to waken into life as powerful machines tore it apart – trees and other wildlife would give way to waving fields of grain. There was something wrong in all this! I had a restless feeling that here, in Kordofan, was not the place for such a large-scale enterprise where the tribespeople were likely to finish up as agricultural labourers and the pressures of commerce change the shape of society. To this had to be added the pressure on a sensitive ecology. In the long term, all of life could suffer! This awareness came more easily to me after my observations on erosion in the mountains. Obviously no one else felt like I did; but no other person had witnessed the problem with such a critical eye.

The camp, or rather 'home', was assembled by the time I returned. A net-covered bed stood beside the tent; a set table was prepared close to a fire and Ibrahim hovered in the shadows ready to serve dinner when I gave the word. Late into the night I studied papers on the coming work – lists of equipment; the names of the engineers soon to arrive; they appeared by their names to be a mixed bag of nationalities. It was after midnight when I put out the light and climbed into bed. The lights of an approaching car made me sit up again.

'Who? At this late hour!'

It stopped just yards away and Alex stepped out. He called, rather too cheerfully:

'Sorry to be so late – is there a cup of tea?'

Black figures jumped to the ground and in a few minutes his bed was erected beside mine, the fire stirred up and we were seated at the table talking over the coming programme of work.

'The engineers arrive tomorrow and I thought I should be here to meet them. Also I have sorted out arrangements for contractors; they shall arrive in a day or two . . .'

By 2 a.m., with everything talked over, I was able to return to bed, but sleep was elusive. It had been said that my first urgent job would be to recruit 1000 labourers. 'Mek Adam will advise!' A lot of machinery had reached Um Ruaba station. 'You will have to make sure it gets down here safely . . .'

There was a flicker of dawn in the sky when sleep came, but work got under way as early as ever. We toured the valley – mile after mile of good land; some stretches of forest to be cut. Alex spread out cloth maps to conjecture the likely site for the small dam across the Abu Habl watercourse. 'It is up to the engineers to sort out the technical work – dam, bridges, canals and the like.' I dared to mention the great flood of the previous rains and how it filled the valley, but apparently the engineers knew of the problem and they also knew the answer 'so I could put my mind at ease'.

We waited on the sand at Um Ruaba as the evening train arrived from Khartoum bearing with it the 'experts', my companions in months to come. A compartment door swung open and one by one a group of Europeans or, at least, people clothed in European fashion, stepped down. It was already twilight but I could see that one of the arrivals was a woman – it was hard to believe my eyes, a woman coming to live on the Abu Habl in a tent! She had blond hair, I could tell her eyes were blue; she was quite young, about my own age. As people do, I saw all this in a flash – then I took time to observe the others and join Alex in welcoming them to Kordofan.

The first obvious thing was they spoke virtually no English, and one only, an Egyptian, spoke Arabic. Leader of the group, a grey-haired Hungarian, struggled to exchange greetings and introduce the others using his few words of English. We learned in due course that they had been gleaned from the Middle East, refugees from the war, and had signed contracts to serve in the Sudan. There was a Romanian, a Pole and a strikingly tall

Czechoslovakian with a thin moustache who, in turn, proudly spoke one word – 'Wife!' indicating the silent lady at his side.

The couple were newly married and the journey to the Abu Habl was their honeymoon trip. The wife proved to be Russian. In her arms she held a little black kitten, and ventured to hold out one of its paws towards Alex saying two mysterious words – 'Ivan Ivanovitch!' which turned out to be the kitten's name. Alex looked bemused.

As we talked, a lorry containing kit passed by heading for the campsite and by the time we arrived there was a bustle of people struggling with poles and canvas in the darkness. The boys had a long table set for a meal so together, dust and all, we sat down to monkeynut soup followed by stringy meat and the usual produce of the suq. It was eaten hungrily but in relative silence as we struggled to find a common language with which to communicate. Alex prodded words here and there and heads nodded as he spoke, but only when the Russian wife held up a knife and named it in her language did conversation take off, with the purpose of learning Arabic. Guttural sounds rolled round their tongues and the evening blossomed into smiles.

'Knife . . . spoon . . . pencil . . .!'

With the ice broken and nervous tension released, the arrivals became more human, making prospects for the future seem more agreeable.

When we separated to go to our various tents I was surprised to see two boys struggling under the weight of a most unusual article, a high-backed white enamel bath. It was carried into my neighbours' 'home'; that of the newly-weds. To get sufficient water to fill it could be a future problem, yet flaps were no sooner tied down than singing came from the tent, the kind that can only come from a bath-tub.

The day that followed was spent touring the area in detail and poring over maps, the experts being concerned mainly with land gradients to accommodate the flow of water from the watercourse. The Hungarian engineer walked the dry riverbed to confirm the best place to dam the flow of water and, in a remarkably short time, decisions were made.

My first task was to estimate the amount of timber to be cleared. There were several areas of tall gum trees, one of them populated by a number of monkeys: it was inevitable that the trees had all to be removed for burning into charcoal. I knew that once the timber was felled, the charcoal burners would come from El Obeid.

Machinery arrived from the railway, contractor's vehicles poured in and little more than a day after my arrival, the peace of the valley seemed shattered for ever.

A long string of washing hung outside my neighbours' tent and it appeared as if the Russian wife was busily employed turning her tent into a home, as well as keeping a watchful eye on Ivan Ivanovitch.

With wheels rolling and decisions made, Alex left again for the city where, he assured me, he would provide me with all the backing I needed. To contact him urgently the only link was by telephone at Um Ruaba station – there was no radio or telephone link from the irrigation scheme. It was a period when most decisions had to be made on the spot without reference to higher authority.

A daily routine became quickly established. Work continued from daylight until dusk: there was nothing else to do there except work! A 12-hour day was the norm with only short meal breaks. The engineers were as keen as I to finish the job and get away to somewhere more agreeable. At night a row of beds, 20 or so yards apart, stood out in the cool night air. There was no 'entertaining' or even discussion over drinks, because by nightfall we were all too tired for anything but rest.

Trees were bulldozed, pegs marked canal lines and giant elevating graders scooped out continuous slivers of soil, which in turn made the banks of canals. The valley was quickly scoured and scraped beyond recognition with neither rock nor stone to impede progress. Air became blue with the smoke from charcoal pits and men, like hundreds of ants, worked at scattered sites over the whole area. The engineers worked on the main dam as well as the other smaller structures needed to permit road and rail movement over the scheme.

Mek Adam turned up, as he had promised to advise on where workers could be most readily recruited. It was a thinly populated area with villages many miles apart and it was obvious from the start that 'labour' would prove a limiting resource. He rode in a lorry with a retinue of followers, remaining only a few hours and expressing surprise at the changes to his valley, as if the scale of the operation was unexpected. Then he gave a warning:

'I don't think the jinns will be pleased, keep your eyes wide open just in case.'

So far the jinns had kept clear, so I laughed at his superstition and got on with the work. Jinns! He was as bad as Ibrahim. Yet, one could never tell . . .

With work well established, three of the engineers went off to the city leaving various Sudanese officials to continue their work. There remained only two Europeans in addition to myself; namely the Czech and his wife. The couple continued their prolonged honeymoon, though in daylight hours, she saw little of him. It would be wrong to consider the Abu Habl valley an ideal place to begin married life. The engineer had an excellent voice but singing in the bath-tub became less frequent. In fact, it was easy to tell that life in the tent next door was not always harmonious. On one occasion she came over to my tent and said, hands on hips, in pidgin Arabic, 'Why he work such long hours? This is not life!'

My explanations of the need for urgency to get the dam completed in the short period before the floods was met with an impatient foot-stamp. 'You will kill him!'

I thought this was stretching things rather far, after all, I too was a victim. She marched back to her tent and closed the flap, the nearest possible alternative to slamming the door. It was apparent from this that neighbourly relations had plummeted to rock-bottom. Fortunately I remained on excellent terms with the husband.

Day after day I scoured the villages searching for labourers. I arrived in a village, stood on the rear of the box-car with the local sheikh at my side, then made an impassioned speech. With a white man's arrogance I fully expected the people to drop everything and jump aboard. This is what usually did happen. They squeezed on with only the clothes they were wearing and I took them perhaps 50 or so miles to the camp. Several days later numbers drifted home by foot carrying the few coppers they had earned. At times I was almost frantic in my efforts to find men to keep the job going, as each passing day was one day closer to the Abu Habl floods.

Progress, however, continued steadily – pipes and bridges were laid for the railway to cross over and geometric patterns of canals criss-crossed the valley floor.

Things eventually came to a head 'next door'. I rose one morning to the sound of a loud quarrel, and in spite of language difficulties it was easy to understand what was going on. That the wife was by now dissatisfied with her lot did not surprise me in the least. To be alone in a tent all day contending with heat, dust and flies, then to welcome one's partner home to a meal of goat's meat and yams would have tested a saint.

The Czech stumped off to his work and some moments of silence followed. Then I became aware of a figure just outside my tent – it said, 'You will take me out in your car after work tonight.' With this pert sentence and without waiting for an answer the distraught wife retreated to her tent.

I swallowed hard. Take her out, she had said. Out! When the last time we spoke I had been given a reprimand! And this was no gentle request – it was a command.

At this period of history the day of the permissive society had yet to dawn; to take out the wife of a confederate was a breathtaking improbability fraught with risk, or so I thought. I had a vision of hot-blooded Czecho-slovakian wrath; in any case, where was there to take her? There was only miles and miles of bush with the occasional rocky hillock. Um Ruaba station with its surrounding village held little attraction for an evening out. Perhaps she will change her mind, I thought hopefully. But no, she had the look of a woman decided, there could be no escape.

My first step was obvious. I jumped into the car and headed straight for the watercourse where a concrete barrage already covered its base and one white half-naked figure stood out clearly from the swarm of black workers. He jumped down at my signal and for some moments we discussed the work, then, in as casual a manner as possible I said:

'It seems I am going to take your wife out this evening.'

He straightened his back, grinned in a frozen sort of way then shook my hand. That was all. He climbed on to the dam leaving me to question whether or not the coming expedition had his blessing. I was hardly reassured!

The day passed with the usual frenzy of work though my mind did stray at times to the coming excursion: perhaps I was a little afraid. Any social skills I had in the area of entertaining ladies had withered a bit through lack of use. It was like treading into the unknown.

I returned well before sunset as I saw no point in having an outing in the dark of night. 'Ibrahim,' I commanded, 'prepare the bath – white shirt, flannels! I am going out this evening.'

He was surprised, and daringly asked, 'Where are you going in the Abu Habl valley?'

It was a bit like taking an excursion in the middle of the Sahara.

'I am taking the Lady for an evening's drive.'

He stepped back and grinned all over his face. '*Jenabo*,' he said, with very deep meaning which did not add to my ease of mind.

I left the tent, dressed, and prepared for the worst. As at a signal she too emerged, looking a picture: a tailored costume, silk stockings (or perhaps the new nylon), in fact a most attractive figure which could well have been heading for a local dance hall. The car stood fuelled and ready; we climbed aboard without a word and set off into the wilderness. 'Where to?' I asked. Raised hands and a shrug indicated just anywhere as long as it took her away from the camp. We weaved a way through the scrub, breaking a swathe in the tall dead grass – mile after mile of nothingness.

I drove, only too aware of the neat figure at my side: subtle wafts of perfume had me sniffing deeply. Her arms were folded over her chest and she had the determined look of a woman out to enjoy herself, husband or not!

The silence became difficult. I tried a smile, looking at her, and spoke the Arabic equivalent of the word 'Hello!' but there was no vestige of a response. So we continued until an antelope loped across our path, and at last she showed signs of life, saying some Russian words, apparently not meant for me.

Then a little rocky mound came into view. It was somewhere to head for. I stopped close beside it and she climbed down, smoothed her skirt and set off walking, as if bent on examining the hill. I followed at her heels. She touched the rock – 'Hot!' she said, a little surprised at the heat derived from the lowering sun. I told her the word for rock – at last we were talking!

Together we walked round the hill then climbed to a flat slab offering a view westwards over the flat plain. The Nuba Mountains shimmered in an azure haze on the skyline, land became dappled with purple: all of nature was beautiful and at peace. We sat down side by side watching the sun lowering in shades of crimson and gold until everything was bathed in a soft orange glow. It was a time when conversation would have been an intrusion, so we held a silence which lasted a long time.

I could see her eyes wide in rapture – there were tears! There came a sob and her shoulders quivered. She was very beautiful with light shining in her hair like a halo. Had I put a finger out to touch her then, I knew she would melt away before my eyes as in a dream.

The shadows lengthened then at last she turned her head and began to speak, slowly at first then more rapidly in Arabic, but more often in her native language. Most of what she said I could understand. She had been at university until the German advance into Russia drove her from her people. I could see the hurt her words expressed. By some means she had reached Khartoum then met and married the engineer within a matter of weeks.

For the first time she turned to look at me and said, 'He is really a good man: but . . .' the qualifications to this remark were made in Russian.

I learned that she was an artistic person, a dreamer who spoke with a distant look in her eyes as if longing to fly away to higher and better realms. She was not one to be submerged in the clamour and squalor of an engineering camp.

There were now no barriers separating us. I reached over and held her hand to which she yielded without showing awareness. Time now raced by and darkness gathered round; it was a magic time.

How long we talked is hard to say, but at last she withdrew her hand from mine, we rose and I helped her down from the rock. Slowly we walked to the car where we continued talking before starting for home. I told her my story, of Marion waiting for my return after years of separation, and she nodded her head in understanding. The evening was like a catharsis for both of us as we talked out our loneliness.

We lapsed into silence on the way back to the camp. I could picture the determined set of her chin as she steeled herself for further days of drudgery. She expressed her thanks and disappeared into her tent.

It was over, and how different the evening had proved after all!

Ibrahim brought a cup of tea and I sat motionless for a long time thinking out the evening. A sense of unease gripped me as my mind turned over aspects of life from which I had been deprived for so long: the lack of simple caring relationships. To share one's life continuously, what would it be like? If only leave home to Scotland was possible!

I was brought back to reality by the sound of laughter from the nearby tent. There must have been a reconciliation! I felt drawn towards the cheerful sounds, so I walked over and shook the tent flap. A voice called happily: 'Come in, come in!' The scene within was indeed blissful – there he sat, knees high in the enamel bath, his wife happily removing Abu Habl dust from his back with soap and cloth.

The evening's excursion had been a success for all parties. In weeks to come we shared a few more evenings out. They acted as a safety-valve. We looked at other rock hills and returned refreshed. On each occasion we dressed carefully, then on our return she disappeared into her tent, no doubt to plunge her husband into the enamel bath.

There followed months of work: endless work without a day of rest. From sunrise to sunset I was in continuous movement, always having before me the spectre of the first floods and the job unfinished. It took its toll.

Abu Habl Scheme under construction (railway crossing over canal).

Main Abu Habl barrage (where water is deflected into irrigation canals).

Excavating main canal by elevating grader.

Arguing with contractors, obtaining supplies, finding workers in the sameness of heat and dust turned this period into a nightmare.

On one occasion I made the journey to El Obeid returning with a load which included dynamite, 5 sacks of sugar, spare parts and food-food-food for a work force numbering 1200. There was always sufficient money, but food remained scarce to the end. Fortunately workers ate simply and prepared their own meals from the simple ingredients gleaned from the bounds of Kordofan.

Another day a sandstorm blew in from the northern plains, stopping work while people sheltered from spiralling dust-devils and the all-pervading grit which coated mouths and eyes. Drifts piled against the tents. Newly worked soil became marbled with red dust borne from land in the north where erosion had already done its worst, visible evidence of the encroaching desert. The storm blew itself out and work started again.

By this time the scheme extended over 15 miles in length, with 50 miles of canals excavated and almost ready to carry water. At this point no more food could be found locally and stocks were almost finished. An urgent message went off to Khartoum, and just in time 600 sacks of millet arrived at the station.

Ten heavy tractors and a large range of other machines had to be kept working and there were scarcely any spare parts in the country. A needed part could take several days to come from Khartoum, but miracles of improvisation were performed by Sudanese mechanics in a little workshop where welders and smiths did their invaluable work night and day.

The total weekly wage bill averaged £1,115, a meagre sum today but at that time a day's work earned a few piastres (100 to the pound Egyptian) and workers signed the wages sheet by means of an inky thumb-print.

Occasionally visitors came to inspect the work and they brought with them news of the outside world. They spoke of rapid developments taking place in the war with a second front established in Europe. There was neither radio nor newspaper to keep me up to date with news and by the time information came to the Abu Habl it was already weeks out of date.

A District Commissioner suggested that before very long a start might be made to home leave and it would be a useful exercise for me to write to the Civil Secretary and find out what were my prospects for going home. 'No harm in reminding him you exist,' he added. The Civil Secretary, head of the Political Service and next to the Governor General in importance, watched over the affairs of all departments, so I knew he must be aware of happenings on the Abu Habl. I wrote the letter, then forgot all about it.

It came as a surprise when a week later the following letter was delivered:

Dear Ian,

It is good of you to write me. I note your enquiry about leave to the home country. I am as keen as you to see the old place again.

I hear good reports from the Abu Habl and intend to visit soon to find what you are up to. I may have some news about home leave then.

Yours . . .

With this information to act as a spur, work seemed less oppressive: a chink of light was beginning to brighten up prospects for the future, and as for the Civil Secretary's visit, there was a lot for him to see when he came. A calculation showed that there were by now 90 miles of field channels and over 320 miles of terraces: the main barrage was growing up fast! A remarkable transformation had taken place in a small period of time.

Alex turned up without warning as usual, his first visit for several weeks. 'You are going to have visitors tomorrow so I thought I had better check what is going on!' He reeled off a list of those due to arrive at Um Ruaba station the next morning – it included the Civil Secretary, the Director of

Agriculture, the province Governor and several others. 'They are coming in the Royal Coach and we have to call on them early for breakfast.' The name 'Royal Coach' referred to a luxury rail coach decorated with Victorian splendour and used by travellers of special merit.

There was no time to waste. After a quick lunch we set off on tour; I needed the comforting assurance that work done so far met with Alex's approval. It took several hours to complete the inspection. The by now treeless valley closely resembled the flat Gezira irrigation scheme where I had first worked with Alex. It was certainly an impressive spectacle but his sole positive comment was: 'Yes, there is a difference all right, but time is drawing on. You had better make sure it is all finished before the rains!' As if it was possible to hurry more than in past months! Everyone, including the tractormen, had worked to drop. There had been no 'passengers'.

The intention was to plant 10,000 acres with the first flood, with a possibility of 100,000 in the long term. At one place Alex noticed a driver had continued to work beyond the clay limits leaving a sliver of red sand. He sharply noted there was no point in leading water on to sand where it would disappear – as if I didn't know!

Mainly, however, he was satisfied and we returned in the dark to dine with the engineer and his wife. As always, in the lamplit hours of late evening, Alex relaxed and became a different person, but there was always that barrier to true ease in relationships, perhaps because of the isolated type of life and the need to make do with whatever company was at hand.

I lay into the night staring at the sky. Three years of my life had, by now, been spent in the Sudan and during this time Alex had dodged in and out of my life. I clearly remembered the first descriptions I had been given of him in Khartoum – 'a hard man . . . difficult to get on with!' These descriptions were true: I had quickly learned that friendships and the gentler side of life were not allowed to interfere with work. Yet he was fair, direct and I knew where I stood with him; if only he could speak words of encouragement, words which would have lessened the sense of isolation which came from time to time. Years afterwards I remember these times of gnawing loneliness which had little to do with the solitary trekking life; rather the lack of a warm continuing bond with the one who was my ongoing link with my own race.

Perhaps the Civil Secretary would have some good news about leave home. This was a thought sufficient to remove the gloom and send me to sleep.

With the coming of dawn we rose and set out for our breakfast in the Royal Coach which stood in solitary glory in a siding, looking very important. Alex climbed the carriage steps, knocked on the door, then we were ushered into a richly decorated saloon. Several tables were set for breakfast, a fan already whirred overhead and several servants moved about busily. We sat for ten minutes before the hearty sound of voices warned us the travellers were on the point of entering.

A number of men, smartly clad in bush shirts wearing insignia denoting their status in the country, filed slowly in until the space was full of people. I stood up smartly to meet them as did Alex though with an air of familiar irreverence, because he was well known to those present. Amid much cheerful banter I was introduced all round, then we sat down to eat, sharing a table with the Civil Secretary and the Director of Agriculture. Millet porridge was followed by the rarest of delicacies seldom seen in Kordofan – bacon and eggs; talk went on meanwhile about the new irrigation scheme.

'Very impressive,' the Civil Secretary commented. 'I got a glimpse of it from the train last night.'

For an hour or more discussion went on – costs, equipment, supply of labour; providing a golden opportunity to raise the issues which limited progress and at every point there were words of support. The political service was already attending to matters of land tenure in co-operation with tribal chiefs. There was little enough time left to complete the work before the arrival of the Abu Habl flood and seed time. The various topics were well aired.

I was asked: 'Will you beat the rains?' I could but answer 'Yes,' although there was still some element of doubt. Alex discussed matters of finance with the Financial Secretary of the Government as this was Alex's special area of responsibility with regard to the scheme.

Then we set off in a procession of cars. I led them to the main dam which was already up to the level of the banks of the watercourse, and for some time the black workers stood back as the party examined it from top to bottom. In terms of dam construction it was not large, as its purpose was to deflect the coming flood into the new main canal rather than provide a reservoir of water. Nevertheless, it was an impressive structure which brought words of praise from the party. And it had another role to fulfil – never again would the Buggara be trapped by the Abu Habl; it bridged the watercourse and the 'long swim' would never be re-enacted.

For some hours the party toured the entire scheme, stopping at times to examine particular features. Whether or not it was going to be successful, it looked good. Apparently I, alone, had inner doubts as the past flood was still too fresh in the memory. The jinns might still have a card to play!

A long table was set out at the campsite for a late lunch with an army of 'boys' in attendance. Talk continued on the prospect of thousands of tons of grain coming out of the scheme to meet the country's pressing need for food.

I became exhausted from the press of conversation and sat passively listening, faintly aware that a malarial sweat was gathering and making the scene unreal. The Civil Secretary addressed me on the subject of soldiers returning to the mountains, and it took an effort to make an adequate answer; even when he raised the subject of home leave, the matter which mattered most, it was as much as I could do to take it in. My name was on a list and when the time came I would be given sufficient notice: this I did understand. It came as a great relief when the party set off again for the station.

A train was waiting with the Royal Coach coupled on and ready to leave for Khartoum. We waved our farewells then Alex set off for El Obeid, leaving me to return alone to the tent where I lay down in the misery of the illness, indifferent to the scheme, to the world, even to life itself.

A few days later when it had run its course I staggered from bed to be told that after returning to Khartoum the Civil Secretary died. I felt then that I had lost a friend, but so did many other people throughout this vast country.

There was no time to convalesce. People kept coming to the door of the tent so that I started working in the fierce heat of day when I should have rested. A telegram went off to Alex in the hope that he could take over for a spell but he was off on trek in far Darfur. Khartoum sent a Sudanese agriculturalist, so this took away some of the immediate load of work, but I went about in a daze with my body and mind drained. It led to an inevitable and inglorious climax. In the island of life, surrounded as I was by a limitless ocean of work and now weakened by the effects of malaria, something snapped inside me. With hindsight the picture is clear enough but then, when nothing existed for me save this burning hot valley with little time for rest, something had to give.

The entire set-up was unjust, but when one is young it is all too easy to do appointed duties without question. A friend, or a sympathetic ear would have been of help, but I felt there was no one! A night came when I walked into the bush without evening meal; without washing off the day's grime and sweat. I walked and walked seeing nothing: numbed. My limbs ached, fevered imaginings tortured my mind. It was irrational and it felt like failure. I had to hide: not from people, more from myself. At last my legs gave and I fell face down with eyes tightly closed, clawing at the ground as if to dig a hole and escape from everything.

I must have been there a long time. If there is an ultimate depth of desolation which the mind tests for a split moment of time before recoiling, I reached such a depth in that lonely spot. A shivering cold racked my body like pain. Slowly – although there is little memory of this, I must have rolled over, and now looking up, the stars were bright, like friends I had known for long – the Southern Cross, the Scorpion, Heavenly Twins: Venus low in the west . . . Mars: supreme order – the eternal heavens.

Again, a long interval of time passed. My senses gathered awareness of the surrounding scene – the gentle sigh of an evening breeze. The black shadow of trees, the Nuba Mountains dimly visible on the skyline. Then I thought of people, friendly people. Pictures, long since remembered, flashed through my mind. There was even love . . .! Love to give: love to receive. I drew in a long breath.

It all happened in this strange way. Nothing like it ever happened to me again; in this experience there was a lesson to last a lifetime, but a lesson difficult to frame in words.

I sat up shaking my head from side to side and allowing a smile. Where was I? What was I doing here sitting on the ground? I rose and with aching muscles but lighter mind, returned to the camp. The boys were standing beside the tent talking anxiously, and came towards me as I reached the lamplight.

'Are you all right, *Jenabo*?' The question was asked gently.

I was. Yes, gratefully, I was.

A wire came from Alex on his return to El Obeid: 'Take a few days rest in the mountains I will keep things going.'

The boys shared my pleasure: indeed, they almost danced with joy. 'Are we finished with this place?' Ibrahim asked hopefully.

'No, we have much still to do. I cannot leave for good until the water comes and the scheme is tested.'

'This is a bad place, this Abu Habl . . .'

I had heard it said on so many occasions, but was not prepared to argue the point.

High in its mountain fastness Rashad looked splendid. The dilapidated shacks of the suq seemed familiar and friendly, and the office building looked every bit a castle. The flag was flying showing that Neil was at home.

An exciting pile of mail from home waited my attention and I was settling to an evening's reading when there was a tap on the door and Neil walked in. It was remarkable how seldom our paths crossed, and only rarely were we in Rashad at the same time. The great area of the mountains was sufficient to swallow up two travellers, even though their work was interconnected. His face radiated good humour. 'Welcome home again: wasn't expecting you! Come and meet the family. His wife and children lived most of the year in Khartoum and came only rarely to Rashad. They were on holiday.

I put the mail aside a shade reluctantly and we walked to his house a short distance away. To sit down for afternoon tea in an 'English' home with lively children was a rare experience, one I had not enjoyed for so long. There followed carefree days taking the children riding along dry watercourses, and on one occasion having a picnic surrounded by baboons, watching us closely from neighbouring rocks. This was a world apart, which had a dream-like quality. My mind and body grew in strength, until a return to the plain seemed less of a nightmare.

Ibrahim brought his family to the house for me to meet, particularly the new baby of whom he was extremely proud. During this brief visit the wife remained hidden in her robes, but she timidly held out fingers for me to shake. I observed silver rings and bangles: the wife obviously of an affluent servant.

There was, however, one cloud: Gamr, the second riding horse, had a wasting illness from which it could never recover. The head groom carried with him the smell of beer, and voices whispered that he left the horses to the care of the younger grooms, and was seldom sober. I had him on the carpet and would have sacked him, but for his plea – 'My family, my parents, aunts and uncles will all starve if I lose my job!' He got off with a last-chance warning and was on the point of leaving my presence when he brightened up remarkably quickly.

'*Jenabo*, I have good news. The Omdah has an excellent horse he wants to sell. He asked me to tell you as he thought you would be interested.'

Why should I want to buy a horse? I might not be trekking in the coming rains, particularly if home leave was a possibility. I was in no mood to trust the groom no matter how good his news.

'It is a pure white stallion, one of the best in the mountains, and it's going cheap!' he persevered.

In exasperation now I shouted, 'Go! Let him bring the horse if he wants.' He left in a hurry and I forgot the incident.

It was the last day of my short stay in Rashad so I decided to enjoy a rare novelty – an afternoon's siesta. I lay down naked in bed while the afternoon sun beat down outside in its usual merciless way. In a few moments I fell asleep.

It might only have been seconds later, I wakened to the sound of voices and clattering hooves as if the entire village was paying a visit. Then it dawned on me – the Omdah, already! Why had I not sacked the groom on the spot?

Feeling very naked indeed I peered out of the window: yes, there he was, an erect proud figure clad in dazzling white, and mounted on a splendid white charger. He held his seat easily, almost imperiously, as the horse pawed the ground impatiently – what might be termed a fiery steed, all activity, as if impatient to be off taking the high compound wall in its stride. In my dazed state it presented an intimidating spectacle, more so because he had with him what amounted to a retinue of warriors all well mounted on strong Arab horses, obviously waiting for the young inspector to emerge and demonstrate his equestrian talents.

Ibrahim turned up and said quite superfluously:

'*Jenabo*, you have got visitors.'

I swallowed hard, slipped on bits of clothing and went out into the glaring light with whatever composure I could muster. The Omdah dismounted and walked over to greet me affably.

'You wish to buy my horse? The best horse in Africa! Just look, to you alone I will sell it.'

'Well . . .' I commented, looking at its fiery eyes and stepping back a pace.

He patted it here, he stroked it there. I watched bemused; there could well have been smoke coming from its nostrils. Instinct told me that my standard of horsemanship could only offend the creature.

'Try it!' he said. 'Mount! You will find the horse can gallop faster than any in the country.'

He said this by way of tempting me. The retainers looked on and the boys stood in an expectant knot. The head groom leaned against a wall with a complacent smile on his face – Just wait, I thought, just you wait. To ride a horse, the first time in months, and on a beast like this!

It stood still, ears pricked – an expectant hush settled on the compound. I saw my scraggy leg and clumsy sandal as I lifted them over the saddle. Gently I tugged the reins; nothing happened except it shook its head as if in irritation. I pulled again, stronger this time, and dug in my heels, then we were off!

We reached open country, then, as promised, it galloped like the wind, its hooves seeming scarcely to touch the ground. I held my seat only just, barely aware of the blurred shapes of familiar landmarks as they raced by. Far in the rear, excited whoops spoke of retainers trying to keep me in sight.

These were hectic moments: they could well have been my last. The horse ran until it was tired, only then could I turn it back towards Rashad, where I rode it in with its mouth frothing.

'See, did not I say this is the best horse in Africa?'

I was off in a flash and stepping out of harm's way.

'You will buy? I offer it to you out of respect for our friendship.'

The thought of this creature walking docilely in a line of trek ponies – never! But tact was called for.

'My friend,' I said, 'how right you are to be proud of this magnificent animal. Nothing in the world could persuade me to deprive you of it; that would not be the act of a friend.'

'Forty pounds!' he ventured.

'Call your friends and let's enjoy a cup of coffee together.'

'Thirty-five pounds!'

'Ibrahim,' I called, 'coffee for the guests.'

'For you alone thirty-three pounds!'

I had become temporarily deaf so, in resignation, he held up his hands to Allah and we all sat down in relative harmony to enjoy our coffee.

The white horse passed from my life. Gamr the riding horse sadly died and the groom in due course, and after further infringements, was banished from the establishment.

Written records of these days remind me that some time later I bought a mule!

The holiday over, and by now much restored in health and spirit, I said my goodbyes to Neil and family and then headed back to the Abu Habl valley. More grinding work lay ahead, but time was passing and it would not be long before the rains came, and the job was finished. But what then? There were many uncertainties with regard to the future – leave, home to Scotland, or more horse-trekking? Perhaps a posting to another area of Kordofan!

There were more immediate anxieties however – would the irrigation scheme actually work? Perhaps the canal could not cope with the flood . . . and the dam . . .? But these were the responsibilities of the engineers. I still had my doubts about its success, as a watercourse was a different proposition from a continually flowing river like the Nile. What if all this work proved to be in vain?

Alex was back in El Obeid when I reached the camp. The engineer and his wife invited me to dine with them in their tent as it was a cool evening. 'We have missed you: so has Ivan Ivanovitch,' I was told. The black cat, for it was no longer a kitten, seldom left Madame's arms as if it was her lifeline to a more normal world. The Czech looked as lean and as tanned as a man can be from months of incessant labour. If he had felt he had a debt to pay for his new life in the Sudan, by now he had certainly paid it in full. His wife on the other hand wore a look of resignation, as if the life of the camp had defeated her. They spoke very little and I left to go to my tent wondering at the force that had kept them together in this hopeless place.

Then, even at this late date, a series of disasters struck the scheme. First of all, a loud explosion from the workshop shocked me as I was stepping from the car. I hurried over to the scene and found two men lying dead beside an exploded oil drum. They had been burning it open with a gas torch, making the one obvious and careless mistake which ended their lives. There followed the sad and difficult duty of arranging transfer of the bodies to Khartoum.

Next, there came a message from one of the temporary villages erected for labourers on the scheme that there was an outbreak of illness and men were dying. That disease had come was not remarkable, as conditions there were the poorest that can be imagined, a situation exacerbated by scarcity of water. It is a sad reflection of the times that workers were given such scant regard. They were paid, fed and watered – all at subsistence level – then left to fend for themselves. The workers were employed by contractors who, in the end, were responsible – it is always comfortable to be able to put blame on others! The Government did respond urgently, however, by sending a strong medical team to contain the situation, which it did with its usual efficiency. The workers and their few belongings were thoroughly cleansed, the village was razed to the ground, and a new ramshackle village grew on a fresh piece of ground. Five men died.

Work continued as if nothing unusual had happened.

Then came another disaster; at least it was so for the engineer's wife. Ivan Ivanovitch disappeared. Madame was distraught. She wandered into the bush repeatedly calling the name, but in vain.

The husband returned from the dam at twilight worn out as usual and flopped into a chair outside the tent. His wife appealed to him to go out in search of the cat but he was unsympathetic: 'Perhaps,' he said, 'it will come back. In any case it is only a cat!'

She stopped motionless for a second then rushed into her tent. The next I knew was the sound of a resounding thump. I looked up – there she stood over the body of her husband with a saucepan in her hand. He lay in Abu Habl dust, out for the count!

I decided to remain passively neutral and averted my eyes. She stumped over to me, saucepan still in hand. I waited, eyes tight shut expecting the worst.

'You! You!' she said. 'You will take me to the station tonight. I leave this place!'

She did not wait for an answer and it did not seem safe to argue the point. In a matter of minutes she came back, suitcase in hand, and took a seat in the car staring straight before her. Her husband by now sat nursing his wounds – there were no farewells. I drove her to the station where she boarded the evening train to Khartoum. So, one might think, ended a marriage! Many marriages have ended from lesser cause than this.

It became obvious in the days that followed that the engineer had lost his sense of drive. He drifted about the job as in a cloud of gloom. I tried my best to cheer him with words of encouragement, but nothing could change him. A week of this and work was suffering. I had visions of the watercourse in flood sweeping everything away.

I became almost desperate, then one afternoon something new and previously unknown happened: he asked for a few hours off work. At first I thought: This is it! He is leaving as well. Then I saw he was unusually active around the tent; boys were being directed hither and thither. A 'spring clean' was taking place. Now he spruced himself up in a way hitherto unknown – hair slicked down, black patent shoes and other extravagant manifestations; nor would he enlighten me as to the reason for his eccentricity.

I left to get on with my work, to return again after dark. Cheerful voices came from my neighbours' tent. It could only be . . .!

I paid a social call and found the lovers reunited and showing every sign of bliss – 'Madame had enjoyed her holiday in the city but it was nice to be back!' Next day the engineer was working as hard as ever before and to all intents and purposes Ivan Ivanovitch was quite forgotten.

By now it was the end of May 1945. Local wisdom said that the first flood was not due until the first week in July so there remained a month to complete the work. Two little round stone houses had been built beside the barrage, so I left the tent and went to live in one of them while the boys occupied the other. The structure still swarmed with workers as there remained stonework to complete with heavy iron gates waiting to be winched into place.

I knew only too well from past experience that the Abu Habl was unpredictable, as a rainstorm striking any part of the northern mountains could send down a tidal wave of water any time in the near future. But there was no way of hurrying things: hand labour and simple equipment could only do so much and no more.

Ibrahim became more anxious with each passing day. 'You know, *Jenabo*, we should not be here. Remember what happened to you last year!'

This became a monotonously repeated theme, then one night he stepped into the lamplight, his eyes rolling and looking furtively around as if jinns might be listening and waiting to pounce. 'If you do not leave this place I will leave you and return to Rashad,' he said, with trembling voice. He was in a highly emotional state, another victim of the Abu Habl, having had too much time to think over his problems.

This was going too far: to think that after the years together he should suggest such a thing! Mahomed came in and took Ibrahim's arm, as if to lead him away. '*Jenabo*, sorry about this,' he said to me. 'Come away Ibrahim, leave *Jenabo* in peace.' But Ibrahim shook off his grip.

I said in the most beguiling way I could, 'Ibrahim, just give me three more days, then we can return to the tent. See, we are high on the canal bank, there is no danger from the flood.'

It was, however, apparently not the physical danger of the flood that was his problem, it was something deep in his nature; the fear of the supernatural.

'Three more days only!' I repeated, and they left, with Ibrahim apparently resigned to a further period on the dam.

The three days quickly passed, and on the evening prior to moving, masonrywork at the dam was completed and it remained only to winch the heavy iron flood-gates into position. This last day was oppressively hot, giving shapes a double image in the brassy light. dust-devils flitted round and over the dam as if to search and probe this new monstrosity which was changing the age-old shape of the valley. I looked to the mountains and noticed they were topped by a black shroud. As the wind stilled, silence became hurtful to the ears, making sounds, when they came, crack like bullets.

If only we could get away from this place which had taken so much from us and given so little in return. This place, the antithesis of all I had hoped for in coming to the Sudan. There was no adventure here, no sense of romance or discovery, just oppressive labour in an inhospitable world.

I stood at the end of the great main canal, seeing it stretch far into the distance until it melted into a shimmering haze – it came as a shock to see it apparently rising upwards and disappearing into the sky. There must be something wrong: water could never flow in this channel. Had the surveyors made a mistake? It took an effort for me to know this was an optical illusion – it was time that I was going from the Abu Habl for good!

As the sun sank lower, cool air poured in from the west with a suddenness that caused me to shiver. I retreated into the little house to write up my notes – the only kind of recreation I had been able to enjoy for a very long time. Without the availability of a pen and paper to release my pent-up thoughts and emotions, life here would have been closer to purgatory. In resurrecting these notes it is difficult to avoid the mood of anxiety recorded at the time: in fact, much of the Abu Habl record was torn up and destroyed many years ago because it told of a time I wanted to forget.

With bed set up indoors, I fell asleep as soon as my head touched the pillow. It was as well I did not know that a black snaking mass of water was rushing towards the dam. A rogue storm in the western mountains poured out its torrents, the first violent rainfall of the year, sufficient to stir up the jinns of the valley.

I struggled to waken from a nightmarish dream – a roaring sound – could it be part of the dream? At last I jerked into wakefulness: the noise was all too real, confusing the senses. Mahomed was approaching, a lamp in his hand. He cupped his hand and shouted.

'Quick, *Jenabo*! It has come! The flood has come!'

I jumped from bed to feel cold water swilling over the hut floor. Ibrahim too was there, cowering behind Mahomed. I grasped the lamp from Mahomed and splashed from the hut to the edge of the dam. White water poured in torrents over the structure then swirled down the *khor* out of sight. In these moments it looked as if the entire uncompleted structure was about to be swept away.

There was terror in the scene, lit as it was by the weak light of the lamp. Yet as I watched, it slowly dawned on me that the dam had withstood a first violent surge, and had the work only been finished, these same waters would be feeding the new canals. Yes, there was really no fear in this! If we were only given a few more days, the iron gates would be fixed on the sluices and the flood brought under control.

With some enthusiasm I shook Mahomed's hand. Ibrahim stood in silence, his eyes wide.

'Look, Ibrahim, isn't it beautiful?'

There was no response from him.

I watched the flood for some time – already there were signs it was lessening: inch by inch it dropped. But this was what happened to such rivers in the Sudan. Early storms before the rains really got under way, sent down short-lived rushes of water, only to dry up until the next flood came.

At first light of dawn the engineer came on the scene, taken by surprise at the sight of rushing water, but he seemed to be exhilarated.

'See,' he said, 'the cement is not yet fully mature but it withstood the flood; isn't it splendid?'

'But what of the damage to equipment: the material lying in the water-course?'

'What does it matter? The job is almost done. Now, when it dries we can lift on the gates – then – goodbye Abu Habl!' His eyes, like my own, were alight at the prospect of moving on to other places, as far from here as possible.

The flow lessened and by mid morning the water reduced to a mere trickle as the dry soil soaked up the year's first flood. The large gates lay where they had been tossed by the water, hidden beneath a mound of soft mud: cement mixers and other equipment were all but invisible. There was no great loss. Once the clay dried most of it would be quickly cleaned and restored.

Workers returned to the site and, with the engineer in their midst, they set about arranging the last heavy-lift of the gates which would signify the end of construction. By midday the car was loaded and we returned to the camp with a feeling of excitement that the job was finished. What would happen next? There was still a big question mark where the future was concerned.

It came as a surprise when I found Alex just arrived at the tent and apparently moving in. Yes! He had known about the storm, hurrying from El Obeid to see what had happened, and he intended to remain for a spell.

There was more pressing information, which stopped me in my tracks. 'You are going home on leave in a month or so; there is a berth for you on a ship sailing from Port Said.'

This came so suddenly I could hardly take it in: home leave at last! Back to Marion, my family and Scotland! I had no sense of joy – the war years, what would these have done? Would people have changed? Perversely it took time, then slowly a feeling of relief and happiness crept in. Home and freedom! It was not that the Sudan and Africa had lost its hold on me, in spite of the Abu Habl: no, it was the problem of breaking the bonds which had kept me so long from those I loved at home. In any case Marion would come back with me when leave was over.

I broke the news to the boys, whose happiness was immediate and spontaneous. They too would have time, at last, to spend with their families.

I remained there with Alex long enough to hand the work over then one evening we made yet another journey to the station, to see off the engineer and his wife. I felt a little sad that after the months of living close and working together we were parting for good. The engineer and I had made a good team, there had been no cross words and we had shared the same urge to see the job through. His wife! I held her hand again: I kissed her cheek, she laughingly flashed her blue eyes at me then they were gone.

My diary runs out at this point. There was now too much on my mind – too much to prepare for. My letters home, which had also been written faithfully day after day, dried up: it was a thrilling thought that, in any case, I could well be home before them, so there was no point in writing.

Alex asked me to do a final trek of the mountains before setting off home on leave. The rains were about to start so a number of tasks needed urgent attention.

The main events of this trek remain clear in the memory.

I spent two days at Rashad emptying my desk and riding the trails around the village. The Rashad Omdah came for afternoon tea and brought with him a present: 'For your wife,' he said. He handed over a carved donkey stick, a present the significance of which I found difficult to grasp. Perhaps it was a response to my afternoon's ride on his white steed.

The village school appeared to be thriving under the care of the new female teacher. She welcomed me to the school, face uncovered and smiling, showing that there had been at least one step forward in the mountains since my arrival. The children sang their song and I said my piece, so here, at least, was continuity!

We trekked southwards through a parched dead landscape where, once again, the whole of nature awaited the coming of rain. I stopped at the *hafirs* to find that most of them still held traces of water but had been taken over by wild animals and cattle for use as water-holes. Looking at the crumbling walls and the slime, it was easy to read failure: what was there left of the high ideal? Soil conservation: had it just been a dream? If only the concept had been fashionable with the Government for longer! If only more funds had been provided! If only the *hafirs* had been maintained and developed. If . . . But the Government had got its pound of flesh in the shape of increased output of grain from land that was, in fact, slowly dying.

Sad? Yes, it was very, very sad!

Some little homes were still standing close to the *hafirs* but the people looked as impoverished as any in the mountains – here was the indictment, the forgotten people, yet it was people such as they who *were* the Sudan.

At Kologi I called on the dancing Sheikh Mahomed, but he was prostrate in bed shivering with malaria and soaked with perspiration. He shook my hand and turned groaning to the wall of his hut. There was no dance that night.

I found the Resettlement Scheme for Returning Soldiers at Talodi in fine heart and looking good. Two soldiers, wounded in the earlier years of the present war but now recovered, had moved in with their families and the village had grown to receive them. Another good report was sent off to Khartoum. Here, at least, there were grounds for optimism. The people at the club gave me my usual welcome, not to mention a teasing that I was soon going to be married.

A meeting with the senior ginnery engineer, Bob Bass by name, had been arranged previously, so I found him already in residence at the rest-house. His role in the mountains was to visit the ginneries before and after the rains, twice in the year, to make sure the native mechanics had the machinery in good order.

In our first evening together for many months, I told him of my swim over the Abu Habl a year before. He was a very stoical and sober person and I was surprised when he roared with laughter, beat his hands on his knees, and almost doubled up. He too had come from the mountains then, and had a good tale about the Abu Habl. The story impressed me because I wrote it down at length afterwards – it went like this:

The Race

Bob Bass was the visiting engineer who kept the ginnery equipment in order. He was a typical loner, devoted to his own company, and when we occasionally met on trek our camp-beds were erected within hailing distance and we exchanged a few informal words of conversation. It is not that we were unfriendly to one another, it was just that we both got so that we did not need company. Bob had been on the job for so many years now that he was a completely self-contained unit provided he had three items with him – his servant, his trek kit and his dictionary.

I have a rock-hard memory of Bob sitting at night in the light of a little lamp being served faithfully by a tall servant while he endlessly read his dictionary. If it is an eccentricity to relax by reading through the pages of a dictionary night after night, Bob was eccentric in the extreme. He was a veteran in years of service, but according to Civil Service status at that time, he occupied a 'junior' post; the juniors being the craftsmen and tradesmen who kept the various services in trim. Whether Bob was frustrated at this state of affairs or whether he stoically carried a great personal secret was difficult to tell, but he was a singularly uncommunicative gentleman as far as events outwith his work were concerned. I had learned somewhere he had been a works mechanic in Bradford in his youth, but to all intents and purposes he had no past and might well have been a white Sudanese. There was something almost frightening about the mechanical rhythms of his life which repeated themselves in exact patterns each day. He would have made a wonderful 9 to 5 bank clerk as he had succeeded in taking all the irregularities out of the trekking life – perhaps that was why he kept everyone at some distance. He was over 50 years old and must have been close to retiring age, although it was impossible to visualise him changing his life pattern merely for retirement.

Bob sat at the table with a pillar-straight back as if moulded into the camp chair and his tough frame showed none of the weakening consequences of tropical illness. A faded moustache protruded from his weathered features, but his eyes, narrowed by the sun, were an intense youthful blue.

It was his custom to trek the mountains at the very end of the dry season, and to escape across the Abu Habl before the arrival of the flood.

Like me, he had not been prepared for the early coming of the rainy season!

With his servant and driver he was approaching the end of his last circuit of the factories before the rains. On the trail north from Talodi to Um Berrembeita he let himself be driven, while he half dozed, quite indifferent to the scene. To him, the Nuba Mountains was merely an endless succession of hot days over familiar routes, which had long since lost their novelty. He had never seen the magical transformation of the rains with the forests in leaf, and the carpets of short-lived flowers – perhaps he would not have recognised the change, as he was no naturalist!

The track led through groves of palms where a group of Nuba waved a friendly salute as he passed. Bob waved back with scrupulous care and enthusiasm. His response to the native people was always more particular than that to his own race. He had a feeling for the people and was touched by their simplicity and their poverty.

In a swirl of dust the box-car entered the compound in front of the brick-built rest-house and soon the well-ordered routine commenced. The driver kindled a fire in the little cookhouse, the servant set up table and chair then unrolled the bedding. Bob stretched himself and walked into the experimental garden to see what fruit was ready for collecting. The products of the various gardens on his route were a perquisite he made full use of. By the time he returned to the house with an armful of fruit, tea was ready and the lamp lit. There, on the table, the dictionary was carefully laid. Bob sat down to commence his first session of reading. After tea, and in strict order, came bath, short walk, dinner and finally a last study of the book before settling down for the night.

In the little world made visible by the lamp Bob sat like a statue, scarcely moving, his eyes fixed on the book, when suddenly he became aware of a new sensation. From the village, just a quarter of a mile away, drums were pounding and excited shouts repeatedly pierced the night air. Some ceremony was taking place which might bear investigation. It was against his habit to leave camp at this time, but he felt impelled towards the noise. The village lay at the opposite side of a deep, dry watercourse. Climbing up to the village he sensed a change in the atmosphere. He was panting and sweating from a wave of humid heat which seemed to engulf him, making him pause for breath. Even as he halted a sudden electric storm sent repeated flashes across the sky. For the first time he realised the possibility that the rains might come early, breaking up the roads, and trapping him in this corner of the mountains.

On the fringe of the village, concealed by some low trees, he stopped to see what was happening in the clearing. A wood fire was burning nearby, a wide circle of natives were swaying their bodies and chanting to the rhythm of drums. With each flash of lightning shouts arose from the crowd, and in the centre a figure darted about frantically, waving its arms wildly as if beckoning for the clouds to fall. To Bob's mind there was something ominous about the whole scene; something alien to him which made him think his presence would be unwelcome.

A rainmaker at work! Often he had heard of this important aspect of witchcraft which regulated much of the life in the mountains. Here in Um Berembeita were a mixture of Moslems and Nuba who often combined the practices of both groups at the appropriate times. The coming of the rains was a time when the gods or the spirits must be motivated to the full, as rain was the source of life to both crops and man. Bob watched for a short time then slipped back to the rest-house, glad that he had not been seen by the excited villagers.

In bed at the usual time, he lay and listened, only too aware of the changes around him. Soft dank winds moved his mosquito net, fanning the sweat beading on his forehead. A first distant clash of thunder was following on the heels of the electric storm which had been sparking over the sky the whole evening.

Through the years he had been caught several times by rainstorms when sleeping in the open, but tonight this did not come into his scheme of things; it was really much too early in the season for rain! He pulled the thin sheet close to his chin as another sharp crackle echoed and re-echoed through the night air. There appeared to be flashes descending from the sky on all sides, and already the dark shapes of the trees were writhing at the onslaught of a sudden wind.

The first wet blobs of rain beat against the net, sending a fine mist over his face. He jumped up as if ejected by a spring, and struggled to gather his bedding before the frail structure was torn away by the storm. A final crash! The rain beat down as he struggled the last few yards to the shelter of the rest-house verandah. The servant arrived those few seconds too late. Together they resurrected the bed. The air was now cold, as Bob lay down in the damp sheets to listen to the storm, and strive for sleep. Then, as if a switch had been pulled, rain and wind ceased. Only the heavy drips of water from the roof remained to punctuate the ever more distant echoes of thunder.

The midnight nightmare of being trapped by the rains now gave Bob real cause for worry. Broken roads and flooded watercourses would put paid to his leave, and it was a long journey to the Abu Habl and the escape beyond to the railway. The new stillness, however, comforted him at last, and he slipped into his usual deep sleep.

There was no further rain in Um Berembeita that night and Bob rose with an easier mind to commence the routine of the day. The cotton ginnery stood a mile away on the far side of the watercourse, and he reckoned that a couple of hours would see him finished and on his way. The driver had the engine ticking over and they set off down the steep slope and across the floor of the watercourse. He noticed with mild interest that a little trickle of water, the first for many months, was flowing across their path. The car splashed easily through, up the other side, and along the clay track to the factory. There were slight corrugations where last night's rainfall had moved some of the clay, but it was only sufficient to cause vibrations in the steering and gave no cause for anxiety. The dust was laid, and this alone made travelling much more pleasant.

The little factory was in excellent shape, the local mechanic being particularly efficient. Bob went through his usual routine of checking and calculating, not that it was particularly necessary on this occasion, but it was his habit. He also knew the importance of showing an active interest to his local staff, and he scarcely took time to notice that once again the weather outside was changing dramatically.

A shroud of stillness cloaked everything, and trees hung motionless and limp in a shimmering heat-haze. Even in the tall factory building Bob finally sensed the change. His bush-shirt was stained with sweat, and mopping his brow he moved to the door to call his driver. His voice sounded hollow in the still air, like speaking in a confined space.

A dark haze had gathered in the western sky and even as he was making hurried farewells to the staff, the fetid smell of wet soil was carried in by a new wind which brought the trees to frantic life. Now everything happened in a breathtaking rush which stunned the mind, and drove Bob and his staff into the safety of the factory. Darkness, almost of night, clamped down and brought an air of unreality. A searing flash, following simultaneously by a violent crash of thunder, heralded rain so violent that in seconds, sheets of water were swilling over the clearing with a mist spray blanketing the whole ground. It was as if a cloud had paused over the factory and was pouring down its entire contents of water. A confusion of repeated flashes and continuous thunder made the walls of the ginnery vibrate, while even above this noise could be heard the howl of the wind. Even within the factory fine waves of rain spray were dampening the machinery. There was a strange, almost sulphurous smell. Bob shivered in the chilled air. There was nothing he could do now but merely watch, wait, and trust that the roads would still be open when the storm was past.

This violence was too strong to last. Slowly the intervals between flashes and the noise of the thunder increased, as the storm moved on. The rain lost some of its violence and then, as only tropical storms can do, it stopped almost in an instant, leaving only the sound of water spewing from gutters. Every hollow was now a pool, every crack a runnel of water, and all this load of water was draining into the mighty Abu Habl. The sun seemed unnaturally hot in this completely saturated air, making the heart pump violently as sweat poured from every pore in the body.

Walking towards the car now, his shoes sunk into the clay of the road, he realised that they could never progress on this surface. There was nothing for it but to wait. He paced about and fretted as, gradually, the surface visibly dried in the hot sun. Fortunately the sky was now clear without any other storm signs.

The fear of being trapped here with the roads broken by floods was more than he could bear – here was something completely out of rhythm, quite out of his expected pattern of things. His mind wrestled with the problems of riding the 100 miles by camel to the railway – no! This could not possibly be, so early in the season – there must be another answer. Throwing reason to the winds, he jumped into the driving seat and revved the car across the compound. The wheels spun and the car slewed from side to side, leaving a deep zig-zag track behind. The driver and some of the ginnery staff put their shoulders to the car and were rewarded by a spray of mud thrown up by the wheels. Slowly they moved forward until the road became more sandy and able to bear the load. Now, bumping over new water cracks, they moved slowly towards the watercourse beside the village. Bob held his breath at the spectacle. A swirling mass of muddy water was tumbling over the bed of the previously empty river.

Before his nerve failed him he quickly drove the car, slithering and slipping, down the bank and into the water, about 18 inches in depth. The car bounded and jolted along for a short distance with water spilling across the floor at his feet, and then the engine shuddered to a stop. Violently he pulled the starter, but without effect. He jumped into the river almost in desperation. The water was getting deeper as all the tributaries poured their contribution into the watercourse.

Fortunately several natives witnessed his predicament and without hesitation they rushed to the scene and laboriously pushed the stranded vehicle to the far bank. This they did with only minutes to spare, because even as they looked behind them, they witnessed a new torrent racing down the course like a small tidal wave. It would surely have washed the car out of sight. Bob knew only too well that this watercourse, big as it was, was only a minor branch of the great Abu Habl. At this very moment hundreds of tributaries were pouring their complements into the main river and a vast torrent of surging water was racing round the mountains to trap him. His way across this awesome barrier was almost 100 miles from here, close to the railway at Rahad. Could he reach this point before the flood? It would be a race — but what of the car?

The driver was struggling to get some life into the engine but with no success. The servant had already loaded the kit and was perched on top, equally anxious to get away from this place before it was too late. Almost dancing in his anxiety to be gone, Bob watched helplessly as the normally capable driver carefully dried points and went through his entire repertoire. He was rewarded at last. Blue smoke clouds exploded from the exhaust for a few moments, then the engine settled to a steady rhythm. In a few seconds they were away, leaving the villagers and the ginnery staff to their own problems. There was only one thought now — to race the flood to the railway at Rahad.

The track from Um Berembeita was stony and reasonably firm. At two places in the first few miles Bob had to level out the surface where little channels of water had gashed the road. One wide stretch of clay was rutted deeply by the wildly spinning wheels, but the driver was able to keep the car in motion at little more than walking speed. Bob suddenly sensed the pain of fingernails digging hard into the palms of his hands with the build-up of tension at this slow progress.

On firmer ground once more; several miles at a good speed, then another watercourse about six feet wide barred the road. There were a few ramshackle village huts here whose occupants crowded out to inspect the new arrivals. The driver, shoes and all, waded knee-deep into the middle of the stream to test its depth. The help of the villagers was recruited and as the car was slowly driven into the fast waters a dozen willing shoulders heaved until they reached the other bank none the worse.

With each passing mile the ground was becoming firmer. The storm had scarcely reached this part of the country. Bob urged the driver to greater speed and relaxed a little for the first time. No river could flow at this speed. He smiled to himself when he thought of his recent predicament – this country! It had not got the better of him yet! They were by now crossing a wide plain, parallel to the twisting course of the Abu Habl some 20 miles further north. Bob noticed a thin sheen of green in some of the hollows indicating that a shower of rain had germinated pockets of grass. Two gazelles leaped off at great speed as the car raced by. A variety of wild animals would soon graze over this area as the new season's grass became established.

With half of the journey behind them the hollow of a little watercourse showed ahead, an innocent-looking depression partly concealed from the driver. He remembered this hollow from previous journeys and he knew that it was quite safe to take it at fair speed. Too late – flowing water had cut the surface at its base. He jammed on brakes; the car lurched violently down, ejecting both Bob and the servant to the ground. The driver's head crashed against the cab roof, stunning him. A cloud of dust settled on the group as Bob sat up in a daze, scarcely able to comprehend this change in their situation. It took him some seconds to appreciate that the unexpected had taken command, and, after all, he was by no means master of the situation.

The others were stirring and, marvellously, no bones were broken – even the windscreen was intact. They examined the car, rubbing their bruised limbs, but found no cause for joy. The bonnet was dug into the bank of the watercourse, one tyre flat, and it seemed as if a spring was broken as a wheel was bent over at an awkward angle. A distant rainstorm had sent a stream of water through this wilderness, sufficient to make a deep gash where the smoothed-out road surface should have been. The watercourse was dry again but another flood could come at any time.

Bob grabbed the spade in panic, attacking the earth in front of the car. Hard dry clay can have a physical consistency of concrete. In a few minutes he stood back, panting, realising that another way must be found. This might have been the centre of an oven. On all sides shimmering mirage lakes reflected, like great mirrors lying on the ground. He sat down, his shirt black with sweat and dust.

Looking around him he could see scarcely a shrub to break the flatness of this arid plain. Some of last season's dead grass stood in desolate broken tufts, and on the horizon to the south there appeared the low line of a hill – or was it another mirage? The prospect of the rushing waters of the Abu Habl was serious, but this present predicament was trouble enough. There would be no traffic on this road until after the rains; there was no village for at least 25 miles. The driver suggested jacking the car up in stages – there were no stones, no wood to make a lever. This heavy box-car with its steel-plate sides would take some lifting. They started again with the spade, taking it in turns.

It was already evening when the exhausted travellers sat down to consider the small inroads on the bank. At this rate it would take many hours of labour, and even then, what of the damaged car in this awkward tilted situation? Bob studied his blistered palms – perhaps the best thing to do would be to start walking. They just could not wait on here indefinitely. Never before had he been in such a spot. The servant produced some food from the trek-box and disconsolately they sat in silence watching the sun dropping lower in the sky.

The driver jumped up in great excitement pointing to the east. A short string of camels could be seen moving single file into the gathering gloom. All three shouted at once but in this great arena their voices were puny. The camels paced slowly on, the drivers apparently sound asleep — motionless in the saddles. Bob pounded the car horn and then in final despair, forgetting his years, set off at a trot towards the little caravan.

Fortunately by now it was cooler, but soon he was gasping for breath, his legs moving as if outwith his control. Somehow he kept going and what seemed an immense distance gradually narrowed. He would never have survived half the distance, especially as the camels were moving in the same direction, but by good fortune, one driver turned to look at the last rim of the setting sun and saw his stumbling form. The line of camels halted at the same moment as Bob, run to a complete standstill, now stood with his arms dangling by his side, unable to move. The Arabs studied the stationary body with suspicion – he was still a mile away and his form was melting into the shadows of the night. This spectral figure might be a jinn – why did it only stand there? Bob lifted his arm to beckon and the most courageous Arab swung his camel in the direction of the travellers. Muttering, the others followed and eventually they looked down from their high mounts on this white man – not quite certain yet whether he was shadow or substance.

He had recovered his breath a little by now and the situation was quickly explained to them. They were rather reluctant to retrace their steps further – no doubt they too had the Abu Habl in mind and were keen to get over in time. Bob might have promised them half his wealth at this moment. He suggested instead that if they helped him he would reward them with a payment of one pound. To his joy they immediately agreed and now, more slowly, he walked beside the camels back to the car.

They soon reached the scene of the accident where by dint of considerable ingenuity, and pulling by the camels roped to the rear bumper, the vehicle was slowly dragged back on to level ground. The camel men, duly rewarded, now left the scene. Bob and the driver dismantled the broken spring shackles in the poor light of a paraffin lamp. In the Sudan, trek cars carry spare springs as well as spare tyres so that the damage was eventually repaired.

The early light of dawn was showing in the east as the last nut was tightened and they were ready to move again. The road being by now levelled out at the watercourse, they moved slowly across and set off at speed towards the Abu Habl. It was impossible to judge whether the water would have travelled this distance since the storm, almost a full day before. The main watercourse attracted water from such a vast area of country that a storm in any one district could be sufficient to generate a flood down beyond Rahad.

The sun had risen when at last the nature of the countryside changed. Thick groves of thorn trees in the distance showed that they were approaching the Abu Habl at last. The car slowly climbed a crest and Bob held his breath as the deep bed of the watercourse came to view. The road across was dry, but even as they paused to look they caught the glimpse of water a mere hundred yards from the crossing point. The driver drove furiously to the other side, bumping up the north bank and into safety at last. Bob was overjoyed at their victory, and he returned to the bank to enjoy the spectacle of the flood roaring past.

Fascinated, they watched and awaited the approach of the water which, unexpectedly, was crawling along foot by foot. Finally the flow ceased, only a few steps from the roadway, leaving only a tide-mark of froth to show the limit of the flood. The force had been dissipated by the cracked dry soil. The rush of water from the mountains had travelled all this distance to stop just at the crossing place to the railway.

The travellers looked ruefully at one another. Bob felt the blisters on his hands, the ache in his back. He sat back and smiled – the Sudan had not beaten him yet!

I left Talodi to trek north in the direction of home. In spite of its hard reputation and not so distant strife, Talodi had turned out to be a good place after all, with its mixture of races and traditions always giving some air of excitement. I left the rest-house questioning in my mind whether I would ever return again. Never could I have guessed that a time would come when I would feel sorry to leave this bare stone house with its associations of pain and hardship – the white gravestones in the garden – British soldiers long forgotten; that 'corner of a foreign field'.

Why was I ever there; or rather, why were we ever there? in the mountains? in the Sudan? It is all too easy to raise questions like this years after the event, but for me, well – it was a place to work or, to be more specific, it was a place to work towards an ideal. To pursue the question further, what was that ideal? This is more difficult to answer! One might as well ask why did David Livingstone the missionary and General Gordon of Khartoum go to Africa – to convert, to stop slave traffic, to show compassion, to meet a challenge — motives are usually complex, but my ideal, though in a lesser scale, was possibly a mixture of some of these, and more. Many people in the Anglo-Egyptian Sudan had similar ideals which may no longer be fashionable in modern times yet, in their day, they represented the highest attainable goals in life.

Later that day I stopped at a rest-house in a Nuba village, name long forgotten; there was an unusual stir of excitement with people running towards a central hut. A man, apparently the mek, was loudly banging a large gong and shouting to his naked audience. I hurried over to find the cause of the stir and it was there in the heart of the Nuba Mountains I learned the war with Germany was won and Hitler was dead.

We made one last camp in the open beside a typical rock outcrop before returning to Rashad. It was a warm night, but to celebrate victory the boys built a great celebration bonfire. We had it all to ourselves as the site was far from any village. We sat around reminiscing over past events and making plans for the future. As the evening wore on I climbed to the top of the little hill to look down on our camp illuminated by the firelight. The air was redolent with the perfume of burning wood, and fairy sparks lifted past me into the air. Below, I could see Ibrahim clearing the table and Mahomed sitting occupied with his pots. Here was the picture I would carry in my memory for the rest of my life.

Celebrating victory over Hitler at Heiban.
Front row, left to right: Self, two missionaries, Mrs Mills (the missionary of the story), Neill DC, missionary, the Mamur.

The ship arrived one week late at Port Said because of the difficulties placed on shipping by armies returning from the war. My bunk was one among hundreds in a crowded hold in the ship. There were thousands of soldiers cramming every part of it.

In the middle of the Mediterranean, a voice called us to attention:

'An atomic bomb has been dropped on Japan.'

Dead silence followed. What was this; what did it signify?

Approaching England I joined an excited crowd to see a welcoming light flashing from the Needles, and in the following morning the ship berthed at Southampton. It took many hours to empty the ship and I was waiting my turn to go ashore when a great cheer tore the air:

'The war is over, Japan has surrendered!'

I stood in a long queue for a telephone to phone Marion who was stationed near London. Her voice was soft, I knew that she also was apprehensive; we were too nervous to say anything meaningful to each other, but arranged to meet the following morning near her place of work.

From a railway carriage window, the English countryside looked impossibly green. Trees stood bold against the sky, fields sagged beneath their weight of crops. I arrived at the appointed place an hour late, due to a confusion over the bus route.

So anxious now, I looked from the bus window – would she be waiting for me? A small, solitary figure in uniform stood at the corner of a road – the gap of the years had closed and we were together.

Yes, she was beautiful, just as I remembered. Her faded photographs were still in my pocket: they were a complete understatement! Hand in hand we walked for a time just anywhere. But this was also a special day throughout the length of the country – VJ day. The war was over and everyone was celebrating. Every eye smiled; it was as if the entire population of London celebrated our reunion.

We travelled by subway to the heart of the city to join in the celebration. One 'parcel' of memory lives on, a memory as near to ecstasy as I can ever imagine for myself – in the train I could not take my eyes from Marion's face. I pressed her hand until it hurt and swallowed tears. This was happiness complete!

In Trafalgar Square we were arm in arm with the dancing crowds. That entire day we did nothing but dance, sing and laugh.

One week later, in a little Scottish country church, we were married. Ahead of us were weeks, months and years together, there was Africa and all that was to lie beyond.

Finale

The account of *Trek Into Nuba* actually happened – I know, because the old records and memory verify, for me at least, that each successive event did take place. Yet now, after the passage of years, it reads like a dream.

Were they futile misspent years? A mere chimera, yielding nothing? No, for me it was an epic time, making the remaining years lesser, when compared with them. The Nuba experiences greatly moulded my view of life; not because of achieving the childhood ambition of trek, or even because of testing the limits of youthful adventure: no, there is much more to it than that.

What lingers and even torments is the memory of challenge unfulfilled – such an impossibly large challenge – namely to stay the spread of erosion and to improve the life of the Nuba people. Part of the torment is the view that the challenge can be met and that there are solutions. *Trek Into Nuba* does toss around some of the potential answers.

Today – now so very late, the principles of soil conservation are well understood; the great African drought has focused minds on this subject. The drought of Ethiopia, Sudan and elsewhere can be partly attributed to cyclical climatic change, but man, particularly in semi-arid North Africa, is the primary culprit.

Man, Erosion and Drought are close partners. But – the answers? Are there any answers? I can only think there are. For example – read the report on Dam Gamad Village Project for Returning Soldiers (following). Establish new communities on good land (the Nuba Mountains has an abundance) then further the important work of conserving water stocks – combine all this with good husbandry practice and a real effort at community education. There are answers here for many of the people of Kordofan!

The critic could well say 'this is obvious! – simplistic!' That is true, but it is a remarkable fact that many intractable human problems have simple solutions: it is the devious mind of man that makes them apparently insoluble.

It took me years of hard trek even to begin to understand! Yes, political will, the provision of resources and a groundswell of concern from the affluent west are all needed. The Sudan Government today, despite its difficulties, must have at heart the welfare of its people: perhaps the work

*Omer M. Shurkian, a Nuba exile from the Western Mountains. He is a B.Sc.
(Hons) in Textile Technology, 1988: was a member of the University of Gezira
teaching staff. he got a British Council scholarship to pursue further studies in
Britain, 1989, studied in the Scottish College of Textiles, and was awarded M.Phil.
in Textile Technology, 1992. Unable, because of the persecution, to return to the
Sudan, he is currently (1994) pursuing a Ph.D. degree at UMIST. Like many
other Sudanese exiles, it is a struggle for him to find resources to continue his stay in
Britain. He has written a comprehensive book on his country,* The Sudan: The
Way Through the Tragedies, *and is seeking a publisher. Omer Shurkian is a
typical example of those Sudanese who, when the present oppressive regime passes
away, will be poised to lead his country into a new era. He is an example to all of
how, when given the chance, and whatever the ethnic origins, a person can attain the
highest honours.*

started in 1942 is being furthered today, but it seems more likely that I have to accept that the 'torment' will remain.

Today (in the year 1994) the Sudan is torn apart by war. As in all wars no one party has the monopoly of right or of wrong. At first glance it appears to be a war between north and south: between Arabs in the north and the Christian/animist blacks in the south, but it is much more complex than that.

In the Arabic-speaking north, large sections of the population are opposed to the 'fundamentalist' government party and its military rule. In the south, effective opposition to government forces is minimised because of warfare between the tribal groupings there. Such divisions have permitted the government to continue its cruel oppression of people such as the Nuba.

In the present circumstances, a clear-cut, just solution to the people's agonies seems impossibly out of reach. At the root of the tragedy is the government's imposition of Sharia Law (a code of law demanding acceptance of fundamental Moslem principles which, in effect, debars or at least reduces the standing of the large non-Moslem population). It is a rule of law which makes co-operation by the black people with the government a virtual impossibility, implying as it does their acceptance of the Moslem faith.

Of all the black races in the Sudan, the Nuba suffer most, because the mountains are nearer to the centre of government and they are virtually surrounded by Arab tribes. The southern races have at least got the barriers arising from the Sudd and distance to protect them partially.

One possible long-term solution will be to separate north from south, allowing the southern peoples to form unions with countries surrounding, where there are tribal associations. But this will not ease the lot of the Nuba.

There is, of course, one real hope for the future, namely that the British Government, together with the world community, will waken to the human rights position in the Sudan and the fact that death and suffering in that country are on a scale greater than the combined disasters of Bosnia and Somalia. The vast scale and the remoteness of the Sudan tragedy is such that politicians hesitate to face up to it, but if countries become alert to the situation, perhaps appropriate pressure can be put on the Sudan Government to change its behaviour – so that people such as the Nuba may be saved from the 'ethnic cleansing' to which they are currently subjected.

It is the earnest desire of the author of *Trek Into Nuba* that each and every reader will share his concern for the current state of the lovely Nuba people.

Footnote

On December 13th 1942 a Soil Conservation Committee was set up in the Sudan to report on the situation with regard to soil erosion, desiccation, and water supplies, and to make recommendations and draw up a programme of work. The Committee submitted its report in April 1944, which proposed a number of projects for each province in the country. As a result, a Rural Water Supplies and Soil Conservation Board was formed in October 1944.

A Specialist Soil Conservation Officer was appointed in January 1945 and a series of projects was launched. These included:

i.   A large forest reservation programme (with an initial target of 3762 square miles area)

   (a) part of this area was for the purpose of protecting water catchment areas

   (b) part was to provide timber and firewood in a controlled, self-regulating way.

ii. A programme to improve water supplies was inaugurated. This consisted of sinking deep bores, building storage tanks and excavating reservoirs (*hafirs*).

iii. Work was begun on perimeter protection round towns and villages by means of controlled grazing, planting of tree belts – using the following species – neem, eucalyptus and mesquite.

iv. Forest plots for building poles to be established close to centres of population.

By the end of 1956, fourteen reservoirs and tanks, 38 deep bores and wells were completed as part of the programme.

By the year 1947 a first forest reservation of 200 square miles area had been established.

The work of SOIL CONSERVATION in the Sudan progressed until the British left, and the Sudan became independent.

Appendices

A Report on the first SOIL CONSERVATION meeting ever held with the Sudanese people, and showing an awareness of the erosion problem as early as 1944. Also, from this event came the first positive steps by the people to work on the erosion problem – and produce results.

B Report on Dam Gamad Resettlement Experiment (for returning soldiers) first year's work.

A study of resettlement needs for displaced people (in this case Nuba). Using such methods, together with supervised husbandry, can provide answers to current 'hunger' problems in many areas of north Africa.

Appendix A

No. NMT/26N3   Talodi, 18th May, 1944.

Senior Inspector Of Agric.,
El -Obeid.

As a consequence of decisions made at Abbassia regarding the establishing of two Agricultural committees for the Tegali area the two first meetings have been held at Kologi and Abbassia respectively, and it is believed that on this foundation some attempts at furthering good agricultural methods may be based. There was a complete interest in such problems as fires, erosion, stock improvement, and although all matters will not result in immediate concrete action, useful discussion resulted in the various representatives taking new ideas to their districts. It was agreed to appoint agricultural sheikhs at various villages with an elected support of good cultivators, and these village units would be responsible for propagating advancement, and supervising measures decided by main committees.

I detail the topics and decisions of the respective committees.

Kologi   Under the leadership of Nazir Abdel Eshiem the following matters were surveyed:

1/ Fire control   This was recognised as the major problem, and the following was decided.

(a)   After each fire there would be an administrative investigation as to cause and perpetrator, and offender, if caught, would be adequately punished. The people would recognise the serious manner in which the matter is being tackled, and fire raising would be deterred.

(b)   Each village would be held responsible for fires occurring in its own area and an attempt at organising fire fighting would be made in each locality. Should any district make no attempt at fire suppression, the local agricultural authority would hold responsibility.

(c)   Each village will undertake the making of fire lines in its own agricultural area starting at the end of October. This work will be supervised by the agricultural sheikh with the necessary advice and help of the agricultural effendis.

(d) Propaganda against fire raising will be forced everywhere.

2/ <u>Afforestation</u> The evils of haphazard tree destruction were understood and means of forest preservation were discussed, as well as means of establishing forests.

(a) Explaining and enforcing of the local Order which states that trees in immediate village proximity must not be removed.

(b) When fresh agricultural holdings are prepared, tree stumps must not be burned, but, after chopping, should be left alive so that when cultivation is over a quick soil protecting cover may grow. This point is very important, as at present many areas are great masses of destroyed tree stumps which had they been left alive, would still have held the soil and have minimised erosion. It was agreed that eventually this unnecessary destruction should become a punishable offence, and the population must be informed when clearing holdings, to burn weeds and scrub apart from the trees.

(c) A small demonstration forest will be started in both Kologi and Abu Gubeiha of say 2 feddans, and in coming years it is hoped all villages will create such a forest.

(d) At present, much cultivation takes place on khor banks so that with recent rains, many khores have changed their courses and destroyed good land. As in the case of roads, it shall be forbidden to cut trees within 20 metres of khor banks.

(e) The cutting and destruction of young immature trees e.g. Doleib and Ardeeb is to be deplored and those who destroy should be warned against it.

(f) Many villages want young trees for planting in gardens and in suks; attempt will be made to provide all these young trees.

(g) General propaganda as to the value of trees will be furthered.

3/ <u>Animal damage</u> A small Zareeba will be made in villages and should animals cause repeated damageto young trees and crops they shall be put in this Zareeba. A small fine of 2 piastres per donkey and 3 piastres per goat was suggested. this being to cause a greater control over animals and minimise the damage they cause.

4/ Ingle hedging will be made available to all who wish it, within the limits of supply – particularly at Abu Gebeiha and Kologi. Its value as permanent hedging is understood.

5/ Cattle improvement   The need for mass stock selection is realised and a policy of castration will be started in January when cattle start coming to the wells. It is agreed that at least 90% of all bulls will be castrated; a committee for this work will be formed of Agricultural Sheikh, Veterinary Assistant and any one cultivator, and castration will be according to their judgement. The administration will undertake to attend to the assembling of the bulls, and all bulls left entire will be branded and will be available for servicing all village cattle.

A start will now be made in explaining this to cultivators so that when the work is to be started, the object will be understood by all. Meanwhile the assistance and advice of the Veterinary Department will be asked.

6/ Every attempt to further vegetable growing will be made. The following possible garden areas were listed and attempts will be made to visit them, that their possibilities may be examined.

El Shug, Miheila, Dub Dob; also of course, Abu Gebeiha and Abu Tuleih and villages in El Liri area.

There was a strong demand for metal sagias[1] for developing these districts and it is hoped that such can eventually be made available.

7/ Rotations

(a)   The advantages and need for rotational agriculture were emphasised and propaganda to the effect that land should not be continuously cropped more than a period of 4 years would be started.

(b)   The quick establishment of good harig by means of grass sowing at the beginning of kharif of first resting season, is recognised as being a very sound idea, and attempts will be made to establish this new method.

8/ Communal farming   The following villages undertake the starting of communal plots not merely to provide seed, but to establish methods of co-operation.

Abu Gebeiha; El Sahl; Gadied; Abu Nuware; Kologi; Gedir; Gereda; El Lokha; Moring; El Diri.

---

1 Sagia – for raising subterranean water

The Agricultural Sheikh and committee will organise this, and the plot will be run as an agricultural club, in which the work and products will be shared between all members. To establish this spirit of co-operation and understanding by means of an agricultural club will be of great value and deserves particular consideration.

9/ Rotational grazing   Means of grass conservation for animal feed were discussed particularly in relation to ingle hedging, and outside Zareebas, and, although the ideals were appreciated it was agreed to postpone attempts till a later date.

Meanwhile it is intended that an experiment in hay-making will take place in various areas, the object being to provide good grass for milk production.

10/ Wells and Hafirs   Various areas where development or improvement of water supplies might be advantageous were suggested, and it is thought these might be inspected with this aim in view – Moring, Koro, Um Dowal Sinaf, Kaw Nayaro, Um El Sheikh, Rusersa.

11/ The general question of soil preservation will be given full consideration, and Tayeb Eff. Gazouli who will attend and co-ordinate all meetings will explain and further attempts at conservation.

The meeting of the main committee at Abbassia under Mek Adam Geili took place later and decisions were as for the earlier meeting with the following exceptions.

1/ As above.

(2)   An experiment in permanent fire lines using Ingle will be made at Um Berembeita.

2/ Demonstration forests will be started in Em Berembeita and Abbassiya.

(4) As for other meeting
(5) As for other meeting
(6) As for other meeting
(7) As for other meeting

3 and 8   It was agreed to wait a period before tackling these questions; the experience gained in other half of the district could be used for the good when a start is made.

9/ Members of the committee undertook to experiment in grass conservation – both hay and silage, and work according to instruction to be supplied later. The fodder conserved would be used in production of milk.

Appendix B

A First Annual Report on
Dam Gamad Settlement Experiment

A first year's working of the Dam Gamad Settlement Experiment has now been satisfactorily completed and much information of value for large-scale settlement has been obtained. The object of the experiment is to find the agricultural requirements of the Nuba and to learn how best this knowledge can be applied to larger agricultural settlements. Further information can be obtained regarding the degree of co-opera-tion and initiative the Nuba is capable of evidencing in an organised community. Naturally, to get complete statistical proof of the above points, many years would be required, but this season's work shows definite trends on which fairly sound opinions can be based. The land chosen for this scheme was originally the 'Dam Gamad Investigation Area' where experiments, particularly in Harig grasses, had gone on for a number of years, so land was already cleared, and there remained only the division of this land and construction of village, to complete the site of settlement.

The area was split into 9 holdings of various sizes and Nuba ex-sol-diers were appointed to these holdings. At least 2 of these cultivators were old men whose soldiering days were long forgotten, but the nine of them made a typical little Nuba community whose efforts might be considered almost typical of the Nuba as a whole. In the first year's working of such a new system difficulties were naturally expected, but the only real difficulty that arose was, that during the rains, in spite of what they had been told to the contrary, the cultivators concluded the government must have part right to the crops, and effort consequently slackened. Towards the end of the rains when this fear was quietened, and they fully appreciated that what they grew was their own, they got down to it with renewed energy and a very fine spirit has prevailed ever since. Of the original nine cultivators, six of them completed the year and the other three did not last because of absenteeism, old age and mental imbalance respectively; two of these would almost certainly have remained but for the above-mentioned imagined snag. Now that the principle is fully understood there should be no shortage of volunteers for holdings in coming years.

At no time were the cultivators driven to a job, but they were left to manage their holdings as best they thought fit. The official present kept daily records of all that was going on, and at period meetings held in the village under the leadership of the agricultural sheikh, any advice required was given, and any defaulting and laziness was discussed. The six remaining cultivators with their families make a very contented community and their cultivations have generally been good; the not so good areas were generally due to the excessive areas dictated by the experiment. They all take a pride in the fine little village and they have cared well for all stock in their charge.

2. Outline of the Experiment

As the cultivators came without any source of income, and there was naturally a period of several months before crops matured, they were given a monthly subsidy of £1. While in recept of this subsidy they worked in the preparation of their land and building of their houses, and some little skilled help in house building was given by the government. The village completed, the cultivators elected a sheikh and cultivation proceeded according to a plan and rotation worked out in advance. First year's seed was supplied by the government, then the cultivator worked as he pleased, used his family or employed labour as he thought fit, and the ultimate crops were all his own property. The only marketing condition is that cotton must be brought into ginnery, in order to minimise any pest damage. Implements and bulls were loaned to the cultivators and these may be bought by them in instalments through a period of years. A canteen and a communal holding were incorporated, and care and development of the village was left to the cultivators.

3. Details of the holdings:

	Cotton	Dura	Sim Sim	Earth Nut	Resting under grass
3 holdings of 17 feddans	4	3	1	½	8½
3 holdings of 21 feddans	5	4	1	½	10½
3 holdings of 25 feddans	6	5	1	½	12½

4. Notes on Season's Working:

As may be expected, the cultivators did not strain themselves with overwork nor was their effort at any time exceptional, yet the little organisation and slight supervision provided has resulted in production of quite good crops of much bigger acreage than is ever normally grown by single natives. The crops naturally varied with the individual effort of the cultivator and of the six completed holdings, at least 3 were very good while one of them was an outstandingly fine piece of cultivation.

The bulk of work was done by cultivator and his family but at rush periods, as between heavy rainfalls, when weed growth was high, labour was occasionally employed at his own expense. Very often the 'Naffir' system was used whereby a group of the cultivators worked on any one holding and the owner of that holding provided free 'Marisa' and a goat to celebrate. This is proof also of the good spirit which prevailed.

5. Cultivation:

The rain started late but came heavily so that a minimum of resowing was required and well-spaced rainfall assured a firm establishment. It was necessary only to resow the cotton in part once.

The harig grass was burned when young grass was already well germinated, and sowing, with the aid of a plough, quickly followed; this simple process consists of drawing shallow lines at a spacing of 1 metre and sowing the seed in the hollow produced.

Hoeing presented much more difficulty as, on several holdings, there was standing water for a considerable period due to the excessive flooding of the neighbouring khor. Holdings thus affected were the larger ones of 25 and 21 feddans, and these remained more backward for the rest of the season.

Inter-row cultivation was done with the aid of a simple horse-hoe implement which saved much hand cultivation. Some cultivators did not adequately resow their grain and the crop suffered as a result, but generally the dura is good.

Harvesting was leisurely done by cultivator and his family; sim sim was quickly cut then stacked tidily near the village before threshing. Cotton was picked and brought into Talodi ginnery with the aid of a bull cart. Grain was cut and stacked most neatly outside the village where, indeed, at moment of writing some still remains to be threshed. This neat stacking was one of the features of the village and the three grains – White McCoy; Red Kideika, and yellow Kurgi – were stacked on platforms according to the method applied by the different communities from which the cultivators came. The Earth Nuts were not efficiently harvested as the heavy clay was allowed to become too dry before being tackled and some of the crop is still in the soil.

The cultivation on the 17 feddans holdings was best in all cases while one of these holdings was a model piece of cultivation. From this year's working it would seem that the 25 feddans holdings were too big and several operations were left uncompleted. The 21 feddan holdings were worked quite well and it seems that the ideal is somewhere between 17–21 feddans. If the opinion of cultivators can be taken as a criterion, the 21 feddans area is most suitable as there is a demand among them for holdings of this size next season.

6. Implements:

The following implements were loaned to the cultivators:

1 iron-wheeled single-bull cart
1 single raw horse-hoe
1 plough
1 hoe per cultivator
1 axe per cultivator

The horse-hoe and plough along with the services of a skilled ploughman were put at their convenience from the start; the machines, which caused a great saving in labour, may be bought by them in instalments over a period of years. Several of the cultivators took an active interest in the ploughing and, it is hoped, will operate the machine in coming years. The bull cart was put at their disposal after the rains and has been invaluable in bringing crops to market; one such cart would suffice for twenty cultivators. The plough and horse-hoe unit is sufficient probably only for three or four cultivators because of the sudden and extreme pressure which comes at the first rains. These implements for such work can cover 2½ feddans, working from 6 a.m. to 11 a.m., a period sufficient to tire the bulls. The hoes and axes were taken from cultivators at the end of the year's cultivation, as they were prepared to buy their own light implements.

Bulls were also put at the disposal of the cultivators. It is not yet clear how many holdings one pair of bulls can efficiently cope with – possibly from 3 to 5 – and it is hoped that this coming season will give more evidence on this point. Bulls could also become the property of the cultivators by gradual payment over a period of years.

7. Communal Holding:

The communal holding throughout the whole season has been fairly well tended and cultivators have worked well together; the cotton was flooded at one stage and because of heavy rains and pressure of work on the holdings it suffered from the start. The other crops were quite good.

This holding was worked mainly on Friday holidays and in the afternoon, and commonly the cultivators went in groups under the direction of the agricultural sheikh. The products of this holding were harvested and are being disposed of in a way decided upon by all. In addition, the grain and sim sim of two of the departed cultivators was also worked communally and profits from these will also go to their welfare fund. One ideal of this holding is to build up a useful village reserve which will ultimately benefit the community. The returns for this first year were not exceptional, but now the idea is appreciated and they realise that 'even this' is their very own, good results should follow.

8. Canteen:

The canteen was started with the payment by each cultivator of a 30 PT share, and with this initial capital of £2.700 produce was bought. One cultivator has had responsibility for the canteen, which has had its ups and downs and is keeping a proper cash book. Two of the cultivators who did not finish the season removed their shares on departure so that capital was somewhat reduced; by the end of the year, however, the realisable capital was £3.100. At one stage 500 m.m. was stolen from the canteen by a 'visitor', and for a period the activity of the canteen was rather reduced as produce was loaned to cultivators and there was considerable delay in repaying these loans. This matter is now under control and the canteen is now quite an institution in the community. When the number of cultivators and capital increase, the function and effectiveness of the canteen will similarly grow.

Some very good cross Rhode Island poultry are communally owned and are breeding prolifically; any excess stock will later be sold to augment the canteen funds. Pigeons, which in their little loft adorn the 'village square', are also breeding profusely.

9. Village:

The construction of the village was late in starting and was thus prejudiced because of cultivation going on at the same time. The cultivators all did their share in the building and one of them proved to be an expert at the job. This sudden rush, however, was not an encouraging start for the new cultivators although, soon after the rains came, all houses were complete. A cow shed which was in existence before the settlement started was incorporated in the village, and a fine henhouse was built.

The village has been well cared for and is always clean and everyone does his bit to this end. They divide the duties with bulls and poultry so that each one has his day on duty and looks after the stock.

The amenities of the village are at present being increased at their own wish and by their own effort. They have cut and sunk a suitable piece of wood for an oil press, and are employing a man to shape it, and it is expected this will be in operation soon. Also they are about to build a grain store in the centre of the village and to this end they are collecting wood and grass, and shall soon start on the mud walls. This particular development is most satisfying. Some goats and sheep have been bought by individuals, and the agricultural sheikh has bought a donkey.

10. Social Activities

Each month a cultivation meeting presided over by the sheikh and attended by the cultivators, the agricultural effendi, and a crowd of onlookers, is held. During the rains when anything of particular note happened, an extra meeting took place. At these meetings all social and agricultural matters, as well as policy regarding canteen, animal management and communal plot, were discussed. Any arguments were settled in good atmosphere. A considerable number of friends and relations visited the community, particularly during the rains.

Many parties of visitors – soldiers, administration and other notable people – have been shown round the settlement.

As much as possible the cultivators have been left to themselves with a minimum of interference, and the life of the village has been that of a Nuba community, only set round a new environment.

11. Subsidies and Individual Finances up to the period of Crop Maturity:

(a) Each cultivator received a monthly subsidy of £1 for the six-month period May–October, i.e. from the settlement of scheme before rains to the month the first crops matured. Thus expenditure was £6 per head.

(b) To find the suitability of this subsidy, note was kept by the agricultural effendi of the domestic finances of each cultivator, from May to October.

Holding	Clothes	Grain	Luxuries	Labour	Animals	Total
1 of 17 fedds.	750	1.500	230	885	1.070	4.435
2 –do–	270	1.800	1 640	375	220	4.305
3 –do–	770	1.800	840	415	400	4.225
5 of 25 fedds.	1.240	1.800	900	2.250	250	6.440
8 of 21 fedds.	1.215	1.800	440	1.310	1.500	6.265
9 –do–	230	1.200	640	965	1.620	4.655

Some minor transactions took place, e.g. buying then selling of animals. This has been taken into account in the above list. It would seem the subsidy has adequately met all requirements. In an earlier Interim Report the totals given as expenditure for clothes and grain were for the period May to December, for comparison with actual subsidy the above figures are only for period subsidy was given.

More money unaccountably went for such luxuries as 'Marisa', while divorces and pensions boosted the revenue of at least two others.

It will be observed that the bigger cultivators found it necessary to employ more labour and indeed, a large part of their subsidy was so expended. Further, one of the 21 feddan cultivators is unmarried and that explains his low domestic expenses. The other cultivator of 21 feddans has a large family and it will be noted his expenses are considerably higher.

The families are as follows:

	Elders	Male Children	Female Children
Holding 1 –	2	1	1
2 –	2	1	3
3 –	2	–	–
5 –	2	1	1
8 –	2	1	2
9 –	1	–	–

The average grain consumption of a Nuba family was found to be ½ ardeb per month, but they are capable of consuming very much more; thus, from the subsidy an average of 300 per month went on grain alone. The cultivator of No. 2 holding who spent a large sum on 'other foods' (tea, sugar, etc.) has a pension.

12. Yields and Marketing of Crops:

Grain:

Holding number		Total		Yields per Feddan	
		Ardebs	*Keila*	*Ardebs*	*Keila*
Holding 1	3 fedds.	4	2	1	4½
2	3 –do–	10	–	3	4
3	3 –do–	11	3	3	9
5	5 –do–	13	–	2	7
6	5 –do–	10	–	2	0
8	4 –do–	10	6	2	8
9	4 –do–	9	–	2	3
Communal Cultivation		7	8	2	7

The grain of holding No. 6 was still worked by the 'mentally unbalanced' cultivator who was permitted to remove his crop. As much of the grain still remains to be threshed and some is being consumed immediately after threshing some of the above figures are only close estimates.

Cultivator of holding No. 1 was much absent at the beginning of season when his son was ill in hospital and that probably accounts for his bad grain. Otherwise it is interesting to note that the other 17 feddan holdings yielded as much as most of the other bigger holdings and certainly gave much higher average yields. The trend can be seen that the greater the area worked the lower the yield of grain, and the optimum with this cropping seems to be either 3 or 4 feddans. Taking the average grain consumption as ½ ardeb a month, this average production of 10 ardebs and extra per holding would suffice to meet requirements, e.g. 6 ardebs for food: seed: and a reasonable surplus at his disposal.

The three varieties of grain used – Kideika, McCoy and Kurgi – are all high yielders and most suited to the conditions existing here. The cultivators are still debating what to do with their surplus grain but it is thought they may bring it in to market.

Sim Sim:

	Total yield		
	Ardeb	Keila	Roba
Holding 1 of 17 feddans	1	1	1
2 –do– 17 –do–	1	6	–
3 –do– 17 –do–	1	–	–
5 –do– 25 –do–	1	2	1
8 –do– 21 –do–	1	1	1
9 –do– 21 –do–	1	2	1
Communal Cultivations	1	9	–

All holdings had only 1 feddan of sim sim. A good average yield for Talodi district is 1 ardeb so that results here are particularly good. The communally owned sim sim includes some which came from one of the empty holdings. Some of this sim sim has already been sold by them, but they are reserving a quantity for when their press is ready.

Cotton:

		Total Yield		Average per feddan		Total Returns
		Kantars	Rotts	Kantars	Rotts	
Holding 1: 4 fedds.	Cotton	5	60	1	40	£2.350
2: 4 –do–	–do–	6	90	1	73	£2.906
3: 4 –do–	–do–	21	30	5	33	£8.945
5: 6 –do–	–do–	11	85	1	98	£4.975
8: 5 –do–	–do–	15	8	3	2	£6.335
9: 5 –do–	–do–	10	13	2	3	£4.340
Communal Plot		6	71	2	27	£2.820

Kantars of 100 Rotts

Earth Nuts:

It was impossible to estimate the returns from the ½ feddan area of earth nuts as this crop was only partly harvested and was consumed at any odd moment. It is safe to say this area of crop met all the needs of the community.

Disposal of Communal Plot Crops:

The cultivators have already sold all their cotton and after discussion they decided to convert the grain and sim sim into money all of which is being kept for future use. Only sufficient seed was stored for next year's sowing. From this fund they bought 10 petrol tins, as much water has to be carried for the building of a new store house.

13. Resting Area:

The area sown under grass has established a very good harig in one year. To further understanding of harig grasses, the opportunity was taken to sow grasses in a simple strip experiment – one strip was left to natural regeneration, one was sown a grass seed mixture, and individual grass varieties were sown on the other strips. What is outstanding and obvious in this experiment is the tremendous advantage of sowing grass compared to natural regeneration. Whereas the former now provides an almost satisfactory harig, the latter is still naked soil apart from a sparse covering of tufted grasses and undesirable weeds.

14. Notes on Coming Cultivation Year:

The original 9 holdings will this year be increased to 12 as an area of cleared land is being incorporated into the settlement. Some of the cultivators express desire for a different area of cropping, as, for example, the cultivator who has made such good work on his 17 feddan holding; also they have offered suggestions for altering slightly the present plan of cropping. This will be taken into account and considered in the coming season's plan.

There now exists a demand for holdings, and what is more pleasing, younger ex-soldiers are keen, so that this also predicts better results for the coming year. All people who have visited Dam Gamad have expressed satisfaction of the experiment, and further state that such schemes would be of considerable value throughout their various districts.

15. Conclusions:

I. It seems that 17–21 feddans including half resting is a suitable holding area range. If cultivation were done from good harig land it is considered that 21 feddans could be easily managed. The cultivators present have been asked what area they themselves think they are capable of working and almost all of them wish for 21 feddans. The exception is an old man who considers he cannot work more than his existing 17 feddans. To judge their capacities this year from actual cultivation is difficult, because the full understanding and spirit of the scheme was not present till late in the season, when doubts that the government had part right to their efforts were removed.

II. It is now taken that average grain consumption of a Nuba family is ½ ardeb per month although they are capable of consuming very much more. 3 or 4 feddans would therefore meet the grain requirements of an average family. The average grain yield for Talodi is just under three ardebs per feddan.

III. Some cultivators wish to grow more cotton for some reason. As cotton requires much more labour than other crops, and from the present season's showing, it is considered better not to increase this crop. This year has proved that a small area well worked can produce much better returns than a big area badly worked. The return of £7.400 obtained by the best cultivator is a considerable sum of money, and in view of his new wealth this cultivator is now exercising considerable influence in the community.

IV. Sim sim proved a very easy crop for them requiring a minimum expenditure of effort; now that their own oil press is under way some of them express desire to increase this crop to 2 feddans.

V. The area of ½ feddan Earth Nut is probably suitable for all requirements.

VI. The canteen is doing quite well, in view of the few cultivators, and it can certainly work well in a village economy.

VII. Communal cultivation produced quite good results for a first season, and, provided they see some benefit accruing from their efforts here, it shall become important and fundamental in the scheme. The choice of cropping was a happy one, which may be slightly increased this coming season with more cultivators.

VIII. Simple bull implements were of great assistance to them, and made it possible to cultivate greater areas of crop. It is probable an improved E.T. Plough could perform the functions of both plough and cultivator employed there this season.

IX. The subsidy of £1 has proved fair and meets the needs of the settlers.

X. The construction of the village was late in starting and was thus prejudiced because of cultivation going on at the same time. For such a scheme the village should be established before cultivation got under way.

XI. The most satisfying feature of the settlement is perhaps the new co-operative life; they are getting the idea of communal property and are taking an unselfish share in the care and increase of that property. At first they had to be much encouraged to this end as the idea was quite new to them, but they now know that individual benefit comes from communal effort and they pull together very well.

It is pleasing that the settlers, who arrived in tatters, are now among the better dressed of the community and show signs of utilising profits from their crops to the best of advantage.

It may be considered by some that six cultivators from a total of nine is a poor representation on which to draw the above conclusions, and perhaps this is true, so that final conclusion must await the experience of coming seasons.

Finally, great credit is due to the resident agriculturist Tahr Eff. Suleiman. He proved the ideal man for the work in hand and, although an Arab, he treated the Nuba cultivators with understanding, and much of the experiment's success comes from his patience and guidance.

Epilogue

A Collection of Poems Written on Trek, 1943

The Lonely Man

Loneliness in solitude is acceptable
But in a crowded place becomes
A torture to the mind.
The crowd moves on its way
Enmeshed with webs of friendship
Which seem to bind all people
And yet counts the stranger out.

The city is there
To hurt the lonely man.

The Mob – Nuba

I saw a crowd which turned into a mob
Hot fired and violent from some righteous cause:
Not with the fire of new-tempered steel
But with the random heat
Of molten iron which breaks down all cohesion
And sends its particles out in violent disarray.

Its voice, once tamped with reason, was stirred up
And patient order quickly brushed aside
The flame of passion glowed from every eye
There was no law
To halt them from the violence of their deeds.
A time for glory, and an ecstasy to die.

Unspoken Words

The words we speak
When with our dearest friends
Are very often those
Which come from shallow thought
And are of small account.

But there are other words
Deep planted in the soul
The words we would express
Yet cannot speak
As if the burden of their utterance
Were too great.

Or is it when our love is deep
Words are not moulded into speech?
Some inhibition holds the reins
And drives those words beyond our reach.

And so it often is
That people meet and part
Who never really know
The yearnings of the heart.

The Sum

I added it up and found
The amount was very small.
What was the sum and substance of my life.
A birth, a childhood, and long years
Of learning, yearning, striving for some goal.
The sum is small,
For what is there to show?

At Abu Gubeiha, 1944

I saw a man standing motionless
On a bare hillside, his back straight
With a long spear stuck into the ground.
There seemed no reason for his stillness
Or why he should be there at all.

Before him stretched out barren miles
Devoid of living things. Nothing but sand and rock
And solitary stems of twisted scrub
To catch his eye, and glue him to the spot.

Yet still he stood nor did he care
That I was near at hand.
A witness to his deeds. Was he perhaps
A philosopher deep sunk in thought
Pondering out the purpose of his life?

Or praying to his God who placed him
In this barren wilderness?
Now here was I as motionless as he.
Awaiting his first movement
As if to break a spell.
And so at last it came.

With spear on shoulder he turned and walked away
As to another world.
I never saw him more.

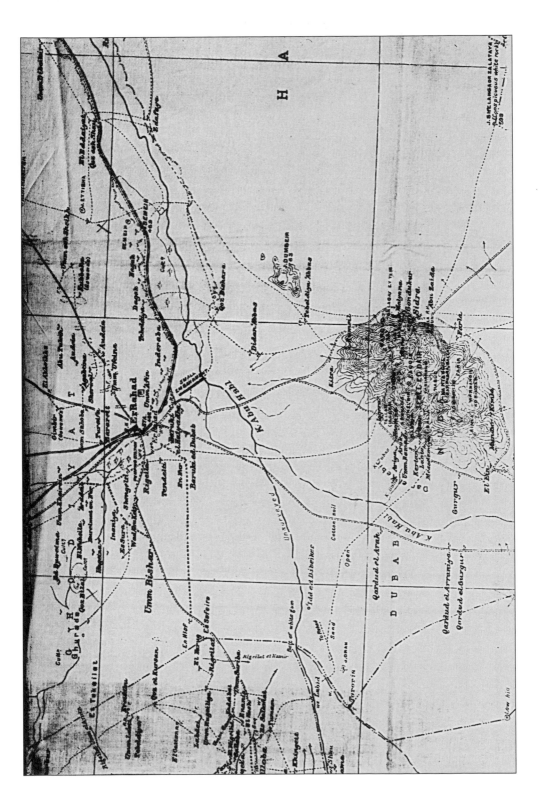

411

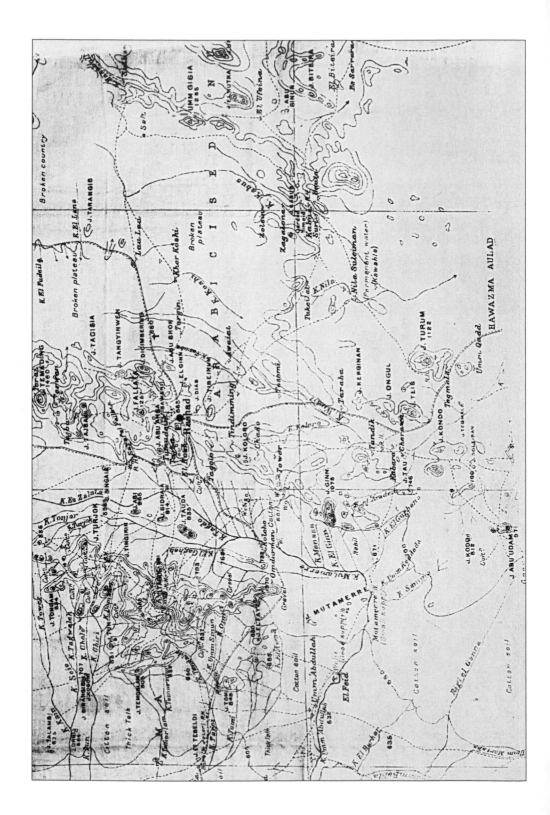

413

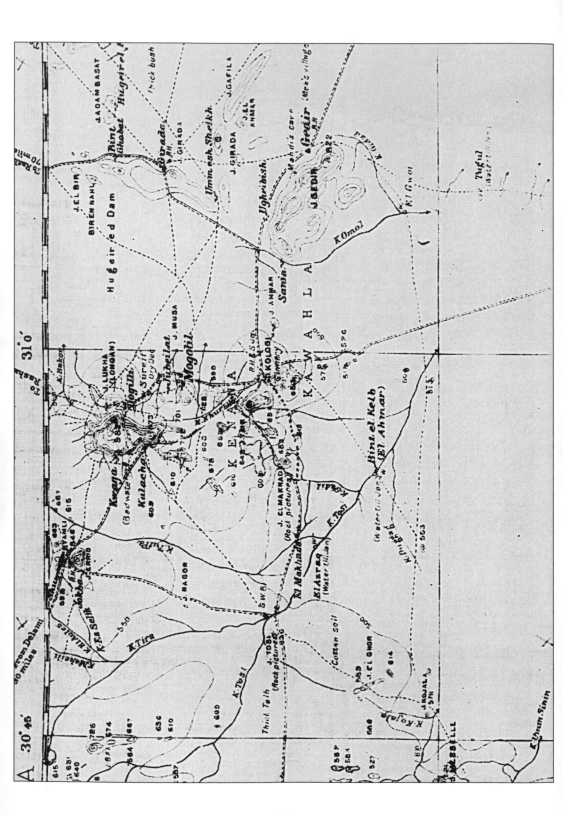

414

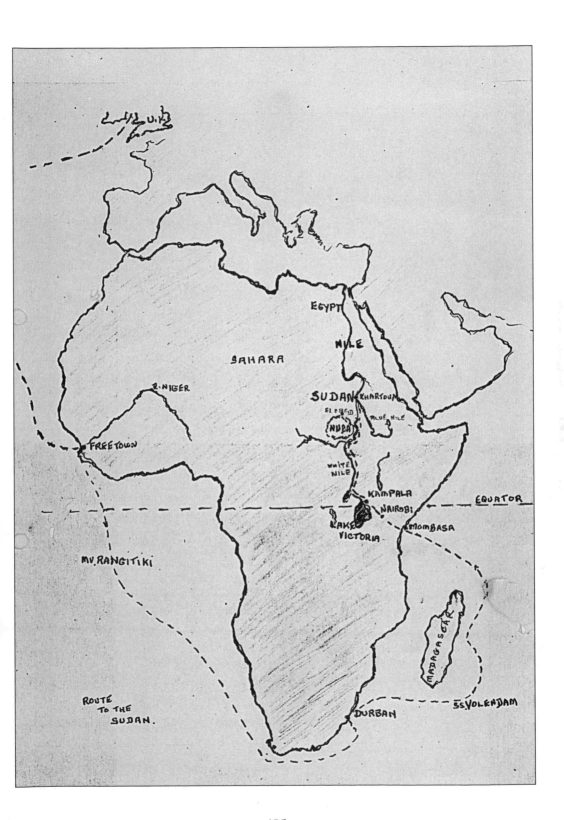

EGYPT

NILE

SAHARA

R.NIGER

SUDAN KHARTOUM

EL OBEID

NUBA

BLUE NILE

FREETOWN

WHITE NILE

KAMPALA

NAIROBI

EQUATOR

LAKE VICTORIA

MOMBASA

MV.RANGITIKI

MADAGASCAR

ROUTE
TO THE
SUDAN.

DURBAN

SSVOLENDAM

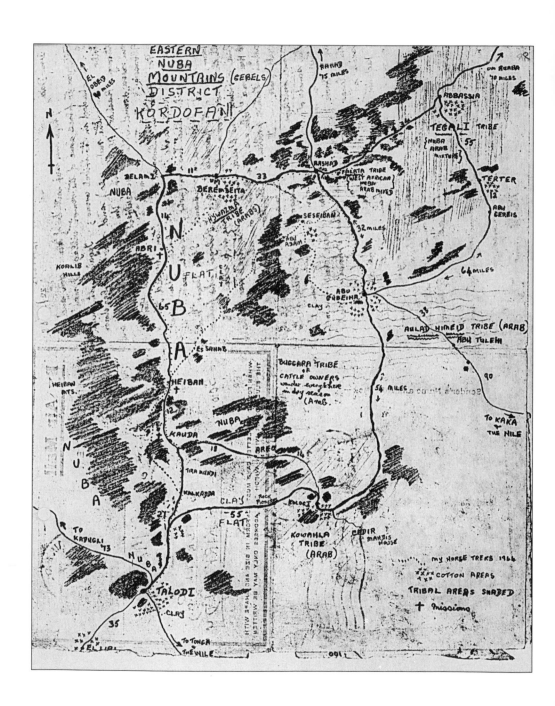

EASTERN
NUBA
MOUNTAINS (GEBELS)
DISTRICT
KORDOFAN

N

EL OBEID MILES

BELANI

NUBA

ABRI

KORLIB HILLS

N
U
B
A
FLAT
65

B
A
ES SAHAB

HEIBAN MTS.

N
U
B
A
HEIBAN
12
NUBA
KAUDA
18
TIRA RUNDI
KALKADDA
27
NUBA

TO KADUGLI 73

TALODI
35
EL LIRI
CLAY

BEREM SEITA

11°
33

KWALEB TRIBE (ARABS)

ABU ASAM

SESEIBAN

ABU GUBEINA
CLAY

RASHAD

FALATA TRIBE (WEST AFRICAN NUBA ARAB MIXED)

32 MILES

BUGGARA TRIBE OR CATTLE OWNERS wander everywhere in dry season (Arab)

NUBA AREA
14

CLAYS
55
FLAT

ROCK PICNICS
KELOGI

KOWAHLA TRIBE (ARAB)

GEDIR MANDIS HOUSE

TO TONGA & THE NILE

RAHAD 75 MILES

UM RABA 70 MILES

ABBASSIA

TEGALI TRIBE
(NUBA ARAB MIXTURE)
55

TERTER 12

ABU GEREIS

64 MILES

38

AULAD HIMEID TRIBE (ARAB
ABU TULEH

90

54 MILES

TO KAKA & THE NILE

my horse treks 1944
COTTON AREAS
TRIBAL AREAS SHADED
missions